Starting a Business

FOR

DUMMIES

A Wiley Brand

4th Edition

by Colin Barrow

FOR

DUMMIES

A Wiley Brand

Starting a Business For Dummies,® 4th Edition

Published by: **John Wiley & Sons, Ltd.,** The Atrium, Southern Gate, Chichester, www.wiley.com

This edition first published 2014

© 2014 John Wiley & Sons, Ltd, Chichester, West Sussex.

Registered office

John Wiley & Sons Ltd, The Atrium, Southern Gate, Chichester, West Sussex, PO19 8SQ, United Kingdom

For details of our global editorial offices, for customer services and for information about how to apply for permission to reuse the copyright material in this book please see our website at www.wiley.com.

Wiley publishes in a variety of print and electronic formats and by print-on-demand. Some material included with standard print versions of this book may not be included in e-books or in print-on-demand. If this book refers to media such as a CD or DVD that is not included in the version you purchased, you may download this material at www.dummies.com. For more information about Wiley products, visit www.wiley.com.

Designations used by companies to distinguish their products are often claimed as trademarks. All brand names and product names used in this book are trade names, service marks, trademarks or registered trademarks of their respective owners. The publisher is not associated with any product or vendor mentioned in this book.

For general information on our other products and services, please contact our Customer Care Department within the U.S. at 877-762-2974, outside the U.S. at (001) 317-572-3993, or fax 317-572-4002. For technical support, please visit www.wiley.com/techsupport.

A catalogue record for this book is available from the British Library.

ISBN 978-1-118-83734-4 (paperback); ISBN 978-1-118-83724-5 (ebk);

ISBN 978-1-118-83729-0 (ebk)

Printed in the UK

Contents at a Glance

Table of Contents

Part II: Making and Funding Your Plan 83

Chapter 5: Structuring Your Business 85

Introduction

· ·

*I*f you pulled this book down from the shelf or had it passed to you by a friend or loved one as a gift, you don't have to be psychic to know something about your current business situation. You may be in need of this book for any number of reasons:

- ✔ A relative, hopefully a distant and elderly one, has died and left you, rather than the government or a dogs' home, a pile of dosh and you don't fancy leaving it to your stockbroker to lose on your behalf.

- ✔ Your employer is in the middle of a major downsizing operation as well as proposing to close its final salary pension scheme and relocate to somewhere with lousy schools and no healthcare facilities.

- ✔ You've a great idea for a world-beating product, bigger than Google and Facebook combined, that no one has ever thought of but every one of the world's billion-plus Internet users desperately needs – when they hear the good news, they're going to click a path to your website.

- ✔ Your brother, sister, father, mother or best friend – or worse still, all of them – has started his or her own business and retired to a chateau in France to breed horses, tend the vines and sail on a luxury yacht.

- ✔ You've heard that the Entrepreneurship Barometer, by accountancy firm Ernst & Young, has revealed that Britain is the best place in Europe to start, grow and run a business. Fired up with enthusiasm, you've decided it's now or never to get your business off the ground.

If your present situation is founded largely on luck and serendipity, that isn't enough to get you through the business start-up process unaided. Good ideas, hard work, relevant skills and knowledge about your product and its market, though essential, on their own aren't enough. The 400,000 small firms that close their doors every year in the UK, a figure that rose sharply in the recent recession, are evidence enough that the process is a tough one.

This book is aimed at you if you want to start up a business or to review your prospects in the small-business world. It brings together, from a wide variety of sources, the essential elements of knowledge that are a prerequisite to understanding the world of small business and to achieving financial and personal success, whatever the economic weather.

About This Book

Most business failures occur within the first 18 months of operation. That fact alone has made it increasingly clear that small businesses need special help, particularly in their formative period. The most crucial needs for owners and managers include the following:

✔ Help in acquiring business skills in such areas as basic bookkeeping and accounting. Most failing businesses don't know their financial position. Even if the order book is full, the cash can still run out.

✔ Knowledge of what sorts of finance are available and how to put themselves in the best possible position to raise money. Surprisingly, funds aren't in short supply. Rather, problems lie in the business proposition itself or, more often, in the way in which the owner makes the proposition to the financier.

✔ Information with which to make realistic market assessments of the size and possibilities of their chosen market. Over-optimism about the size and ease with which a market can be reached is a common mistake.

✔ Skills and tools to grow their businesses into valuable assets to pass on to family members or to sell and then sail off into the sunset.

This book gives you help in all these areas.

In addition, every business needs a *business plan,* a statement of business purpose, with the consequences of each element of that purpose spelled out in financial terms. You must describe what you want your business to do – who its potential customers are, how much they're likely to spend, who can supply you and how much their supplies cost. Then you must translate those plans and projections into cash – how much your business needs, how much you already have and how much you expect 'outsiders' to put in. This plan also helps you to avoid catching the 'common cold' of small businesses – underestimating the amount of start-up capital you need. Going back to a bank and asking for 30 per cent more funding six months after opening your doors and retaining any credibility at all is difficult, if not impossible. Yet, new businesses consistently underestimate how much money they need to finance their growth. Many people have never prepared a business plan, don't know how to start and need information. That's where this book comes in. It gives you the information you need to formulate and follow a business plan.

The book is also invaluable to innovators, who have special problems of communication and security when they try to translate their ideas into businesses. All too often, their inventions are left for other countries to exploit, or they feel unhappy about discussing ideas, believing that a patent is their only protection. However, more often than not, these business owners simply don't know who to talk to, little realising that sophisticated help is often close at hand. Thus this book illuminates a path from the laboratory to the market place so that small firms and inventors can see a clear route.

Starting a Business For Dummies can help you succeed no matter what kind of business expertise you're looking for. If you have a great and proven business idea, you may want to plug straight into finding out how to raise finance. If you need more than just yourself to get your great business idea off the ground, you may want to discover how to find great employees or perhaps a business partner to take some of the financial and emotional strain. This book is set up so that you can dip in and out of it in a number of ways depending on your situation.

- ✔ If you haven't started a business before, or been profit accountable for part of an enterprise, you may want to start at the beginning and work your way through.

- ✔ If you're more experienced, you may start by selecting the areas you're less knowledgeable about to fill in the gaps, and then work outwards from there.

- ✔ If you're quite confident in the business world, you can use this book as a guide and mentor to review a particular topic. You can even use it to plan to sell your business after it's established and move on to a different challenge.

- ✔ If you learn by example, you may want to flip through the book, using the True Story icon as your guide. The text next to this icon highlights 'straight from the horse's mouth' examples of how entrepreneurs have tackled specific situations successfully, be it finding a partner, raising finance or getting a free grant from the government.

Foolish Assumptions

This book gathers together the essential, need-to-know information about getting a business up and running. It assumes that you've not yet been in business but that you're giving some serious thought to starting one. It also assumes that you can produce and deliver products or services that people will be willing to pay you for. These products and services can be anything – you're limited only by your imagination. Finally, this book assumes that you don't already know everything there is to know about starting your own business but that you're eager to get cracking.

Icons Used in This Book

To help you pinpoint vital information, I've placed icons throughout the text that highlight nuggets of knowledge.

This icon calls your attention to particularly important points and offers useful advice on practical topics.

The Remember icon serves as a friendly reminder that the topic at hand is important enough for you to make a note of.

Business, like any specialist subject, is awash with specialised terms and expressions, some of which may not be familiar to you. This icon draws your attention to these.

When you see this icon, I'm alerting you to the fact that I'm using a practical example showing how another business starter has tackled a particular topic. These examples are usually businesses facing today's difficult environment, and often you can apply the example to your own business.

Proceed with caution; look left and right before crossing. In fact, think carefully about crossing at all when you see this icon, which alerts you to potential dangers.

This icon refers to specialised business facts and data that are interesting as background data but not essential for you to know. You can skip paragraphs marked by this icon without missing the point – but reading them may help you build credibility with outside investors and partners.

Beyond the Book

As you travel on your journey of discovery through starting up a business, you can augment what you read here by checking out some of the access-anywhere extra information that is hosted online. You can find the book's e-cheat sheet at www.dummies.com/cheatsheet/startingabusinessuk, and by going to www.dummies.com/extras/startingabusinessuk you can access three bonus articles and an extra Part of Tens chapter.

Where to Go From Here

Take a minute to thumb through the table of contents and get comfortable with the topics the book covers. Pick a chapter that strikes a particular chord with the aspect of starting a business that's uppermost in your mind, such as finding the money or doing business online. Read that and see where it leads you.

You can also use Chapter 6, 'Preparing a Business Plan', as a framework for gathering knowledge and dive into the other chapters as you go.

If all else fails, start at the beginning. That technique has a pretty good track record.

Part I
Getting Started with Your New Business

 For Dummies can help get you started with lots of subjects. Visit www.dummies.com to learn more and do more with For Dummies.

In this part . . .

- ✔ Use your knowledge of business cycles to get your business off to the best possible start, and appreciate the effect that the state of the wider economy will have on your business.

- ✔ Lay the groundwork for opening your doors for business either at home or in dedicated premises.

- ✔ Check out your skills and aptitudes and see how they compare to the business idea you have in mind.

- ✔ Investigate your idea and its market in detail.

Chapter 1

Preparing for Business

. . . .

In This Chapter

▶ Getting to grips with the basics of business strategy

▶ Working up to opening up

▶ Measuring your business's viability

▶ Growing for success

. . . .

*W*hen you're starting a business, particularly your first business, you need to carry out the same level of preparation as you would for crossing the Gobi Desert or exploring the jungles of South America. You're entering hostile territory. A stroll down any high street in the land shows you just how tough it is out there. Since the last edition of this book, Comet, JJB Sports, Clinton Cards, Game, Borders, Barratts, Jane Norman, Habitat, Oddbins, Adams Childrenswear, Principles, Sofa Workshop, Allied Carpets, Viyella, Dewhursts, Woolworths, MFI and Zavvi/Virgin Megastore have hit the rocks. Some 53 retailers have closed 4,000 stores.

Your business idea may be good, it may even be great, but such ideas are two a penny. The patent office is stuffed full of great inventions that have never returned tuppence to the inventors who spent so much time and money filing them. And failure is pretty much a norm for business start-ups. Over the past three years, nearly half a million small firms have shut up shop in the UK alone. As if that wasn't bad enough, the small-business population has actually grown by over a quarter of a million, at a time when the economy has shrunk by around 6 per cent. That means thousands more businesses are chasing a shrinking pot of customer spending power.

How you plan, how you prepare and how you implement your plan makes the difference between success and failure. This chapter sets the scene to make sure that you're well prepared for the journey ahead.

Understanding the Enduring Rules of Business Strategy

When you're engulfed by enthusiasm for an idea for a new business or engaged in the challenge of getting it off the ground, you can easily miss out on the knowledge you can gain by lifting your eyes up and taking the big picture on board too. You won't gain much from taking aim at the wrong target from the outset!

Credit for devising the most succinct and usable way to get a handle on the big picture has to be given to Michael E. Porter, who trained as an economist at Princeton, taking his MBA at Harvard Business School where he's now a professor. Porter's research led him to conclude that two factors above all influence a business's chances of making superior profits – surely an absolute must if you're going to all the pain of working for yourself:

- ✔ **The attractiveness or otherwise of the industry in which it primarily operates.** That's down to your research, a subject I cover in Chapters 2 and 4.

- ✔ **How the business positions itself within the industry in terms of an organisation's sphere of influence.** In that respect, a business can only have a cost advantage if it can make products or deliver services for less than others. Alternatively, the business may be different in a way that matters to consumers, so that its offers are unique, or at least relatively so.

Porter added a further twist to his prescription. Businesses can follow a cost advantage path or a differentiation path industry wide, or they can take a third path – they can concentrate on a narrow specific segment with cost advantage or differentiation. This path he termed *focus strategy*, which I discuss in the following sections.

Focusing on focus – and a bit more besides

Whoa up a minute. Before you can get a handle on focus, you need to understand exactly what the good professor means by *cost leadership* and *differentiation*, because the combination of those provides the most fruitful arena for a new business to compete.

Cost leadership

Don't confuse low cost with low price. A business with low costs may or may not pass those savings on to customers. Alternatively, the business can use low costs alongside tight cost controls and low margins to create an effective barrier to others considering entering or extending their penetration of that market.

Businesses are most likely to achieve low-cost strategies in large markets, requiring large-scale capital investment, where production or service volumes are high and businesses can achieve economies of scale from long runs. If you've deep pockets, or can put together a proposition that convinces the money men to stump up the cash, this avenue may be one to pursue. (I cover everything you need to put together a great business plan in Chapter 6.)

Ryanair and easyJet are examples of fairly recent business start-ups where analysing every component of the business made it possible to strip out major elements of cost (meals, free baggage and allocated seating, for example) while leaving the essential proposition – we fly you from A to B – intact. This plan proved enough of a strategy to give bigger, more established rivals such as British Airways a few sleepless nights.

Differentiation

The key to *differentiation* (ensuring that your product or service has a unique element that makes it stand out from the rest) is a deep understanding of what customers really want and need and, more importantly, what they're prepared to pay more for. Apple's opening strategy was based around a 'fun' operating system based on icons, rather than the dull MS-DOS. This belief was based on Apple's understanding that computer users were mostly young and wanted an intuitive command system and the 'graphical user interface' delivered just that. Sony and BMW are also examples of differentiators. Both have distinctive and desirable differences in their products. Neither they nor Apple offer the lowest price in their respective industries; customers are willing to pay extra for the idiosyncratic and prized differences embedded in their products.

Consumers can be a pretty fickle bunch. Dangle something faster, brighter or just plain newer and you can usually grab their attention. Your difference doesn't have to be profound or even high-tech to capture a slice of the market. Book buyers rushed in droves to Waterstones for no more profound a reason than that its doors remained open in the evenings and on Sundays, when most other established bookshops were firmly closed.

Focus

Your patience is about to be rewarded. Now I can get to the strategy that Porter reckoned was the most fruitful for new business starters to plunge into.

Focused strategy involves concentrating on serving a particular market or a defined geographic region. IKEA, for example, targets young, white-collar workers as its prime customer segment, selling through 235 stores in more than 30 countries. Ingvar Kamprad, an entrepreneur from the Småland province in southern Sweden, who founded the business in the late 1940s, offers home furnishing products of good function and design at prices young people can afford. He achieves this quality and price by using simple cost-cutting solutions that don't affect the quality of products. (You can read more about Kamprad in the sidebar 'Less is more'.)

Warren Buffett, one of the world's richest men, knows a thing or two about focus. His investment company combined with Mars to buy US chewing gum manufacturer Wrigley for $23 billion (£11.6 billion) in May 2008. Chigago-based Wrigley, which launched its Spearmint and Juicy Fruit gums in the 1890s, has specialised in chewing gum ever since and consistently outperformed its more diversified competitors. Wrigley is the only major consumer products company to grow comfortably faster than the population in its markets and above the rate of inflation. Over the past decade or so, for example, other consumer products companies have diversified. Gillette moved into batteries used to drive many of its products by acquiring Duracell. Nestlé bought Ralston Purina, Dreyer's, Ice Cream Partners and Chef America. Both have trailed Wrigley's performance.

Businesses often lose their focus over time and periodically have to rediscover their core strategic purpose. Procter & Gamble is an example of a business that had to refocus to cure weak growth. In 2000 the company was losing share in seven of its top nine categories, and had lowered earnings expectations four times in two quarters. This situation prompted the company to restructure and refocus on its core business: big brands, big customers and big countries. Procter & Gamble sold off non-core businesses, establishing five global business units with a closely focused product portfolio.

Less is more

Furniture company IKEA was founded by Ingvar Kamprad when he was just 17, having cut his teeth on selling matches to his nearby neighbours at the age of 5, followed by spells selling flower seeds, greeting cards, Christmas decorations and eventually furniture. Worth £16 billion, Kamprad still lives frugally, in keeping with the functional nature of the IKEA brand. He lives in a bungalow, flies easyJet and drives an 18-year-old Volvo. When he arrived at a gala dinner recently to collect a business award, the security guard turned him away because he saw Kamprad getting off a bus. He and his wife Margaretha are often seen dining in cheap restaurants. He does his food shopping in the afternoon when prices are lower and even then haggles prices down.

Appreciating the forces at work in your sector

Aside from articulating the generic approach to business strategy, Porter's other major contribution to the field was what has become known as the Five Forces Theory of Industry Structure. Porter postulated that you have to understand the five forces that drive competition in an industry as part of the process of choosing which of the three generic strategies (cost leadership, differentiation or focus) to pursue. The forces he identified are:

- ✔ **Threat of substitution:** Can customers buy something else instead of your product? For example, Apple – and to a lesser extent Sony – have laptop computers that are distinctive enough to make substitution difficult. Dell, on the other hand, faces intense competition from dozens of other suppliers with near-identical products competing mostly on price alone.

- ✔ **Threat of new entrants:** If it's easy to enter your market, start-up costs are low and no barriers to entry exist, such as intellectual property protection, then the threat is high.

- ✔ **Supplier power:** Usually, the fewer the suppliers, the more powerful they are. Oil is a classic example where less than a dozen countries supply the whole market and consequently can set prices.

- ✔ **Buyer power:** In the food market, for example, just a few, powerful supermarket buyers are supplied by thousands of much smaller businesses, so the buyers are often able to dictate terms.

- ✔ **Industry competition:** The number and capability of competitors is one determinant of a business's power. Few competitors with relatively less attractive products or services lower the intensity of rivalry in a sector. Often these sectors slip into *oligopolistic behaviour,* preferring to collude rather than compete. You can see a video clip of Professor Porter discussing the Five Force model on the Harvard Business School website (http://hbr.org/2008/01/the-five-competitive-forces-that-shape-strategy/ar/1).

Recognising the first-to-market fallacy

People use the words 'first mover advantage' like a mantra to justify a headlong rush into starting a business without doing enough basic research. That won't happen to you – after all, you're reading this book and by the end of this section you'll be glad you paused for thought.

The idea that you've the best chance of being successful if you get in first is one of the most enduring in business theory and practice. Entrepreneurs and established giants are always in a race to be first. Research from the 1980s claimed to show that market pioneers have enduring advantages in distribution, product-line breadth, product quality and, especially, market share.

Beguiling though the theory of first mover advantage is, it's probably wrong. Gerard Tellis, of the University of Southern California, and Peter Golder, of New York University's Stern Business School, argue in their research that previous studies on the subject were deeply flawed. In the first instance earlier studies were based on surveys of surviving companies and brands, excluding all the pioneers that failed. This fact helps some companies to look as though they were first to market even when they weren't. Procter & Gamble boasts that it created the USA's disposable-nappy (diaper) business. In fact, a company called Chux launched its product a quarter of a century before Procter & Gamble entered the market in 1961.

Also, the questions used to gather much of the data in earlier research were at best ambiguous and perhaps dangerously so. For example, researchers had used the term 'one of the pioneers in first developing such products or services' as a proxy for 'first to market'. The authors emphasise their point by listing popular misconceptions of who the real pioneers were across the 66 markets they analysed:

- **Online book sales:** Amazon (wrong); Bookshop.co.uk (right). Amazon opened on 16 July 1995. Bookshop.co.uk opened in 1992 and was bought out by WH Smith in 1998 for £9.4 million.

- **PCs:** IBM/Apple (both wrong); Micro Instrumentation Telemetry Systems (right) – it introduced its PC, the Altair, a $400 kit, in 1974 followed by Tandy Corporation (Radio Shack) in 1977.

- **Search engines:** Google (wrong); Archie (right). The credit for developing the first search engine goes to Alan Emtage, a student at McGill University in Montreal, who in 1990 created Archie, an index for archiving computer files. The following year, Mark McCahill, a student at the University of Minnesota, used hypertext to create Gopher, which was able to search for plain text references in files. Then the search engine race was on, starting with Excite (1993), followed by Yahoo!, WebCrawler, Infoseek and Lycos (1994), AltaVista (1995), Inktomi (1996) and Ask Jeeves, now Ask (1997). Google didn't come on the scene until 1997, making it 11th in the race, but nevertheless the winner.

In fact the most compelling evidence from all the research is that nearly half of all firms pursuing a first-to-market strategy are fated to fail, but those following fairly close behind are three times as likely to succeed. Tellis and Golder claim the best strategy is to enter the market a few years after pioneers, learn from their mistakes, benefit from their product and market development and be more certain about customer preferences.

Getting in Shape to Start Up

You need to be in great shape to start a business. You don't have to diet or exercise, at least not in the conventional sense of those words, but you do have to be sure that you've the skills and knowledge you need for the business you have in mind, or know how to tap into sources of such expertise.

The following sections help you through a pre-opening check-up so that you can be absolutely certain that your abilities and interests closely align to those that the business you have in mind requires. The sections also help you to check that a profitable market exists for your products or services. You can use these sections as a vehicle for sifting through your business ideas to see whether they're worth the devotion of time and energy that you need to start up a business.

You may well not have all the expertise you need to do everything yourself. Chapter 7 introduces you to the zillions of agencies and advisers who can fill in the gaps in your expertise.

Assessing your abilities

Business lore claims that for every ten people who want to start their own business, only one finally does. It follows that an awful lot of dreamers exist who, while liking the idea of starting their own business, never get around to taking action. Chapter 3 looks in detail at how you can assess whether you're a dreamer or a doer when it comes to entrepreneurship. For now, see whether you fit into one of the following entrepreneurial categories:

- **Nature:** If one of your parents or siblings runs a business, successfully or otherwise, you're highly likely to start up your own business. No big surprise here, because the rules and experiences of business are being discussed every day in such families and some of this knowledge is bound to rub off. It also helps if you're a risk-taker who's comfortable with uncertainty.

- **Nurture:** For every entrepreneur whose parents or siblings have a business, two don't. If you can find a business idea that excites you and has the prospect of providing personal satisfaction and wealth, then you can assemble all the skills and resources you need to succeed in your own business. You need to acquire good planning and organisational skills (Chapter 6 covers all aspects of writing a business plan) and develop a well-rounded knowledge of basic finance, people management, operational systems, business law, marketing and selling, or get help and advice from people who have that knowledge.

✔ **Risk-taker:** If you crave certainty in everything you do, then running your own business may be something of a culture shock. By the time the demand for a product or service is an absolutely sure-fire thing, there may already be too many other businesses in the market to leave much room for you. Don't confuse risk-taking with a pure gamble. You need to be able to weigh matters up and make your risk a calculated one.

✔ **Jack-of-all-trades:** You need to be prepared to do any business task at any time. The buck definitely stops with you when you run your own business. You can't tell a customer that his delivery is late just because a driver fails to show up. You just have to put in a few more hours and do the job yourself.

Discovering a real need

You may be a great potential entrepreneur, but you still need to spell out exactly what it is you plan to do, who needs it and how it can make money. A good starting point is to look around and see whether anyone is dissatisfied with their present suppliers. Unhappy customers are fertile ground for new businesses to work upon.

One dissatisfied customer isn't enough to start a business for. Make sure that unhappiness is reasonably widespread, because that gives you a feel for how many customers may be prepared to defect. After you have an idea of the size of the potential market, you can quickly see whether your business idea is a money-making proposition.

Aside from asking around, one way to get a handle on dissatisfaction levels is to check out websites that allow consumers to register their feelings, such as www.complaints.com. Then scour blogs (short for weblogs), where irate people can complain their hearts out. Check out websites such as www. technorati.com, www.totalblogdirectory.com and www.bloghub. com, which all operate blog-indexing services that can help you filter through the 70 million plus blogs and reach the few dozen that serve the sector you're interested in.

The easiest way to fill a need that people are going to pay to have satisfied is to tap into one or more of these triggers:

✔ **Cost reduction and economy:** Anything that saves customers money is always an attractive proposition. Lastminute.com's appeal is that it acts as a 'warehouse' for unsold hotel rooms and airline tickets that you can have at a heavy discount.

✔ **Fear and security:** Products that protect customers from any danger, however obscure, are enduringly appealing. When Long-Term Capital Management (LTCM), one of the USA's largest hedge funds, collapsed and had to be rescued by the Federal Reserve at a cost of $2 billion, it nearly brought down the US financial system single-handedly. Two months later, Ian and Susan Jenkins launched the first issue of their magazine *EuroHedge*. At the time 35 hedge funds existed in Europe, but investors knew little about them and were rightly fearful for their investments. *EuroHedge* provided information and protection to a nervous market – five years after its launch the Jenkinses sold the magazine for £16.5 million.

✔ **Greed:** Anything that offers the prospect of making exceptional returns is always a winner. *Competitors' Companion,* a magazine aimed at helping anyone become a regular competition winner, was an immediate success. The proposition was simple: subscribe and you get your money back if you don't win a competition prize worth at least your subscription. The magazine provided details of every competition being run that week, details of how to enter, the factual answers to all the questions and pointers on how to answer any tie breakers. It also provided the inspiration to ensure success with this sentence: 'You have to enter competitions in order to have a chance of winning them.'

✔ **Niche markets:** Big markets are usually the habitat of big business – encroach on their territory at your peril. New businesses thrive in markets that are too small even to be an appetite whetter to established firms. These market niches are often easy prey to new entrants because businesses have usually neglected, ignored or served them badly in the past.

Checking the fit of the business

Having a great business idea and possessing the attributes and skills you require to start your own business successfully are two vital elements to get right before you launch. The final ingredient is to be sure that the business you plan to start is right for you.

Before you go too far, make an inventory of the key things that you're looking for in a business. These things may include working hours that suit your lifestyle, the opportunity to meet new people, minimal paperwork or a chance to travel. Then match those up with the proposition you're considering. (Chapter 3 talks more about finding a good business fit.)

Confirming Viability

An idea, however exciting, unique, revolutionary and necessary, isn't a business. An idea is a great starting point, and an essential one, but you have to do a good deal more work before you can sidle up to your boss and tell him exactly what you think of him.

The following sections explore the steps you need to take so that you don't have to go back to your boss in six months and plead for your old job back (and possibly eat a large piece of humble pie at the same time).

Researching the market

However passionate you are about your business idea, you're unlikely to have the answers to all the important questions concerning your marketplace already. Before you can develop a successful business strategy, you have to understand as much as possible about your market and the competitors you're likely to face.

The main way to get to understand new business areas, or areas that are new to you at any rate, is to conduct market research (head to Chapter 4 for all the details). The purpose of this research is to ensure that you have sufficient information on customers, competitors and markets so that your market entry strategy or expansion plan is at least on target, if not on the bull's-eye itself. In other words, you need to explore whether enough people are attracted to buy what you want to sell at a price that gives you a viable business. If you miss the target altogether, which you may well do without research, you may not have the necessary resources for a second shot.

The areas to research include the following:

- **Your customers:** Who may buy more of your existing goods and services and who may buy your new goods and services? How many such customers exist? What particular customer needs do you meet?

- **Your competitors:** Who are you competing with in your product/market areas? What are those firms' strengths and weaknesses?

- **Your product or service:** How can you tailor your product or service to meet customer needs and give you an edge in the market?

- **The price:** What do customers see as giving value for money, so encouraging both loyalty and referral?

✔ **The advertising and promotional material:** What newspapers, journals and so forth do your potential customers read and what websites do they visit? Unglamorous as may be, analysing data on what messages actually influence people to buy, rather than just to click, holds the key to identifying where and how to promote your products and services.

✔ **Channels of distribution:** How can you get to your customers and who do you need to distribute your products or services? You may need to use retailers, wholesalers, mail order or the Internet. These methods all have different costs, and if you use one or more, each wants a slice of your margin.

✔ **Your location:** Where do you need to be to reach your customers most easily at minimum cost? Sometimes you don't actually need to be anywhere near your market, particularly if you anticipate most of your sales coming from the Internet. If you're in this position, you need to have a strategy to make sure that potential customers can find your website (see Chapter 15).

Inflated numbers on the Internet

If you plan to advertise on an Internet site, make sure that you check out the different sites you're considering. Be aware that some sites publish a fair amount of gobbledygook about the high number of 'hits' (often millions) they receive. Millions of hits don't mean that the site has millions of visitors. Some Internet sites increase their hit rate by the simple expedient of leading each viewer through a number of pages, each of which adds to the number of hits. Another mildly meaningless measure of the advertising value of a site is the notion of a *subscriber.* In Internet parlance anyone visiting a website and giving over an email address becomes part of that company's share price! Compare that to the suggestion that anyone passing a shop and glancing in the window turns into hard cash the following day.

Any real analysis of website use starts with *page impression,* which is a measure of how many times an individual page has been viewed. The Audit Bureau of Circulations, which started its life measuring newspaper response, has now turned its attention to auditing websites (www.abc.org.uk). Also check out the World Internet Usage website (www.internetworldstats.com/stats.htm) for the latest statistics on Internet penetration by continent and country. That gives you a realistic measure of the maximum traffic and relative importance of each market you're interested in.

Try to spend your advertising money wisely. Nationwide advertisements or blanketing the market with free CD-ROMs may create huge short-term growth, but little evidence exists that indiscriminate blunderbuss advertising works well in retaining customers. Certainly, few people using such techniques make any money. Chapter 10 contains lots of tips on advertising.

Doing the numbers

Your big idea looks as though it has a market. You've evaluated your skills and inclinations and you believe that you can run this business. The next crucial question is – can it make you money?

You absolutely must establish the financial viability of your idea before you invest money in it or approach outsiders for backing. You need to carry out a thorough appraisal of the business's financial requirements. If the numbers come out as unworkable, you can then rethink your business proposition without losing anything. If the figures look good, you can go ahead and prepare cash flow projections, a profit and loss account and a balance sheet, and put together the all-important business plan. (Chapters 6 and 13 cover these procedures.)

You need to establish the following for your business:

- ✔ Day-to-day operating costs
- ✔ How long it will take to reach breakeven
- ✔ How much start-up capital you need
- ✔ The likely sales volume
- ✔ The profit level you require for the business not just to survive, but also to thrive
- ✔ The selling price of your product or service

Many businesses have difficulty raising start-up capital. To compound this, one of the main reasons that small businesses fail in the early stages is that they use too much start-up capital to buy fixed assets. Although some equipment is clearly essential at the start, you can postpone other purchases. You may be better off borrowing or hiring 'desirable' and labour-saving devices for a specific period. The higher your fixed costs, the longer it usually takes to reach breakeven point and profitability. Time isn't usually on the side of the small, new business: it has to become profitable relatively quickly or it simply runs out of money and dies.

Raising the money

Two fundamentally different types of money that a business can tap into are debt and equity.

- ✔ **Debt** is money borrowed, usually from a bank, and that you have to repay. While you're making use of borrowed money, you also have to pay interest on the loan.

- ✔ **Equity** is the money that shareholders, including the proprietor, put in and money left in the business by way of retained profit. You don't have to give the shareholders their money back, but shareholders do expect the directors to increase the value of their shares, and if you go public they probably expect a stream of dividends too.

    If you don't meet the shareholders' expectations, they won't be there when you need more money – or, if they're powerful enough, they may take steps to change the membership of the board.

Alternative financing methods include raising money from family and friends, applying for grants and awards, and entering business competitions. Check out Chapter 8 for a review of all these sources of financing.

Writing up the business plan

A *business plan* is a selling document that conveys the excitement and promise of your business to potential backers and stakeholders. These potential backers can include bankers, venture capital firms, family, friends and others who may help you launch your business if they only know what you want to do. (Chapter 8 considers how to find and approach sources of finance.)

Getting money is expensive, time consuming and hard work. Having said that, you can get a quick decision. One recent start-up succeeded in raising £3 million in eight days, after the founder turned down an earlier offer of £1 million made just 40 minutes after he presented his business plan.

Your business plan should cover what you expect to achieve over the next three years. (Chapter 6 gives full details on how to write a winning business plan.) Most business plans are dull, badly written and frequently read only by the most junior of people in the financing organisations they're presented to.

One venture capital firm in the USA went on record to say that in one year it received 25,000 business plans asking for finance and invested in only 40. Follow these tips to make your business plan stand out from the crowd:

- **Hit them with the benefits.** You need to spell out exactly what you do, for whom and why that matters. One such statement that has the ring of practical authority is: 'Our website makes ordering gardening products simple. It saves the average customer two hours a week browsing catalogues and £250 a year through discounts not otherwise available from garden centres. We have surveyed 200 home gardeners who rate efficient purchasing as a key priority.'

- **Make your projections believable.** Sales projections always look like a hockey stick – a straight line curving rapidly upwards towards the end. You have to explain exactly what drives growth, how you capture sales and what the link between activity and results is. The profit margins are key numbers in your projections, alongside sales forecasts. Financiers tend to probe these figures in depth, so show the build-up in detail.

- **Say how big the market is.** Financiers feel safer backing people in big markets. Capturing a fraction of a percentage of a massive market may be hard to achieve – but if you get it, at least the effort is worth it. Going for 10 per cent of a market measured in millions rather than billions may come to the same number, but the result isn't as interesting.

- **Introduce yourself and your team.** You need to sound like winners with a track record of great accomplishments.

- **Include non-executive directors.** Sometimes a heavyweight outsider can lend extra credibility to a business proposition. If you know or have access to someone with a successful track record in your area of business who has time on his hands, you can invite him to help. If you plan to trade as a limited company (Chapter 5 has details on legal structures) you can ask him to be a director, without specific executive responsibilities beyond being on hand to offer advice. But non-executive directors do need to have relevant experience or be able to open doors and do deals. Check out organisations such as Venture Investment Partners (www.ventureip.co.uk) and First Flight Placement's non-exec search site (www.nonexecutivedirector.co.uk) for information on tracking down the right non-executive director for your business.

- **Provide financial forecasts.** You need projected cash flows, profit and loss accounts and balance sheets for at least three years ahead. No one believes them after Year 1, but the thinking behind them is what's important.

- **Demonstrate the product or service.** Financiers need to see what the customer is going to get. A mock-up is okay or, failing that, a picture or diagram. For a service, show how customers can gain from using it – that it can help with improved production scheduling and so reduce stock holding, for example.

> ✔ **Spell out the benefits to your potential investors.** Tell them that you can repay their money within *x* years, even on your most cautious projections. Alternatively, if you're speaking to an equity investor, tell him what return he may get on his investment when you sell the business in three or five years' time.

Going for Growth

Growth is as natural a feature of business life as it is of biological life. People, animals and plants all grow to a set size range and then stop. A few unusually small and particularly large specimens come to fruition, but the vast majority fits within a fairly narrow size band.

Businesses follow a similar formula: most successful new businesses (those that survive, that is) reach a plateau within five to seven years. At that stage the business employs 5 to 20 people and has annual sales of between £250,000 and £1 million. Of the 4.8 million private businesses operating in the United Kingdom, fewer than 125,000 have a turnover in excess of £1 million a year. That doesn't represent a bad result. Viewed from the position of a one-man-band start-up, having a couple of hundred thousand pounds in sales each year is an admirable (and unusual) success.

The following sections demonstrate the great benefits of growth (Chapters 15, 16, 17 and 18 contain more advice on how to make your business grow).

Gaining economies of scale

After a business starts to grow, you can spread overhead costs over a wider base. You can buy materials and services in larger quantities, which usually means better terms and lower costs. The combination of these factors generally leads to a higher profit margin, which in turn provides funds to improve the business, which in turn can lead to even lower costs. This *virtuous circle* can make a growing firm more cost competitive than one that's cautiously marking time.

Securing a competitive advantage

A new business can steal a march on its competitors by doing something vital that established businesses can't easily imitate. For example, a new hairdressing shop can locate where customers are, but an existing shop has to content itself with its current location, at least until its lease expires.

A growing firm can gain advantages over its slower competitors. For example, launching new products or services gives a firm more goods to sell to its existing customer base. This situation puts smaller competitors at a disadvantage, because they're perceived as having less to offer than the existing supplier. This type of growth strategy can, if coupled with high-quality standards, lead to improved customer retention, which can lead to higher profits – a further push on the momentum of the virtuous circle.

Retaining key staff

The surest way to ensure that a business fails is to have a continual churn of employees coming and going. You have to invest valuable time and money in every new employee before he becomes productive, so the more staff you lose, the more growth you sacrifice. Most employers believe that their staff work for money and their key staff work for more money. The facts don't really support this hypothesis. All the evidence is that employees want to have an interesting job and recognition and praise for their achievements. In Chapters 11 and 18, you can find out how to get the best out of your staff.

By growing the business, you can let key managers realise their potential. In a bigger business you can train and promote your staff, moving them up the ladder into more challenging jobs, earning higher salaries on merit, while they stay with you rather than leaving for pastures new. So, if employees are good at their jobs, the longer they stay with you, and the more valuable they become. You save time and money on recruitment and you don't have to finance new managers' mistakes while they find out how to work in your business.

Gaining critical business mass

Bigger isn't always better, but a growing business has a greater presence in its market, and that's rarely a bad strategy. Large businesses are also more stable, tending to survive better in turbulent times. Bigger businesses can and do sometimes go bust, but smaller, 'doing nicely' businesses are far more likely to go bump.

A small company often relies on a handful of customers and just one or two products or services for most or all of its profits. If its main product or service comes under competitive pressure, or if a principal customer goes bust, changes supplier, or spreads orders around more thinly, then the small company is in trouble. Expanding the number of customers so that you break out of the 80/20 cycle – in which 80 per cent of the business comes from just 20 per cent of customers – is a sensible way to make your business safer and more predictable.

One-product businesses are the natural medium of the inventor, but they're extremely vulnerable to competition, changes in fashion and technological obsolescence. Having only one product can limit the growth potential of the enterprise. A question mark must inevitably hang over such ventures until they can broaden their product base. Adding successful new products or services helps a business to grow and become a safer and more secure venture.

Chapter 2

Doing the Groundwork

· ·

· ·

*I*f you've worked in a big organisation, you know that small and medium enterprises (SMEs) are different kinds of animal from big businesses. SMEs are more vulnerable to the vagaries of the economy, but are vital to its vigour.

In this chapter, you can find out how to come up with a great business idea and avoid the lemons. You can also look at the most common mistakes that businesses starting up make and how you can avoid them.

Understanding the Small Business Environment

During one of the all too many periods in recent history when the business climate was particularly frigid (the recent global credit crunch being a good example), some bright spark claimed that the only sure-fire way to get a small business safely down the slipway was to start out with a big one and shrink it down to size. I can't deny that that's one way to get started, but even as a joke the statement completely misses the point. Small businesses have almost nothing in common with big ones. Just because someone, you perhaps, has worked in a big business, however successfully, that's no guarantee of success in the small business world.

Big businesses usually have deep pockets, and even if those pockets aren't actually stuffed full of cash, after years of trading under their belt they can get the ear of their bank manager in all but the most extraordinary of circumstances. Even if unsuccessful at the bank, big firms can generally extract credit from suppliers, especially if the suppliers are smaller and susceptible to being leaned on in order to retain them as a customer. If all else fails, big businesses may have the option to tap their shareholders or go out to the stock market for more boodle – options a small business owner can only dream about. Of course, if the business is huge, in times of extreme hardship it can expect a sympathetic hearing from the government. The UK government shrank from letting Northern Rock fold, the US government threw General Motors a lifeline and France's Nicholas Sarkozy used public cash to keep Renault and Peugeot Citroën in business so long as they kept their French factories open. The boss of a big firm has legions of staff to carry out research, and to do all those hundred and one boring but essential jobs, like writing up the books, that are essential preludes to tapping into credit.

In contrast, small business founders have to stay up late, burning the midnight oil and poring over those figures themselves. To cap it all, they may even have to get up at dawn and make special deliveries to customers in order to ensure that they meet deadlines. Big business bosses have chauffeurs and travel business class; after all, they don't own a large proportion of the business's shares, so however frugal they are, they won't be much richer. Small firm founders, however, are personally poorer every time an employee makes a phone call at work, books a business trip or takes a client out to lunch, unless that call, trip or lunch generates extra business. The question that separates owners from employees (which is, after all, what bosses of big businesses really are, however powerful they look from below) is: if it was your money, would you spend it on that call, business trip or lunch? Seven times out of ten the answer is, 'No way, not with my dosh.'

Defining Small Business

Small business defies easy definition. Typically, people apply the term *small business* to one-man bands such as shops, garages and restaurants, and apply the term *big business* to such giants as IBM, General Motors, Shell and Microsoft. But between these two extremes fall businesses that you may look upon as big or small, depending on the yardstick and cut-off point you use to measure size.

No single definition exists of a small firm, mainly because of the wide diversity of businesses. One wit claimed that a business was small if it felt it was, and a grain of truth exists in that point of view.

In practical terms the only reason to be concerned about a business's size, age or business sector is the support and constraints imposed by virtue of those factors. The government, for example, may offer grant aid, support or even constraints based on such factors. For instance, a business with a small annual sales turnover, less than £15,000, can file a much simpler set of accounts than a larger business can.

Looking at the Types of People Who Start Businesses

At one level, statistics on small firms are precise. Government collects and analyses the basic data on how many businesses start (and close) in each geographic area and what type of activity those businesses undertake. Periodic studies give further insights into how new and small firms are financed or how much of their business comes from overseas markets. Beyond that the 'facts' become a little more hazy and information comes most often from informal studies by banks, academics and others who may have a particular axe to grind.

The first fact about the UK small business sector is how big it is. Over 4.8 million people now run their own business, up from 1.9 million three decades ago.

The desire to start a business isn't evenly distributed across the population as a whole. Certain factors such as geographic area and age group seem to influence the number of start-ups at any one time. The following sections explore some of these factors.

Making your age an asset

Research by the Global Entrepreneurship Monitor (www.gemconsortium.org) and the UK Office for National Statistics (www.statistics.gov.uk) reveals a number of interesting facts about the age of small business starters:

- ✔ Every age group from 18 through to 64 is represented in the business starter population.

- ✔ Between 6 and 9 per cent of each age group run their own businesses.

- ✔ The youngest age group (16–24), particularly in Scotland and Wales, is now among the most likely to be running a business. The reason may be the high levels of youth unemployment and a decline in opportunities for graduates.

- ✔ The older age group (55–64) is seeing a surge in interest from people wanting to keep at work after leaving employment. (In the US, this group has the highest rate of entrepreneurship, and people over 55 are almost twice as likely to found successful companies than those between 20 and 34.)

Zandra Johnson, 67, launched her company Fairy Tale Children's Furniture, making bespoke furniture for children, five years ago. Her start-up capital was £12,000 saved up over a decade while working in the voluntary sector. With no business experience, she augmented her skills by attending business courses and seminars and reading copiously. By 2013, her website (www.fairytalechildrensfurniture.co.uk) was packed full of products.

Gaming his way to fame

David Darling, a schoolboy entrepreneur, created a multi-million-pound company from modest beginnings – his first venture operated from his grandparents' garden shed. As a teenager growing up in the early 1980s, he developed his first digital game and placed an advert in a specialist magazine. The exercise was a success. David, founder of Codemasters, owns a substantial slice of a business that has grown to span the globe. With its central campus and studios in the heart of the UK, the company operates through its network of European offices, its art and animation studio in Kuala Lumpur, Malaysia, and its US office in Los Angeles, the capital of the USA's entertainment industry. The company has significantly strengthened its international distribution reach, including a partnership with Warner Bros. Home Video in North America.

David and his brother Richard were fascinated by the new technology of computer games. They were avid readers of *Popular Computing Weekly*, a specialist magazine for Atari, Commodore and Sinclair users. One section of the publication was devoted to programming, featuring the computer codes for popular games as well as tuition and advice. The technology was primitive and with the help of the magazine the two brothers were able to copy simple codes for games such as Space Invaders. Next they started to develop games, initially for themselves.

They decided to test the market and saved up the money for a half-page advertisement in *Popular Computing Weekly*. The price was £70, which they raised by missing school dinners for weeks. They created their own advert and logo – a Superman-type character – with the help of a friend whose father ran an advertising design company. Under the name Galactic Software, they offered '14 great games from America' for £10. Although they had merely hoped to make enough money to cover the cost of the advert, in the event 40 readers replied, generating £400 of sales. Encouraged by their success, the brothers ran a second and third advert in consecutive issues. After the third, 500 orders came in, which was more work than two people could manage, especially with exams approaching. In response, David employed the services of a music-duplication business in Bridgwater, Somerset that made copies of tapes for local bands. He struck a deal, paying the company to copy the games at the rate of 50p per tape.

After the Darling brothers sat their exams, they went into business full time.

Considering location

More than three times as many people in London start a business as do those in the North East of England. So, at the very least you're more likely to feel lonelier as an entrepreneur in that area, or in Wales and Scotland, than in, say, London or the South East.

According to the UK Office for National Statistics, the chances of your business surviving are best in Northern Ireland, where just over 70 per cent are still going after three years, and worst in London, where around 60 per cent of businesses remain after three years.

Select Database, a direct marketing firm, has a nifty database that can tell you how many businesses have been set up recently in any postal district in the UK (www.selectabase.co.uk).

Winning with women

Figures from the Office of National Statistics show that 614,000 women in the UK ran their own business full time in July 2013, a 10.3 per cent increase on the 556,000 a year earlier. Some 2,399,000 men ran their own business full time, a 2.5 per cent drop from the preceding year.

The British Association of Women Entrepreneurs (www.bawe-uk.org) and Everywoman (www.everywoman.com) are useful starting points to find out more about targeted help and advice for women starting up a business.

Self-employment, a term used interchangeably with starting a business, tends to be a mid-life choice for women, with the majority starting up businesses after the age of 35. Self-employed women usually have children at home (kudos to these super-mums), and many go the self-employment route *because* they have family commitments. In most cases, self-employment grants greater schedule flexibility than the rigors of a nine-to-five job.

The types of businesses that women run reflect the pattern of their occupations in employment. The public administration, education and health fields account for around a quarter of self-employed women, and distribution, hotels and restaurants another fifth.

In financing a new business, women tend to prefer using personal credit cards or remortgaging their home, and men prefer bank loan finance and government and local authority grants.

Being educated about education

A popular myth states that under-educated self-made men dominate the field of entrepreneurship. Anecdotal evidence seems to throw up enough examples of school or university drop-outs to support the theory that education is unnecessary, perhaps even a hindrance, to getting a business started. After all, if Sir Richard Branson (Virgin) dropped out of full-time education at 16, and Lord Sugar (Amstrad), Sir Philip Green (BHS and Arcadia, the group that includes Topshop and Miss Selfridge), Sir Bernie Ecclestone (Formula One – Britain's tenth richest man) and Charles Dunstone (Carphone Warehouse) all gave higher education a miss, education can't be that vital.

However, the facts, such as they are, reveal a rather different picture. Research shows that the more educated the population, the more entrepreneurship takes place. Educated individuals are more likely to identify gaps in the market or understand new technologies. After all, Stelios Haji-Iannou, founder of easy-Jet, has six degrees to his name, albeit four are honorary. Tony Wheeler, who – together with his wife Maureen – founded Lonely Planet Publications, has degrees from Warwick University and the London Business School. Jeff Bezos (Amazon) is an alumnus of Princeton, and Google's founders, Sergey Brin and Larry Page, graduated from Stanford.

So if you're in education now, stay the course. After all, a key characteristic of successful business starters is persistence and the ability to see things through to completion. Chapter 3 outlines more entrepreneurial attributes.

Coming Up with a Winning Idea

Every business starts with the germ of an idea. The idea may stem from nothing more profound than a feeling that customers are getting a raw deal from their present suppliers.

In this section, you can find out tried-and-tested ways to help you come up with a great idea for a new business.

Ranking popular start-up ideas

The government's statistics service produces periodic statistics on the types of businesses operating in the UK.

In terms of the sheer number of business enterprises, the UK is more a nation of estate agents than of small shopkeepers, as demonstrated in Table 2-1, which shows the types of businesses currently being operated the UK and regions, according to government statistics. (You can find out more at the www.gov.uk website by entering 'business population' in the search pane.)

Table 2-1	Businesses Operating by Sector, 2012
Sector	*Total*
Construction	907,480
Wholesale and retail trade; repairs	514,805
Admin and support service	378,735
Human health and social work	303,540
Information and communication	289,075
Transportation and storage	269,945
Education	243,220
Manufacturing	230,970
Arts, entertainment and recreation	209,430
Accommodation and food service	166,555
Agriculture, forestry and fishing	152,085
Real estate	91,810
Finance and insurance	76,380

You can take one of two views on entering a particularly popular business sector: it represents a great idea you're mad to resist, or the business is already awash with competition. In practice, the best view to take is that if others are starting up, at least a market opportunity exists. Your task is to research the market thoroughly, using Chapter 4 as your guide.

Going with fast growth

Entrepreneur.com produces an annual list of hot business sectors to enter (www.entrepreneur.com/article/224977). The 2013 list includes:

- ✔ **Beauty:** When it comes to anti-aging solutions, beauty seekers are in favour of 'cosmeceuticals', personal-care products with supposed skin-enhancing ingredients. Growth is driven by products advertising 'active and natural' ingredients like rice-enzyme powders and rainforest plant extracts.

- ✔ **Education:** The lack of jobs has sent millions around the globe back to college to train or retrain. Universities in the UK are full to bursting point. Unsurprisingly, a boom is occurring in online learning, tutoring and other private learning facilities.

- **Energy-enhancing products:** Red Bull started the trend. Launched in 1987 in Austria, it didn't hit the USA and mainstream Europe until 1997, but since then Red Bull and other energy-enhancing products have grown into a multi-billion-dollar industry fuelled by young consumers.

- **Green energy and renewables:** A growing sector because governments the world over are chucking what little money they have at this.

- **Senior market:** With the population of over-64s exploding, this sector is a no-brainer to serve. Academics, always quick to latch on to opportunities, have singled out *gerontology* (the study of social, psychological and biological aspects of aging with the view of extending active life while enhancing its quality) as a hot area, and a university is scheduled to debut a new master's degree in aging-services management to meet the growing interest in the field.

You can use this information to help pick a fast-growing business area to start your business in. Beginning with the current flowing strongly in the direction you want to travel can make things easier for you from the start.

Spotting a gap in the market

The classic way to identify a great opportunity is to see something that people would buy if only they knew about it. The demand is latent, lying beneath the surface, waiting for someone – you, hopefully – to recognise that the market is crying out for something no one is yet supplying.

The following are some of the ways to go about identifying a market gap:

- **Adapting:** Can you take an idea that's already working in another part of the country or abroad and bring it to your own market?

- **Locating:** Do customers have to travel too far to reach their present source of supply? This situation is a classic route to market for shops, hairdressers and other retail-based businesses, including those that can benefit from online fulfilment.

- **Size:** If you made things a different size, would that appeal to a new market? Anita Roddick of The Body Shop found that she could only buy the beauty products she wanted in huge quantities. By breaking down the quantities and sizes of those products and selling them, she unleashed a huge new demand.

- **Timing:** Are customers happy with current opening hours? If you opened later, earlier or longer, would you tap into a new market?

Cleaning up in the kitchen

What do Guy's Hospital and The Wolseley, a grand café-restaurant located in St James's on London's famous Piccadilly, have in common? They're both clients of Olive Services, which maintains their kitchens. The business was started by Sol Goodall, a professional chef who'd experienced at first hand how maintenance problems impact productivity and profitability.

Until Goodall started up, anyone running a commercial kitchen could find companies doing parts of the maintenance, but no one brought it all together. This, Goodall reasoned, was a clear gap in the market. He set out to provide chefs with a one-stop shop for everything they needed to keep their kitchens running and for them to stay up to date with the latest environmentally friendly and efficient processes. By 2013 Olive Services had over 70 regular clients, and as well as maintenance it offered refrigeration, air conditioning and building services.

Revamping an old idea

A good starting point is to look for products or services that used to work really well, but have stopped selling. Ask yourself why they seem to have died out and then try to establish whether, and how, you can overcome that problem. Or you can search overseas or in other markets for products and services that have worked well for years in their home markets but have so far failed to penetrate into your area.

Sometimes with little more than a slight adjustment you can give an old idea a whole new lease of life. For example, the Monopoly game, with its emphasis on the universal appeal of London street names, has been launched in France with Parisian *rues* and in Cornwall using towns rather than streets.

Using the Internet

Many of the first generation of Internet start-ups had nothing unique about their offer – the mere fact that the business was 'on the net' was thought to be enough. Hardly surprisingly, most of them went belly-up in no time at all.

All the basic rules of business apply to Internet businesses. You need a competitive edge – something better and different about your product or service that makes you stand out from the crowd.

Winning on the net

In 1999, Simon Nixon had dropped out of studying accountancy at university (because it was 'boring'), and he had the idea for a new business: an Internet-based price comparator that saves you hours surfing the net yourself. He persuaded Duncan Cameron, a computer whizz and his girlfriend's brother, to give up a computer studies course at university to write the software programs that were crucial to the launch of Moneysupermarket.com.

By the summer of 2007, on the eve of the company's stock market float, it was valued at around £1 billion. Today the site covers a myriad of sectors, including utilities, travel and general shopping, and Nixon recently landed £200 million from the sale of 100 million shares. A further £20 million is scheduled in dividends to add to the £100 million Nixon banked when the website joined the stock market.

However, you also need something about the way you use the Internet to add extra value over and above the traditional ways in which your product or service is sold. Online employment agencies, for example, can add value to their websites by offering clients and applicants useful information such as interview tips, prevailing wage rates and employment law updates.

But using the Internet to take an old idea and turn it into a new and more cost-efficient business can be a winner. Check out the example in the 'Winning on the net' sidebar. Chapter 15 is devoted exclusively to the subject of making a success of getting online and making money.

Solving customer problems

Sometimes existing suppliers just aren't meeting customers' needs. Big firms often don't have the time to pay attention to all their customers properly because doing so just isn't economic. Recognising that enough people exist with needs and expectations that aren't being met can constitute an opportunity for a new small firm to start up.

Start by recalling the occasions when you've had reason to complain about a product or service. You can extend that by canvassing the experiences of friends, relatives and colleagues. If you spot a recurring complaint, that may be a valuable clue about a problem just waiting to be solved.

Next, go back over the times when firms you've tried to deal with have put restrictions or barriers in the way of your purchase. If those restrictions seem easy to overcome, and others share your experience, then you may well be on the trail of a new business idea.

Creating inventions and innovations

Inventions and innovations are all too often almost the opposite of identifying a gap in the market or solving an unsolved problem. Inventors usually start by looking through the other end of the telescope. They find an interesting problem and solve it. There may or may not be a great need for whatever it is they invent.

The Post-it note is a good example of inventors going out on a limb to satisfy themselves rather than to meet a particular need or even solve a burning problem. The story goes that scientists at 3M, a giant American company, came across an adhesive that failed most of their tests. It had poor adhesion qualities because it could be separated from anything it was stuck to. No obvious market existed, but they persevered and pushed the product on their marketing department, saying that the new product had unique properties in that it stuck 'permanently, but temporarily'. The rest, as they say, is history.

Never go down the lonely inventor's route without getting plenty of help and advice. Chapter 7 gives you details of organisations that can smooth your path from the bench to the market. You should also make sure that someone else hasn't already grabbed your innovation, and that you can put a legal fence around it to keep rustlers out. I deal with copyrights, patents and the like in Chapter 5.

Marketing other people's ideas

You may not have a business idea of your own, but nevertheless feel strongly that you want to work for yourself. This approach isn't unusual. Sometimes an event such as redundancy, early retirement or a financial windfall prompts you to searching for a business idea.

Business ideas often come from the knowledge and experience gained in previous jobs, but take time to come into focus. Usually, you need a good flow of ideas before one arrives that appeals to you and appears viable.

You can trawl for ideas and opportunities in any number of ways:

- ✔ **Browse websites.** The Internet is a great source of business ideas. Try Entrepreneurs.com (www.entrepreneur.com/bizopportunities), which lists hundreds of ideas for new businesses, together with information on start-up costs and suggestions for further research. It also has a series of checklists to help you evaluate a business opportunity to see whether it's right for you. Home Working (www.homeworkinguk.com) lists dozens of current business ideas exclusively aimed at the British market.

> ✔ **Read business magazines.** Periodicals such as *Start Your Business* magazine (`www.startyourbusinessmag.com`) present the bones of a number of ideas each month.
>
> ✔ **Scan papers and periodicals.** Almost all papers and many general magazines too have sections on opportunities and ideas for small businesses.

When answering advertisements for other people's business ideas, take precautions to ensure that you aren't about to become a victim of a fraudulent venture. The Advertising Standards Authority (ASA) warns that not all 'get rich quick' offers are genuine. These advertisements can lure even quite sophisticated people into bogus schemes. The ASA believes that 'fooling all of the people all of the time' is entirely possible when the product or service is interesting or persuasive enough. Recent complaints include those about a mailshot saying: 'No more telephone bills for you – ever.' For £7.50, GP Services of Huntingdon offered to disclose details of a technique that had been 'tried, tested and proven', required no equipment or capital and was 'currently being used throughout the UK'. The method was just to contact British Telecom's customer services department and ask to be disconnected. Upholding complaints against the firm, the authority ruled that it 'exploited consumers' credulity'.

The ASA (`www.asa.org.uk`) publishes a quarterly list of complaints that it has considered or is investigating. Also check out websites such as `www.scambusters.org`, `www.scam.com` and `www.fraudguides.com`, which track the latest wheezes doing the rounds both on- and offline.

Being better or different

To have any realistic hope of success, every business opportunity must pass one crucial test: the idea or the way the business is to operate must be different from or better than any other business in the same line of work. In other words you need a *unique selling proposition* (USP), or its Internet equivalent, a *killer application*.

The thinking behind these two propositions is that your business should have a near-unbeatable competitive advantage if your product or service offers something highly desirable that others in the field can't easily copy: something that only you can offer. Dyson's initial USP was the bagless cleaner, and Amazon's was 'one-click' shopping, a system for retaining customer details that made buying online a less painful experience.

Inventors need to be persistent. James Dyson took five years and 5,127 prototypes to produce the world's first bagless vacuum cleaner. The result was so successful that, despite patent protection, Hoover tried to imitate the product. Dyson then had an 18-month legal battle on his hands before he finally won a victory against Hoover for patent infringement.

The trick with USPs and killer applications doesn't just lie with developing the idea in the first place, but making it difficult for others to copy it. (Chapter 5 suggests ways to protect your USP.)

If neither you nor the product or service you're offering stands out in some way, why on earth would anyone want to buy from you? But don't run off with the idea that only new inventions have any hope of success. Often just doing what you say you'll do, when you say you'll do it, is enough to make you stand out from the crowd.

That was all Tom Farmer did when he founded Kwik-Fit. He put his finger on the main criticisms people had of garages. The experience of getting an exhaust fitted or tyres changed was made seriously unpleasant simply because you couldn't rely on the garage's cost estimate or be sure when your car would be ready. The message always was: ring us at 4:00 p.m. and we'll let you know. Farmer's big idea was simply to make promises he could keep, to meet deadlines and to keep to estimated costs. And wow, that was enough to build a business that the Ford Motor Company thought was worth the billion pounds they paid for it.

I point out ways to test the feasibility of your business idea in Chapter 4.

Finding a contract in the public sector

However tough the economic climate, one sector of customers is always buying: the public sector. Roads have to be built, hospitals run, soldiers armed and legislation extended and enforced. The government invests a lot of money, and is eager to encourage small, new and owner-managed firms to grab a slice of the action.

Check out Contracts Finder (`www.gov.uk/contracts-finder`). Using this free online tool you can find detailed information about contracts with the government and its agencies.

Banning Bad Reasons to Start a Business

You may have any number of good reasons to start a business, but make sure that you're not starting a business for the wrong reasons – some of which I explore in the following sections.

Steering clear of bad assumptions

You need to be sure that your business idea isn't a lemon. You can't be sure that you've a winning idea on your hands, but you can take steps to make sure that you avoid obvious losers. Much as you want to start a business, don't get in over your head because you start from a bad premise, such as those in the following list:

- ✔ **The market needs educating.** You may think that you have a situation in which the market doesn't yet realise it can't live without your product or service. Many early Internet businesses fitted this description and look what happened to them. If you think that customers have to be educated before they purchase your product, walk away from the idea and leave it to people with deep pockets and a long-time horizon; they'll need them.

- ✔ **We're first to market.** Gaining 'first-mover advantage' is a concept used to justify a headlong rush into a new business, but as I explain in Chapter 1, the idea is probably incorrect.

- ✔ **If we can get just 1 per cent of the market, we're on to a winner.** No markets exist with a vacant percentage or two just waiting to be filled. Entering almost any market involves displacing someone else, even if your product is new. Po Na Na, a chain of late-night souk bars, failed despite being new and apparently without competitors. If the company had captured just 1 per cent of the dining market instead of 100 per cent of the souk-eating student market, it may have survived. But the dining market had Italian, Indian, Greek and French competitors already in place. This, when combined with the vastly improved range of ready-to-eat meals from the supermarket, means that companies fight bitterly over every hundredth of a per cent of this market.

Every business begins with an idea, but it doesn't necessarily have to be your own idea. It has to be a viable idea, which means that the market has to contain customers who want to buy from you. And enough of them have to exist to make you the kind of living you want. It may be an idea that you've nursed and investigated for years, or it may be someone else's great idea that's just too big for her to exploit on her own. A franchised business is one example of a business idea that has room for more than one would-be business starter to get involved. Franchises can be run at many levels, ranging from simply taking up a local franchise, through to running a small chain of two to five such franchises covering neighbouring areas.

Avoiding obvious mistakes

Your enthusiasm for starting a business is a valuable asset as long as you don't let it blind you to practical realities. The following list contains some reasoning to resist.

✔ **Starting in a business sector of which you've little or no previous knowledge or experience.** The grass always looks greener, making business opportunities in distant lands or in technologies with which you've only a passing acquaintance seem disproportionately attractive. Taking this route leads to disaster. Success in business depends on superior market knowledge from the outset and sustaining that knowledge in the face of relentless competition.

✔ **Putting in more money than you can afford to lose, especially if you have to pay upfront.** You need time to find out how business works. If you've spent all your capital and exhausted your capacity for credit on the first spin of the wheel, you're more of a gambler than an entrepreneur. The true entrepreneur takes only a calculated risk. Freddie Laker, who started the first low-cost, no-frills airline, bet everything he could raise on buying more planes than he could afford. To compound the risk, he bet against the exchange rate between the pound and the dollar – and lost. Learn from Mr Laker's mistake.

✔ **Pitting yourself against established businesses before you're strong enough to resist them.** Laker also broke the third taboo: he took on the big boys on their own ground. He upset the British and American national carriers on their most lucrative routes. There was no way that big, entrenched businesses with deep pockets would yield territory to a newcomer without a fight to the death. That's not to say that Laker's business model was wrong. After all, Ryanair and easyJet have proved that it can work. But those businesses tackled the short-haul market to and from new airfields and, in the case of easyJet, at least started out with tens of millions of pounds of family money that came from a lifetime in the transportation business.

Recognising that the Economy Matters

The state of the economy in general has an effect both on the propensity of people to start a business and on their chances of survival. Although business cycles have no doubt been in existence for centuries, a serious study of the subject is barely 150 years old. Joseph Schumpeter, the American economist who more or less invented the subject of economics, defined the cycle itself as 'the economic ebb and flow that defines capitalism'. 'Cycles,' he wrote, 'are not, like tonsils, separable things that might be treated by themselves, but are, like the beat of the heart, of the essence of the organism that displays them.' In a later work, he went on to claim that business enterprises operate in 'the perennial gale of creative destruction'. This creative destruction – the term for which Schumpeter is perhaps best remembered – is the by-product of the continuous stream of innovation; the more radical the innovation – steam, electricity, the Internet – the more violent the cycle.

Spotting cycles

Seeing a business cycle on the horizon would be a doddle if there weren't so many of them and they weren't all so different! At least four competing, overlapping and even contradictory theories exist about the shape and form of business cycles, including:

- ✔ **The Juglar Cycle,** named after Clement Juglar, a French economist who studied interest rate and price changes in the 1860s and observed boom and bust waves of 9 to 11 years going through four phases in each cycle:

    - **Prosperity:** Where investors rush into new and exciting ventures.

    - **Crisis:** When business failure rates start to rise.

    - **Liquidation:** When investors pull out of markets.

    - **Recession:** When the consequences of these failures begin to be felt in the wider economy in terms of job losses and reduced consumption.

- ✔ **The Kitchin Cycle,** also known as the inventory cycle, named after Joseph Kitchin who discovered a 40-month cycle resulting from a study of US and UK statistics from 1890 to 1922. When demand appears to be stronger than it really is, companies build and carry too much inventory, leading people to overestimate likely future growth. When that higher growth fails to materialise, inventories are reduced, often sharply, so inflicting a 'boom, bust' pressure on the economy.

- ✔ **Kondratieff's theory** was that the advent of capitalism had created long-wave economic cycles lasting around 50 years. His theories received a boost when the Great Depression (1929–1933) hit world economies. The idea of a long wave is supported by evidence that major enabling technologies, from the first printing press to the Internet, take 50 years to yield full value, before themselves being overtaken.

- ✔ **Kuznet's Cycle,** proposed by Simon Kuznet, is based around the proposition that it takes 15 to 25 years to acquire land, get the necessary permissions, build property and sell. Also known as the building cycle, this theory has credibility because so much of economic life is influenced by property and the related purchases of furniture and associated professional charges, for example for lawyers, architects and surveyors.

Since 1900, 27 *bull markets* have existed in the UK, roughly corresponding to the upswing of an economic cycle, when brands can rise sharply with the incoming economic tide. (In summer 2013, the UK was gripped by the latest one.) For every bull market, a corresponding *bear market* exists (though predicting its timing accurately is rarely easy) when over-optimistic firms get mauled because the bottom drops out of stock markets.

Readying for the ups and downs

Clearly, it would be helpful if a business starter could have warning in advance about the likelihood of a downturn. In much the same way as a shipping forecast helps sailors trim their boats before a storm, some advance warning would let businesses do the same. Sailors don't need to have a detailed knowledge of what causes tides, currents and winds, just an indication of when a change is likely to occur and how serious and prolonged the event will be. Information on the timing, strength, shape and path of the downturn stage of an economic cycle would help managers.

People generally understand and recognise the broad shape of the effect of the economic cycle on output: in other words, total demand for goods and services (see Figure 2-1). But a few caveats to this pattern exist. A *double dip* can occur with two downturns before recovery gets properly underway, and occasionally long periods of *flat-lining* can occur, where the economy virtually stands still, neither growing nor contracting.

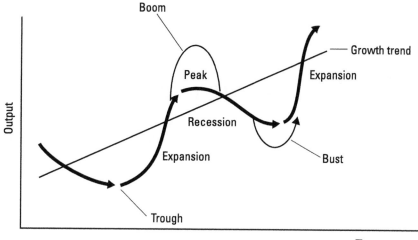

Figure 2-1:
Typical
path of an
economic
cycle.

Unfortunately, no one has yet come up with a reliable way of anticipating the turning points in cycles. Only two economists, Friedrich von Hayek and Ludwig von Mises, forecasted the stock market crash of 1929. The Harvard Economics Society concluded in November after the 1929 crash that 'a depression seems improbable; we expect a recovery of business next spring with further improvements in the fall'. In fact, the Society was to dissolve itself before the depression was halfway through its life. 'All economic cycles are easy to predict, apart from the one you're in' is the helpful guidance on offer from most academic economists.

Maynard Keynes, the famous British economist, described the cause of the violent and unpredictable nature of the business cycle as 'animal spirits', or people's tendency to let emotions, particularly swings from excessive optimism to excessive pessimism, influence their economic actions. In short, the business cycle is all down to how millions of people feel!

Two schools of thought exist on whether starting a business is more difficult when the economy is contracting, corresponding to whether you subscribe to the belief that a glass is half full or half empty. On the one hand, fewer competitors are in the market, because many have failed. But on the other hand, those remaining are both seasoned warriors and more desperate to keep what small amount of business exists to themselves.

Most people start a business when they want to and not at a favourable stage in the economic cycle. That, however, doesn't mean that you can simply ignore the economy. In much the same way as a prudent sailor pays attention to the state of the tide, you need to see whether the general trend of the economy is working with or against you.

If you've a choice of when to start up, having the current working for you is usually better than having it against you, so choose to open your business during an economic upswing, if possible.

Preparing to Recognise Success

To be truly successful in running your own business, you have to both make money and have fun. That's your pay-off for the long hours, the pressure of meeting tough deadlines and the constant stream of problems that accompany most start-up ventures.

One measure of success for any business is just staying in business. That's not as trite a goal as it sounds, nor is it easily achieved, as you can see by looking at the number of businesses that fail each year. However, survival isn't enough. Cash flow, which I look at in Chapter 8, is the key to survival, but becoming profitable and making worthwhile use of the assets you employ determine whether staying in business is worth all your hard work.

Measuring business success

No one in their right mind sets out to run an unsuccessful business, although that's exactly what millions of business founders end up doing. Answering the following questions can act as a check on your progress and keep you on track to success.

✔ **Are you meeting your goals and objectives?** In Chapter 6 I talk about setting down business goals. Achieving those goals and objectives is both motivational and, ultimately, the reason you're in business.

✔ **Are you making enough money?** This question may sound daft, but it may well be the most important one you ask. The answer comes out of your reply to two subsidiary questions:

- **Can you do better by investing your time and money elsewhere?** If the answer to this question is yes, go back to the drawing board with your business idea.

- **Can you make enough money to invest in growing your business?** The answer to this question only becomes clear when you work out your profit margins, which I cover in Chapter 13. But the fact that many businesses don't make enough money to reinvest in themselves is pretty evident when you see scruffy, run-down premises, worn-out equipment and the like.

✔ **Can you work to your values?** Anita Roddick's Body Shop had a clearly articulated set of values that she and every employee bought into. Every aspect of the business, from product and market development down to the recruitment process, promoted this value system – if you weren't green, you didn't join. Ms Roddick's philosophy may have been a little higher than you feel like going, but values can help guide you and your team when the going gets tough.

Exploring the myth and reality of business survival rates

Misinformation continually circulates about the number of failing businesses. The most persistent and wrong statistic is that 70 per cent (some quote 90 per cent) of all new businesses fail. The failure rate is high, but not that high. And in any case the term *failure* itself, if people use the word to mean a business closing down, has a number of subtly different nuances.

Millions of small businesses start up, but many survive for a relatively short time. Over half of all independently owned ventures cease trading within five years of starting up. However, if you can make it for five years, the chances of your business surviving increase dramatically from earlier years.

The Office of the Official Receiver lists the following causes for business failures:

✔ **Bad debts:** Unfortunately, having great products and services and customers keen to buy them is only half the problem. The other half is making sure that those customers pay up on time. One or two late or non-payers can kill off a start-up venture. In Chapter 13, you can find strategies to make sure that you get paid and aren't left in the lurch.

✔ **Competition:** Without a sound strategy for winning and retaining customers, your business is at the mercy of the competition. In Chapter 10, you can discover how to win the battle for the customer.

✔ **Excessive remuneration to the owners:** Some business owners mistake the cash coming into the business for profit and take that money out as drawings. They forget that they have to allow for periodic bills for tax, value added tax (VAT), insurance and replacement equipment before they can calculate the true profit, and hence what they can safely draw out of the business. In Chapter 13 you can discover how to tell profit from cash and how to allow for future bills.

✔ **Insufficient turnover:** This situation can occur if the fixed costs of your business are too high for the level of sales turnover achieved. Chapter 13 shows how to calculate your break-even point and so keep sales levels sufficient to remain profitable.

✔ **Lack of proper accounting:** Often business founders are too busy in the start-up phase to keep track of the figures. They pile up invoices and bills to await a convenient moment when they can enter these figures in the accounts. However, without timely financial information, you may miss key signals or make wrong decisions. In Chapter 13, you can read about how to keep on top of the numbers.

✔ **Not enough capital:** You, along with most business start-ups, may hope to get going on a shoestring. But you need to be realistic about how much cash you need to get underway and stay in business until sales volumes build up. In Chapter 8, you can see how to plan your cash flow so that you can survive.

✔ **Poor management and supervision:** You may well know how your business works, but sharing that knowledge and expertise with those you employ isn't always that easy. In Chapter 11, you see how to manage, control and get the best employees to give of their best.

Chapter 3

Can You Do the Business?

In This Chapter

▶ Understanding whether being your own boss is right for you

▶ Checking out various ventures

▶ Setting up your business at home

▶ Figuring out your profit motive

▶ Taking a skills inventory to identify any gaps

*G*overnments are keen to foster entrepreneurship: new businesses create jobs for individuals and increased prosperity for nations, which are both primary goals for any government. If these new firms don't throw people out of work when recessions start to bite, supporting them becomes doubly attractive.

But people, you included, don't start businesses or grow existing ones simply to please politicians or to give their neighbours employment. They've many reasons for considering self-employment. The idea of escaping the daily grind of working for someone else and being in charge of their own destiny attracts most people. But despite the many potential benefits, they face real challenges and problems, and self-employment isn't a realistic option for everyone.

The questions you need to ask yourself are: Can I do it? Am I really the entrepreneurial type? What are my motivations and aims? How do I find the right business for me? This chapter can help you discover the answers.

Deciding What You Want From a Business

See whether you relate to any of the most common reasons people give for starting up in business:

✔ Being able to make your own decisions

✔ Having a business to leave to your children

✔ Creating employment for the family

✔ Being able to capitalise on specialist skills

✔ Earning your own money when you want

✔ Having flexible working hours

✔ Wanting to take a calculated risk

✔ Reducing stress and worry

✔ Having the satisfaction of creating something truly your own

✔ Being your own boss

✔ Working without having to rely on other people

The two central themes connecting all these reasons seem to revolve around gaining personal satisfaction – making work as much fun as any other aspect of life – and creating wealth – essential if an enterprise is going to last any length of time.

Even when your personality fits and your goals are realistic, you have to make sure that the business you're starting is a good fit for your abilities.

The following sections explore these reasons in more detail.

Gaining personal satisfaction (or, entrepreneurs just wanna have fun)

No one particularly enjoys being told what to do and where and when to do it. Working for someone else's organisation brings all those disadvantages. When you work for yourself, the only person to blame if your job is boring, repetitive or takes up time that you should perhaps spend with family and friends is yourself.

Another source of personal satisfaction comes from the ability to 'do things my way'. Employees are constantly puzzled and often irritated by the decisions their bosses impose on them. All too often, managers in big firms say that they'd never spend their own money in the way the powers that be encourage or instruct them to do. Managers and subordinates alike feel constrained by company policy, which seems to set out arbitrary standards for dealing with customers and employees in the same way.

The high failure rate for new businesses suggests that the glamour of starting up on their own seduces some people who may be more successful and more contented in some other line of endeavour.

Running your own firm allows you to do things in a way that you think the market, and your employees, believe to be right at the time.

'Create fun and a little weirdness': Zappos

Nick Swinmurn pitched his proposal to sell shoes online to investment firm Venture Frogs. Though initially doubtful, the venture capitalists were wooed after Swinmurn showed them that foot-wear in the USA was a 40-billion-dollar market with a sizeable piece of that, 5 per cent, already being sold through conventional mail-order catalogues. With an investment of $2 million, Swinmurn launched Zappos (a variation of *zapa-tos*, the Spanish word for shoes). By 2013, Zappos was a success and had branched out into cloth-ing, sports equipment and a wedding shop, with the hint of more to come.

Part of Swinmurn's success comes down to the ten core principles he devised for Zappos. Principle number 3 – create fun and a little weirdness – aims to ensure that everyone working in the company can share something of the same experience that Swinmurn has in run-ning his own business. To that end, Zappos has a host of zany ways to make working life more fun. Aside from throwing birthday parties for their staff, for example, they open their doors for safe trick or treating at Halloween, and turn their office into a haunted house and spend the day scaring their visitors!

Making money

Apart from winning the lottery, starting your own business is the only pos-sible way to achieve full financial independence. But it isn't risk-free. In truth, most people who work for themselves don't become mega rich. However, many do, and many more become far wealthier than they'd probably have become working for someone else.

You can also earn money working at your own pace when you want to and even help your family to make money too.

Running your own business means taking more risks than you do if you're working for someone else. If the business fails, you stand to lose far more than your job. If, like most owner managers, you opt for *sole trader status* – someone working usually on his own without forming a limited company (find more on business categories in Chapter 5) – you can end up personally liable for any business debts you incur. This debt can mean having to sell your home and other assets to meet your obligations. In these circumstances, not only is all your hard work to no avail, but you can end up worse off than when you started. Also, winding up a business is far from fun or personally satisfying.

I don't want to discourage you, just to apply a reality check. The truth is that running your own business is hard work that often doesn't pay well at first. You have to be okay with those facts in order to have a chance of success.

Saving the planet

Not everyone has making money as their sole aim when setting up in business. According to the government's figures, around 20,000 'social entrepreneurs' run businesses aiming to achieve sustainable social change and trade with a social or environmental purpose. They contribute almost £25 billion to the national economy and assist local communities by creating jobs, providing ethical products and services using sustainable resources, and reinvesting a share of the profits back into society.

Ethical businesses have unique advantages. For example, according to those running such firms, they can relatively easily attract and retain intelligent people. Over 70 per cent of students say that a potential employer's ethical track record is an important factor in job choice. Customers also like ethical firms. According to a recent European Union survey on sustainable consumption, 86 per cent of those polled in the UK, Spain, Germany, Greece and Italy said that they felt strongly about wanting companies to produce and market things responsibly. They also blamed brands for not providing more environmentally and socially friendly products.

If you want to explore the prospects for starting a social enterprise, contact the School for Social Entrepreneurs (website: www.the-sse.org; tel: 020 7089 9120), which can help with specific and tailored support. If you need funds to start a social enterprise, contact Bridges Community Ventures (website: www.bridgesventures.com; tel: 020 7262 5566), a venture capital firm with a social mission. Its founding principle is that all the funds it invests go to businesses with a clear social purpose as well as the aim of achieving financial returns for investors.

Fighting poverty through trade

Traidcraft's mission is to fight poverty through trade, practising and promoting approaches to trade that help poor people in developing countries transform their lives. The company has more than 450 different products sourced from more than 100 producer groups in almost 30 developing countries, selling through its nationwide network of fair traders and online shop. Traidcraft raises funds and gives aid and advice to the tune of £1.5 million a year to help enterprises in developing countries. Projects include improving market access for women producers in Vietnam; helping Indian tea workers achieve sustainable livelihoods; and analysing the dairy sector in Kenya, identifying key constraints affecting smallholder dairy farmers and their access to markets. Traidcraft received the Queen's Award for Industry for Sustainable Development, along with a host of other awards. Oh, and it does a pretty good job of making money too – with a £15-million turnover each year, business has been growing at an average of 18 per cent a year, making a return on capital of 10 per cent. More details are on the company's website, www.traidcraft.co.uk.

Exploring Different Types of Business

At one level, all businesses are the same – they sell something to people who want to buy from them, while trying to make an honest buck along the way. At another level, many different types of business and ways of doing business exist, even within what superficially can appear to be similar fields.

Selling to other businesses

Business-to-business (B2B) enterprises, such as those selling market research, database management, corporate clothing, management consultancy, tele-marketing or graphic design, involve one business person selling to another. The attractions are that you're dealing with other people who have a definite need and usually buy in relative large quantities and at regular intervals. For example, an individual may buy envelopes in packs of a dozen a few times a year, but a business buys hundreds, perhaps even thousands, and puts in an order every month. Corporate customers are harder to win, but are often worth more when you have them. And unlike private individuals, businesses like to forge relationships that endure over time.

Some downsides exist too. Business customers expect credit, perhaps taking between 60 and 90 days to pay up. If they go bust, they may owe a lot of money and take some of their suppliers down with them. You may have to attend exhibitions to make your presence known, a costly and time-consuming process, or advertise in trade directories. Check out these websites to find out more about these topics: www.greatbritishbusinessshow.co.uk and www.b2bindex.co.uk.

Opening all hours

Conventional shops, restaurants and the like have long opening hours and have to meet the expectations of increasingly savvy consumers, whose access to the Internet has made them aware of competitive prices as well as high specifications and standards of service. The upside of any form of retailing is that you're almost invariably paid up front. But just because you get the cash in your hand doesn't mean that you don't have to meet exacting standards. Customers are protected in their dealings in a myriad of ways. If you fall short of their legal entitlement, you can end up with a bigger bill than a simple cash refund. (I cover legal issues in Chapter 10, 'Marketing and Selling Your Wares'.) In conventional retailing, you also have to rent premises and stock them with products, both factors that can add significantly to the business risk.

Increasingly, new retail business start-ups are Internet-based. The website is in effect the shop window and the stock of products being sold may even be in a warehouse owned by a third party. This arrangement keeps upfront costs down but means keeping abreast of fast-changing technologies – the Internet, servers and computer hardware and software. (I look at these topics in more depth in Chapter 15.)

Making products

One of the attractions of manufacturing is that you've a greater degree of control over the quality, cost and specification of the end product than a retailer or wholesaler might. But with those advantages come some hefty penalties. Factories, equipment, stocks of raw materials and employees are costly overheads. You have to incur these expenses well before you're certain of any orders – an unlikely way into business for someone without previous manufacturing experience and a deep wallet. Such owners also bear significant risks towards their employees. The UK manufacturing sector reports over 32,000 work-related accidents to the Health and Safety Executive each year. This figure includes over 6,200 major injuries, such as fractures and amputations, as well as around 40 fatalities.

A more likely route to manufacturing for a new business is subcontracting, where you're working for a manufacturer on part of a product. The most common examples of subcontractors are plumbers, electricians and carpenters in building work, metal and plastic casing production and the like in civil engineering, and a wide range of activities in the information technology sector.

Servicing customers

Service industries now dominate the British economy and account for around 70 per cent of gross domestic product (the value of the goods and services that the country produces). Services include financial intermediaries; hairdressing; real estate; computer services; research and development; education; health and social work; refuse disposal; recreational, cultural and sporting activities; and an extensive range of other activities where no physical goods play a major part in any transaction. In truth, however, most manufactured goods include a service element, though the business functions are often separated. For example, manufacturing businesses produce cars but are quite separate from the garage chains that repair those vehicles. However, some manufacturers go further – Dell manufactures computers and also carries out delivery and many other service functions.

Service businesses require a high degree of personal involvement and as such call for founders who see their people skills as pivotal. In a nutshell, if you don't enjoy understanding the intimate details of what makes customers tick and then going out of your way to meet their needs, running a service business may be of little appeal.

Working from Home

Few dedicated statistics exist on the number of people operating home-based enterprises as distinct from those setting up in dedicated premises. IDC, a US-based research firm, claims that around 18 million of the 29 million owner-managed businesses in US are home-based. US census data shows that 17.6 million businesses employ no one but the boss. Put these two facts together and, working on the reasonable assumption that the majority of home-based businesses are one-man (and one-woman) bands, around two thirds of all small business would appear to be home-based. Even those not working from home now often start out from there, like Simon Nixon, who founded the price comparison site Moneysupermarket.com (see Chapter 2).

Starting a business from home gives you a number of distinct advantages over those plumping for premises straight away. Here are three big advantages that a home-based business has over its peers that give it an edge:

- **Lower costs:** Starting from home saves most of the £35,000 start-up costs that the average business incurs even before it takes its first order. The chances are that you've nearly everything you need to start up your business already somewhere around your home. You can press into service a garage, loft, spare bedroom or garden shed for a whole host of business-related tasks from holding stock to being a dedicated office space away from the normal hustle of home life. Your computer, however old, is almost definitely just fine, unless you're starting a business at the cutting edge of design or on the Internet.

- **More time:** Money can buy lots of things, but time isn't one of them. However close to your business premises you are, you'll spend an hour or more a day travelling to and from it. I'm sure if your shop, restaurant or office is only a couple of miles away, you won't believe that proposition. How on earth is it possible to take an hour to travel just a mile? Well, an immutable law says that the closer your home is to your business premises, the more often you travel between the two. Ergo, if you're 20 miles away, you go once a day, covering 40 miles, and if you're only 5 miles away, you come home for lunch and return once or twice more each week to collect things you've forgotten. Whatever the distance, the average weekly travel time is about the same. Working from home gives you back all that wasted time spent travelling, and you can invest the time in your business.

- **Less stress:** Commuting to work on a daily basis is stressful. In any vibrant and successful economic area, road works, accidents, delays and traffic jams are pretty much the norm. Few people are fortunate enough to work in a car-free area or where parking is never a problem. Even if you can find such a paradise, the chances are it would be useless as a business proposition. Depopulated areas are equally devoid of customers, suppliers and people to employ.

Finding the space

As a first step, list all the activities involved in getting your business to the point where it has something to sell. If you're going to run a bookkeeping service, this list may be quite short. You need a computer, some software and perhaps a leaflet setting out your prices and the range of services on offer. But if you're going to repair musical instruments, say, then you may need much more space, including perhaps a workshop.

Clearly, if you live in a cul-de-sac at the end of a narrow lane surrounded by other houses, you're unlikely to be allowed to manufacture using hazardous chemicals and have articulated vehicles delivering and collecting in the middle of the night. You also have to consider how your neighbours may be affected, even if you're legally allowed to operate your business.

You don't, of course, have to carry out every activity related to your business yourself, nor do you have to do it all on your premises. If you think about it, you can see that no business does everything itself.

When you know how much space you need for business and what you'll be doing in that space, you can start to scour your home and garden for space to convert to business use. The following sections outline areas to consider – not an exhaustive list, but enough ideas to kick-start your thinking.

Using the garage

The most obvious discreet space that's separate from the house and likely to be free of family traffic is your garage (if you have one). You can move cars onto the drive or a neighbouring street, subject to your insurance company being happy with that arrangement. According to the RAC Foundation, although 71 per cent of motorists have a garage, only 41 per cent use it to park their car. Most people use it as storage for junk or are too lazy to open the garage doors.

The Garage Conversion Company has sample plans and information on any possible restrictions that may apply (www.garageconversion.com; go to Conversion Ideas and then Home Office).

Parking in the parking space

This area and any private drive could be used for a caravan-based office, although you need to keep in mind that visitors, suppliers and of course you and your family still need to get access to your home.

If you do think that a caravan is worth considering, check out that your house deeds allow you to have one. Covenants were introduced into the title deeds of new properties from the 1960s onwards to prevent people keeping caravans at home. Even if you're legally allowed to keep a caravan at home, you should consider any possible impact on your neighbours and discuss your plans with them. Caravans that can be used as a home office, though probably not as touring caravans, sell for upwards of £1,000.

Planting yourself in the garden

You can install a shed up to 4 square metres without planning consent under certain circumstances. The exact rules are a little complicated; for example the shed can't be bigger than 50 per cent of your garden, you can't erect one in a conservation area and your title deeds can't expressly prohibit you. Great Little Garden (www.greatlittlegarden.co.uk) and Leisure Buildings (www.leisurebuildings.com) both offer advice on planning issues and have sections on using garden sheds as home offices. Sheds that you can use for home office purposes sell at garden centres for £800 upwards.

A further alternative, if space allows, is to rent or buy a portable 'room'. Portakabin (www.portakabin.co.uk) and Foremans Relocatable Building Systems (www.foremansbuildings.co.uk) have selections of new and second-hand cabins for rent and sale.

Climbing into an attic

Converting an attic to usable space is likely to be an expensive option and something to consider later after your business is up and running: £10,000 is the entry level price including a ladder and a window; double that if you want to include a WC, plastered walls and a power supply.

You may not need planning permission, but as with garden sheds the rules are complicated. Check out the Planning Portal (www.planningportal.gov.uk/permission/commonprojects/loftconversion) which has information on the rules and much besides.

Guidelines for using space at home

Keep these factors in mind when deciding on an area of your home to work from:

✔ The room or area needs to be well lit, warm in winter and cool in summer.

✔ The space shouldn't be claustrophobic because you may be in it 12 hours a day.

✔ Somewhere you can close the door, shut your business off and get on with normal family life is a great asset.

✔ Allow room for modest expansion. Try to anticipate what your business may look like a year down the line and make sure that the space you allocate can accommodate such growth. Moving is disruptive, time consuming and expensive.

✔ You need power, a telephone line and access to the Internet.

Doubling up in the spare room

If you do have a spare or under-utilised room, your search for office space is probably over. It will have heat, light and power and may also be out of the way of general family traffic. If this room is currently a bedroom, you could get the best of both worlds by putting in a sofa bed and desk with locked drawers. In that way occasional guests can still use the room and you can have it for most of the time. Though far from ideal, this option can be a low-cost one that you can implement quickly.

Options (www.optionsfit.com) provides guides and products for turning your spare room into an office.

Checking out the rules

Whatever business you plan to run from home, and whether the space you use is inside or outside of your property, you need to check out a number of important rules and regulations before you start up.

Planning consent and building regulations

The extent to which the use of your home and the land it stands on changes determines whether or not you need planning consent or to consider building regulations. You may need permission for any structural alterations, an increase in traffic, noise or smells, or anything such as operating unreasonable hours or a disturbance that can affect your neighbours.

You can find out informally from your local council before applying, and the Communities and Local Government website (www.gov.uk/government/topics/planning-and-building) has detailed information on all these matters. You can also get free answers to specific questions from UK Planning, whose site offers planning advice written specifically for your region (www.ukplanning.com).

Looking at health, safety and hazards

If you're working with materials that are flammable, toxic, give off fumes or are corrosive, you should check the website of the Health and Safety Executive (www.hse.gov.uk/risk), where you'll find detailed guidance and advice on all aspects of safety at work.

Considering insurance

Your home insurance policy won't cover any business activity, so you must inform your insurer what you plan to do from home. You can find out more about whether or not what you plan to do from home needs special insurance cover and where to find an insurance company on the Confused.com website (www.confused.com/home-insurance/guides/home-insurance-for-home-based-workers).

Managing the mortgage

Unless you own fully the freehold of your property, some other party such as a mortgage lender, landlord or freeholder may need to give their permission for you to run a business from home. Even as a freeholder, you may find that a covenant has been included in your title deeds to prevent you operating certain activities from your home.

Realising business rates

You currently pay council tax on your home, but after you start using part of it or your grounds for business purposes you may be liable to pay business rates on the part of the property you use for work. You can see examples of how business rating applies to home-based businesses on the Valuation Office Agency website (go to `www.voa.gov.uk/corporate/Publications/workingFromHome.html`). Some types of small business, particularly those in rural areas providing products or services of particular benefit to the community, are exempt from paying business rates, or pay at a reduced rate. Your local council has details of such schemes.

Anticipating capital gains tax implications

Any increase in value of your main home is usually free of capital gains tax (CGT) when you sell. However, if you set aside a room or particular area solely for working in then you may be liable for CGT on that proportion of any gain. If you expect to use a large (over 10 per cent) part of your home for business, take professional advice from your accountant and check the HM Revenue and Customs website (`www.hmrc.gov.uk/cgt`) for more information on CGT and how to calculate any possible liability.

Tax rates and their methods of payment are always in a state of flux, so it pays to check out the current situation.

Readying for refuse

If your business creates additional or different refuse from that of a normal domestic nature, you should check your local council's policy on collecting for businesses. Also check on NetRegs (`www.netregs.org.uk`), the government website that provides free environmental guidance for small businesses in the UK, what your responsibilities are for disposing of waste and hazardous substances.

Keeping in with the neighbours

After you've satisfied yourself that you're complying with all the relevant rules and regulations, you're prudent to advise your immediate neighbours of your plans. They may be concerned when they see any unusual comings and goings from your home and a timely word sets their minds at rest. Talking with neighbours is especially important if you're doing building work.

The government website Gov.uk has useful pointers on what can cause problems with neighbours and how to resolve such issues (www.gov.uk/how-to-resolve-neighbour-disputes/overview).

Dealing with the family

You may be inclined to slop around just because you're working at home. The dangers here are twofold:

✔ You give out the wrong signals to everyone around you. As far as they can see you're just 'at home' and as such available for more or less anything that they'd usually expect in a domestic environment.

✔ You may not feel as though you're at work yourself. The operative word here is *appropriate*. That doesn't have to mean a suit and tie, but 'smart casual' is a good yardstick and certainly a notch up from what you wear around the house normally, say at weekends.

Dress is a powerful way of sending signals to those around you that you're 'at work'. Here are a few other tools to help harmonise business and personal life while you work.

Negotiating with your partner

Your spouse, partner or housemate, whether or not he has a part to play in your business, will be affected and expect to be consulted on how you plan to make use of what he probably sees as his premises. The effect is double if he's picking up the financial slack until your business gets going. These measures help keep your loved one onside:

✔ Tell him about your business ideas early on and why you think that you'll succeed without disrupting home life unreasonably.

✔ Discuss the space you need, why you need it and if necessary 'trade' space. If you have to have one of the bedrooms, see what can you offer as compensation. In one rather dramatic case, a boat builder needed all the downstairs rooms for 12 months to build a prototype. The boat builder agreed with his partner to build a patio and conservatory the year his first boat sold.

✔ See whether you can provide a 'quick win' for everyone in your home. For example, if you need broadband Internet, offer access to everyone either by setting time aside on your computer or by providing another wireless-enabled computer. Or if you're painting and redecorating your office, get other rooms done too.

✔ Explain the upside potential of what success can mean for everyone in your family when your business gets established: more money, part-time employment for those who want it and eventually perhaps a move to business premises.

Handling children

One of the advantages of starting your business from home is that you can adopt a great work–life balance from the outset. You can take the kids to school, be home when they get back, share meals with them and handle emergency trips to doctors and dentist yourself, rather than having to call in favours from relatives and friends. Few working more conventionally out of an office an hour or more's commute away can look after family matters with such relative ease.

Pre-school children who are going to be at home when you need to work are a different matter altogether. Sometimes they're asleep or resting and you're free to work at will. Otherwise, you've two options. The simplest is to have a nanny to cover your peak working hours. Make sure that the nanny knows you're working and find somewhere in the house where any noise won't disturb you. Alternatively, find a childminder or nursery nearby.

Vanquishing visitors

You may live in an area besieged by door-to-door salespeople, over-friendly neighbours who now know you're working from home or politicians after your vote. You can't be certain than no one is going to call uninvited to discuss business so you have to answer each time. Dealing with an unwanted visitor may only take a couple of minutes, but the interruption to your work flow may add as much as 20 minutes to that wasted time. Three visitors a week and you've lost an hour's output, mounting up to nearly seven man days over the year. That's probably equivalent to half the amount of holiday you're able to take in your first year or so in business, so you need to find a way to isolate yourself from such distractions.

Assessing Yourself

Business isn't just about ideas and market opportunities. Business is about people too, and at the outset it's mostly about *you*. You need to make sure that you have the temperament to run your own business and the expertise and understanding required for the type of business you have in mind.

The test at the end of this section requires no revision or preparation. You may find out the truth about yourself and whether running a business is a great career option or a potential disaster for you.

Discovering your entrepreneurial attributes

Business founders are frequently characterised as people who are bursting with new ideas, highly enthusiastic, hyperactive and insatiably curious. But the more you try to create a clear picture of the typical small business founder, the fuzzier that picture becomes. In reality, the most reliable indicator that a person is likely to start a business is that he has a parent or sibling who runs a business – such people are highly likely to start businesses themselves.

That being said, commentators generally accept some fairly broad characteristics as desirable, if not mandatory. Check whether you recognise yourself in the following list of entrepreneurial traits.

- **Accepting of uncertainty:** An essential characteristic of someone starting a business is a willingness to make decisions and to take risks. This risk-taking doesn't mean gambling on hunches. It means carefully calculating the odds and deciding which risks to take and when to take them.

  Managers in big business tend to seek to minimise risk by delaying decisions until they know every possible fact. They feel that working without all the facts isn't prudent or desirable. Entrepreneurs, on the other hand, know that by the time the fog of uncertainty has completely lifted, too many people are able to spot the opportunity clearly. In fact, an entrepreneur is usually only interested in decisions that involve accepting a degree of uncertainty.

- **Driven to succeed:** Business founders need to be results oriented. Successful people set themselves goals and get pleasure out of trying to achieve them as quickly as possible and then move on to the next goal. This restlessness is highly characteristic.

- **Hardworking:** Don't confuse hard work with long hours. At times an owner-manager has to put in 18-hour days, but that shouldn't be the norm. Even if you do work long hours, as long as you enjoy them that's fine. Enthusiasts can be productive. Workaholics, on the other hand, have a negative, addictive, driven quality where outputs (results) are less important than inputs. This type of hard work is counterproductive. Real hard work means sticking at a task, however difficult, until you complete it. It means hitting deadlines even when you're dead-beat. It means doing some things you don't much enjoy so you can work your way through to the activities that you enjoy most.

- **Healthy:** Apart from being able to put in long days, successful small business owners need to be on the spot to manage the firm every day. Owners are the essential lubricant that keeps the wheels of small business turning. They have to plug any gaps when other people are ill or because they can't afford to employ anyone else for that particular job. They can't afford the luxury of sick leave. Even a week's holiday is something of a luxury in the early years of a business's life.

✔ **Innovative:** Most people recognise innovation as the most distinctive trait of business founders. They tend to tackle the unknown; they do things in new and difficult ways; they weave old ideas into new patterns. But they go beyond innovation itself and carry their concept to market rather than remain in an ivory tower.

✔ **Self-disciplined:** Owner-managers need strong personal discipline to keep themselves and the business on the schedule the plan calls for. This discipline is the drumbeat that sets the timing for everything in the company. Get that wrong and you send incorrect signals to every part of the business, both inside and out.

One of the most common pitfalls for novice businesspeople is failing to recognise the difference between cash and profit. Cash can make people feel wealthy, and if it results in a relaxed attitude to corporate status symbols, such as cars and luxury office fittings, then failure is just around the corner.

✔ **Totally committed:** You must have complete faith in your business idea. That's the only way in which you can convince all the doubters you're bound to meet along the route. But blind faith isn't enough. You have to back your commitment up with a sound business strategy.

✔ **Well rounded:** Small business founders are rarely geniuses. Some people in their business nearly always have more competence in one field than they can ever aspire to. But the founders have a wide range of abilities and a willingness to turn their hand to anything that has to be done to make the venture succeed. They can usually make the product, market it and count the money, but above all they've the self-confidence that lets them move comfortably through uncharted waters.

Working out a business idea that's right for you

Take time to do a simple exercise that can help you decide what type of business is a good match with your abilities. Take a sheet of paper and draw two columns. In the left-hand column, list all your hobbies, interests and skills. In the right-hand column, translate those interests into possible business ideas. Table 3-1 shows an example of such a list.

Table 3-1	Matching a Business Idea to Your Skills
Interest/ Skills	**Business Ideas**
Cars	Car dealer; repair garage; home tuning service; valet and cleaning; taxi
Cooking	Restaurant; home catering service; providing produce for home freezers
Gardening	Supplying produce to flower or vegetable shops; running a nursery; running a garden centre; landscape design; running a gardening service
Using a computer	Typing authors' manuscripts from home; typing back-up service for busy local companies; running a secretarial agency; web design; bookkeeping service; selling online

When you've done this exercise, balance the possibilities against the criteria that are important to you in starting a business.

Figuring out what you're willing to invest

I'm not just talking about money here. How much are you willing to invest of your time, your interest and your education, as well as your (and your investors') money?

Spending time

How much time are you willing to devote to your business? That may sound a basic enough question, but different businesses done in different ways can have quite different time profiles. One business starter I know opened a French bakery in London. He was determined to make his own croissants and did so for the first three months. But making his own bread meant starting work at 4:00 a.m. Because he didn't close until city workers passed his door on their way home, by the time he cleaned up and took stock, he was working a 15-hour day. But he still had the books to do, orders to place and plans to prepare. He eventually settled for a ten-hour day, which meant that he had to buy in ready-baked croissants.

Furthering your education

You may have identified a market opportunity that requires skills over and above those that you currently have. There may, for example, be a gap in the market for Teaching English as a Foreign Language (TEFL), but to do so requires a month of intensive study plus a £1,000 course fee. Doing the TEFL certificate may involve you in more skill upgrading than you want to commit to, at the outset at least. So, you need to find customers who don't require you to have that qualification, or you need to think about a less educationally challenging business.

Keeping things interesting

If you want to start a restaurant and have never worked in catering, get a job in one. That's the best way to find out whether you like a particular type of work. You may find that a restaurant looks different from behind the chair as opposed to on it. Some businesses are inherently repetitive, with activities that follow a predictable pattern. If that suits you, fine, but if not then perhaps you need to consider a business venture with a shifting range of tasks.

Weighting your preferences

After you've an idea of some of the businesses you may want to start, you can rank those businesses according to how closely they match what you want from starting a business. Go through the standards you want your business to meet and assign a weight between 1 and 5 to each, on a range from not important at all to absolutely must have. Next, list your possible business opportunities and measure them against the graded criteria.

Table 3-2 shows a sample ranking for Jane Clark, an imaginary ex-secretary with school-aged children who needs work because her husband has been made redundant and is looking for another job. Jane isn't in a position to raise much capital, and she wants her working hours to coincide with her children's school day. She wants to run her own show and she wants to enjoy what she does.

Table 3-2	Weighing Up the Factors
Criteria	*Weighting Factor*
Minimal capital required	5
Possibility to work hours that suit lifestyle	5
No need to learn new skills	4
Minimal paperwork	3
Work satisfaction	2
Opportunity to meet interesting people	1

Because minimal capital was an important criterion for Jane she gave it a weight of 5, whereas meeting interesting people, being less important to her, was only weighted 1. Jane gave each of her three business ideas a rating, in points (out of five) against these criteria. A secretarial agency needed capital to start so she gave it only 1 point. Back-up typing needed hardly any money and she allocated 5 points to it. Her worked-out chart is shown in Table 3-3.

Table 3-3		Scoring Alternatives				
		Secretarial Agency		Back-up Typing		Authors' Manuscripts
	Weighting Factor	Points	Score	Points	Score	Points	Score
Criteria							
Minimal capital	5 ×	1	5	5	25	4	20
Flexible hours	5 ×	1	5	3	15	5	25
No new skills	4 ×	2	8	5	20	5	20
Work satis-faction	3 ×	4	12	1	3	3	9
Minimal paper-work	2 ×	0	0	4	8	5	10
Meeting people	1 ×	4	4	3	3	4	4
Total score			34		74		88

The weighting factor and the rating point multiplied together give a score for each business idea. The highest score indicates the business that best meets Jane's criteria. In this case, typing authors' manuscripts scores over back-up typing, because Jane can do it exactly when it suits her.

Chapter 4

Testing Feasibility

*Y*ou need to decide whether or not starting up your own business is for you. Maybe you've reached a tentative decision on whether to go it alone or to join forces with others who have valuable resources or ideas to add to your own, and now you've the bones of an idea of what type of business you want to start, buy into, franchise or enter in some other way.

So all you have to do now is wait for the customers to turn up and the cash to roll in. Right? Wrong, regrettably. Although you're beyond square one, you've a good few miles to cover before you can be confident that your big business idea is actually going to work and make money. This chapter gives you the right questions to ask to make you as sure as you can be that you've the best shot at success.

Finding Enough Product or People

The first test of feasibility is whether you can get enough goods to sell or enough people to provide the service you're offering. You need to be sure that you can get your product manufactured at the rate and quantity to meet your needs. Likewise, if you're starting a service business, you need to be sure that you can hire people with the skills you need, whether they're house-cleaners or web page designers.

Of course, if you're buying into a franchise or joining an existing business or co-operative, these issues are already addressed for the most part. Still, it never hurts to do your own assessment of the *supply chain* linking you to your source of materials and onwards to your end customers, if only to famil-iarise yourself with the process.

How much is enough?

The amount of goods or services you need depends in part on the scale of your ambitions and also on what you believe the market can bear. If the area in which you plan to open a restaurant has a total population of 100 people within a 50-mile radius, that fact alone limits the scale of your venture.

It makes sense to work backwards to answer this question. For example, if you want to make at least as much money from your business as you have in wages from your current job, then you can use that figure to work out the initial scale of your level of output. As a rough rule of thumb, if you want to make £10,000 profit before tax, a business involved in manufacturing or processing materials needs to generate between £80,000 and £100,000 worth of orders. Taking away your anticipated profit from the sales target leaves you with the value of the goods and services you need to buy in.

Buying in equipment and supplies

There are four main areas to check out:

- ✔ **Consumable materials:** If you're making things yourself, you need to check out suppliers of raw materials. Even if, like mail-order firms, you're buying in finished product, you should check that out too. You can search on Google, Yahoo!, Bing, Ask Jeeves or any of the major search engines for almost any product or service. However, unless the quantities are large and significantly better terms can be had elsewhere, you're better sticking to local suppliers for consumables. This is an inexpensive way to build up goodwill in the local community and may even create business for you. See *Kellysearch* and *Kompass* directories for details of suppliers of consumables (see the next bullet for details).

- ✔ **Equipment:** If you're going to make any or all of your products yourself, you need to check out suppliers, delivery times, payment terms and so forth for the equipment you need for the production processes. You first need to check out the output levels and quality standards of any equipment you want, to make sure that it meets your needs. You can find equipment suppliers in *Kellysearch* (www.kellysearch.co.uk) or *Kompass* (http://gb.kompass.com). These two directories between them contain information on 23 million products and services from 2.7 million suppliers in over 70 countries. These directories are available both in your local business library and, to a limited extent, online.

- ✔ **Finished goods:** It's usually a better use of scarce cash for a new business to buy in product that's as close to its finished state as possible, leaving you only the high-value-added tasks to complete. Few niche mail-order catalogue businesses make any of their own product; their key skills lie in merchandise selection, advertising copy, web design or buying in the right mailing lists. *Kellysearch* and *Kompass* directories list almost every finished goods supplier.

✔ **Premises:** Finding the right premises can be the limiting factor for some businesses. If, for example, you need to be in a particular type of area, as with restaurants, coffee shops and night clubs, it can take months for the right place to come on the market and even longer to get planning or change-of-use consent if you require that. When you've a clear idea of the type of premises you want, check out all the commercial estate agents in the area. It makes sense to have a few alternative locations in your plans too.

Hiring in help

Unless you plan to do everything yourself on day one, you need to confirm that people with the skills you need are available in your area at wage rates you can afford. Start by looking in the situations vacant section of your local newspaper under the appropriate headings. If you need kitchen staff for your new restaurant and the paper has 20 pages of advertisers desperately looking for staff, you may have a problem on your hands. Chapter 11 looks at finding employees for your business.

Sizing Up the Market

You need to ensure that enough customers, with sufficient money to spend, exist to create a viable marketplace for your products or services. You must also see who's competing against you for their business. In other words, you need to research your market.

Market research is something that potential financial backers – be they banks or other institutions – insist on. In this, they're doing you a favour. Many businesses started with private money fail because the founders don't thoroughly research the market at the outset.

Whatever your business idea, you must undertake some well-thought-out market research before you invest any money or approach anyone else to invest in your venture.

Market research has three main purposes:

✔ **To build credibility for your business idea:** You must prove, first to your own satisfaction and later to outside financiers, that you thoroughly understand the marketplace for your product or service. This proof is vital to attracting resources to build the new venture.

✔ **To develop a realistic market entry strategy:** You must base a successful marketing strategy on a clear understanding of genuine customer needs and on the assurance that product quality, price and promotional and distribution methods are mutually supportive and clearly focused on target customers.

✔ **To gain understanding of the total market, both customers and competition:** You need sufficient information on your potential customers, competitors and market to ensure that your market strategy is at least on the target, if not on the bull's-eye itself. If you miss the target altogether, which you may well do without research, you may not have the necessary cash resources for a second shot.

The military motto 'Time spent in reconnaissance is rarely time wasted' holds true for business as well.

Before you start your research:

1. **Define your objectives.**

   Figure out what you absolutely have to know. For example, how often do people buy whatever it is you're selling and how much do they buy?

2. **Identify the customers to sample for this information.**

   Decide who you want to sample and how you can best reach them. For example, for do-it-yourself products, an Ideal Home Exhibition crowd may be best.

3. **Decide how best to undertake the research.**

   Choose the research method best suited to getting the results you need. For example, face-to-face interviews in the street may allow you direct access to potential customers.

4. **Think about how you can analyse the data.**

   If your research involves complex multi-choice questions or a large sample size, you may need to plan in advance to use a computer and the appropriate software to help you process the data, which in turn means coding the questions. An even better idea is to keep the research so simple that you don't need a computer!

You can analyse the raw market research data and turn it into information to guide your decisions on price, promotion, location and the shape, design and scope of the product or service itself.

The following sections cover the areas you need to consider to make sure that you've properly sized up your business sector.

Figuring out what you need to know

Before embarking on your market research, set clear and precise objectives. You don't want just to find out interesting information about the market in general, and you don't want to spend time and money exploring the whole market when your target is merely a segment of that market. (I talk about segmenting the market in the later section 'Finding your segment of the market'.)

You have to figure out who your target customers are and what you need to know about them. For example, if you're planning to open a shop selling to young, fashion-conscious women, your research objective may be to find out how many women between the ages of 18 and 28, who make at least £25,000 per annum, live or work within two miles of your chosen shop position. That gives you an idea of whether the market can support a venture such as yours.

You also want to know what the existing market is for your product and how much money your potential customers spend on similar products. You can get a measure of such spending from Mintel reports (`www.mintel.com`). Mintel publishes over 400 reports every year covering key sectors such as fast-moving consumer goods (FMCG), financial services, media, retail, leisure and education. Worldwide office locations include London, Chicago, New York, Shanghai, Tokyo and Sydney.

Figuring out the size of the market may require several different pieces of information. You may want to know the resident population of a given area, which may be fairly easy to find out, and also something about the type of people who come into your area for work, for leisure, on holiday or for any other purpose. A nearby hospital, library, railway station or school, for example, may pull potential customers into your particular area.

You need to research in particular:

- ✔ **Your customers:** Who's going to buy your goods and services? What particular customer needs does your business meet? How many of them are there, are their numbers growing or contracting, how much do they spend and how often do they buy?

- ✔ **Your competitors:** Which established businesses are already meeting the needs of your potential customers? What are their strengths and weaknesses? Are they currently failing their customers in some way that you can improve on? For the lowdown on competitor research, see the later section 'Checking out your competition'.

- ✔ **Your product or service:** Can, or should, you tailor it to meet the needs of particular groups of customers? For example, if you're starting up a delivery business, professional clients may require a same-day service, but members of the public at large may be happy to get goods in a day or two, provided this is less costly.

- ✔ **The price you should charge:** All too often, small firms confine their research on pricing to seeing what the competition charges and matching it or beating it. That may be a way to get business, but it's not the best route to profitable business. You need to know what customers think: What price is too cheap? What represents good value for money? What's a rip-off? Then you can pitch in at the right price for your offering.

- ✔ **Which promotional material will reach your customers:** What newspapers and journals do they read and which of these papers is most likely to influence their buying decision?

✔ **Your location:** From where can you reach your customers most easily and at minimum cost?

✔ **Most effective sales method:** Can you use telesales, the Internet or a catalogue, or do customers only buy face to face from a salesperson or a retail outlet?

Research isn't just essential in starting a business but should become an integral part in the ongoing life of the business. Customers and competitors change; products and services don't last forever. When started, however, ongoing market research becomes easier, because you have existing customers (and staff) to question. Make sure that you regularly monitor their views on your business (as a sign in a barber shop stated: 'We need your head to run our business') and develop simple techniques for this purpose (for example, questionnaires for customers beside the till, or suggestion boxes with rewards for employees).

Finding your segment of the market

Market segmentation is the process whereby you organise customers and potential customers into clusters of similar types, such as by age, sex, education level or location.

The starting point for your business may be to sell clothes, but 'every person who buys clothes' is too large and diverse a market to get a handle on. So you divide that market into different segments – clothes for men, women and children, for example – and then further divide those segments into clothes for work, leisure, sports and social occasions. You just segmented your market.

Taking the segmentation process a stage further can involve dividing the market by age group, income, geography or social group, such as yuppie (young, upwardly mobile, professional), bump (borrowed-to-the-hilt upwardly mobile professional show-off) and jolly (jet-setting oldie with lots of loot). There are no hard-and-fast rules on how to segment markets. If any particular group of people has different needs or expectations of a product or service, hey presto – you have a new segment.

Above all, customers increasingly want products and services tailored to their needs and are prepared to pay for the privilege.

Use the following guidelines to help determine whether a market segment is worth trying to sell into:

✔ **Accessibility:** Can you communicate with these customers, preferably in a way that reaches them alone? For example, you can reach the over-50s through advertising in a specialist magazine, with reasonable confidence that young people don't read it, so that you can tailor your message and language accordingly.

✔ **Measurability:** Can you estimate how many customers are in the segment? Are there enough to make it worth offering something different for?

✔ **Open to profitable development:** The customers must have money to spend on the benefits you propose offering. Once upon a time 'oldies' were poor, so they weren't good targets for upmarket, expensive products. Then they became rich and everyone had products aimed at older markets.

Checking out your competition

Finding out about your competitors is easier if you divide them into categories.

✔ **Direct competitors:** These offer something similar to what you have in mind. So direct competitors to a new restaurant are eateries within a *reasonable radius* (how far you think that people will travel to get what you're offering).

List your key competitors only (you may start with a long list and then classify to primary, secondary, potential and so on) so that you limit the number of firms that you research to a workable number. If you end up with more than 10 or 12 primary competitors, think carefully about whether or not this market is a good one to get into, because the level of rivalry may make it hard to make a profit.

✔ **Indirect competitors:** No easy way exists to identify what indirect competition you may face. Use these categories to generate ideas:

  • **Substitutes:** If you're running an Indian restaurant, your customers may be easily tempted to go to a nearby or Chinese if they offer superior service, lower prices, better food or some other benefit such as live entertainment or free parking.

  • **Close substitutes:** Coca-Cola faces direct competition from Pepsi, but it faces indirect competition from juices, tea, coffee, milk, chocolate drinks, bottled water and many other products that provide customers with the same benefit – getting their thirst quenched.

  • **Partial substitutes:** Cinemas, theatres, television, subscription TV, film hire and sales of DVDs all occupy roughly the same space in the entertainment market. Each of these products has loyal customers and some who move seamlessly between two or more of them. The threat may be weak, but is nevertheless real.

  • **Alternatives:** These are products that are nearly below the radar. A classic example is the array of convenience products placed near the end of a supermarket checkout till. The link between chocolate, chewing gum, a torch, a cut-price DVD and a disposable barbeque isn't obvious. However, these items all compete for the same discretionary spending power, so a customer buying one of these products may not buy another.

Budgeting for your research

Market research isn't free, even if you do it yourself. At the very least, you have to consider your time. You may also spend money on journals, phone calls, letters and field visits. And if you employ a professional market research firm, your budgeting shoots to the top of the scale.

For example, a survey of 200 executives responsible for office equipment purchasing decisions cost one company £12,000. In-depth interviews with 20 banking consumers cost £8,000.

Doing the research in-house may save costs but limit the objectivity of the research. If time is your most valuable commodity, getting an outside agency to do the work may make sense. Another argument for commissioning professional research is that it may carry more clout with investors.

Whatever the cost of research, you need to assess its value to you when you're setting your budget. So if getting it wrong costs £100,000, spending £5,000 on market research may be a good investment.

Doing the preliminary research

Research methods range from doing it all from your desk to getting out in the field yourself and asking questions – or hiring someone to do it for you. The following sections explore the various methods you can use to find out what you need to know.

Researching from your desk

When you know the questions you want answers to, the next step is finding out whether someone else has the answers already. Much of the information you need may well be published, so you can do at least some of your market research in a comfortable chair, in your home or in a good library. Even if you use other research methods, doing a little desk research first is worthwhile.

Gathering information at the library

Thousands of libraries in the UK and tens of thousands elsewhere in the world between them contain more desk research data than any entrepreneur ever requires. Libraries offer any number of excellent information sources. You can take yourself to your local library or bring the library's information to you via the Internet if you're dealing with one of the reference libraries in a larger city or town.

As well as the fairly conventional business books, libraries contain many hundreds of reference and research databases. For example, the official Census of Population supplies demographic data on size, age and sex of the local populace. You can also find a wealth of governmental and other statistics that enable you to work out the size and shape of the market nationwide and how much each person spends.

You can find details of every journal, paper and magazine's readership in *BRAD* (British Rate and Data). In addition, every company has to file details of its profits, assets, liabilities and directors at Companies House, the place where all business details and accounts are kept (www.companieshouse. org.uk). Their WebCHeck service offers a free-of-charge, searchable Company Names and Address Index that covers 2 million companies by name or unique company registration number. Some market information data costs hundreds of pounds and some is available only to subscribers who pay thousands of pounds to have it on tap. Fortunately for you, your library (or an Internet link to a library) may have the relevant directory, publication or research study on its shelves.

Librarians are trained to archive and retrieve information and data from their own libraries and increasingly from Internet data sources as well. Thus they represent an invaluable resource that you should tap into early in the research process. You can benefit many times from their knowledge at no cost, or you may want to make use of the research service certain libraries offer to business users at fairly modest rates.

Apart from public libraries, you can access hundreds of university libraries, specialist science and technology libraries, and government collections of data with little difficulty.

Using the power of the Internet

The Internet can be a powerful research tool. However, it has some particular strengths and weaknesses that you need to keep in mind when using it.

Strengths of the Internet include:

- ✔ Access is cheap and information is often free.
- ✔ It helps you gather good background information.
- ✔ You can access information quickly.
- ✔ It covers a wide geographic scope.

Weaknesses of the Internet include:

- ✔ The bias is strongly towards the USA.
- ✔ Coverage of any given subject may be patchy.
- ✔ Authority and credentials are often lacking.

It would be a brave or foolhardy entrepreneur who started up in business or set out to launch new products or services without at least spending a day or two surfing the Internet. At the very least, this surfing tells you whether anyone else has taken your business idea to market. At best, it may save you lots of legwork around libraries, if the information you want is available online.

You can gather market research information on the Internet in two main ways:

- Use directories, search engines or telephone directories to research your market or product.
- Use blogs, bulletin or message boards, newsgroups and chat rooms to elicit the data you require.

These two useful search portals can help get you started:

- Business.com (www.business.com)
- Easy Searcher 2 (www.easysearcher.com)

Here are a few of the most useful online sources of information on markets:

- **Blogs** are sites where people, both informed and uninformed, converse about a particular topic and, as a result, the information you find on blogs is more straw in the wind than hard fact. Globe of Blogs (http://globeofblogs.com), launched in 2002, claims to be the first comprehensive world weblog directory. It links up to some 70,000 blogs, which you can search by country, topic and just about any other criteria you care to name. Google (www.google.com/blogsearch) is also a search engine through which you can access the world's blogs.

- **Corporate Information** (www.corporateinformation.com; go to Tools and then Research Links) is a business information site covering the main world economies, offering plenty of free information. This link takes you to sources of business information in over 100 countries.

- **Doing Business** (www.doingbusiness.org) is the World Bank's database that provides objective measures of business regulations across 185 countries and produces occasional reports on major cities within those countries. You can find out everything from the rules on opening and closing a business to trading across borders, tax rates, employment laws, enforcing contracts and much more. The site also has a tool for comparing countries to rank them by the criteria you consider most important.

- **Google Trends** (www.google.co.uk/trends) provides a snapshot of what the world is most interested in at any one moment. For example, if you're thinking of starting a bookkeeping service, entering that term into the search pane produces a snazzy graph showing how interest, measured by the number of searches made, has grown or contracted since January 2004 (when Google started collecting the data). You can tweak the graph to show seasonality, geographical information and 'demand' peaks.

✔ **Google News** (`http://news.google.co.uk`) contains links to any newspaper article anywhere in the world. You can search for articles covering a particular topic from over the last decade or list them by year. Asking for information on baby clothes, for example, reveals recent articles on how much the average family spends on baby clothes, the launch of a thrift store specialising in second-hand baby clothes and the launch of an organic baby clothes catalogue.

✔ **The Internet Public Library** (`www.ipl.org`) is run by a consortium of American universities whose aim is to help Internet users with finding information online. The website has extensive sections on business, computers, education, leisure and health.

✔ **MarketResearch.com** (`www.marketresearch.com`) claims with some justification to be the world's largest continuously updated online collection of market research, offering over 250,000 market research reports from over 700 leading global publishers. Whether you're looking for new product trends or competitive analysis of a new or existing market, alerts from this source keep you on top of the latest available intelligence.

✔ **NationMaster.com** (`www.nationmaster.com`) provides a compilation of data from such sources as the *CIA World Factbook,* the United Nations and the Organisation for Economic Co-operation and Development. Using the tools on the website, you can generate maps and graphs on all kinds of statistics with ease. Their aim is to be the web's one-stop resource for country statistics on everything.

✔ **Pew Internet** (`http://pewinternet.org/Trend-Data-(Adults)/Whos-Online.aspx`) is a non-profit 'fact tank' that provides information on issues, attitudes and trends. At this site, you can find Internet user demographics and information about what those users do online. (If you'd like to get information on how use of the Internet has changed over time, for example, you can download a large spreadsheet that contains data stretching back to online activity surveys done in 2000.)

✔ **Trade Association Forum** (`www.taforum.org`; go to Directories and then Trade Association) is the online directory of trade associations on whose websites are links to industry-relevant online research sources. For example, you can find the Baby Products Association listed, at whose website you can find details of the 238 companies operating in the sector with their contact details.

✔ **Udini** (`http://udini.proquest.com`) provides an article store for entrepreneurs, consultants, educators and everyone else who needs quality research. This site contains 150 million articles from 12,000 publications. You can buy articles on a pay-as-you-go basis from as little as 99 cents, while $30 buys you 14 days' access to the whole caboodle – enough time to thoroughly research any topic.

✔ **Warc** (`www.warc.com`) claims to provide the most comprehensive marketing information service in the world. Their online guide to world advertising trends is based on the annual advertising expenditure data across all main media for more than 100 countries, outlining key trends in media investment over the last ten years.

By running surveys online you can find out more about your customers' needs, check out whether new products or services would appeal to them and monitor complaints, so preventing them from becoming problems. Zoomerang (www.zoomerang.com) and Instant Survey (www.instantsurvey.com) are among a host of companies that provide a free or nearly free online survey tool.

Getting to the grass roots

If the market information you need isn't already available, and the chances are that it isn't, then you need to find the answers yourself.

Going out into the marketplace to do market research is known as *field research,* or sometimes *primary research,* by marketing professionals.

Field research allows you to gather information directly related to your venture and to fine-tune results you get from other sources. For example, entrepreneurs interested in opening a classical music shop in Exeter aimed at young people were encouraged when desk research showed that of a total population of 250,000, 25 per cent were under 30. However, the research didn't tell them what percentage of this 25 per cent was interested in classical music nor how much money each potential customer may spend. Field research showed that 1 per cent was interested in classical music and would spend £2 a week, suggesting a potential market of only £65,000 a year (250,000 x 25% x 1% x £2 x 52)! The entrepreneurs sensibly decided to investigate Birmingham and London instead. But at least the cost had been only two damp afternoons spent in Exeter, rather than the horror of having to dispose of a lease on an unsuccessful shop.

Most field research consists of an interviewer putting questions to a respondent. No doubt you've become accustomed to being interviewed while travelling or resisting the attempts of an enthusiastic salesperson on your doorstep posing as a market researcher (*slugging,* as this practice is known, has been illegal since 1986).

The more popular forms of interviews are

- ✔ Personal (face-to-face) interview (especially for consumer markets)
- ✔ Telephone (especially for surveying businesses)
- ✔ Postal survey (especially for industrial markets)
- ✔ Test and discussion groups
- ✔ Internet surveys

Personal interviews and postal surveys are clearly less expensive than getting together panels of interested parties or using expensive telephone time. Telephone interviewing requires a highly positive attitude, courtesy, an ability not to talk too quickly and to listen while sticking to a rigid questionnaire. Low response rates on postal surveys (normally less than 10 per cent) can be improved by including a letter explaining the purpose of the survey and why respondents should reply; by offering rewards for completed questionnaires (a small gift); by associating the survey with a charity donation based on the number of respondents; by sending reminder letters; and, of course, by providing pre-paid reply envelopes.

Internet surveys using questionnaires similar to those conducted by post or on the telephone are growing in popularity. On the plus side, the other survey methods involve having the data entered or transcribed at your expense, but with an Internet survey the respondent enters the data. Internet survey software also comes with the means of readily analysing the data, turning it into useful tables and charts. Such software may also have a statistical package to check out the validity of the data itself and so give you an idea how much reliance to place on it.

Buying the software to carry out Internet surveys may be expensive, but you can rent it and pay per respondent for each survey you do.

Check out companies such as Free Online Surveys (`http://free-online-surveys.co.uk`) and Zoomerang (`www.zoomerang.com`) – both provide software that lets you carry out online surveys and analyse the data quickly. Most of these organisations offer free trials – Free Online Surveys, for example, allows you to create a survey of up to 20 questions and receive up to 50 responses over a ten-day period, beginning when you start creating your survey. An upgrade to their SurveyExtra lets you ask as many questions as you want with up to 1,000 responses for £19.95 per month, discounted to £9.95 for students.

Once upon a time samples of Internet users were heavily biased towards students, big companies and university academics. Not any more. In 2013, according to the Office for National Statistics, 36 million adults (73 per cent) in Great Britain accessed the Internet every day, 20 million more than in 2006. This means that you can canvas almost everyone's views.

Conducting the research

Field research means that you have to do the work yourself: decide the questions, select the right people to ask those questions and then interpret the data when you have it. This is completely different from desk research, where all that work has been done for you. But field research can be worth every ounce of sweat that goes into it. You get information that no one else is likely to have at their finger tips, and knowledge in the business start-up arena is definitely power. When you come to writing up your business plan (see Chapter 6), you have the evidence to support your belief in your business.

Setting up a sample

It's rarely possible or even desirable to include every potential customer or competitor in your research. Imagine trying to talk to all pet owners before launching Petfeed.com! Instead, you select a sample group to represent the whole population.

Sampling saves time and money and can be more accurate than surveying an entire population. Talking to every pet owner may take months. By the time you complete your survey, the first people questioned may have changed their opinions, or the whole environment may have changed in some way.

You need to take care and ensure that you've included all the important customer segments you've targeted as potential users or buyers of your products or services in your research sample.

The main sampling issue is how big a sample you need to give you a reliable indication of how the whole population behaves. The accuracy of your survey increases with the sample size, as Table 4-1 shows. There you see that a sample of 250 is generally (95 per cent of the time) accurate only to between plus 6.2 per cent to minus 6.2 per cent. This means that 12.4 per cent of the time it's generally above or below the true figure. Up the sample to 6,000 and the error range drops to between plus 1.2 per cent and minus 1.2 per cent, a range of just 2.4 per cent. You need to include each of your main customer segments – for example, the over-50s, people earning between £20,000 and £30,000 a year or those without university degrees, if those are groups of people whose views are important to your strategy – in the sample in numbers sufficient to make your sample reasonably reliable.

Table 4-1	Sample Size and Accuracy
Number in Sample	**Percentage Accuracy of 95% of Surveys**
250	Accurate to a range of + to – 6.2% of true figure
500	Accurate to a range of + to – 4.4% of true figure
750	Accurate to a range of + to – 3.6% of true figure
1,000	Accurate to a range of + to – 3.1% of true figure
2,000	Accurate to a range of + to – 2.2% of true figure
6,000	Accurate to a range of + to – 1.2% of true figure

For most basic research, a small business may find the lower sample sizes accurate enough, given the uncertainty surrounding the whole area of entering new markets and launching new products.

Asking the right questions

To make your field research pay off, you have to ask the questions whose responses tell you what you need to know. Writing those questions is both an art and a science – and you can master both aspects by using the following tips:

- ✔ Keep the number of questions to a minimum. A dozen or so should be enough – 25 is getting ridiculous.

- ✔ Keep the questions simple. Answers should be Yes/No/Don't Know or somewhere on a scale such as Never/Once a Month/Three or Four Times a Month/Always.

- ✔ Avoid ambiguity. Make sure that the respondent really understands the question by avoiding vague words such as *generally, usually* and *regularly.* Seek factual answers; avoid opinions.

- ✔ Make sure that you have a cut-out question at the beginning to eliminate unsuitable respondents. You don't want to waste time questioning people who never use your kind of product or service.

- ✔ Put an identifying question at the end so that you can make sure that you get a suitable cross-section of respondents. For example, you may want to identify men from women, people living alone from those with children or certain age groups.

The introduction to a face-to-face interview is important. Make sure that you're prepared, carrying an identifying card (maybe a student card or watchdog card) or with a rehearsed introduction (such as 'Good morning. I'm from Cranfield University [show card] and we're conducting a survey and would be grateful for your help'). You may also need visuals of the product you're investigating (samples, photographs) to ensure that the respondent understands. Make sure that these visuals are neat and accessible.

Try out the questionnaire and your technique on your friends prior to using them in the street. You may be surprised to find that questions that seem simple to you are incomprehensible at first to respondents!

Remember, above all, that questioning is by no means the only or most important form of fieldwork. Also get out and look at your competitors' premises, get their catalogues and price lists, go to exhibitions and trade fairs relevant to your chosen business sector and get information on competitors' accounts and financial data. One would-be business starter found out from the company's accounts, obtained from Companies House (www.companieshouse.org.uk), that the 'small' competitor near to where he planned to locate was in fact owned by a giant public company that was testing out the market prior to a major launch itself.

All methods can be equally valid depending only on the type of market data you need to gather. Carefully record the results of each piece of market research for subsequent use in presentations and business plans.

After the primary market research (desk and field research) and market testing (stalls and exhibitions) are complete, if you're investing a substantial amount of money upfront in your venture you should pilot test the business in one location or with one customer segment before launching fully into business. Only then can you make a reasonably accurate prediction of sales and the cash-flow implications for your business.

Finding test subjects

Now you need someone to ask your questions of. If you're doing a street survey, you have to make do with whoever comes along. Otherwise, to carry out a survey your best bet is to buy or rent a mailing list. Typically, you pay a fee to the list owner, such as a magazine with its list of subscribers. You negotiate a fee for how many times you're allowed to use the list. Note that you aren't the owner of the list.

Several individual freelancers specialise in brokering lists and building lists. You may want to consider hiring an individual for a consultation or to manage the entire process. Marketing professionals claim that buying lists is a science, but you can master this science on your own, especially if you're trying to reach a local or regional market. Think of publications, organisations and businesses whose lists are most likely to contain people who may buy your product or service. Don't overlook trade magazines, regional magazines or non-competing businesses with a similar customer base. You can then select and narrow your lists by looking at nearly any demographic variable, to arrive at as close to your description of your target market as possible. Listbroker (www.listbroker.com) and Electric Marketing (www.electricmarketing.co.uk) between them can provide lists of all types.

Working Out Whether You Can Make Money

Trying to get a new business off the ground is pointless if doing so is going to take more money than you can raise or take longer to reach breakeven and turn in a profit than you can possibly survive unaided. I look in more detail at financial matters such as profits and margins in Chapter 13, but you can't start looking at the figures soon enough. Doing some rough figures at the outset can save you a lot of time pursuing unrealistic or unprofitable business opportunities.

Estimating start-up costs

Setting up a business requires money – you can't get away from that. You have rent to pay, materials and equipment to purchase, and all before you receive any income. Starting a business on the road to success involves ensuring that you've sufficient money to survive until the point where income continually exceeds expenditure.

Raising this initial money and the subsequent financial management of the business are therefore vital, and you should take great care over these matters. Unfortunately, more businesses fail due to lack of sufficient day-to-day cash and financial management than for any other reason.

The first big question is to establish how much money you need. Look at every possible cost and divide them into one-off, fixed or variable categories. The *fixed costs* are those that you have to pay even if you make no sales (rent, rates, possibly some staff costs, repayments on any loans and so on) as well as some *one-off costs,* or one-time purchases such as buying a vehicle or computer, which you won't repeat after the business is up and running. *Variable costs* are those that vary depending on the level of your sales (raw materials, production and distribution costs, and so on).

Your finance requirements are shown clearly on your cash-flow forecast, which is a table showing, usually on a monthly basis, the amount of money actually received into the business and the amount of money paid out.

According to the Bank of England's report on small business finance, the average start-up cost for a new business in the UK is just over £35,000. However, that average conceals wide variations. Some start-ups, particularly those in technology or manufacturing, may require hundreds, thousands or even millions of pounds, but others, such as those run from home, may cost little or nothing.

Six out of every ten people starting up a business use personal funds as their initial source of finance. Naturally, using your own money – your savings, your un-mortgaged property, your life insurance and your other assets – is a logical starting point. You may not feel you can put all your worth behind a business because of the risks involved, but whichever route you go down you're normally expected to invest some of your own assets. Banks seek personal guarantees, and venture capitalists like to see owners taking risks with their own money – why should they risk their clients' money if you aren't risking yours?

If you can fund the project from your own resources, doing so presents some attractions. Only in this way do all the rewards of success flow to you. As soon as you bring in other sources of finance those sources slice off some of the reward, be it interest, share of the value on the sale of the business or dividends. They may also constrain the business through the use of covenants, borrowing limits and placing financial obligations on the business – potentially not only carving off part of your rewards but also capping them by restricting your operation.

Forecasting sales

All forecasts may turn out to be wrong, but you must demonstrate in your strategy that you've thought through the factors that affect performance. You should also show how you can deliver satisfactory results even when many of these factors work against you. You need this information to give you comfort, and both your backers and employees alike measure the downside risk to evaluate the worst scenario and its likely effects, and look towards an ultimate exit route.

Here are a few guidelines to help you make an initial sales forecast:

- **Credible projections:** Your overall projections have to be believable. Most lenders and investors have extensive experience of similar business proposals. Unlike you, they've the benefit of hindsight and can look back several years at other ventures they've backed and see how they fared in practice as compared with their initial forecasts.

  You can gather useful knowledge on similar businesses yourself by researching company records (at Companies House, `www.companies house.gov.uk`, where the accounts of most British companies are kept) or by talking with the founders of similar ventures who aren't your direct competitors.

- **Customers:** How many customers and potential customers do you know who are likely to buy from you, and how much might they buy? Here you can use many types of data on which to base reasonable sales projections. You can interview a sample of prospective customers, issue a press release or advertisement to gauge response and exhibit at trade shows to obtain customer reactions. If your product or service needs to be on an approved list before it can be bought, as is the case for public sector bodies, then your business plan should confirm that you have that approval or, less desirably, show how you can get it.

  You should also look at seasonal factors that may cause sales to be high or low at certain periods in the year. This is particularly significant for cash-flow projections. You should then relate your seasonal, customer-based forecast to your capacity to make or sell at this rate. Sometimes your inability to recruit or increase capacity may limit your sales forecasts.

- **Desired income:** This approach to estimating sales embraces the concept that forecasts may also accommodate the realistic aims of the proprietor. Indeed, you can go further and state that the whole purpose of strategy is to ensure that the business achieves certain forecasts. This is more likely to be the case in a mature company with proven products and markets than in a start-up.

Nevertheless, an element of 'How much do we need to earn?' must play a part in forecasting, if only to signal when a business idea isn't worth pursuing.

One extreme of the desired income approach to forecasting comes from those entrepreneurs who think that the forecasts are the business plan. Such people cover the business plan with a mass of largely unconnected numbers. With reams of computer printouts covering every variation possible in business, complete with sensitivity analysis, these people are invariably a big turn-off for financiers.

✔ **Market guidelines:** Some businesses have accepted formulas you can use to estimate sales. This is particularly true in retailing, where location studies, traffic counts and population density are known factors.

✔ **Market share:** How big is the market for your product or service? Is it growing or contracting and at what rate, as a percentage per annum? What is the economic and competitive position? These are all factors that can provide a market share basis for your forecasts. An entry market share of more than a few per cent is most unusual. But beware of turning this argument on its head. Unsubstantiated statements such as 'In a market of £1 billion per annum we can easily capture 1 per cent, which is £1 million a year' impress no investor.

Exceeding breakeven

So far I've taken certain decisions for granted and ignored how to cost the product or service you're marketing – and, indeed, how to set the selling price.

Your goal is to get past breakeven, the point at which you've covered all your costs, and into the realm of making profits as quickly as possible. So these decisions are clearly important if you want to be sure of making a profit.

At first glance, the problem is simple. You just add up all the costs and charge a bit more. The more you charge above your costs, provided the customers keep on buying, the more profit you make. Unfortunately, as soon as you start to do the sums the problem gets a little more complex. For a start, not all costs have the same characteristics. Some costs, for example, don't change however much you sell. If you're running a shop, the rent and rates are relatively constant figures, completely independent of the volume of your sales. On the other hand, the cost of the products sold from the shop is completely dependent on volume. The more you sell, the more it costs you to buy in stock. You can't really add up those two types of costs until you've made an assumption about how much you plan to sell. You can find out more detail about this subject in Chapter 13.

Part II
Making and Funding Your Plan

Addressing the Five Cs

Bankers like to speak of the *five Cs of credit analysis,* factors they look at when they evaluate a loan request. When applying to a bank for a loan, prepare to address the following points:

- ✔ **Capacity:** This is a prediction of the borrower's ability to repay the loan. For a new business, bankers look at the business plan. For an existing business, bankers consider financial statements and industry trends.

- ✔ **Capital:** Bankers scrutinise a borrower's net worth, the amount by which assets exceed debts.

- ✔ **Character:** Bankers lend money to borrowers who appear honest and who have a good credit history. Before you apply for a loan, it makes sense to obtain a copy of your credit report and clean up any problems.

- ✔ **Collateral:** Bankers generally want a borrower to pledge an asset that can be sold to pay off the loan if the borrower lacks funds.

- ✔ **Conditions**: Whether bankers give a loan can be influenced by the current economic climate as well as by the amount requested.

Head online and visit www.dummies.com/extras/startingabusinessuk for a free bonus article that looks at the measurable part of a business plan – the *objectives*.

Part II

Making and Funding
Your Plan

In this part . . .

- ✔ Get the best legal structure in place.
- ✔ Write a winning business plan.
- ✔ Find out all about money – where it is and how to get some to start up or grow your business.
- ✔ Access the many sources of help available.
- ✔ Find the best way to develop and communicate your marketing strategy, set a selling price, decide on a place to operate from, and determine how and where to advertise.

Chapter 5

Structuring Your Business

. . . .

. . . .

*W*hen you start your business, you have to make a decision more or less from the outset on the legal structure you're going to use to trade. Although that's an important decision, luckily, it's not an irrevocable one. You can change structures as your business grows – though not without some cost and paperwork.

The simplest structure is to make all the business decisions yourself and take all the risk personally. You don't have to shoulder all the responsibilities when you start a business, though most people initially do so. It may be great doing everything your way, at last, after the frustrations of working for someone else. But it can be lonely or even scary with no one with whom you can talk over the day-to-day problems and share the responsibility of decision making.

If your business requires substantial investment, or involves other people who have a more or less equal hand in the venture alongside you, then your decision about the legal structure of the business is a little more complicated.

In this chapter, you can find all the important factors to consider when deciding on the legal structure for your business. And while on the subject of legalities, I look at other areas of interest, from intellectual property to dealing with unpaid invoices.

Choosing the Right Structure

Different legal frameworks exist for the ownership of a business and not all are equally appropriate for everyone.

Most small businesses in the UK start out as sole proprietorships; however, by the time they register for VAT (value added tax) – in other words, after they're up and running – then owners tend to seek the shelter of limited liability (see Table 5-1.)

Table 5-1	Popular Business Structures (%)	
	2009	*2012*
Limited companies	24.4	28.0
Sole proprietorships	58.2	62.7
Partnerships	13.5	9.3

One of the many factors you have to consider when deciding on the legal structure of your business is tax, including VAT and its implications, and I talk about how to manage your tax position in Chapter 14.

But even more compelling reasons than tax may exist to choose one structure over another. Not all sources of finance are open to every type of business. When you know how much money you need to start up or to grow a business and what you need that money for, you're in a better position to make an informed choice about the best way to structure your business. If you need to raise large sums of money from the outset for research and development, for example, then a limited company may be your only realistic option, with its access to risk capital. And if you're nervous about embroiling your finances with other people's, a partnership isn't an attractive option.

In general, the more money you require and the riskier the venture, the more likely it is that a limited company is the appropriate structure.

The good news is that you can change your legal structure at more or less any time. Even if you go the full distance and form a company and get it listed on the stock exchange, you can delist and go private. Richard Branson (Virgin) and Alan Sugar (Amstrad) have both gone down this route. That's not to say you'll find it easy to dissolve partnerships or shut down companies, but you can do it.

Both your accountant and your lawyer can help you with choosing your legal form. The types of business structures and some of their advantages and disadvantages are shown in Table 5-2.

Table 5-2   Pros and Cons of Various Organisational Structures

Type of Entity	Main Advantages	Main Drawbacks
Sole proprietorship	Simple and inexpensive to create and operate.	Owner is personally liable for business debts.
	Profit or loss is reported on owner's personal tax return.	No access to outside capital.
		Life of business is restricted to life of owner.
		Limited potential for value creation.
General partnership	Simple and inexpensive to create and operate.	Partners are personally liable for business debts.
	Partners' share of profit or loss is reported on personal tax returns.	The business is dissolved when a partner dies.
	Potential for some value creation.	Only partners can raise outside capital.
Limited partnership	Non-managing partners have limited personal liability for business debts.	General partners are personally liable for business debts.
	General partners can raise cash without involving outside investors in the management of the business.	More expensive to create than a general partnership.
	Wider access to outside capital than for a sole proprietor.	Life of business is restricted to life of first partner to die.
	Potential for some value creation.	
Limited company	Owners have limited personal liability for business debts.	More expensive to create and run than partnership or sole proprietorship.
	Some benefits (such as pensions) can be deducted as a business expense.	Owners must meet legal requirements for stock registration, account filing and paperwork.
	Owners can share out the profit and can end up paying less tax overall.	
	Access to full range of outside capital.	

(continued)

Table 5-2 (continued)

Type of Entity	Main Advantages	Main Drawbacks
	Business can live on after founder's death.	
	Potential for value creation.	
	Separate taxable entity.	
Co-operative	Owners have limited personal liability for business debts.	More expensive to create than a sole proprietorship.
	Owners' share of corporate profit or loss reported on personal tax returns.	Owners must meet legal requirements for account filing, registration and paperwork.
	Owners can use corporate loss to offset income from other sources.	Restricted access to outside capital.
		Limited potential for value creation.

Going into Business by Yourself

You may want to develop your own unique ideas for a product or service, and if so, setting up your own business from the drawing board may be your only option. You may want to start a home-based business that you can run in your own time. You may want to start a business because you want to do things the right way, after working for an employer who goes about things in the wrong way.

Doing things your own way is much easier if you're working alone, rather than, say, buying someone else's business that already has its routines and working practices established.

Advantages

Working for and by yourself has several things going for it:

✔ It may be possible to start the business in your spare time. Doing so allows you to gain more confidence in the future success of your proposed venture before giving up your job or pumping your life savings into the business.

✔ If you've limited money to invest in your new venture, you may not need to spend it all at the start of the project. If you're working on your own, it also means that if things do start to go wrong, restricting the losses is easier.

✔ Starting a business isn't just about money. Setting up and running a successful business has the potential to give you a feeling of personal achievement, which may not exist to quite the same extent if you buy someone else's business, for example.

Disadvantages

Going it alone isn't all fun and games. Some of the disadvantages include the following:

✔ Your business will take time to grow. It may not be able to support your current personal financial obligations for many months or years.

✔ A lot of one-off administration is involved in setting up a new business, such as registering for VAT and PAYE (pay as you earn, or income tax), getting business stationery, setting up phone, fax and Internet connections at your trading premises and registering your business name, in addition to actually trading.

These tasks can be time consuming and frustrating in the short term, and costly in the long run if you get them wrong. Unfortunately, you can't delegate these tasks easily and getting other people to do them can be expensive. If you buy a business or take up a franchise, these basic administrative tasks should have already been dealt with.

✔ You've no one to bounce ideas off, or to share responsibility with when things go wrong.

✔ As a result of the perceived riskiness, generally you may have more difficulty borrowing money to fund a start-up than to invest in an established, profitable business.

Settling on sole-trader status

The vast majority of new businesses are essentially one-man (or one-woman) bands. As such, they're free to choose the simplest legal structure, known by terms such as *sole trader* or *sole proprietor.* This structure has the merit of being relatively formality free and having few rules about the records you have to keep. As a sole proprietor, you don't have to have your accounts audited or file financial information on your business.

If you're a sole trader, no legal distinction exists between you and your business. Your business is one of your personal assets, just as your house or car is. It follows that, if your business should fail, your creditors have a right not only to the assets of the business but also to your personal assets, subject only to the provisions of local bankruptcy rules (these rules often allow you to keep only a few absolutely basic essentials for yourself and family). You may be able to avoid the worst of these consequences by distancing your assets.

The capital to start and run the business must come from you, or from loans. In return for these drawbacks you can have the pleasure of being your own boss immediately, subject only to declaring your profits on your tax return and if necessary applying for a trade licence. (In practice, you'd be wise to take professional advice before starting up.)

Often people who start up on their own don't have enough money to buy into an existing operation, so the do-it-yourself approach is the only alternative.

Building up to Network Marketing

Network marketing, multilevel marketing (MLM) and *referral marketing* are the names used to describe selling methods designed to replace the retail outlet as a route to market for certain products. Although referral marketing has been around since the early part of the last century, for many people this type of marketing is still unfamiliar territory.

Network marketing is one way of starting a profitable, full-time business with little or no investment; and also a method of starting a second or part-time business to run alongside your existing business or career. Network marketing is one of the fastest-growing business sectors. Industry turnover has grown from £1 billion ten years ago to £2 billion today.

In most cases, network marketing involves selling a product or service that a parent company produces and supplies. You take on the responsibilities of selling the products and introducing other people to the company. You get paid commission on the products/services you sell yourself and a smaller commission on the products/services that the people you've introduced to the company sell. In addition, you often get a percentage commission based on the sales of the people that the people you introduced to the company also introduce, and so on.

Advocates of network marketing maintain that, when given identical products, the one sold face to face (without the cost of maintaining a shop and paying employees and insurance) is less expensive than the same product sold in a store. Additionally, network marketing fans believe that buying a product from someone you know and trust makes more sense than buying from a shop assistant behind a retail counter.

A wide variety of good-quality network marketing companies from all over the world exist for you to choose from. They offer products and services from a wide range of industries – health, telecommunications, household products, technology, e-commerce, adult products and so on. Household names include Amway, Avon, Betterware, Herbalife, Kleeneze and Mary Kay Cosmetics. Choose a product or service that you're interested in, because when it comes to sales nothing beats enthusiasm and confidence in the product.

Evaluating the pros and cons

Like any other type of business, network marketing has its upside and its downside. Some of the positives are:

- **Little or no start-up costs:** With most companies, the investment in a business kit and a range of sample products rarely exceeds £100. The law governing network marketing doesn't allow an investment of more than £200 in the first seven days.

- **The potential to build a substantial business:** By recruiting more and more people to join the company and by those people recruiting more people, your percentages of their sales grow and grow. And, of course, you're still selling at a high rate yourself.

- **A proven business formula:** Network marketing has been around since the early 1900s.

- **Low risk:** Unlike a brand-new business idea that you may have uncovered, network marketing products and services are usually tried-and-tested business concepts. That doesn't mean they can't fail, but if you follow the rules, you're less likely to hit the buffers than you would on your own.

- **You often get a great deal of support and advice:** The parent company and the person who brought you into the company have a vested interest in helping you succeed because the more you sell, the more money they make.

- **Flexible hours:** You can sell on a full-time or part-time basis during the hours that suit you and your customers.

- **Highly expandable:** You don't have territory restrictions like conventional salespeople, and with e-commerce capabilities most parent companies can supply to many countries.

- **Location:** You can run the business from your own home.

- **Personal development:** You build your confidence and increase your communication skills.

Again, as with any business, network marketing isn't all good. The following list shows some of the disadvantages:

- Restrictions on your business practices may exist; for example, recruitment, advertising and so on.

- Your business relies heavily on the success of one parent company and its ability to deliver its products/services on time.

- You may not feel comfortable selling to your friends or to strangers.

- Even the best network marketing companies may be thought of as pyramid schemes – see the next section.

One characteristic of network marketing that leads to its all-too-frequent excesses is that everyone can get in for little money upfront; thus, everyone does get in.

Distinguishing pyramids from network marketing

Pyramid selling schemes are sometimes disguised to look like network marketing schemes, but commonly have the following characteristics:

- ✔ They encourage participants to make substantial investments in stocks of goods, by offering rewards to participants for getting others to do the same.

- ✔ They make little reference to direct selling and the need to achieve consumer sales. Instead, they imply that the main source of rewards comes from getting others to make substantial initial investments.

- ✔ They don't offer contracts to participants, nor cancellation rights or the opportunity to buy back unsold goods – all of which are required under UK law.

Quality network marketing companies make sense for people who really believe in a particular product and want to sell it but don't want to, or can't, tie up a lot of money buying a franchise or other business, or who don't have a great idea of their own. Just remember to check out the network company using trade associations such as the Direct Selling Association (`http://dsa.org.uk`). You won't get rich in a hurry, or probably ever. But if you take care, you probably won't lose your shirt either.

Working with a Limited Number of Other People

Unless you're the self-contained type who prefers going it alone, you have to work alongside other people to get your business going. Not just suppliers or employees or bankers and the like – everyone in business has to do that to a greater or lesser extent.

The upside of going into business with others is that you've someone on your side to talk to when the going gets tough, and it will do from time to time. Two heads are often better than one. Also, you've the advantage of extra physical and mental resources when they matter most, from the outset.

However, the equation isn't one-sided, unfortunately. With other people come other points of view, other agendas and the opportunity to disagree, argue and misunderstand.

Taking on an existing business

If you don't have a solid business idea of your own, with a clear vision and strategy, you can consider using someone else's wholly formed business. You can think of such ventures as virtually a business-in-a-box. Just buy it, take it home, open it up and start trading. Of course nothing is quite that easy, but in broad principle that's what network marketing, franchising and co-operative ventures are all about.

Forming a partnership

A *partnership* is effectively a collection of sole traders or proprietors. Few restrictions apply to setting up in business with another person (or persons) in partnership, and several definite advantages exist:

✔ Pooling your resources means that you've more capital.

✔ You bring several sets of skills to the business, hopefully, instead of just one.

✔ If one of you is unable to work, the business can still carry on.

Partnerships are a common structure that people who started out on their own use when they want to expand.

The legal regulations governing partnerships in essence assume that competent businesspeople should know what they're doing. The law merely provides a framework of agreement, which applies 'in the absence of agreement to the contrary'.

In the absence of an agreement to the contrary these rules apply to partnerships:

✔ All partners contribute capital equally.

✔ All partners share profits and losses equally.

✔ No partner shall have interest paid on his capital.

✔ No partner shall be paid a salary.

✔ All partners have an equal say in the management of the business.

All these provisions probably won't suit you, so you're well advised to get a partnership agreement drawn up in writing before opening for business.

Partnerships have three serious financial drawbacks that merit particular attention:

- ✔ If one partner makes a business mistake, perhaps by signing a disastrous contract without the others' knowledge or consent, every member of the partnership must shoulder the consequences. Under these circumstances, your personal assets can be taken to pay the creditors even though the mistake was no fault of your own.

- ✔ If a partner faces personal bankruptcy, for whatever reason, his creditors can seize his share of the partnership. As a private individual you aren't liable for your partner's private debts, but having to buy him out of the partnership at short notice rather than gaining an unwanted replacement may put you and the business in financial jeopardy.

- ✔ If one partner wants to quit the partnership, that partner will want to take the value of his part of the business with him. The remaining partner(s), in effect, has to buy out the partner who's leaving. The agreement you have on setting up the business should specify the procedure and how to value the leaver's share, otherwise resolving the situation is costly. Several options for addressing this issue exist. Here are a few:

  - The traditional route to value the leaver's share is to ask an independent accountant but doing so is rarely cost effective. The valuation costs money and, worst of all, it's not definite and consequently room for argument remains.

  - You can establish a formula; say, eight times the last audited pre-tax profits. This approach is simple but difficult to get right. A fast-growing business is undervalued by a formula using historic data unless the multiple (eight times or whatever) is high; a high multiple may overvalue 'hope' or goodwill, thus unreasonably profiting the leaver.

    You can arrive at the multiplier by looking up the performance of a business similar to the one in question that's listed on a stock market. Such a business has a *P/E (price/earnings) ratio* published in both its accounts and the financial sections of national newspapers. You calculate the P/E ratio by dividing the share price into the amount of profit earned for each share. For example, if a business makes £100,000 profit and has 1,000 shares, the profit per share is £100. If the share price of that company is £10, its P/E ratio is 10 (100/10). So much for the science, now for the art. Because any business quoted on a stock market is big and its shares are liquid – that is, easy to buy and sell – such a business is considered more valuable than a small private company. In any event, private firms don't have a published share price. To compensate, you usually discount the P/E ratio by a third. So, using this example, a private firm in the same line of work as the one listed on a stock market would be given a P/E of approximately 7 (2/3 x 10).

  - You can value the assets of the business and use that as a basis for dividing the spoils.

Even death may not release you from a partnership and in some circumstances your estate can remain liable for the partnership's obligations. Unless you take public leave of your partnership by notifying your business contacts and legally bringing your partnership to an end, you remain liable indefinitely.

Gerard Hogkinson, a professor of strategic management and behavioural science at Warwick Business School, advises:

> *If you have two people with exactly the same outlook, experience and skill set and the only basis for them going into business together is that they get on, then there is no value added to that partnership. You are just adding a financial burden to the business that need not be there.*

Looking at limited partnerships

One option that can reduce the more painful consequences of entering a partnership is to have your involvement registered as a limited partnership. A *limited partnership* works as follows: one or more general partners must be involved with the same basic rights and responsibilities (including unlimited liability) as in any general partnership. In addition, you can have one or more limited partners who are usually passive investors. The big difference between a general partner and a limited partner is that the limited partner isn't personally liable for debts of the partnership so long as he plays no active part in the business. The most a limited partner can lose is the amount that he

✔ Paid or agreed to pay into the partnership as a capital contribution

✔ Received from the partnership after it became insolvent

The advantage of a limited partnership as a business structure is that it provides a way for business owners to raise money (from the limited partners) without having to take in new partners who are active in the business, or to form a limited company. Often, a general partnership that's been operating for years creates a limited partnership to finance expansion.

Checking out co-operatives

If making money is much lower on your list of priorities for starting up in business than being involved in the decisions of an ethical enterprise, then joining a co-operative or starting your own is an idea worth exploring.

A *co-operative* is an autonomous association of people united voluntarily to meet their common economic, social and cultural needs and aspirations through a jointly owned and democratically controlled enterprise.

You must have at least seven members at the outset, though they don't all have to be full-time workers at first.

Like a limited company, a registered co-operative has limited liability for its members and must file annual accounts.

Although the most visible co-operatives are the high-street shops and supermarkets, pretty much any type of business can operate as a co-operative.

If you choose to form a co-operative, you can pay from £90 to register with the Chief Registrar of Friendly Societies. Not all co-operatives bother to register because doing so isn't mandatory, but if you don't register, the law regards your co-operative as a partnership with unlimited liability.

You can find out everything you need to know about the size, structure and prospects of co-operatives in the UK in a free 36-page report that you can download from www.uk.coop/document/uk-co-operative-economy-2010.

Finding Your Way to Franchising

Franchising can be a good first step into self-employment for those with business experience but no actual experience of running a business – often the case with those who are looking for something to do following a corporate career.

Franchising is a marketing technique used to improve and expand the distribution of a product or service. The franchiser supplies the product or teaches the service to you, the franchisee, who in turn sells it to the public. In return, you pay a fee and a continuing royalty, usually based on turnover. The franchiser may also require you to buy materials or ingredients from it, which gives it an additional income stream. The advantage to you is a relatively safe and quick way of getting into business for yourself, but with the support and advice of an experienced organisation close at hand.

The franchising company can expand its distribution with minimum strain on its own capital and have the services of a highly motivated team of owner-managers. Franchising isn't a path to great riches, nor is it for the truly independent spirit, because policy and profits still come from on high.

Although franchising eliminates some of the more costly and at times disastrous bumps in the learning curve of working for yourself, the system is not an easy way to riches. Ninety-one per cent of franchisees report they're trading profitably, but the number of those claiming high levels of profitability remains low, at around 4 per cent. Still, this performance compares well with the depth of the 1990 recession when just 70 per cent of franchises traded profitably.

Facts about franchising in the UK in 2012

The following statistics are from the National Westminster Bank and the British Franchise Association annual franchise survey 2012 (www.thebfa.org/about-franchising/franchising-industry-research):

✔ The industry annual turnover is £13.4 billion (20 years ago, the figure was just £5 billion).

✔ The number of franchisor brands (McDonald's, Domino's Pizzas, Kall Kwik and the like) operating in the UK is 929.

✔ Some 40,100 franchisee outlets exist.

✔ The number of people employed in franchising is 594,000.

✔ Ninety-one per cent of units are profitable (including new businesses).

✔ Men account for 72 per cent of franchisees (in 2005 the figure was 78 per cent).

✔ The mean age of a franchisee is 49, compared to 47 in 2010 and 46 in 2005.

✔ The majority of franchisees are single-unit businesses (73 per cent), but a growing proportion of franchisees own now multiple units (27 per cent compared to 22 per cent in 2010).

✔ London and the South East, the South West, the North West and the West and East Midlands are the main regions for franchising activity. The London and South East region alone accounts for 30 per cent of all franchise units.

Some people make wild claims about how much safer a franchise is when compared to a conventional start-up. The long-established, big franchise chains are relatively safe – though a few big names have got into trouble – but the smaller and newer ones are as vulnerable as any other venture in the early, formative years.

Looking at franchise types

Franchises can be clustered under these three main headings:

✔ **Business franchises:** These businesses typically have premises and employees. They require a higher level of investment, typically in the range of £20,000–£120,000, in stock, equipment and premises. Large numbers of business franchises are available in such areas as retailing, food services and business services such as high-street printing shops.

✔ **Investment franchises:** Here, you're talking about initial investments of over £120,000. Hotels and some of the larger and more-established fast-food outlets come into the top range of this category at around £750,000.

The essence of this type of franchise is that the franchisee is unlikely to work in the business day to day. People operating investment franchises typically operate several similar franchises in nearby areas.

✓ **Job franchises:** These franchises are where you're buying the rights to operate what's essentially a one-person business, such as plumbing, building services or a recruitment business. These franchises require a financial investment in the £7,000–£20,000 range and can be described as 'buying a job'. However, with back-up in the way of training, customer leads, advertising and so on from the franchiser, these kind of franchises are suitable for someone with little capital but who has a specific area of expertise or is willing to be trained in it, such as cleaning or vehicle repair and maintenance services.

Defining a franchise

A franchise agreement is just like any business contract, in that it sets out what each party is expected to do and what can happen if he doesn't.

The main ingredients of the franchise agreement are

✓ Permission to use a business name and so be associated with that bigger enterprise

✓ The right for the franchiser to set and enforce business and product standards, such as the use of ingredients, cooking processes, opening times, staff uniforms and so forth

✓ An obligation for the franchiser to provide help, training and guidance in all aspects of operating the business

✓ A definition of how the franchisee is to pay for rights to operate the franchise; for example, royalties on sales, initial purchase fee, marketing levy, mark-up on goods and services provided, and so forth

The British Franchise Association expects its members to follow its code of practice, and you can find out more on its website: www.thebfa.org.

Evaluating a franchise opportunity

Although membership of the BFA and adhering to a code of practice are helpful, they're not a guarantee of success for your franchise. You should be looking for a shortlist of as many as six opportunities, acquiring as much advice as you can get from franchisers, from franchisees, from your bank and from other professional advisers.

Before deciding on a particular franchise, you must consult your legal and financial advisers, as well as ask the franchiser searching questions such as the following:

✔ Has the franchiser operated at least one unit for a year or so as a pilot unit in the UK? They must have done so before selling franchises to third parties. Otherwise, how can the franchiser really know all the problems, and so put you on the right track?

✔ What training and support is included in the *franchise package,* the name given to the start-up kit provided by the franchiser? This package should extend to support staff over the launch period and give you access to back-up advice.

✔ How substantial is the franchise company? Ask to see the balance sheet (take it to your accountant if you can't understand it). Inquire into the track record of the directors (including their other directorships).

Sometimes a major clearing bank offers financial support to buy a particular franchise, which is an encouraging sign that the company is in good financial health. At least you know that the concept is tried and tested and, to some extent, the business is reputable. However, as with everything to do with starting up a business, the buck stops with you.

You can meet franchisers and hear their pitch at one of the dozen or so franchise exhibitions held around the country each year. The BFA Diary page (`www.thebfa.org/events/seminars`) gives details of dates and venues.

Popping into a pop-up

Temporary businesses have been around a long time, in one form or another – charity shops taking short-term leases on vacant high-street sites and car parks springing up on bomb sites awaiting planning consent are two of the most high-profile examples. But recently, these ventures have acquired their own brand name – *pop-ups.* Now pop-ups house artists looking for temporary space to exhibit work, stage shows or create studio spaces. You can find pop-up gardens and parks, pop-up cinemas and theatre shows, and pop-up cafes and restaurants. London is probably the best market for pop-ups, with great media, a large tourist market and property in a constant state of flux – indeed, at the last count 74 pop-up restaurants existed in London, including one established by a Michelin-starred chef.

A number of websites are dedicated to the pop-up phenomenon, including `www.londonpopups.com`, `www.popupspaceblog.com`, `http://popupcity.net`, `www.spareplace.com` and `www.theplacestation.org.uk`. You can even find websites that focus on specific business needs, such as the following that offer insurance: `www.popupspace.com` and `www.hencilla.co.uk`. For national funding for pop-ups, `www.fundingcentral.org.uk` is a good starting point; search 'pop-up' and you find loads of sources of funds.

For a good look at the subject, read *Pop Up Business For Dummies* by Dan Thompson (Wiley).

Founding a Larger Company

If your business looks like it needs a substantial amount of money from the outset and will be taking on the risk of customers owing money, then, as with any manufacturing venture, the legal structures in the preceding sections may not be right for you. In this section you can find out about the advantages and disadvantages of going for a limited company, or buying out a company already in business.

Opting for a limited company

As the name suggests, in this form of business your liability is limited to the amount you contribute by way of share capital.

Two shareholders, one of whom must be a director, can form a limited company. You must also appoint a company secretary, who can be a shareholder, director or an outside person such as an accountant or lawyer. You can buy a company 'off the shelf' from a registration agent, and then adapt it to suit your own purposes. To do so involves changing the name, shareholders and articles of association and takes a couple of weeks to arrange. Alternatively, you can form your own company.

A limited company has a legal identity of its own, separate from the people who own or run it. So, in the event of failure, creditors' claims are restricted to the assets of the company. The shareholders of the business aren't liable as individuals for the business debts beyond the paid-up value of their shares. This lack of liability applies even if the shareholders are working directors, unless of course the company has been trading fraudulently. In practice, the ability to limit liability is restricted these days because most lenders, including the banks, often insist on personal guarantees from the directors. Other advantages include the freedom to raise capital by selling shares.

Disadvantages include the legal requirement for the company's accounts to be audited and filed for public inspection.

When a company is first registered, it must send to Companies House (www.companieshouse.org.uk), the place where all business details and accounts are kept, a copy of its memorandum and articles of association and Form 10, which contains the address of the company's registered office and details of its directors and company secretary. The directors' details are current names, any former names, date of birth, usual residential address, occupation, nationality and other directorships. For the secretary only, the name and address are required. Companies House organises or attends a variety of seminars and exhibitions to support and advise businesses and to support new directors and secretaries. You can find details of these events on the events section of the Companies House website (www.companieshouse.org.uk/about/chEvents.shtml).

Buying out a business

Buying out an existing business is particularly well suited to people who have extensive experience of general business management but lack detailed technical or product knowledge. When you buy an established business, you not only pay for the basic assets of the business, but also the accumulated time and effort that the previous owner spent growing the business to its present state. You can think of this extra asset as *goodwill*. The better the business, the more the 'goodwill' costs you.

Advantages of buying a business include the following:

- ✔ You acquire experience and expertise that you don't have. Learning from the mistakes other people have made in the past is much easier, and almost invariably less costly, than making all these mistakes yourself.

- ✔ You gain both access to your potential customers and the credibility of a trading history from the outset, which can save months if not years of hard work in building relationships.

- ✔ If the business you buy is already profitable, you can pay yourself a living wage from the outset.

- ✔ Bank financing may be easier to acquire for an established business than for a riskier start-up business.

Disadvantages of buying a business include the following:

- ✔ You run the risk of acquiring the existing unsolved problems and mistakes of the person who's selling it.

- ✔ Identifying the right potential acquisition and negotiating a purchase can take a long time, and you've no guarantee that you'll succeed at your first attempt.

- ✔ The professional fees associated with buying a business can be a significant, though necessary, cost. If you buy a small business, the total professional fees associated with the transaction are a major percentage of the total cost of your investment, perhaps as much as 15 or 20 per cent. Experienced solicitors and accountants are vital to this process. They're your safeguards to ensure that you know exactly what you're buying.

Contact these organisations to find out more about buying a business and to see listings of businesses for sale:

- ✔ Businesses For Sale (www.businessesforsale.com) has over 64,000 businesses for sale in the UK, as well as listings of firms in Spain, the USA, Australia, Canada, India, Ireland, New Zealand and France.
- ✔ Christie & Co (www.christie.com) claims to have the largest database of businesses for sale in Europe. This organisation is the recognised market leader in the hotel, catering, leisure and retail markets, and is also expanding into healthcare.
- ✔ Daltons (www.daltonsbusiness.com) has an online database of over 30,000 businesses for sale around the UK and some overseas countries.

Looking at Legal Issues in Marketing

Nothing in business escapes the legal eye of the law and marketing is no exception. If anything, marketing is likely to produce more grey areas from a legal point of view than most other aspects. You have patent and copyright issues to consider, for example.

A number of vital aspects of your business distinguish it from similar firms operating in or near to your area of operations. Having invested time, energy and money in acquiring these distinguishing factors, you need to take steps to preserve any benefits they provide you with. Intellectual property, often known as IP, is the generic title covering the area of law that allows people to own their creativity and innovation in the same way that they can own physical property. The owner of intellectual property can control and be rewarded for its use, and this control encourages further innovation and creativity.

The following four organisations can help direct you to most sources of help and advice across the entire intellectual property field. They also have helpful literature and explanatory leaflets and guidance notes on applying for intellectual property protection:

- ✔ Intellectual Property Office (www.ipo.gov.uk)
- ✔ European Patent Office (www.epo.org)
- ✔ US Patent and Trade Mark Office (www.uspto.gov)
- ✔ World Intellectual Property Association (www.wipo.int)

I cover the most common types of intellectual property in the following sections.

Protecting your intellectual property in the UK may not be of much help in a global world. This lack of protection can be a problem, particularly when it comes to patents where disclosure is a part of the application process. Your details and those of your idea will be included in the government's searchable patents journal when it publishes your application. Both are available to the public on its website and can be found using most standard search engines. The Intellectual Property Office provides guidance on getting worldwide protection for your IP at `www.ipo.gov.uk/types/patent/p-manage/p-abroad/p-worldwide.htm`.

Naming your business

The main consideration in choosing a business name is its commercial usefulness. You want one that lets people know as much as possible about what your company does. So choose a name that conveys the right image and message.

Whichever business name you choose, it has to be legally acceptable and abide by the rules of the Business Names Act 1985. Detailed information on this subject is available from the Business Names section at the Companies House website. Go to `www.companieshouse.gov.uk` and click on Guidance and then Incorporation and Names.

Looking at logos

You don't have to have a logo for your business, but it can build greater customer awareness. A *logo* may be a word, typeface, colour or shape. The McDonald's name is a logo because of its distinct and stylistic writing. Choose your logo carefully. It should be easily recognisable, fairly simple in design and able to be reproduced on everything associated with your business. As far as the law is concerned, a logo is a form of trademark (see 'Registering a trademark', later in this chapter).

Protecting patents

Patents can be regarded as contracts between inventors and the state. The state agrees with the inventor that if he's prepared to publish details of his invention in a set form and if it appears that he's made a real advance, the state then grants him a monopoly on his invention for 20 years. The inventor can use the monopoly period to manufacture and sell the innovation;

competitors can read the published specifications and glean ideas for their research, or they can approach the inventor and offer to help to develop the idea under licence.

If you want to apply for a patent, you mustn't disclose your idea in non-confidential circumstances. If you do, your invention is already 'published' in the eyes of the law, and this fact can invalidate your application. Ideally, you write down the confidentiality of the disclosure you make in a confidentiality agreement, which the person to whom you're making the disclosure signs. The other way is to get your patent application on file before you start talking to anyone about your idea. You can talk to a chartered patent agent in complete confidence because they work under strict rules of confidentiality.

The process of filing an application, and publishing and granting the patent takes two and a half years. The associated costs can be high: subject matter searches cost upwards of £500, validity searches from £1,000 and infringement searches from £1,500. The relevant forms and details of how to patent are available from the Patent Office at www.ipo.gov.uk, and you can find more information in Trevor Baylis Brands' and Henri Charmasson's *Patents, Copyrights & Trademarks For Dummies* (Wiley).

Registering a trademark

A *trademark* is the symbol by which the goods of a particular manufacturer or trader can be identified. It can be a word, a signature, a monogram, a picture, a logo or a combination of these.

To qualify for registration the trademark must be distinctive, must not be deceptive and must not be capable of confusion with marks already registered. Excluded are national flags, royal crests and insignia of the armed forces. A trademark can only apply to tangible goods, not services (although pressure is mounting for this ruling to be changed). To register a trademark, you or your agent should first conduct preliminary searches at the Trade Marks Branch of the Patent Office to check that no conflicting marks are already in existence. You then apply for registration on the official trademark form and pay a fee (currently £200, or £170 if you apply online). Registration is initially for ten years. After this time, you can renew for further periods of ten years at a time, with no upper time limit.

If you've been using an unregistered trademark for some time and it can be construed that customers closely associate it with your product, the trademark has acquired a 'reputation' that gives it some protection legally, but registration makes it much simpler for the owner to have recourse against anyone who infringes the trademark.

Detailing your design

You can register the shape, design or decorative features of a commercial product if it's new, original, never published before or – if already known – never before applied to the product you have in mind. Protection is intended to apply to industrial articles to be produced in quantities of more than 50.

Design registration only applies to features that appeal to the eye – not to the way the article functions.

To register a design in the UK, you apply to the Design Registry at www. ipo.gov.uk/types/design.htm and send a specimen or photograph of the design plus a registration fee (currently £60 plus £40 for each additional design). To protect your design outside the UK, you generally have to make separate applications for registration in each country in which you want protection.

Controlling a copyright

Copyright gives protection against the unlicensed copying of original artistic and creative works – articles, books, paintings, films, plays, songs, music and even engineering drawings. To claim copyright, the item in question should carry the symbol © with the author's name and date. No other action is required to take out copyright, if that copyright is relevant to your business. For further information, you can access the Copyright Service through the Patent Office website (www.ipo.gov.uk/types/copy.htm).

Copyright doesn't last forever. Its duration depends on the type of copyright involved and can be anything from 25 to 70 years after the creator's death.

Abiding by fair business rules

The whole way in which businesses and markets operate is the subject of keen government interest. Don't, for example, gang up with others in your market to create a *cartel*, in which you all agree not to lower your prices or to compete with each other too vigorously. Any such action may be brought to the attention of the Office of Fair Trading (OFT; www.oft.gov.uk). The OFT's job is to make markets work well for consumers. Markets work well when businesses are in open, fair and vigorous competition with each other for the consumer's custom.

The OFT

✔ Ensures that consumer legislation and regulations are properly enforced

✔ Takes action against unfair traders

✔ Encourages codes of practice and standards

✔ Offers a range of information to help consumers understand their rights and make good choices

✔ Liaises closely with other regulatory bodies that also have enforcement powers

Setting terms of trade

All business is governed by terms of trade, which are in turn affected by contractual relationships. Almost everything done in business, whether it's the supply of raw materials, the sale of goods and services or the hire of machinery, is executed under contract law. This is true whether the contract is in writing or verbal – or even merely implied.

Only contracts for the sale of land, hire purchase and some insurance contracts have to be in writing to be enforceable. To make life more complicated, a contract can be part written and part oral. So statements made at the time of signing a written contract can legally form part of that contract. For a contract to exist, three events must take place:

✔ An offer

✔ An acceptance

✔ A consideration – some form of payment

When selling via the Internet or mail order, the contract starts when the supplier 'posts' an acceptance letter, a confirmation or the goods themselves – whichever comes first.

Goods purchased via the Internet or mail order are also covered by the Distance Selling Regulations, under which customers have seven working days after they've received the goods to change their minds and return them. They don't need a reason and can get a full refund.

You must also give customers

✔ Information about the company they're dealing with, such as the business name, registered and trading addresses and directors' names

✔ Written confirmation of the order – by fax, letter or email

✔ A full refund if the goods don't arrive by the date agreed in the original order; if no date was agreed, they must be delivered within 30 days

✔ Information about cancellation rights

✔ Protection against credit card fraud

You have to meet certain standards by law for the supply of goods and services. Over and above these, you need your own terms and conditions to avoid entering into 'contracts' you didn't intend. You need help to devise these terms. The following four basic propositions govern your conditions:

✔ The conditions must be brought to the other party's attention before he makes the contract.

✔ The last terms and conditions specified before acceptance of an offer apply.

✔ If any ambiguity or uncertainty exists in the contract terms, they're interpreted against the person who inserted them.

✔ The terms may be interpreted as unreasonably unenforceable, in breach of various Acts of Parliament.

The Office of Fair Trading (www.oft.gov.uk) and the Trading Standards Institute (www.tradingstandards.gov.uk) can provide useful information on most aspects of trading relationships.

Describing your goods

You can't make whatever claim you like for the performance of your goods or services. If you state or imply a certain standard of performance for what you're selling, your customers have a legally enforceable right to expect that to happen. So if you state that your new slimming method not only makes people lose weight but also makes them happier, richer and more successful, you'd better deliver on all those promises.

The Trade Descriptions Acts and related legislation make it an offence for a trader to describe goods falsely. The Acts cover everything from the declared mileage of second-hand cars to the country of manufacture of a pair of jeans.

The Trading Standards Service operates at county level throughout the UK to ensure that trading laws are met. You can contact your branch by phone or via the website (www.tradingstandards.gov.uk).

Dealing with payment problems

Unless you're able to insist on payment before you send your product or supply your service, getting paid isn't always as simple as sending a bill and waiting for the cheque. Customers may dispute the bill, fairly or unfairly.

A government service gives you an opportunity to collect money when you find a regular court too expensive. True, for particularly small cases the process isn't always cost effective, and occasionally you have problems collecting on your judgement. But the Small Claims Court, as this service is sometimes referred to, should still be part of your business's collection strategy. (See `https://www.gov.uk/make-court-claim-for-money/overview` for more info.) The Department of Justice also offers a mediation service, providing members of the public and businesses with a simple, low-cost method of resolving a wide range of civil disputes out of court. Costs range from £50 to £425, plus VAT, for disputes over amounts between £5,000 and £50,000. For details visit `www.civilmediation.justice.gov.uk`.

One other route to less painful debt recovery (or problem resolution) is to go to arbitration. That's where an independent person listens to both sides of the case and makes a decision based more on common sense, fairness and practicalities than merely on the law. Arbitration is a cheaper, quicker and less intimidating process. You can find out all about the process and locate an arbitrator from the Chartered Institute of Arbitrators (`www.ciarb.org`).

Chapter 6

Preparing the Business Plan

*P*erhaps the most important step in launching any new venture or expanding an existing one is the construction of a *business plan*. If the 2 million plus results that come from putting those words into Google are anything to go by, plenty of interest in the subject exists, and rightly so. Such a plan must include your goals for the enterprise, both short and long term; a description of the products or services you offer and the market opportunities you anticipate; and finally, an explanation of the resources and means that you need to achieve your goals in the face of likely competition.

Preparing a comprehensive business plan along these lines takes time and effort – the Cranfield School of Management estimates anywhere between 200 and 400 hours, depending on the nature of your business and how much data you've already gathered. Nevertheless, such an effort is essential if you're to both crystallise and focus your ideas, and test your resolve about starting or expanding your business.

The core thinking behind business plans and their eventual implementation is strategic analysis. The strategic analysis refines or confirms your view of what's really unique about your proposition. Or to put it another way, 'Why on earth would anyone want to pay enough for this to make me rich?'

After completion, your business plan serves as a blueprint to follow that, like any map, improves users' chances of reaching their destination.

Finding a Reason to Write a Business Plan

A number of important benefits arise from preparing a business plan. All these benefits add up to one compelling reason: businesses that plan make more money than those that don't and they survive for longer too.

The research on planning generally shows a positive relationship between planning and business performance. Businesses that follow a well-thought-out plan generally out-perform businesses with no plans or informal plans in every relevant category. Businesses that continue to update their plans throughout their life enjoy significantly more success than businesses that don't.

I cover key reasons for writing up your business plan in the following sections.

Building confidence

Completing a business plan makes you feel confident in your ability to set up and operate the venture because you've put together a plan to make it happen. It may even compensate for lack of capital and experience, provided of course that you've other factors in your favour, such as a sound idea and a sizeable market opportunity for your product or service.

Testing your ideas

A systematic approach to planning enables you to make your mistakes on paper, rather than in the market place. One potential entrepreneur made the discovery while gathering data for his business plan that the local competitor he thought was a one-man band was in fact the pilot operation for a proposed national chain of franchised outlets. This discovery had a profound effect on his market-entry strategy!

Another entrepreneur found out that, at the price he proposed charging, he would never recover his overheads or break even. Indeed, *overheads* and *break even* were themselves alien terms before he embarked on preparing a business plan. This naive perspective on costs is by no means unusual. (I cover this whole area in Chapter 13.)

Showing how much money you need

Your business plan details how much money you need, what you need it for, and when and for how long you need it.

Because under-capitalisation and early cash-flow problems are two important reasons for new business activities failing, if you have a soundly prepared business plan, you can reduce these risks of failure. You can also experiment with a range of alternative viable strategies and so concentrate on options that make the most economic use of scarce financial resources.

To say that your business plan is the passport to sources of finance is an exaggeration. It does, however, help you to display your entrepreneurial flair and managerial talent to the full and to communicate your ideas to others in a way that's easier for them to understand so that they appreciate the reasoning behind your ideas. These outside parties can be bankers, potential investors, partners or advisory agencies. As soon as they know what you're trying to do, they're better able to help you.

Providing planning experience

Preparing a business plan gives you an insight into the planning process. This process – not simply the plan that comes out of it – is itself important to the long-term health of a business. Businesses are dynamic, as are the commercial and competitive environments in which they operate. No one expects every event recorded on a business plan to occur as predicted, but the understanding and knowledge created by the process of business planning help prepare the business for any changes it may face, and so enable it to adjust quickly.

Satisfying financiers' concerns

If you need finance, examining what financiers expect from you is important if you're to succeed in raising those funds. (For more on approaching finance, see Chapter 8.)

The media often claim that no shortage of money exists for new and growing businesses, and that the only scarce commodities are good ideas and people with the ability to exploit them. A potential entrepreneur may find this claim hard to believe. One major venture capital firm alone receives several thousand business plans a year (*venture capitalists* put up risk capital to invest in other businesses on behalf of institutions such as pension funds). It examines only 500 or so in any detail, pursues fewer than 25 to the negotiating stage and only invests in 6 of those.

To a great extent, the decision of whether to proceed beyond an initial reading of the plan depends on the quality of the business plan used in supporting the investment proposal. The business plan is your ticket of admission, giving you your first, and often only, chance to impress prospective sources of finance with the quality of your proposal.

To have any chance at all of getting financial support, your business plan must be the best that you can write and it must be professionally packaged. The plans that succeed meet all the following requirements.

Presenting evidence of market orientation and focus

You need to demonstrate that you recognise the needs of potential customers, rather than simply being infatuated with an innovative idea. Financiers usually cold-shoulder business plans that occupy more space with product descriptions and technical explanations than with explaining how products are going to be sold and to whom. They rightly suspect that these companies are more of an ego trip than an enterprise.

But market orientation isn't enough in itself. Financiers want to sense that entrepreneurs know the one or two things their business can do best and that they're prepared to concentrate on exploiting these opportunities.

Demonstrating customer acceptance

Financiers like to know that your new product or service is going to sell and is being used, even if only on a trial or demonstration basis. For example, the founder of Solicitec, a company selling software to solicitors to enable them to process relatively standard documents such as wills, had little trouble getting support for his house-conveyancing package after a leading building society had tried and approved his product for its panel of solicitors.

If you're only at the prototype stage, financiers have no immediate indication that, when made, your product is going to appeal to the market. They have to assess your chances of succeeding without any concrete evidence. Under these circumstances, you have to show that the problem your innovation seeks to solve is a substantial one that a large number of people are prepared to pay for.

As well as evidence of customer acceptance, you need to demonstrate that you know how and to whom your new product or service may be sold, and that you've a financially viable means of doing so.

Owning a proprietary position

Exclusive rights to a product through patents, copyright, trademark protection or a licence help to reduce the apparent riskiness of a venture in financiers' eyes, because these things can limit competition, for a while at least.

One participant on a Cranfield enterprise programme held patents on a revolutionary folding bicycle that he'd designed at college. No financial institution was prepared to back him in manufacturing the bicycle, but funds were readily available to enable him to make production prototypes and then license the design to established bicycle makers throughout the world.

However well protected legally a product is, marketability and marketing know-how generally outweigh 'patentability' in the success equation. A salutary observation made by an American professor of entrepreneurship revealed that less than 0.5 per cent of the best ideas contained in the *US Patent Gazette* in the last five years have returned a dime to the inventors.

Making believable forecasts

Entrepreneurs are naturally ebullient when explaining the future prospects for their businesses. They frequently believe that the sky's the limit when it comes to growth, and that money (or rather the lack of it) is the only thing standing between them and their success.

When you're looking for venture capital, the providers of that capital are looking for rapid growth in your business. However, remember that financiers deal with thousands of investment proposals each year, and already have money tied up in hundreds of business sectors. Therefore, they already have a perception of what the accepted financial results and marketing approaches currently are for any sector. Any new company's business plan showing projections that are outside the ranges perceived as acceptable within an industry is going to raise questions in the investor's mind.

Make your growth forecasts believable – support them with hard facts where possible. If they're on the low side, approach the more cautious lending banker, rather than a venture capitalist. The former often sees a modest forecast as a virtue, lending credibility to the business proposal as a whole.

Writing Up Your Business Plan

In the following sections, I give you some guidelines to make sure that your plan attracts attention and succeeds in the face of fierce competition. More than 1,000 businesses start up in the UK each day, and many of those are looking for money or other resources that they're hoping their business plan can secure for them. Making your business plan the best it can be gives it a chance to stand out.

Defining your readership

Clearly, a business plan is more effective if you write it with your readers in mind. Doing so involves research into the particular interests, foibles and idiosyncrasies of those readers. Bankers are more interested in hearing about certainties and steady growth, and venture capitalists are also interested in dreams of great things to come. *Business angels,* who put their own money at risk, like to know how their particular skills and talents can be deployed in the business.

You can benefit from carrying out your reader research before the final editing of your business plan, because you should incorporate something of this knowledge into the way you present it. You may find that you have to create slightly different versions of the business plan for different audiences. This differentiation makes readers feel that you're addressing the proposal to them rather than them just being the recipient of a 'Dear Sir or Madam' type of missive. However, the fundamentals of the plan remain constant.

Creating the plan

The following sections help you prepare the plan itself.

Deciding on content

No universal business plan format exists. That being said, experience has taught me that certain styles are more successful than others. Following these guidelines results in an effective business plan that covers most requirements. Not every subheading may be relevant to you, but the general format is robust.

The following list contains the elements of an effective business plan, one that covers most requirements. You may not need all these sections, and you may need others to cover special requirements.

- ✔ The **cover** should show the name of your business, its website, Facebook/Twitter pages, physical address, phone number(s) including a mobile, fax number(s), email address, contact name and the date on which this version of the plan was prepared. It should confirm that this document is the current view on the business's position and financing needs.

- ✔ The **title page,** immediately behind the front cover, should repeat the cover information and also give the founder's name, address and phone number. A home phone number can be helpful, particularly for investors, who often work irregular hours.

- ✔ The **executive summary** is ideally one page, but certainly no longer than two, and contains the highlights of your plan. Writing this summary is a difficult task, but is the single most important part of your business plan. Done well, it can favourably dispose the reader from the outset. If you do the executive summary badly, or not at all, then the plan may not get beyond the investor's mail room. This one page (or two pages) must explain

- The current position of the company, including a summary of past trading results

- A description of the products or services, together with details of any rights or patents and of your competitive advantage

- The reasons that customers need this product or service, together with some indication of market size and growth

- A summary of forecasts of sales and profits, together with short- and long-term aims and the strategies that you'll employ

- How much money you need to fund the growth and how and when the provider of that finance can benefit

Write the executive summary only after you complete the business plan itself.

✔ The **table of contents,** with page numbers, is the map that guides readers through the business plan. If that map is obscure, muddled or even missing, you're likely to end up with lost or irritated readers who are in no mind to back your proposal. You should list and number each main section and give it a page number. Elements within each section should also be numbered: 1, 1.1, 1.2 and so on.

✔ Details of the **business and its management** should include a brief history of the business and its performance to date, if any, and details of key staff and their work experience, current mission, legal entity, capital structure and professional advisers.

✔ The description of **products and services,** their applications, competitive advantage and proprietary position must include details of the state of readiness of new products and services, and development cost estimates.

✔ The **marketing** section should provide a brief overview of the market by major segment showing size and growth. Explain the current and proposed marketing strategy for each major segment, covering price, promotion, distribution channels, selling methods, location requirements and the need for acquisitions, mergers or joint ventures, if any.

✔ Information on **management and staffing** should give details of current key staff and any recruitment needs. Include information on staff retention strategies, reward systems and training plans.

✔ The **operations** section describes how you make your products and services and fulfil orders, how you assure quality standards and how you can meet output.

✔ The summary of the key **financial data** includes ratios together with a description of the key controls used to monitor and review performance.

✔ Include **financing requirements** needed to achieve the planned goals, together with how long you need the money for. Also demonstrate how the business would proceed using only internal funding. The difference between these two positions is what the extra money helps to deliver.

✔ **E-commerce** isn't just about selling goods and services online, though that's important. It covers a range of activities that you can carry out online to make your business more efficient. These solutions extend across the supply chain, from ordering your raw materials right through to after-sales service. It can incorporate market intelligence gathering, customer relationship management and a whole range of back-office procedures. Your business plan should show how you plan to tackle this area.

✔ Include **major milestones** with dates; for example, get prototype for testing by 20 December, file patents by 10 January or locate suitable premises by such and such a date.

✔ **Risk assessment** features high on your reader's list of concerns, so you should anticipate as many as you can, together with your solution. For example: 'Our strategy is highly dependent on finding a warehouse with a cold store for stock. But if we can't find one by the start date, we will use space in the public cold store 10 miles away. This isn't as convenient but it will do.'

✔ Detail an **exit route** for venture capitalists and business angels. Typically, they're looking to liquidate their investments within three to seven years, so your business plan should show them how much money they can make and how quickly.

If you think that you need long-term investment (see Chapter 8 for more about equity financing), you need to say something about who may buy the business and when you may be able to launch it on a stock market.

✔ **Appendices** include CVs of the key team members, technical data, patents, copyrights and designs, details of professional advisers, audited accounts, consultants' reports, abstracts of market surveys, details of orders on hand and so on.

Writing and editing

The first draft of the business plan may have several authors and it can be written ignoring the niceties of grammar and style. The first draft is a good one to talk over with your legal adviser to keep you on the straight and narrow, and with a friendly banker or venture capitalist. This discussion can give you an insider's view of the strengths and weaknesses of your proposal.

When you've revised the first draft, then comes the task of editing. Here grammar, spelling and a consistent style do matter. The end result must be a crisp, correct, clear, complete plan no more than 20 pages long. If you're not an expert writer, you may need help with editing. Your local librarian or college may be able to put you in touch with a local editor. You can also use websites such as People Per Hour (www.peopleperhour.com) and Elance (www.elance.com) to help you find editors.

Checking on readability

Many business plans are difficult to read. Two things make life hard for readers: long sentences and long words. Back in 1952, Robert Gunning, a business language expert, devised a formula called the Fog Index to measure just how tough a memo, letter or report is to read. Following are the four steps:

1. Find the average number of words per sentence. Use a sample at least 100 words long. Divide total number of words by number of sentences to give you the average sentence length.

2. Count the number of words of three syllables or more per 100 words. Don't count words that are capitalised; combinations of short, easy words like *bookkeeper;* or verbs that are made up of three syllables by adding –ed or –es, like *created* or *trespasses.*

3. Add the two factors above and multiply by 0.4. This calculation gives you the Fog Index. It corresponds roughly with the number of years of schooling a person would require to read a passage with ease and understanding.

4. Check the results against this scale:

   ✔ 4 and below; very easy – perhaps childish

   ✔ 5 fairly easy; tabloid press, hard-selling letters

   ✔ 7 or 8 standard; *Daily Mail,* most business letters and business plans

   ✔ 9–11 fairly difficult; *The Times, Daily Telegraph,* good product literature

   ✔ 12–15 difficult; *The Economist,* technical literature

   ✔ 17 or above: very difficult; *New Scientist* – don't use in business plans

You can find a neat tool to calculate the Fog Index at `http://gunning-fog-index.com`. Just copy and paste the text you want checked into the box. Microsoft Word has its own readability statistics tool listed as an option when you select the spelling and grammar checker.

Laying out and packaging

Your business plan should be visually appealing. Dense text, poor layout and clutter all serve to put your reader off. Create a favourable impression from the outset and you'll have the reader onside. Here are the most important guidelines to make your written business plan stand out from the crowd:

✔ **Layout:** The reasoning behind good layout is to entice the reader to read your words and take the action you want – back your proposition. Give your text room to breathe by leaving plenty of white space around it. You can achieve this look by having wide margins and double line-spacing. Also use headings to break up the text and different font sizes and styles to differentiate between sections of your business plan.

✔ **Font:** Don't be tempted to use a fancy font in the body of the business plan. Stick to *serif* fonts, those with slight 'tails' on the letters that lead the eye from letter to letter. Times Roman, Book Antiqua and Century are good examples of texts that cause less eye strain. Sans-serif fonts like Arial, Calibri and Helvetica can cause eye fatigue, so save these fonts for headings, bullets or short paragraphs outside the main body of your text. Never use a font smaller than 10 point, unless your readership is mostly under 30. For over-70s, the recommended size to cause the least pain is 14 point. However, most business plan writers settle on 12 point as the preferred size.

✔ **Images and charts:** Pictures, images, charts, tables, graphs and pictures are powerful ways to convey large amounts of information quickly and efficiently. A picture, so the saying goes, is worth a thousand words– which is excellent because they usually only need the space of 200! Using images and charts is also a great way to break up the text and retain the reader's attention.

The University of Leicester has a useful guide to the role of text, tables, graphs and charts in presenting numerical data; visit www2.le.ac.uk/offices/ld/resources/numeracy/numerical-data.

✔ **Packaging:** Appropriate packaging enhances every product and a business plan is no exception. Most experts prefer a simple spiral binding with a clear plastic cover front and back. This presentation makes it easy for the reader to move from section to section, and it ensures that the document survives the frequent handling that every successful business plan is likely to get.

Maintaining confidentiality

Finding an investor or a bank to lend to your business may take weeks or months. During that time, potential investors diligently gather information about the business so that they don't have surprises later about income, expenses or undisclosed liabilities. The business plan is only the starting point for their investigations.

If you and the prospective financiers are strangers to one another, you may be reluctant to turn over sensitive business information until you're confident that they're serious. (This issue isn't as sensitive with banks as it is with business angels and venture capital providers.) To allay these fears, consider asking for a confidentiality letter or agreement.

A confidentiality letter suffices in most circumstances. But if substantial amounts of intellectual property are involved, you may prefer to have a lawyer draft a longer, more formal confidentiality agreement, also known as a non-disclosure agreement (NDA). The confidentiality letter should be limited to their agreement to treat the information as strictly confidential and to use the information only to investigate lending or investing in the business, and to the other terms set out in the letter.

The Intellectual Property Office provides a guide that can help you put together an NDA; see (www.ipo.gov.uk/nda.pdf).

Doing due diligence

Don't be surprised if the investor wants to find out about your personal financial status, job or business history. Investors are interested in your financial stability, your reputation for integrity and your general business savvy because they will, in effect, extend credit to you until you deliver them the interest or return they're expecting on their money. That's what the *due diligence* process is all about.

Usually, the due diligence process, which involves a thorough examination of both the business and its owners, takes several weeks if not longer. But that depends on how much money your plan calls for and from whom you're trying to raise it. (I cover raising finance in Chapter 8.)

Accountants and lawyers usually subject your track record and the business plan to detailed scrutiny. You're then required to warrant that you've provided *all* relevant information, under pain of financial penalties. The cost of this due diligence process, rarely less than a big five-figure sum and often running into six, is borne by the firm raising the money, but is paid out of the money raised, if that's any consolation.

Using Business Planning Software

You may consider taking some of the sweat out of writing your business plan by using one of the myriad software programmes on the market. You need to take care in using such systems, because the result can be a bland plan that pleases no one and achieves nothing worthwhile.

Don't buy a package with several hundred business plans covering every type of business imaginable. The chances are that the person who wrote the plans knows far less than you do about your business sector and can add little or no value to your proposition. Worse still, at least an even chance exists that the reader of your plan has seen the fruits of these packaged plans before and may be less than enthusiastic to see yet another one.

You may well find it beneficial to use the test shown in Figure 6-1 as an uncomplicated form of self-assessment, before becoming bogged down in number-crunching software.

By answering the questions below you will get some idea of how well your business plan is progressing. Score 1, 2, or 3 following the key below for each of the questions. Mark the options closest to your instincts, and be honest. Then add up your scores and refer to the results at the end of the questionnaire to see how you scored and to check the potential of your plan.

Whatever your score, remember that this type of self-assessment test is broad brush. It is designed only to give an indication of whether you have the basic attitude, instincts, and capabilities to make a success of launching a home-based business.

If your score is low, the chances are that you do not. If it is high, the opposite is true.

1 = Made a start   2 = Some data only   3 = Comprehensive

Title page   ☐1 ☐2 ☐3

Name of business contact details, date of business plan, contents

Executive summary   ☐1 ☐2 ☐3

Your details; summary of key strategies; why you are better or different; summary of profit projections; summary of financial needs

The business and its management ☐1 ☐2 ☐3

You and your team's relevant experience; business goals and objectives; legal structure of the business

The marketing strategy   ☐1 ☐2 ☐3

Market segment analysis; pricing strategy; promotion plans; product mix and range; e-commerce strategy; location; selling strategy

Management and staffing   ☐1 ☐2 ☐3

Staff numbers; roles and responsibilities; recruitment needs

Operations   ☐1 ☐2 ☐3

What facilities and equipment are needed; what services will be brought in?

Legal issues   ☐1 ☐2 ☐3

What intellectual protection do you have as a barrier to entry; what other legal issues affect your business?

Financial forecasts   ☐1 ☐2 ☐3

Summary of financial projections; monthly cash flows; profit and loss accounts; balance sheets; break-even analysis

Financing requirements   ☐1 ☐2 ☐3

How much money do you need; what is it needed for; how much money can you provide; how much do you need to raise from outside; what security is available?

Results:

9 points or less:
You still have a lot more information to gather or decisions to make. No serious plan can be drawn up at this stage.
Between 10 and 20 points:
You have made progress, but still have a few gaps to fill. Concentrate your efforts on completing your plan.
More than 20 points:
Your plan is now complete and ready for final editing.

Figure 6-1:
Assessing the content of your business plan.

The following sections help you understand what software can and can't do, and where to start finding software to suit your needs.

Recognising the limits of software

Good business planning software provides a useful structure to drop your plan into and may provide a few helpful spreadsheets and templates for financial projections and market analysis. It also provides a valuable repository for your work in progress as you assemble the evidence to convince yourself and others that your business can succeed.

What software doesn't do is write a convincing business proposition by itself. The maxim 'garbage in, garbage out' applies to business planning software just as it does to everything to do with computers.

The other danger is that you end up with spreadsheet solutions – numbers just pumped into the financials – without any evidence of the underlying logic to support them.

Use business planning software as an aid and not a crutch. Go beyond that and you may end up worse off than if you'd started with a blank sheet of paper.

Reviewing packages

This section tells you how to access business planning software packages and resources that have been used to good effect:

- **Lloyd's** bank offers Sage Business Planning free to anyone opening an account with them. See `http://businesshelp.lloydstsbbusiness.com/starting/business-plan`.

- **NatWest** bank's Business Planner is easy-to-use software that takes the hassle out of planning (it claims to offer a business plan in 60 seconds!). PC and Mac versions are available. On the website, you can also find tips on writing plans. Visit `http://support.natwest.com/business-tools-resources/` where you can find links to their business planning tools. You have to register to get access to them.

- **Bradley University, Illinois,** provides a range of business planning resources at `www.bradley.edu/academic/colleges/fcba/centers/turner/business/planning`.

Presenting Your Plan

Anyone backing a business does so primarily because she believes in the management of the business. She knows from experience that things rarely go according to plan, so she must be confident that the team involved can respond effectively to changing conditions. You can be sure that any financier you're presenting to has read dozens of similar plans and is well rehearsed. She may even have taken the trouble to find out something about your business and financial history.

While the written plan has to be thorough, you need to be equally well prepared to present and defend your proposition in person. That involves thinking through how you'll come across when you make your pitch and how you'll react to the inevitable questions and criticism. Think about how people fare in the BBC's *Dragon's Den* programme, and be prepared.

Starring in show time

What does any actor do before stepping onto a stage? Rehearse, rehearse, rehearse. As you rehearse, keep in mind the guidance in the following sections for how to really connect with your audience.

- ✔ **Be prepared.** You need to have every aspect of your business plan in your head and know your way around the plan forwards, backwards and sideways!

- ✔ **Create empathy between yourself and your listeners.** While you may not be able to change your personality, you can take a few tips on presentation skills. Eye contact, tone of speech, enthusiasm and body language all have a part to play in making a presentation successful (see the sidebar 'Words, tone and body language').

- ✔ **Dress to impress.** Wearing a suit is never likely to upset anyone. Shorts and sandals just set the wrong tone. Serious money calls for serious people and even the Internet world is growing up.

- ✔ **Explain your strategy in a business-like manner.** Demonstrate your grasp of the competitive market forces at work.

- ✔ **Provide the latest information** on sales, profits, product development, market tests or other evidence-based milestones. This information may be too current to include in your written plan, so here's the opportunity to add strength to your proposition.

- ✔ **Use visual aids.** If possible, bring and demonstrate your product or service. A video or computer-generated model or diagram can help bring your proposition to life.

Words, tone and body language

Researchers have shown the value of each of the following in transmitting a message:

✔ **Words – 7 per cent:** Controlling the words is pretty easy when you prepare what you're saying carefully.

✔ **Tone – 35 per cent:** You must work hard to sound professional, interested, open to criticism and friendly, without being over-familiar.

✔ **Non-verbal or body language – 58 per cent:** Subconsciously, your body reveals what you really mean and think. So if you sit with your arms and legs crossed, you indicate a hostile attitude towards the other person and/or the message. If you sit with your arms folded with your thumbs up, you show a superior attitude. Leaning forward indicates interest or intimidation. People who rest their chin on one hand and have a finger in or near their mouth need reassurance. Those who rub their chins are thinking or making a decision and aren't listening. You've limited control over your body language, but it really matters!

Check out *Voice and Speaking Skills For Dummies* by Judy Apps (Wiley), which is crammed full of useful information on everything you need to find your voice and communicate with confidence.

✔ **Allow plenty of time for questions.** Listen to comments and criticisms carefully and make your replies to questions brief and to the point (avoid a defensive attitude when you respond). If your potential investors want more information, they can ask. This approach allows time for the many different questions that must be asked now or later, before an investment can proceed.

Handling feedback

Don't be surprised or disheartened if your business plan doesn't get the reception you hope for. Anita Roddick's Body Shop proposition was turned down flat. It was only when a local garage owner, Ian McGlinn, advanced her £4,000 in return for 25 per cent of her company that she got the money to open a second shop; a deal that netted him a couple of hundred million and her considerably more. Tim Waterstone's business plan was turned down by bank after bank for being too ambitious. They wanted him to open a bookshop, but he'd set his sights on a chain. Eventually, he got backing and went on to build his chain, change the shape of book retailing in the UK and sell his business to his former employers, WH Smith, for £47 million. Business plans are turned down for hundreds of reasons. Venture capitalists turn down 95 propositions for every 100 they receive. Why? Because they're just not convinced that the plan has been well thought through and/or properly researched, and that the person or team are up to the task.

These measures help you to take account of feedback and minimise the chances of ultimate rejection:

✔ Listen carefully to criticisms when you're presenting your business plan. If you can tell at the time that you're going to be turned down, ask two questions:

- Why?

- What can I do to improve my proposition?

✔ Go back over your business plan and see whether you can change anything to make the financial proposition look less risky. Cash pouring out in the early weeks and months on staff, offices and promotion without any significant sales revenue coming in is a big turn-off for financiers.

✔ Consider whether you're pitching your proposition to the right audience. Risky technology-based ventures are more likely to appeal to venture capitalist and corporate venture firms. Bankers are more interested in putting up cash for tangible assets such as property and elements of working capital including stock in trade, and financing quality customers taking credit. I cover these funding options in Chapter 8.

Making an elevator pitch

You never know when the chance to present your business plan may occur – maybe even in a lift between floors (hence the term *elevator pitch*). You need to know your business thoroughly, and it's as well to have a 5-, 10- and 20-minute presentation ready to run at a moment's notice.

One entrepreneur was given a chance to make a presentation of her business plan to the most powerful and influential person in her industry. This person could make or break new businesses, and frequently did. The opportunity was a ten-minute ride in a chauffeur-driven car between the Dorchester hotel and Harrods. She had no room to demonstrate the product, set up flip charts or PowerPoint presentations, or involve the team. She had just enough space and time to convey a handful of powerful facts with passion, conviction and authority. Fortunately, the entrepreneur concerned had rehearsed her impromptu presentation and was completely prepared to seize the opportunity presented. Thanks to this successful pitch, she secured the rights to a product range crucial to the success of her business. Barely a decade after taking that fateful car ride, she had built and sold her business for £20 million.

Chapter 7

Getting Help

*T*he fact that you've decided to start up your own business doesn't mean you have to do everything yourself. Even if you've rejected the idea of taking on a partner or going into a franchise chain, you can still get expert help and advice with nearly every aspect of your business before you start up, while you're starting up and even long after you've established your enterprise.

In taking outside help and advice, you're in good company. Each working day over 12,000 people use the services of a small business advisory organisation. Most are simple telephone enquiries, but others involve face-to-face counselling sessions. Several hundred organisations are specifically concerned with providing help, advice and resources (including finance) for small businesses and those starting them. For the most part, these services are provided free or at a low cost, at least at the outset.

Many of these organisations have been set up, or at least been encouraged to set up, by both national and local governments, who have come to realise how valuable small businesses are to communities and economies. (Chapter 2 addresses these issues in more depth.)

Although lots of people and organisations can help you get started in business, in the end you're the one who has to make the decisions. I don't mean to knock the great advice and wisdom that many in help agencies such as Business Link or Enterprise Agencies and the like have to offer. However, no one can step into your shoes and see the world through your eyes. By the same token, the final responsibility for choice of action rests with you. Listen to advice but take your own decisions.

In this chapter, I introduce some of the organisations to talk to if you want to get an expert outsider's view on the problems you're tussling with and so get off to the best possible start.

Connecting with Government Services

Getting help for your business from the government can be worthwhile. You pay for that help in your taxes, so if you want value for money these schemes are certainly worth exploring. Some of this help is available throughout the country and some is tailored to the needs of a particular region.

Accessing national government support

That the UK government is keen to help small business should come as no big surprise. New small businesses are a key source of new jobs and, eventually, of tax payments. However, just because the government's aims are selfish doesn't mean you shouldn't tap into any help you can get. Exactly what that help is varies from time to time, both in terms of the type of help and its amount and form.

You can expect government help, advice and support in some or all these areas:

- Grants and incentives
- Online information on all aspects of business
- Regulations that apply when starting a business
- Sources of finance, both debt and equity (see Chapter 8 for more on these types of funds)
- The attributes and skills needed to launch and run a business, and how you measure up
- The range of issues that you need to consider in developing your business proposition
- The right sort of finance to start and grow your business
- The steps required for informing public authorities that you're launching your business
- Training schemes
- What type of business is most appropriate

The contact point for access to all government help is the Department for Business Innovation and Skills website (www.gov.uk/government/policies/making-it-easier-to-set-up-and-grow-a-business--6). From this link, you can access information on the full range of help, advice, funding initiatives and other support services provided by or through central government.

Relating to a region

Some support for new and growing businesses is delivered at a national level, but increasingly the governing bodies of the individual countries that make up the UK provide a range of initiatives:

- **England:** National Enterprise Network (NEN) members work across England to offer impartial and independent advice on starting or developing a small business. They operate in over 100 locations around the country. You can find the one closest to you by selecting your region on the homepage of the NEN website (www.nationalenterprisenetwork.org).

- **Northern Ireland:** Invest Northern Ireland business support services are run via this website: www.nibusinessinfo.co.uk/content/starting. The website provides links for all aspects, from generating business ideas through to record keeping, employing people and going for growth.

- **Scotland:** Business Scotland (www.business.scotland.gov.uk/topic/starting-up-a-business) runs a number of country-specific services including a network of Business Gateway offices across Scotland offering support and information to you and your business at any stage (www.bgateway.com/our-services).

- **Wales:** Business Wales (http://business.wales.gov.uk/starting-business) helps you when setting up, from developing your ideas to learning basic business start-up skills and then expanding your potential.

Choosing Small Business Associations

The services of government-supported help agencies are often free, but a growing army of commercial or semi-commercial self-help organisations is present in the field. Their basic premise is that if small firms can band together to buy goods, services or advice, or to influence government policy, they're more likely to be effective than on their own. I cover the more established of these organisations in the following sections.

The Federation of Small Businesses

The Federation of Small Businesses (FSB; website: www.fsb.org.uk; tel: 0808 20 20 888) is a national organisation with offices in Scotland, Wales and Northern Ireland as well as London that protects small firms' interests and fights for their rights. The FSB has the resources to take major test cases of importance to small business through the expensive legal process leading to the House of Lords and the European Courts if necessary. The FSB has been particularly effective when dealing with taxation and employment matters.

The FSB has over 213,000 members and runs a range of business support services, such as guidance on business and marketing planning. Thirty-three regional committees and over 194 branch committees, run by people who themselves operate small businesses and who donate their time to the FSB, complement the professional staffs.

For people thinking of starting their own business, the FSB offers legal, environmental, fire and premises tips, as well as advice on many other issues that small business owners may have to address as the business grows. The FSB also provides information on other agencies that may be of use or assistance when starting up.

Membership costs range from £150 per annum, including a one-off registration fee of £30 for someone working on his own, up to £900 for a firm employing more than 101 people. (Prices exclude VAT.)

Among the valuable services on offer from the FSB is a legal benefits package, providing access to legal advice from qualified lawyers 24 hours a day, 365 days a year; tax advice from Revenue-trained specialists; information and documentation on employment, tax and commercial law; and insurance cover for legal and tax professional fees and statutory awards in the event of an employment dispute or full tax enquiry.

Forum of Private Business

The mission of the Forum of Private Business (FPB; website: www.fpb.org; tel: 0845 130 1722) is to influence laws and policies that affect private businesses and support members to grow profitably. Through its 25,000 members, the FPB researches and distributes a referendum a number of times each year and keeps both members and government aware of how small firms feel about key topical issues.

You can choose between two types of membership. Intermediate membership is best for sole traders and businesses with a few employees, and advanced membership offers complete support for businesses, particularly those with five or more employees. The fees are £175 and £565 respectively, plus VAT. Here are the benefits of membership:

- ✔ A direct influence on laws and policies affecting your business – for example, employment law, uniform business rates, taxation, red tape, bank services and late payment

- ✔ Information on tap when you need it, with unlimited free access to the Member Information Service, on any issue affecting your business

✔ User-friendly management tools to help your business stay within the law – for example, the FPB Employment Guide, the FPB Health & Safety Guide and the FPB Bank Finance Review, which looks at areas such as bank performance, bank switching, tracking transactions and transmission charges

The FPB also has a number of useful tools and calculators to help you with areas such as breakeven, VAT, loan repayments and late payment interest charges.

The British Chambers of Commerce

Though not aimed exclusively at small businesses, the British Chambers of Commerce (www.britishchambers.org.uk) offer an extensive range of services for business starters. Their national network of accredited chambers is managed and developed by their business membership and monitored at the national level to ensure that they deliver appropriate products and services to prescribed standards. They're funded by membership subscriptions.

Currently, over 135,000 businesses belong to a chamber in the accredited network, from growth-oriented start-ups to local and regional subsidiaries of multinational companies, in all commercial and industrial sectors, and from all over the UK.

British Chambers of Commerce have access to a range of benefits geared to help businesses big or small succeed and grow. With over 2,500 staff operating from 53 accredited chambers, their network provides a ready-made management support team for any business anywhere in Britain.

Business training, information resources, networking and savings on essential overheads, all of which are tailored to individual business needs, are on offer from local chambers. Increasingly, many of their services are also available online.

The British Chambers of Commerce are also part of the global network of chambers of commerce, and for existing or potential exporters no better route exists to the global marketplace.

Their regular surveys, consultations and reports provide grass-roots business opinion and have strong influence on government ministers and officials, members of Parliament, and other decision makers and opinion formers.

Chambers of commerce have a long history of providing relevant business training, coaching and support for their members and the wider business community. They're one of the largest training providers in the country, offering a huge range of development opportunities designed to help improve your business performance. To find a course go to www.britishchambers.org.uk/business/training-and-skills.

A few more strings to your bow

Literally hundreds of organisations and associations exist that can help you and your business. Here are a few more whose services may match your needs:

- ✔ **Association of Chartered Certified Accountants** (www.accaglobal.com) is a major accounting body. It offers a range of free articles on many aspects of starting a business and running a business, including access to finance, getting paid and the use of advisors. See in particular www.accaglobal.com/en/research-insights/small-business-resource.html.

- ✔ **National Asian Business Association** (www.nabauk.org) is a national voice for the Asian business community that provides information and advice on anything of interest – from starting a business through to selling goods or services. Membership of NABA is free and comes with benefits such as free training on issues of interest like exporting and financial planning, and, of course, a number of networking opportunities.

- ✔ **Black Business Association** (www.bbassoc.org.uk) focuses on the issues of business and entrepreneurship in the African Caribbean community. Annual fees are £150.

- ✔ **British Association of Women Entrepreneurs** (www.bawe-uk.org) is a peer group for women entrepreneurs who want to be challenged. Associate membership for business starters is £80 per annum.

- ✔ **British Franchise Association** (www.thebfa.org) has a directory of country franchise associations from which you can find information about franchising in each country (go to International and then Franchise Associations).

- ✔ **EveryWoman** (www.everywoman.com). For a fee of £49.99 plus VAT for one year's membership, you gain access to personal development tools, resources and expert insight and advice.

- ✔ **Institute of Directors** (IoD, www.iod.com) is the club for directors, membership of which costs an election fee on joining of £200 and then £360 a year. You get access to a prestigious central London office and other offices around the UK and in their branches in Belgium, Bermuda, Cyprus, France, Germany, Malta, Monaco and the Netherlands. Business information and research is provided for you by the IoD's expert researchers and bespoke business advisers on tax and law. The IoD is also considered one of the best networking associations for entrepreneurs.

- ✔ **PRIME Business Club** (www.prime.org.uk) claims to be the only national organisation dedicated to helping people aged over 50 to set up in business. It has all the usual material on starting a business on its site, but emphasises the issues older people face, such as dealing with tax credits and pensions.

✔ **StartUp Britain** (www.startupbritain.co) is an independent collective of UK entrepreneurs and big businesses, representing the private sector response to the government's ambition for an enterprise-led recovery. Over 60 leading global brands have pledged millions of pounds in support of new entrepreneurs. As well as running events around the country, it offers extensive advice on raising money, carrying out market research, writing a business plan and much more.

✔ **Telework Association** (www.tca.org.uk) costs from £19.95 a year to join. It has 7,000 members who work at or are running a business from home. You get a bi-monthly magazine, a teleworking handbook with ideas for tele-businesses and access to a helpline covering all aspects of working from home.

Universities and Colleges

Universities and colleges around the country offer training programmes, support and other initiatives to help small business founders both before and after start-up. Here are some such initiatives:

✔ **Cranfield School of Management** (www.som.cranfield.ac.uk/som/bgp) runs the Business Growth and Development Programme (BGP), which is the UK's most successful and longest-running programme for ambitious owner managers and managing directors. The programme provides a unique opportunity for you to step back from the day-to-day demands of running your business. By the end of the programme, you've developed a comprehensive and robust strategy and plan for the future. Expect to pay around £8,000 for the privilege, but in return you can expect a substantial payback on your investment. Lord Bilimoria (Cobra Beer) and Angus Thirwell (Hotel Chocolat) are among the alumni of this programme. BGP also operates The Evergreen Fund, established through the generosity of past participants of the programme, to enable aspiring entrepreneurs who need financial support to participate.

✔ **London College of Fashion,** University of the Arts, London (www.fashion.arts.ac.uk) offers a number of business start-up courses, such as Starting Your Own Fashion Label Online, Starting Your Own Lingerie or Swimwear Label, and Starting Your Own Fashion Retail Business.

✔ **London Jewellery School** (www.londonjewelleryschool.co.uk) runs a five-day Set Up Your Own Jewellery Business Intensive Certificate. This course covers business set-up skills including marketing yourself, legal requirements, pricing and selling your jewellery, getting into galleries and shops, and photographing your jewellery. The course costs £630.

Hotcourses (www.hotcourses.com) provides information on some 3,000 business courses run in UK colleges and universities. The company aims to be the best in the world at helping people find the course that's right for them, at whatever stage they are in life. With offices in Chennai, India and London, Hotcourses is the largest publisher of guides to courses, colleges and universities.

Entering an Incubator

Incubators – also known as accelerators, science parks, innovation centres, technology parks and a whole variety of other names coined over the years – are places where new businesses can set up in a benign environment, with support services and advice close at hand. The many names try to describe the tasks that incubators perform.

Finding the right type of incubator

Varieties of incubators now co-exist in the market, with radically different aims and objectives. Some, such as those founded by entrepreneurs and venture capital firms – the 'for profit' variety – only want to get rich by helping entrepreneurs to get rich. That goal at least has the merit of transparency. Some incubators have revenue models that can make the incubator rich without necessarily benefiting anyone else that much. The national governments and local governments are more concerned with job creation than wealth, and universities, another major player, want jobs for the students and funding for faculty research rather than riches themselves. Big corporate firms run private incubators to encourage firms that may buy their products or services, or create career opportunities for their more entrepreneurial and potentially less fickle employees.

These incubators are havens for entrepreneurs with innovative or technology-based business ideas that need more help than most to bring to fruition. Such ventures usually have more potential than other business start-ups, but they're also riskier. No one knows how many entrepreneurs graduate from these incubators each year, but a reasonable supposition is that each of the estimated 4,000 incubators has two or three graduates each year. So, 10,000 or so 'eggs' are hatched in a safe environment each year – not a big number in terms of business start-ups. Across Europe and the USA, somewhere between 3 and 4 million new businesses get going in most years. For at least some of the entrepreneurs who get into an incubator, their chances of success are better than if they go it alone.

Getting into an incubator

You almost invariably face an application process to get into any business incubator. All that varies is the process itself. Some incubators positively invite and encourage the informal approach, some are highly structured, some have their own models and techniques that they believe can sort the wheat from the chaff. All the application processes take time, and if they didn't, you'd have cause for concern. After all, if an incubator takes in anyone without any serious consideration of what the person can do to help their business, that particular incubation process is unlikely to be of much value. Most application processes require some sort of business plan. This plan may be little more than an executive summary created online with your application. Or it may be a more comprehensive written document setting out your latest thinking on what's so special about you and your big idea. Then comes the interview, and after that the decision.

Most incubators have details of their application process on their websites, as well as case examples of successful clients. Some have business plan application templates to help in the process. You can expect to take anything from a couple of weeks to a couple of months to get through the process.

Considering the cost

If you're just paying rent and for services as you use them, the cost of being in an incubator is transparent. Such not-for-profit incubators are usually aimed at non-business-educated people who have good ideas to create traditional small businesses, usually with little technology involved. These incubators are frequently government funded, often in underdeveloped cities, and provide mentoring, business development and office space. The typical equity stake required ranges from none to nominal (some require chief executive officers to give back to the community).

However, if providing an incubator with an equity stake in your business is involved, as it surely is in any for-profit incubator, then the cost can run the scale from a few per cent of the business to an outrageously expensive 30 to 50 per cent. The amount you pay doesn't always relate to the value you receive. It depends on your business needs and the scale of the opportunity that you want to exploit.

Finding out more

Contact UK Business Incubation (www.ukbi.co.uk) or the United Kingdom Science Park Association (UKSPA; www.ukspa.org.uk) to find out all you need to know about incubators or innovation centres that may help you achieve your ambitious goals.

City University operates the London City Incubator (LCI; www.city.ac.uk/
for-business/business-services/london-incubator) that helps
early-stage, high-growth start-up businesses to prepare for investment. It
focuses primarily, but not exclusively, on high-growth sectors, including clean
technology, medical devices and digital media.

Assisting Inventors

Each year over 7,000 hopeful inventors in the UK file patents to protect their
intellectual property from poachers. With a success rate of getting patented
ideas to market of lower than 2 per cent, inventors need all the help they can
get. Check out these organisations that can smooth out the path:

- **Institute of Patentees and Inventors** (website: www.invent.org.uk)
  has among its 1,000 members not only inventors but also patent agents,
  marketers and others who can provide expert advice to its membership on the complex issues relating to invention and innovation. These
  issues cover intellectual property rights and topics as diverse as originality searching, manufacturing practices, pricing practices, presentation techniques, funding and other subjects relating to the exploitation
  of an invention. The Institute also produces a journal titled *Future and
  the Inventor* at least once per annum and issues it to members. The
  journal contains information pertinent to inventors and details the
  forthcoming activities of the Institute. Annual membership is £70 with a
  joining fee of £15.

- **International Federation of Inventors' Societies** (IFIA; website: www.
  invention-ifia.ch) is a not-for-profit, non-governmental organisation created by seven European inventor associations in 1968. Its current
  membership comes from more than 88 countries. IFIA has web links to
  its 100 member organisations and to 345 other organisations of probable
  use to inventors, as well as details of reference books, guides, surveys,
  studies, conferences, seminars, workshops, expert group meetings, lec-
  tures, competitions and awards for inventions.

- **NESTA** (website: www.nesta.org.uk) is the National Endowment for
  Science, Technology and the Arts – an independent body with a mission
  to make the UK more innovative. It helps and invests in early-stage companies, informs policy and delivers practical programmes that inspire
  others to solve the big challenges of the future. NESTA aims to bring
  the best ideas, new flows of capital and talented people together, and
  encourage them to develop further.

✔ **Trevor Baylis Brands** (website: www.trevorbaylisbrands.com) founded by Trevor Baylis, famous for inventing the clockwork radio. Trevor Baylis Brands provides help with ideas and inventions to other inventors. It hopes to help anyone with a good idea or invention to protect and sell it.

If protecting your invention is appropriate for your business, check out Chapter 5.

Helping Young Entrepreneurs

Under-25s are a fast-growing segment of the business start-up market. Even if you aren't in that age group, the organisations in this section can help get your son or daughter off to a flying start.

✔ **Livewire** (www.shell-livewire.org) is a national programme supported by Shell, an oil multinational, to help young entrepreneurs start their own businesses. Established in 1982, the Shell LiveWIRE programme offers free online business advice and start-up awards of £1,000 and £10,000 funding to young entrepreneurs in the UK (England, Scotland, Wales and Northern Ireland). Livewire also runs a monthly £1,000 Grand Ideas Awards and annual £10,000 Young Entrepreneur of the Year Award competitions for new businesses.

✔ **The Prince's Trust** (www.princes-trust.org.uk) helps 14- to 30-year-olds develop confidence, pick up new skills and get into work. It offers opportunities when no one else will. So if you've got an idea for a business but no one will give you the money to get it off the ground, the Prince's Trust may be able to provide you with finance and advice. The Prince's Trust Enterprise programme helps young people interested in self-employment to explore and test their ideas, write plans and start their own businesses, or to achieve alternative outcomes in education, training, volunteering or work.

Not all participants in the Trust's programmes get funding. Individual cases are assessed on the basis of their own merits and the riskiness of the venture. But the Trust has helped more than 80,000 young people set up in business since 1983, and in the year 2012/13 it helped about 55,800 young people, of whom 14,496 went through the Enterprise Programme.

✔ **Young Enterprise** (www.young-enterprise.org.uk) is based on the Junior Achievement model that's been running in the USA since 1919. Its aim is to enable young people to develop skills and knowledge for business and enterprise through setting up and running their own company with the support of representatives from the business community. Young Enterprise programmes also focus on individual development of attitudes and qualities for enterprise, such as problem solving, decision making and management skills.

The Company Programme students set up and run a real firm for a year under the guidance of a business volunteer. They get practical experience of the joys and pitfalls of creating a truly functioning enterprise. They do everything from raising the initial share capital through to designing and making their product or service, selling directly to customers at specially organised trade fairs and, ultimately, winding up the firm and paying taxes.

This renowned programme has been running since 1983 and, in that time, a million 15- to 19-year-olds have taken part. Each year, the business volunteers inspire over 300,000 young people.

Chapter 8

Finding the Money

*B*usinesses need a continuous flow of customers, products or services to sell, and space to work from or store unsold goods. But they need money to make all these things happen. The more the business actually does, the more money it needs.

Even during the recent world credit crunch small businesses needed and, despite some anecdotal evidence to the contrary, accessed money. The latest British Banking Association (BBA; www.bba.org.uk) statistics published in August 2013 showed more than 100,000 finance applications were approved in the preceding year for small and medium-sized enterprises (*SMEs*; that is, businesses with up to 250 employees), providing over £6 billion of funds. All in all, banks had lent £50 billion as at August 2013, and they're the biggest single source of money for small and new businesses in the UK.

Starting a business on the road to success involves ensuring that you have sufficient money to survive until the point where income continually exceeds expenditure. You need a steady flow of money from many different sources along the way. Data from a recent survey by Warwick Business School of SMEs shows that over a three-year period about 55 per cent make use of a personal or business credit card; 53 per cent use an overdraft; 24 per cent use a term loan; 6 per cent have access to a grant; 3 per cent use invoice discounting; and 3 per cent use equity finance. Karan Bilimoria, founder of Cobra Beer and one of my former students, raised money from almost every source imaginable in the decade or so it took to get his business from start-up to £100 million annual turnover. (Check out the Entrepreneurs section of www.startups.co.uk for his story.)

This chapter helps you to find the right type of money for your business and avoid common pitfalls.

Assessing How Much Money You Need

You should work out from the outset how much money you need to get your business off the ground. If your proposed venture needs more cash than you feel comfortable putting up yourself or raising from others, then the sooner you know the better. Then you can start to revise your plans. The steps that lead to an accurate estimate of your financial requirements start with the sales forecast, which you prepare as part of the feasibility testing that I cover in Chapter 4, along with advice on estimating costs for initial expenditure such as retail or production space, equipment, staff and so on.

Forecasting cash flow is the most reliable way to estimate the amount of money a business needs on a day-to-day basis.

Dos and don'ts for creating a cash-flow forecast:

- ✔ Do ensure that your projections are believable. This means that you need to show how you're going to achieve your sales.

- ✔ Do base projections on facts, not conjecture.

- ✔ Do describe the main assumptions that underpin your projections.

- ✔ Do explain what the effect of these assumptions not happening to plan may be. For example, if your projections are based on recruiting three salespeople by month three, what would happen if you can only find two suitable people by that date?

- ✔ Do, for all forecasting, come up with best and worst outcomes as well as the most likely outcomes.

- ✔ Do make sure that you include things like job losses and losses of confidence in the markets that you serve. After all, even if your products and services are excellent, if people have lost confidence because of the bad actions of one of your competitors, you may suffer also.

- ✔ Don't use data to support projections without saying where it came from.

- ✔ Don't forget to allow for seasonal factors. At certain times of the year, most businesses are influenced by regular events. Sales of ice cream are lower in winter than in summer, sales of toys peak in the lead-up to Christmas and business-to-business sales dip in the summer and Christmas holiday periods. So rather than taking your projected annual sales figure and dividing by 12 to get a monthly figure, you need to consider what effect seasonal factors may have.

- ✔ Don't ignore economic factors such as an expanding (or shrinking) economy, rising (or falling) interest rates and an unemployment rate that is so low that it may influence your ability to recruit at the wage rate you want to pay.

- ✔ Don't make projections without showing the specific actions that can get those results.

> ✔ Don't forget to get someone else to check your figures out – you may be blind to your own mistakes, but someone else is more likely to spot the flaws in your projections.

You calculate the cash flow projection by estimating how much cash you expect to get in and pay out every period. By subtracting one figure from the other you arrive at the cash on hand or, if the figure is negative, the amount of the cash you need to raise to stay afloat.

Projecting receipts

Receipts from sales come in different ways, depending on the range of products and services on offer. Aside from money coming in from paying customers, business owners may, and in many cases almost certainly will, put in cash of their own.

You may be drawing on other sources of outside finance, say from a bank or investor, but these sources are best left out at this stage. In fact, the point of the cash-flow projection, as well as showing how much money the business needs, is to reveal the likely shortfall after you, the owner, have put what you can into the business and the customers have paid up.

Be sure to have contingency approaches in place, in case people are late in paying you.

You should total up the projected receipts for each month and for the year as a whole. You're well advised to carry out this process using a spreadsheet program, which saves you from any problems caused by faulty maths.

A sale made in one month may not result in any cash coming into the business bank account until the following month, or even much later if your customers are slow payers. Make sure that you know how quickly people pay their bills in the sectors in which you're working.

Estimating expenses

Some expenses, such as rent, rates and equipment leases, you pay monthly. Other bills, such as telephone, utilities and bank charges, come in quarterly.

If you haven't yet had to pay utilities, for example, put into your forecast your best guesstimate of how much you're going to spend and when. Marketing, promotion, travel, subsistence and stationery are good examples of expenses you may have to estimate. You know that you face costs in these areas, but they may not be all that accurate as projections.

After you've been trading for a while, you can get a much better handle on the true costs you're likely to incur.

Total up the payments for each month and for the year as a whole.

Working out the closing cash balances

This is crunch time, when the real sums reveal the amount of money your great new business needs to get it off the ground. Working through the cash-flow projections allows you to see exactly how much cash you have in hand, or in the bank, at the end of each month, or how much you need to raise. This is the closing cash balance for the month. It's also the opening cash balance for the following month, because that's the position you're carrying forward.

Setting out your cash-flow projection

Figure 8-1 shows the first five-week cash-flow projection for a new business. Sales receipts are £250 in the first week, gradually increasing and resulting in a total of £4,000 cash coming into the business over the five-week period.

Week	1	2	3	4	5	Totals
Receipts: Cash In						
Sales	250	500	750	1,000	1,500	4,000
						0
						0
Total Receipts	250	500	750	1,000	1,500	4,000
Payments: Cash Out						
Stock	500	250	350	500	400	2,000
Advertising	200	200	100	0	0	500
Rent	100	100	100	100	100	500
Utilities	100	0	0	100	0	200
Total Payments	900	550	550	700	500	3,200
Cashflow Surplus/Deficit (-)	-650	-50	200	300	1,000	800
Opening Bank Balance	0	-650	-700	-500	-200	
Closing Bank Balance	-650	-700	-500	-200	800	

Figure 8-1:
A start-up five-week cash-flow projection.

Week one sees payments going out totalling £900, for stock of product to be sold, advertising, rent and utilities such as heat, light and power. Subtracting the total receipts from the total payments leaves the business short of £650.

The following week, the process is repeated. However, this time instead of an opening cash balance of £0, as at the start of week one, week two starts with the negative cash position (–£650) that week one finished with.

Cash receipts in week three are projected to be less than cash payments (£500 – £550 = –£50), which is added to the –£650 brought forward from week one. So the negative cash-flow position in week three is –£700.

The owner-manager can resolve this position by injecting £700 herself, raising £700 from an outside source such as a bank or raising a smaller amount and cutting back on some element in the payment area.

Testing your assumptions

Little disturbs a financier more than a firm that has to go back cap in hand for more finance too soon after raising money, especially if you should've seen and allowed for the additional requirement at the outset.

So, in making projections you have to be ready for likely pitfalls and the unexpected events that knock your cash flow off target. Forecasts and projections rarely go to plan, but you can anticipate the most common pitfalls and to some extent allow for them.

Spotting the pitfalls

You can't really protect yourself against freak disasters or unforeseen delays, which can hit large and small businesses alike. But some events are more likely than others to affect your cash flow.

In particular, watch out for sales taking longer to come in than you thought. Customers take time to make decisions, particularly if they already have a satisfactory alternative supplier.

Also make sure that they'll pay on time. Research by Bacs Payment Schemes Limited (www.bacs.co.uk), the organisation behind Direct Debit and Bacs Direct Credit, published in March 2010, shows that since the credit crunch struck British SMEs are having to wait an average of 25 days longer than their original agreed payment terms before customers pay their invoices.

You can check out potential customers by using a credit reference agency such as Snoop4 Companies (www.snoop4companies.co.uk) for businesses or Experian (www.experian.co.uk) for private individuals. Basic credit reports cost between around £4 and £35 and may save you time and money if you've any reservations about a potential customer's ability to pay.

During periods of economic downturn, recessions to you and me, unsurprisingly customers take longer to settle their bills. Big firms, though perhaps a safer bet and more likely to survive, are rarely sympathetic to a small firm's plight. Expect them to go to the wire when it comes to settling up.

Costs are also a difficult area to predict because not all are easy to anticipate. An increase, for example, in your motor insurance rate as a consequence of using a car for your business is one cost missed from projections.

Allowing for the unexpected

Even if you haven't anticipated events, you can allow for them when estimating financing needs. Analysis using a cash-flow spreadsheet, as shown in Figure 8-1, enables you to identify worst-case scenarios that can knock you off-course, and you can change and insert new figures at will, to test out what may happen to your cash flow under various conditions. After this, you end up with a realistic estimate of the financing requirements of the business or project.

You need to make your cash-flow projection sufficiently far forward so that you can see when you'll start to have positive cash flow. After you've made some reasonably prudent assumptions, such as cash from sales coming in later and for smaller amounts, and for costs to be higher, you can see how much money you need to raise. The sum of money you need to raise is the highest negative cash position in your cash-flow projection. The example in Figure 8-1 shows a business that has to have £700 of additional cash to survive its first five weeks and perhaps a few hundred more as a cushion against unexpected problems.

Reviewing Your Financing Options

Knowing how much money you need to get your business successfully started is an important first step, but only that – a first step. Many sources of funds are available to small firms. However, not all are equally appropriate to all firms at all times. These different sources of finance carry different obligations, responsibilities and opportunities. You have to understand the differences to allow an informed choice.

Most small firms confine their financial strategy to long-term or short-term bank loans, viewing other financing methods as too complex or too risky. In many respects, the reverse is true. Almost every finance source other than banks shares some of the risks of doing business with you to a greater or lesser extent.

You have three main options when it comes to raising money: borrowing it, and paying it back over time with interest added; finding an investor and letting them own a piece of your business; and getting some free money by way of a grant or award.

Deciding between debt capital and equity capital

At one end of the financing spectrum lie shareholders – individual *business angels* who put their own money into a business, or corporate organisations such as *venture capital providers* (also known as venture capitalists or VCs), who provide equity capital that buys a stake in a business. These investors share all the risks and vagaries of the business alongside you and expect a proportionate share in the rewards if things go well. They're less concerned with a stream of dividends – which is just as well because few small companies ever pay them – and instead hope for a radical increase in the value of their investment. They expect to realise this value from other investors who want to take their place for the next stage in the firm's growth, rather than from any repayment by the founder. Investors in new or small businesses don't look for the security of buildings or other assets to underpin their investment. Rather, they look to the founder's vision and the core management team's ability to deliver results.

At the other end of the financing spectrum are debt financiers – banks that try hard to take no risk and expect some return on their money irrespective of your business's performance. They want interest payments on money lent, usually from day one. They too hope that the management is competent, but they're more interested in making sure that you or the business has some type of asset such as a house that they can grab if things go wrong. At the end of the day, and that day can be sooner than the borrower expects, a bank wants all its money back, with interest. Think of bankers as people who help you turn part of an illiquid asset such as property into a more liquid asset such as cash – for a price.

Understanding the differences between *lenders*, who provide debt capital, and *investors*, who provide equity or share capital, is central to a sound grasp of financial management.

In between the extremes of shareholders and the banks lie myriad other financing vehicles that have a mixture of lending or investing criteria. You need to keep your business finances under constant review, choosing the most appropriate mix of funds for the risks you plan to take and the economic climate ahead. The more risky and volatile the road ahead, the more likely taking a higher proportion of equity capital is to be appropriate. In times of stability and low interest, higher borrowings may be more acceptable.

As a rule of thumb, you should use debt and equity in equal amounts to finance a business. If the road ahead looks more risky than usual, go for £2 of equity to every £1 of debt.

Table 8-1 illustrates a few of the differences between risk-averse lenders and risk-taking investors.

Table 8-1	Comparing Benefits of Lenders and Investors	
Category	*Lenders*	*Investors*
Interest	Paid on outstanding loan	None, though dividends sometimes paid if profits warrant it
Capital	Repaid at end of term, or sooner if lender has concerns	Returned with substantial growth through new shareholders
Security	Either from assets or personal guarantees	From belief in founders and their business vision

If your business sector is viewed as particularly risky, and perhaps the most reliable measure of that risk is the proportion of firms that go bust, then financing the business almost exclusively with borrowings is tantamount to gambling.

Debt has to be serviced whatever your business performance, so in any risky, volatile marketplace, you stand a good chance of being caught out one day.

If your business risks are low, profits are probably relatively low too. High profits and low risks always attract a flood of competitors, reducing your profits to levels that ultimately reflect the riskiness of your business sector. Because venture capitalists and shareholders generally look for better returns than they can get by lending the money, they'll be disappointed in an investment in a low-risk, low-return business. So if they're wise, they don't get involved in the first place; or if they do, they don't put any more money in later.

Examining your own finances

Obviously, the first place to start looking for money to finance your business is in your own pockets. You may not have much in ready cash, but you may have assets that you can turn into cash or use to support borrowing.

Start by totalling your assets and liabilities. The chances are that your most valuable *assets* are your house, your car and any life assurance or pension policies you may have. Your *liabilities* are the debts you owe. The difference between your assets and your liabilities, assuming that you've more of the former than the latter, is your *net worth*. That, in effect, is the maximum security you can offer anyone outside the business from whom you want to raise money.

The big questions are: what is your appetite for risk, and how certain are you that your business will be successful? The more of your own money you can put into your business at the outset, the more you're truly running your own business in your own way. The more outside money you have to raise, the more power and perhaps value you have to share with others.

Now you have a simple piece of arithmetic to do. How much money do you need to finance your business start-up, as shown in your worst-case scenario cash-flow forecast? How much of your own money are you willing and able to put into your business? The difference is the sum you're looking to outside financiers to back you with.

If that sum is more than your net worth, you're looking for investors. If less, bankers may be the right people to approach.

If you do have free cash or assets that you can but won't put into your business, you should ask yourself whether the proposition is worth pursuing. You can be absolutely certain that any outsider you approach for money will ask you to put up or shut up.

 Another factor to consider in reviewing your own finances is your ongoing expenses. You have to live while getting your business up and running. So food, heat and a roof over your head are essential expenses. But perhaps a two-week long-haul summer holiday, a second car and membership of a health club aren't essentials – great while you were a hired hand and had a salary cheque each month, but an expendable luxury when you're working for yourself.

Determining the Best Source of Finance for You

Choosing which external source of finance to use is to some extent a matter of personal preference. One of your tasks in managing your business's financial affairs is to keep good lines of communication open with as many sources as possible. The other key task is to consider which is the most appropriate source of finance for your particular requirement at any one time. I explore the main issues that you need to consider in the following sections.

Considering the costs

Clearly, if a large proportion of the funds you need to start your business is going to be consumed in actually raising the money itself, your set-up costs are going to be high. Raising capital, especially if the amounts are relatively small (under £500,000), is generally quite expensive. You have to pay your lawyers and accountants, and those of your investor or lender, to prepare the agreements and to conduct the due diligence examination (the business appraisal). Spending between 10 and 15 per cent of the first £500,000 you raise on set-up costs isn't unusual.

An overdraft or factoring agreement is relatively cheap to set up, usually a couple of per cent or so. However, long-term loans, leasing and hire-purchase agreements can involve legal costs.

Sharing ownership and control

The source of your money helps determine how much ownership and control you have to give up in return. Venture capitalists generally want a large share of stock and often a large say in how the business is run. At the other end of the spectrum are providers of long-term loans, who generally leave you alone so long as you service the interest and repay the capital as agreed. You have to strike the balance that works best for you and your business.

If you don't want to share the ownership of your business with outsiders, then clearly raising equity capital isn't a good idea. Even if you recognise that owning 100 per cent of a small venture isn't as attractive as owning 40 per cent of a business ten times as large, it may not be the right moment to sell any of your shares; particularly if, in common with many business founders, long-term capital gain is one of your principal goals. If you hold on to your shares until profits are reasonably high, you realise more gain for every share sold than if you sell out in the early years or while profits are low.

Parting with shares inevitably involves some loss of control. Letting 5 per cent go may be merely a mild irritation from time to time. However, after 25 per cent has gone, outsiders can have a fair amount of say in how you run things. At that point, even relatively small groups of shareholders can find it easy to call an Extraordinary General Meeting and vote to remove you from the board. Nevertheless, while you have over 51 per cent you're in control, if only just. When you're past the 51 per cent things can get a little dangerous. Theoretically, you can be outvoted at any stage.

Some capital providers take a hands-on approach and may express a view on how you should run the business.

Limiting personal liability

As a general rule, most providers of long-term loans and overdrafts look to you and other owners to provide additional security if the business assets are in any way inadequate. You may be asked to provide a personal guarantee – an asset such as your house. Only when you raise new share capital, by selling more stock in your company, do you escape increasing your personal liability.

Even with the new share capital, you may be asked to provide warranties to assure new investors that you've declared everything in the company's history.

Going for Debt

You can explore borrowing from a number of possible sources in your search for outside finance. Give those I explore in the following sections the once-over.

Most people start and stop at a bank. The other major first source of money is family and friends, but many business starters feel nervous about putting family money at risk, and prefer to deal with professional financiers. *Credit unions* and *mezzanine finance* are fairly unusual sources of finance for a start-up, but finding money to start a business is a tough task, so you shouldn't completely overlook any source. (I explain these terms later in this chapter.)

Borrowing from banks

Banks are the principal, and frequently the only, source of finance for nine out of every ten new and small businesses.

Banks are usually a good starting point for almost any type of debt financing. They're also able to provide many other cash-flow and asset-backed financing products, although they're often not the only or the most appropriate provider. As well as the main clearing banks, a number of the former building societies and smaller regional banks are competing hard for small-firm lending.

If you import raw materials, your bank can provide you with Letters of Credit that guarantee your suppliers payment from the bank when they present proof of satisfactory delivery. If you have a number of overseas suppliers who prefer settlement in their own currency for which you need foreign currency, cheque facilities or to buy money at a fixed exchange rate before you need it, banks can make the necessary arrangements.

Running an overdraft

The principal form of short-term bank funding is an *overdraft*. An overdraft is permission for you to use some of the bank's money when you don't have enough of your own. The permission is usually agreed annually, but can be withdrawn at any time. A little over a quarter of all bank finance for small firms is in the form of an overdraft. The overdraft was originally designed to cover the time between having to pay for raw materials to manufacture finished goods and selling those goods. The size of an overdraft is usually limited to a modest proportion of the amount of money that your customers owe you and the value of your finished goods stock. The bank sees those items as assets, which in the last resort it can use to get its money back.

Starting out in a cleaning business, for example, you need sufficient funds initially to buy the mop and bucket. Three months into the contract, you've paid for these items and so getting a five-year bank loan to cover this expenditure is pointless, because within a year you'll have cash in the bank.

However, if your overdraft doesn't get out of the red at any stage during the year, you need to re-examine your financing. All too often companies utilise an overdraft to acquire long-term assets, and that overdraft never seems to disappear, eventually constraining the business.

The example in Figure 8-1 is a good one of a situation where an overdraft may be appropriate. Funds in the example are only required for three weeks or so before the business is cash-flow positive.

The attraction of overdrafts is that they're easy to arrange, except in the most unusual of circumstances such as during a global credit crunch. Also, they take little time to set up. But their inherent weakness is that the key words in the arrangement document are 'repayable on demand', which leaves the bank free to make and change the rules as it sees fit. (This term is under review and some banks may remove the term from the arrangement.) With other forms of borrowing, as long as you stick to the terms and conditions, the loan is yours for the duration; not so with overdrafts.

Hippychick

When new mother Julie Minchin discovered the Hipseat, she knew she'd found a helpful product. Anything that makes carrying a baby around all day without ending up with excruciating back ache has got to be a benefit. It was only later that she realised that selling the product for the German company that made the Hipseat could launch her into business. At first, Julie acted as their UK distributor, but later she wanted to make major improvements to the product. That meant finding a manufacturer to make the product especially for her business. China was the logical place to find a company flexible enough to make small quantities as well as

being able to help her keep the cost of the end product competitive.

Julie funded the business, Hippychick, with a small family loan, an overdraft facility and a variety of grants secured with the help of Business Link. By its tenth year, the company had a turnover of £3 million a year, selling 14 new and unique products aimed at the baby market. Hippychick supplies national chains such as Boots, Mothercare and Blooming Marvellous, as well as independents. It also sells via a catalogue and website, and is in the process of building a network of distributors for the branded products.

Keeping the money men happy

Most owner-managers don't give much thought to how to deal with their bank, factoring company or venture capitalist. They just jump right into their business and don't consider how they should treat these people, what their bankers can do for them and what their bankers in turn look for in a client. But with a little thought and effort, you can ensure that you get the most from your banking relationships.

Your banker, or any other source of finance, has the ability to influence the success of your business radically. Developing long-term, personal relationships with the banker is important – if you do that, when you hit the inevitable bumps in the road the banker will be there to help you.

Keep in mind when you meet your banker for the first time that you want to develop a long-term relationship with this person. The meeting should be a two-way interview. You should ask yourself: 'Is this person genuinely interested in me? Is this person trying to understand my business? Does this person understand my objectives?' If the answer to any of these questions is 'no', find another banker.

You often hire your lawyer and accountant by the hour or job, but your banker is another matter – your banker makes money off the fees that your business generates. Your banker is usually happy to help you, and can therefore be a source of free consulting, though you do need to be a little more careful today because bankers are beginning to get wise to the idea of charging for services. Shop around for the best-buy bank just as you do for any other product or service. Check out Money Facts (`http://moneyfacts.co.uk/bank-accounts/best-bank-accounts`) or Which 4 U (`www.which4u.co.uk/bank-accounts`) to see who's offering the best deals.

Taking on a term loan

If you're starting up a manufacturing business, you'll be buying machinery to last probably five years, designing your logo and buying stationery, paying the deposit on leasehold premises, buying a vehicle and investing funds in winning a long-term contract. Because you expect the profits to flow over a number of years, they need to be financed over a similarly long period, through a bank loan or by inviting someone to invest in shares in the company – in other words, a long-term commitment.

Term loans, as these long-term borrowings are generally known, are funds provided by a bank for a number of years. The interest can be variable – changing with general interest rates – or fixed for a number of years ahead. In some cases, you may be able to move between having a fixed interest rate and a variable one at certain intervals. You may even be able to have a moratorium (break) on interest payments for a short period, to give the business breathing space. Provided that you meet the conditions of the loan in such matters as repayment, interest and security cover, the money is available for the period of the loan. Unlike having an overdraft, the bank can't pull the rug from under you if your circumstances (or the local manager) change.

Going with the government

The government is often on hand with financial support of one sort or another for small firms. Politicians aren't altruists. They know that helping the 15 per cent of the countries working population that run their own business equates to votes. Also, the government's financial support is pretty small beer: the sums involved are miniscule compared to, say, tinkering with the National Health or education budgets. But who knows? Some, perhaps many, of the businesses getting financial help now will pay it back in taxes or by creating work for other tax payers.

Here are two schemes you should explore first:

- ✔ **The Enterprise Finance Guarantee (EFG):** This is a loan guarantee scheme to facilitate lending to viable businesses that have been turned down for a normal commercial loan due to a lack of security or a proven track record. In instances such as this, EFG may be an option, but is only considered when the lender is satisfied that your business can afford the loan repayments. Applicants can look for finance between £1,000 and £1 million with repayment terms from 3 months to 10 years. Check out full details at www.gov.uk/understanding-the-enterprise-finance-guarantee.

- ✔ **Start Up Loans:** This is a government-funded scheme to provide loans and mentors for entrepreneurs. The scheme is currently only available to those between the ages of 18 and 30, but it may be extended to all age groups. After you receive your loan, you're assigned a mentor who provides ongoing guidance and assistance, answering your questions and ensuring that your business stands the best possible chance of success. You may also be eligible for discounted services such as low-cost offices or free accounting software from a range of global partners. Full details are at www.startuploans.co.uk.

You can find out more about the details of all the finance schemes the government helps with on this section of its website: www.gov.uk/business-finance-support-finder.

Financing cash flow

When your business is trading, two sources of finance open up that can smooth out cash-flow troughs when dealing with business customers. Factoring and invoice discounting are both methods of funding sales after you've submitted an invoice.

Factors provide three related services:

- ✔ Immediate finance of up to 80 per cent of invoiced sales, with the balance (minus administration and finance charges) payable after a set period or when the invoice is paid

- ✔ Managing the sales ledger, including sending out invoices and ensuring that they're paid

- ✔ Advising on credit risk and insuring clients against bad debts

This type of finance is provided against the security of trade debts (the amount of money customers owe you). Normally, when you raise an invoice you send a copy to the factor, who then funds up to 85 per cent against the invoice in advance of the customer paying. The remainder becomes payable on a maturity date or when the customer pays. Because the invoice is assigned to the factor, payment by the customer is direct to the factor.

Invoice discounting operates in a similar way, except the seller retains control of its debtors and is responsible for collecting the money.

These forms of finance are directly related to sales levels and can be particularly helpful during growth spurts.

The Factors and Discounters Association (`www.abfa.org.uk`) provides a list of over 40 members on its website, which has a search facility to help you define which organisations are best placed to meet your individual business requirements.

Getting physical

You can usually finance assets such as vehicles, computers, office equipment and the like by leasing them or buying them on hire purchase, leaving your other funds free to cover less tangible expenses such as advertising or living expenses. You can use a lease to take the risk out of purchasing an asset that becomes obsolete or for taking account of repairs and maintenance costs. In return for this 'certainty', you pay a fee that's added to the monthly or quarterly charge. However, knowing the exact cost of purchasing and using an asset can be attractive and worth paying for. Hire purchase differs from leasing in that you've the option eventually to become the owner of the asset after a series of payments. Important tax implications apply to using these types of finance and you should discuss them with your accountant (I cover finding an accountant in Chapter 13).

The Finance and Leasing Association website (www.fla.org.uk/asset/members) gives more information on the different products on offer to finance assets and has a directory of members and their contact details. You can also use the calculator at www.premlease.co.uk/calculate to get an idea of the monthly repayments over different time periods.

Uniting with a credit union

If you don't like the terms on offer from the *high-street banks*, as the major banks are often known, you may consider forming your own bank. The idea isn't as crazy as it sounds. Credit unions formed by groups of small business people, both in business and aspiring to start up, have been around for decades in the UK, the USA and elsewhere. They're an attractive option for people on low incomes, and provide a cheap and convenient alternative to banks. Some self-employed people such as taxi drivers have also formed credit unions. They can then apply for loans to meet unexpected capital expenditure for repairs, refurbishments or technical upgrading.

Established credit unions usually require you to have a particular trade, have paid money in for a number of months or years and have a maximum loan amount limited to the types of assets people in their trade are likely to need.

Credit union usage in the UK has more than doubled in the past five years, with over 400 unions and over 1 million people using them. Worldwide, 56,000 credit unions operate in 101 countries, enabling 200 million members to access affordable financial services. The Association of British Credit Unions (www.abcul.org) offers information and a directory of providers.

Grabbing cash locally

Many communities, particularly those operating in rundown areas in need of regeneration, have a facility to lend or even invest in businesses that may bring employment to the area. The sidebar 'Destination London' offers one such example. Funding from these sources can be for anything from start-up right through to expansion, or in some cases even rescue finance to help prevent a business from folding, shedding a large number of jobs or relocating to a more benign business environment.

Tapping into community development finance

Community development finance institutions (CDFIs) lend money to businesses and people who struggle to get finance from high street banks. They're social enterprises that invest in customers and communities by, among other things, helping businesses to start and grow. There are currently around 60 CDFIs in all regions of the UK, and in 2012 they lent £30.2 million to 2,608 business customers.

You can find out more about CDFI services at `www.cdfa.org.uk/about-cdfis/icf/community-finance-for-businesses`.

Using a local initiative

Many councils have schemes to help people start and grow businesses in their patch. They've a good reason to do so: the Enterprising Britain Awards, an annual competition, recognises the council with the greatest commitment to supporting SMEs. In 2013, the former mill town of Burnley, Lancashire, was named the most enterprising place in Britain in part for its Bondholder self-help scheme (`http://burnley.co.uk/bondholder`). In 2012, Northamptonshire held the same enterprise crown for its Northamptonshire Enterprise Partnership (`www.northamptonshireep.co.uk`), providing a one-stop shop to offer free business support, funding and access to business networks.

Destination London

Rachel Lowe, a 29-year-old single mother with two children, came up with her winning business idea while working part-time as a taxi driver in Portsmouth. She invented a game involving players throwing a dice to move taxi pieces around a board, collecting fares to travel to famous destinations while aiming to get back to the taxi rank before they ran out of fuel. Being able to run the business from home meant that Rachel could spend more time with her children and still be a breadwinner.

But despite having a business plan written up when she entered a local business competition, she had serious hurdles to cross before she could get started. With a deal from Hamleys, the London toyshop, in the bag and a manufacturer and distributor lined up, all that was missing was a modest amount of additional funding to help with marketing and stock. She pitched her proposal to the BBC's *Dragons' Den* and was given a thorough roasting. To say the dragons weren't enthusiastic would be a serious understatement. They reckoned that Monopoly would wipe the floor with her. Bowed but far from beaten, Rachel then turned to South Coast Money Line, a Community Development Finance Institution and part of the Portsmouth Area Regeneration Trust Group (`www.part.org.uk`). With a loan from them, she propelled her game – Destination London – into the top-ten best-selling games, even beating Monopoly! A deal with Debenhams to stock regional versions of the game and signing up to produce Harry Potter and Disney versions left her with a business worth £2 million, at a conservative estimate.

So, most councils have plenty to offer entrepreneurs through a variety of initiatives that include loans and grants. The whole of Lancashire, for example, has help on tap for those wanting to start up or grow their business through the Regenerate programme (www.regeneratepl.co.uk), and the Cornwall Development Company (www.cornwalldevelopmentcompany.co.uk) has a Business Innovation Fund that provides grant funding to Cornish SMEs for projects seeking £1,000–£50,000, up to 50 per cent of the total project cost.

Try putting the words such as 'business support' or 'help with business start-up' followed by the council name – Cornwall, Northamptonshire, Hackney and so on – into a search engine. Within minutes, you should be able uncover a range of local advice, training and finance on offer.

Borrowing from family and friends

Those close to you may be willing to lend you money or invest in your business. This helps you avoid the problem of pleading your case to outsiders and enduring extra paperwork and bureaucratic delays. Help from friends, relatives and business associates can be especially valuable if you've been through bankruptcy or had other credit problems that make borrowing from a commercial lender difficult or impossible.

Involving friends and family in your business brings a range of extra potential benefits – but also costs and risks that aren't a feature of most other types of finance. You need to decide whether these risks are acceptable.

Some advantages of borrowing money from people you know well are that they may charge you a lower interest rate, you may be able to delay paying back money until you're more established and you may have more flexibility if you get into a jam. But after you agree to the loan terms, you've the same legal obligations as with a bank or any other source of finance.

Borrowing money from relatives and friends can have a major disadvantage. If your business does poorly and those close to you end up losing money, you may damage your personal relationships. So in dealing with friends, relatives and business associates be careful to establish clearly the terms of the deal and put them in writing, and also to make an extra effort to explain the risks. In short, your job is to make sure that your helpful friend or relative doesn't suffer true hardship if you're unable to meet your financial commitments.

When raising money from family and friends, follow these guidelines:

- ✔ Do agree proper terms for the loan or investment.
- ✔ Do put the agreement in writing, and if it involves a limited partnership, share transaction or guarantee, have a legal agreement drawn up.

✔ Do make an extra effort to explain the risks of the business and the possible downside implications to the money your loved ones are lending you.

✔ Do make sure that, when raising money from parents, other siblings are compensated in some way, perhaps via a will.

✔ Do make sure that you want to run a family business before raising money from your family as your experience will not be the same as running your own business. Your family may want a say in how the business is run to make sure that their money is safe.

✔ Don't borrow from people on fixed incomes.

✔ Don't borrow from people who can't afford to lose their investment.

✔ Don't make the possible rewards sound more attractive than you would, say, to a bank.

✔ Don't offer jobs in your business to anyone providing money unless the person is best for the job.

✔ Don't change the normal pattern of social contact with family and friends after they've put up the money.

Sharing Out the Spoils

If your business is particularly risky, requires a lot of upfront finance or involves new technology, you usually have to consider selling a proportion of your business's shares to outside investors.

However, if your business plan doesn't show profit returns in excess of 30 per cent per annum for the next three to five years (see Chapter 13 for more on profit ratios), and you aren't prepared to part with upwards of 15 per cent of your business, then equity finance probably isn't for you.

A number of different types of investor may be prepared to put up the funds if the returns are good enough. I talk about each type in the following sections.

Benefiting from business angels

One source of equity or risk capital is private individuals, with their own funds and perhaps some knowledge of your type of business, who are willing to invest in your company in return for a share in the business.

Such investors have been christened *business angels*, a term first coined to describe private, wealthy individuals who backed theatrical productions, usually a play on Broadway or in London's West End.

By their nature, such investments are highly speculative in nature. The angel typically has a personal interest in the venture and may want to play a role in the company – often an angel is determined to have an involvement beyond merely signing a cheque.

Business angels are informal suppliers of risk capital to new and growing businesses, often taking a hand at a stage when no one else is prepared to take the chance; a sort of investor of last resort. But although they often lose their shirts, business angels sometimes make serious money. The angel who backed software company Sage with £10,000 in its first round of £250,000 financing saw his stake rise to £40 million, and Ian McGlinn, the former garage owner who advanced Anita Roddick the £4,000 she needed to open a second shop in return for about 25 per cent of her company's shares, eventually wound up with a couple of hundred million pounds from his stake in The Body Shop.

In the UK and the USA, hundreds of networks operate with tens of thousands of business angels who are prepared to put several billion pounds each year into new or small businesses. One estimate is that the UK has approximately 18,000 business angels and that they annually invest in the region of £500 million.

These two organisations can put you in contact with a business angel:

- ✔ UK Business Angels Association (www.ukbusinessangelsassociation.org.uk), which is the national trade association representing angel and early-stage investment in the UK.

- ✔ Angel Investment Network (www.angelinvestmentnetwork.co.uk), which operates a service matching entrepreneurs to angels. Its website also has a number of useful tools to help you get investor ready.

Alternatively, you can apply to appear on the BBC's business reality show *Dragon's Den* (www.bbc.co.uk/programmes/b006vq92/features/dd-apply) and put your proposition face to face to 5 angels and 8 million television viewers. Check out the 'Business School' (www.bbc.co.uk/dragonsden/business), an online resource to further your business knowledge.

Going for venture capital

Venture capital is a means of financing the start-up, development, expansion or the purchase of a company. The venture capitalist acquires a share of the company in return for providing the requisite funding. Venture capital firms often work in conjunction with other providers of finance in putting together a total funding package for a business.

Venture capital providers invest other people's money, often from pension funds. They're likely to be interested in investing a large sum of money for a large stake in a company.

Venture capital is a medium- to long-term investment of not just money but also time and effort. The venture capital firm's aim is to enable growth companies to develop into the major businesses of tomorrow. Before investing, a venture capital provider goes through *due diligence*, a process that involves a thorough examination of both the business and its owner (see the later section 'Understanding due diligence'). Accountants and lawyers subject you and your business plan to detailed scrutiny. You and your directors are required to warrant that you've provided *all* relevant information, under pain of financial penalties.

In general, venture capitalists expect their investment to pay off within seven years. But they're hardened realists. Two in every ten investments they make are total write-offs, and six perform averagely well at best. So the one star in every ten investments they make has to cover a lot of duds. Venture capitalists have a target rate of return of 30 per cent plus, to cover this poor success rate.

Raising venture capital isn't a cheap option. The arrangement costs almost always run to six figures. The cost of the due diligence process is borne by the firm raising the money – but is paid out of the money raised, if that's any consolation. Raising venture capital isn't quick either. Six months isn't unusual and over a year has been known. Every venture capitalist has a deal done in six weeks in her portfolio, but that truly is the exception.

Venture capital providers want to exit from their investment at some stage. Their preferred route is via a public offering, taking your company onto the stock market, but a trade sale to another, usually larger, business in a related line of work is more usual.

New venture capital funds are coming on stream all the time and they too are looking for a gap in the market.

The British Venture Capital Association (www.bvca.co.uk) and the European Venture Capital Association (http://evca.eu) both have online directories giving details of hundreds of venture capital providers. VFinance (www.vfinance.com), a global financial services company specialising in high-growth opportunities, has a directory of 1,541 venture capital firms and over 23,000 business angels. Its website also contains a useful business plan template. (See Chapter 6 for more on business planning.)

Karen Darby left school at 16 with just one GCSE. While working in a call centre in 2002, she hit on the idea of helping people find the cheapest gas, electricity and telephone companies and providing a user-friendly way to switch suppliers for free. She pitched her business proposition to Bridges Community Ventures, a venture capital firm, and raised £300,000. Three years down the road, she sold her company, SimplySwitch, to Daily Mail and General Trust, leaving Karen £6 million richer.

Looking to corporate venturing

Alongside the venture capital firms are 200 or so other businesses that have a hand in the risk capital business, without it necessarily being their main line of business. For the most part, these firms have an interest in the Internet or high technology that want an inside track to new developments. Their own research and development operations have slowed down and become less and less entrepreneurial as they've grown bigger. So they need to look outside for new inspiration.

Even successful firms invest hundreds of millions of dollars each year in scores of other small businesses. Sometimes, if the company looks a particularly good fit, they buy the whole business. Apple, for example, while keeping its management team focused on the core business, has a $12 million stake in Akamai Technologies, whose software tries to keep the Web running smoothly even under unusual traffic demands.

Not only high-tech firms go in for corporate venturing. Any firm whose arteries are hardening a bit is on the look-out for new blood. McDonald's, for example – hardly a business at the forefront of the technological revolution – has stakes in over a dozen ventures. At one time it had a 35 per cent stake in Pret a Manger, but when it decided that the Pret model didn't fit well with the McDonald's business, it offloaded its stake to Bridgepoint for £345 million – four times its initial stake; a good result for both parties.

When Alex Cassie was casting around for cash to get his new business making parts for car companies such as Aston Martin, he was steered to an apparently unlikely source: Michelin, the French tyre firm. Since 2003, Michelin has operated a scheme pledged to put £3 million into small firms near its British plants. Michelin put £20,000 into Cassie's business, which within four years employed 68 people and had an annual turnover of £5 million.

Innocent

In the summer of 1998, when Richard Reed, Adam Balon and Jon Wright had developed their first smoothie recipes but were still nervous about giving up their jobs, they bought £500 worth of fruit, turned it into smoothies and sold them from a stall at a London music festival. They put up a sign saying 'Do you think we should give up our jobs to make these smoothies?' next to bins labelled 'YES' and 'NO', inviting people to put the empty bottle in the appropriate bin. At the end of the weekend the 'YES' bin was full, so they went to work the next day and resigned. The rest, as they say, is history. Virtually a household name, Innocent Drinks has experienced a decade of rapid growth.

But the business stalled in 2008, with sales slipping back and European expansion soaking up cash at a rapid rate. The founders, who had an average age of 28, decided that they needed heavy-weight advice and talked to Charles Dunstone, Carphone Warehouse founder, and Mervyn Davies, chairman of Standard Chartered. The strong advice was to get an investor with deep pockets and ideally something else by way of business experience to bring to the party to augment the youthful enthusiasm of the founders. They launched their search for an investor the day that Lehman Brothers filed for bankruptcy. In April 2009 the Innocent team accepted Coca-Cola as a minority investor in their business, paying £30 million for a stake of between 10–20 per cent. They chose Coca-Cola because, as well as providing the funds, the company could help get Innocent products out to more people in more places. They could also learn a lot from Coca-Cola, which has been in business for over 120 years.

Understanding due diligence

Usually, after a private equity firm signs a letter of intent to provide capital and you accept, the firm conducts a *due diligence* investigation of both the management and the company. During this period the private equity firm has access to all financial and other records, facilities and employees to investigate before finalising the deal. The material the firm examines includes copies of all leases, contracts and loan agreements in addition to copious financial records and statements. The firm wants to see any management reports, such as sales reports, inventory records, detailed lists of assets, facility maintenance records, aged receivables and payables reports, employee organisation charts, payroll and benefits records, customer records and marketing materials. It wants to know about any pending litigation, tax audits or insurance disputes. Depending on the nature of the business, it may also consider getting an environmental audit and an insurance check-up.

The sting in the due diligence tail is that the current owners of the business are required to personally warrant that everything they've said or revealed is both true and complete. In the event that this warrant proves not to be so, owners are personally liable to the extent of any loss incurred by those buying the shares.

Finding Free Money

Sometimes, if you're lucky or smart, you can get some of the money you need for free. The following sections tell you how to cash in on government grants, how winning a contest can earn you lots of lovely loot and how to harness the power of crowdfunding.

Getting a grant

Unlike debt, which you have to repay, or equity, which has to earn a return for the investors, grants and awards from the government or the European Union are often non-refundable. So, although they're frequently hard to get, grants can be particularly valuable.

Almost every country has incentives to encourage entrepreneurs to invest in particular locations or industries. The USA, for example, has an allowance of Green Cards (work and residence permits) for up to several hundred immigrants each year who are prepared to put up sufficient funds to start up a substantial business in the country.

Grants often come with strings attached, including you needing to locate in a specific area, take on employees or find matching funding from another source.

Though several grant schemes operate across the whole of the UK and are available to all businesses that satisfy the outline criteria, myriad schemes exist that are administered locally. Thus the location of your business can be absolutely crucial, and funding may strongly depend on the area into which you intend to grow or develop. Additionally, extra grants may well be available to a business investing in an area of social deprivation, particularly if it involves sustainable job creation.

Keep yourself informed about which grants are available at Grants Online (www.grantsonline.org.uk).

Winning money

If you enjoy publicity and like a challenge, then you can look out for a business competition to enter. Like government grants, business competitions are ubiquitous and, like national lotteries, they're something of a hit-or-miss affair. But one thing is certain: if you don't enter, you can't win.

More than 100 annual awards take place in the UK alone, aimed at new or small businesses, and they're mostly sponsored by banks, major accountancy bodies, chambers of commerce, local or national newspapers, business magazines and the trade press. Government departments may also have competitions for promoting their initiatives for exporting, innovation, job creation and so forth.

The nature and amount of the awards change from year to year, as do the sponsors. But looking in the national and local press, particularly the small business sections of *The Times*, *Daily Telegraph*, *Daily Mail* and *The Guardian*, and on the Internet, should put you in touch with a competition organiser.

Money awards constitute 40 per cent of the main competition prizes. For the most part, these cash sums are less than £5,000. However, a few do exceed £10,000 and one British award is for £50,000.

The Design Council (`www.designcouncil.org.uk/our-work/investment`), the National Business Awards (`www.nationalbusinessawards.co.uk`) and the Growing Business Awards (`http://gba.realbusiness.co.uk`) are good websites to visit to find out about competitions.

Following the crowd

Crowdfunding business finance is a new, game-changing concept that puts the power firmly into the hands of entrepreneurs looking to raise finance. Instead of one large investor putting money into a business, larger numbers of smaller investors contribute as little as £10 each to raise the required capital. They then review propositions put up by business owners for loans or investments and make individual decisions on whether and how much to invest.

Venture capital providers and banks use other people's money to invest or lend, a process that provides a layer of bureaucracy and cost, and decisions are generally 'yes' or 'no'. Crowdfunding, however, enables the business owner to make their proposition directly to individual investors and lenders. The more of these people you convince with your business proposition, the more likely you are to secure the full amount of funding you require. The process is quick – think of it as speed dating for business. You can register and apply online in less than 30 minutes and have the money in your bank account in as little as three days. As investors and lenders have to bid for your business, you should get the best terms possible.

Here are a few organisations to check out:

- ✔ **Crowdcube** (`www.crowdcube.com`): The first crowdfunding website in the world to enable the public to invest in and receive shares in UK companies, Crowdcube has more than 10,000 registered members currently seeking investment opportunities and it's partnered with Startups. co.uk. The platform has already raised more than £3 million for small businesses through its principal site (Darlington Football Club raised £291,450 from 722 investors over 14 days to help fend off closure after going into liquidation), and it hosted the world's first £1 million crowd-funding deal in November 2011.

- ✔ **Crowdfunder UK** (`www.crowdfunder.co.uk`): Since its launch in 2010, the Crowdfunder network has raised over £500,000 for ventures. They are strong supporters of community, environmental and social enterprises, among others. Current examples of supported projects include a project to return to the wild a part of the Cambrian Mountains and a social enterprise that helps people living with mental health difficulties by delivering gardening courses.

- ✔ **Funding Circle** (`www.fundingcircle.com/businesses`): Funding Circle is a marketplace where individuals lend to businesses. By cutting out the high costs and complexity of banks, both sides are better off. At the last count, they had over 60,000 people in their funding circle with a total of £200 million to stake in any type of business.

- ✔ **UK Crowdfunding Association** (`www.ukcfa.org.uk`): Formed in 2012 by 14 crowdfunding businesses, this association aims to

  - Promote crowdfunding as a valuable and viable way for UK businesses, projects or ventures to raise funds

  - Be the voice of all crowdfunding businesses in the UK (donations, loans and equity) to the public, press and policymakers

  - Publish a code of practice, adopted by UK crowdfunding businesses, that protects those participating in crowdfunding

You can find out lots more about crowdfunding in *Crowdsourcing For Dummies* (Wiley) by David Alan Grier.

Chapter 9

Considering Your Mission

. . . .

In This Chapter

▶ Pinpointing your concept

▶ Stating your mission

▶ Looking at vision

▶ Tending to goals and objectives

. . . .

To be successful in the market place, you need to have a clear picture of exactly what you want to do and who you're doing it for. In other words, you need a vision and a mission.

Say you want to start your own airline. That idea in itself doesn't make a business. What destinations will you fly to, what type of planes will you use, how will you sell your tickets and to whom will you sell them are all burning questions that set what are known as the *parameters* of your business. You can think of this as a process that narrows down the big universe that starting your own airline begins with, until perhaps you focus down on flying tourists to and from New York, which is where Virgin began.

Defining the parameters of your vision involves getting to know more about your future customers and more about what you plan to do to woo and win them. Every business needs a winning concept, a clear mission, an inspirational vision and achievable objectives and goals – no rocket science in that.

In this chapter, I tell you how to refine your vision and compose a mission statement that you can adjust to suit your goals throughout the life of your business.

Developing Your Concept

When you know the basic concept of what you're selling and to whom, you should refine that by examining the features of the product (or service) and the benefits that customers get when they purchase. *Features* are what a product has or is, and *benefits* are what the product (or service) does for the customer. For example, cameras and even film or memory sticks aren't the end product that customers want: they're looking for good pictures. Finally, include proof that you can deliver these benefits.

You need to decide your business concept, and you really need to get a good handle on it before you can go much further with your business plans.

Composing Your Mission Statement

A *mission statement* explains in clear, concise terms what the business does. To devise a worthy mission statement, focus your attention on your strengths and the value you provide to your customers.

Your mission should be narrow enough to give direction and guidance to everyone in the business. This concentration is the key to business success because only by focusing on specific needs can a small business differentiate itself from its larger competitors. Nothing kills off a business faster than trying to do too many different things too soon. Also, your mission should address a large enough market to allow your business to grow and realise its potential.

Mission statements mustn't be too bland or too general. Anyone reading the statement should be able to tell what your company aims to achieve in the next three years and how it aims to do so.

Your mission statement should explain what business you're in or plan to enter. It should include answers to some or all the following questions:

- ✔ Market/customer needs: who are we satisfying/delighting?

- ✔ What product/service are we offering that meets those needs?

- ✔ What are our capabilities, both particular skills and knowledge, and resources?

- ✔ What market opportunities exist for our product or service, and what threats exist from competitors (and others)?

- ✔ What do we want to achieve both now and in the future?

Above all, mission statements should be realistic, achievable and brief. You certainly don't need to take a long weekend in a country hotel with key staff and management consultants poring over flip charts to develop your mission statement. If you can't distil the essence of what you plan to do in a simple, direct sentence or two, then you'd better hold back on the launch party and definitely don't order champagne and balloons.

Run through the following checklist periodically to make sure that your mission statement is still on track:

- ✔ Is your mission statement current? (You may need to look at a mission statement you wrote before you carried out lots of market research or sold anything much to see whether it's still valid.)

- ✔ Does the mission statement accurately reflect what you do?

- ✔ Would this mission statement stand out in a crowd?

- ✔ Can a 14-year-old understand it? (That is the standard of the average tabloid reader.)

- ✔ Does your mission statement provide a clear guide to action?

- ✔ Does it tell you what businesses you're *not* in?

Write down your company's mission statement from memory. Have your oldest employee and your newest employee do the same, and then compare the three. Use the differences to refine the mission statement or employee training.

Ultimately, your mission statement reflects the unique quality of your business that makes people want to buy from you. That uniqueness may be contained in the product or service, but is more likely to be woven into the fabric of the way you do business. Try telephoning any three car-hire firms, or walking into three restaurants. The chances are that it's not their products but their people and systems that make them stand out.

What the mission statement does is get everyone pulling hard in the same direction. The direction may change slightly over time, but everyone still pulls the same way and the company moves forward, rather than standing still or declining.

You can see a cross section of example mission statements at `www.leadership-tools.com/example-of-mission-statement.html`.

Seeing the Vision Thing

Vision isn't the same as mission. You can think of *mission* as providing direction for the medium term along a line that most people can follow. *Vision* is about stretching the organisation's reach beyond its grasp. Generally, few people concerned with the company can now see how the vision is to be achieved, but all concerned agree that it will be great if it can be. When your vision becomes reality, it may be time for a new challenge, or perhaps even a new business.

Microsoft founder Bill Gates had a vision of a computer in every home at a time when few offices had one. As a mission statement 15 years ago, this vision may have raised a wry smile. After all, only a few decades before IBM had estimated the entire world demand for its computers as seven! Now, Gates's vision has been all but reached.

You need to create the vision with the people who work with you in order to be sure of their wholehearted commitment. You can't get that commitment if the only people who buy into the vision are you, your partner and the management consultant who sold it to you.

As with the mission, only when everyone knows and shares the business's vision is it likely to be achieved. All parts of the organisation are so connected to each other, to the market and to the customer in such a complex series of relationships that the management team can't hope to achieve anything much without everyone's input. Rather, in the way that markets work better with perfect information, businesses work better when everyone knows and believes in the vision.

Setting Objectives and Goals

Missions and visions are vital, but they aren't much good without clear objectives, which are the major measurable tasks for the business and operating goals for individuals. For example, you need an idea of how big you want the business to be – in other words, what your share of the market is likely to be.

Forecasting sales is certainly not easy, especially before you've even started trading. But if you don't set a goal at the start and instead just wait to see how things develop, then one of two problems is likely to occur. You don't sell enough to cover your fixed costs and so lose money and perhaps go out of business, or you sell too much and run out of cash while you wait for your customers to pay up; in other words, you over-trade.

Obviously, before you can set a market share and sales objective, you need to know the size of your market. (See Chapter 4 for information on how to research the market.)

The size you want your business to be is more a matter of judgement than forecast. You make a judgement tempered by the resources you have available to achieve those objectives and by some idea of what's reasonable and achievable and what isn't. The amount of money you can persuade outsiders to pump into your business also limits your ambition.

Set near-term objectives covering the next 18 months or so, and longer-term objectives covering up to three or so years further on.

You can set objectives in any number of areas, but the most vital areas are *profits*, the money you have left after everyone has been paid; *margins*, the profit made per item sold; *return on capital employed*, the profit made for every pound invested and *value added per employee*, the profit made per person employed (see Chapter 13); and *sales volume and value in pounds* and your *percentage share of the market* (see Chapter 17).

You also need to ensure that any objectives set meet these criteria:

- ✔ **Accepted:** This means that whoever you set a goal for must commit to the task. Silence isn't a sufficient response. So, for example, sales staff should sign off acceptance of targets and production staff should confirm that they accept output goals.

- ✔ **Achievable:** If a goal is way beyond any reasonable chance of being achieved, when you fail to get there all concerned, yourself included, are going to be demotivated.

- ✔ **Allocated:** You should leave no objective hanging, without assigning a named person or persons the task of achieving all or part of the task in question.

- ✔ **Challenging:** Objectives need to stretch but not break.

- ✔ **Measurable:** Remember that old saying: 'What gets measured gets done'? Certainly, if you can't measure something, setting goals in that area is pointless.

- ✔ **Time-scaled:** Not great English, but an objective without a date by which it is to be achieved is meaningless. Saying you must get sales of £100,000 a month may be challenging if you're in your first month in business, but altogether too laid-back for year five.

Here are a few real-life examples of goals:

- ✔ Pizza Express set out its goals in June 2011 as aiming to nearly double its number of outlets from 318 to 700 by 2020.

- ✔ Majestic Wine aims to add 12 new stores a year for the next ten years.

- ✔ Daniel Jones, founder of Artisan Chocolatier & Patissier, has a goal that in five years he'll have his own premises in Ludlow, and be thinking about expanding into other areas of the UK.

Chapter 10

Marketing and Selling Your Wares

*E*ntering the market with your product or service involves deciding on what mix of marketing ingredients to use. In cooking, the same ingredients used in different ways can result in really different products. The same is true in business, where the 'ingredients' are product (or service), price, place and promotion. A change in the way you put these elements together can produce an offering tailored to meet the needs of a specific market. For example, a hardback book isn't much more expensive to produce than a paperback. However, with a bit of clever publicity, bringing the hardback out a few months before the paperback edition with a higher price tag, the publisher can create an air of exclusivity that satisfies a particular group of customers.

In this chapter, you find out how to get news about your business to all the people who can help you achieve sales, how to set the right selling price and – if you're selling a physical product – how to get it to your customer.

Making Up the Marketing Mix

The key to successful promotion lies in knowing exactly what you want people to do. A few elements can make or break the successful marketing of your business. The elements you need to consider that go to make up the marketing mix are

✔ *Place* is a general term to cover everything from where you locate your business to how you get your product or service to market. Poor distribution often explains sluggish sales growth. If your type of product gets to market through several channels but you only use one of them, then no amount of price changes or extra promotion makes much difference.

✔ *Pricing* strategies can range from charging what the market may bear, right through to *marginal cost* (just enough to cover direct costs and a small contribution to overheads). Knowing your costs is important, but this element is only one in the pricing decision. You also have to take account of the market place, your competition and your product position (for example, if you offer a luxury item, your place in the market is different to that of someone who sells necessities).

✔ The *product or service* is what people use, but what they buy are the underlying benefits it confers on them. For example, when someone buys a camera she may be considering whether she should buy SLR or digital, what lens it has, even what film it takes in the case of more traditional snappers – but these end products aren't what customers want; what she's looking for is good pictures.

✔ *Promotion* is the means by which you tell your market(s) about your products or services. Promotion includes such elements as your website, leaflets, advertising and even basic items such as business cards and letterheads.

Defining Your Product or Service Parameters

To be successful in any marketplace, you need to have a clear picture of exactly what you want to do and for whom you're doing it. In other words, you need a vision and a mission. (Chapter 9 offers advice on developing your mission statement.)

To market your product effectively, you have to make decisions about factors such as product range and depth before you're ready to enter the market. Having decided to open a corner shop, for example, you still have to decide whether to focus on food only, or to carry household items and perhaps newspapers and flowers too. You also need to decide whether to carry more than one brand and size of each product.

If the key advantages of your corner shop are its location, opening hours, delivery service and friendly staff, all at competitive prices, then perhaps you don't need a wide or deep product range.

Using Advertising to Tell Your Story

You can't be confident that your customers share your zeal for your business proposition, so you need to convince them that they need what you're offering. The way to convince them is to tell potential customers about what you're selling by advertising your wares.

The skill of advertising lies in reducing the global population to your target audience and reaching as many of them as you can at an economic cost. You first analyse the benefits or virtues of your product, isolate the features and translate them into customer benefits. Who has a need for your product? Define exactly who your potential customers are.

Question all the time. Then the advertising process is to set objectives for your campaign, decide on a budget, design the message, pick the medium to reach your target audience and determine how you're going to evaluate the success of your advertising.

When you understand the basics, which I go through in the following sections, you should also be able to analyse advertisements better, break them down into their elements and avoid the all-too-common mistakes that advertisers make every day.

Advertising by itself doesn't sell. It doesn't shift a bad product (or at least not more than once) or create new markets. Sales literature, order forms, a sales force, stocks, distributors and a strategy must back up your advertising.

Considering the customer's point of view

People buy a product or service for what it can do for them. Customers look for the benefits. As the seller, your mission is to answer the question 'What's in it for me?' from your potential customer's point of view.

Every time you compose a sales letter, write an advertisement or plan a trade show, you must get to the heart of the matter. Why should customers purchase your product or service? What benefit may it bring them?

You need to view all your marketing efforts from the prospect's point of view, not just your own. When you know what you're selling and to whom, you can match the features of the product (or service) to the benefits the customers can get when they purchase. A *feature* is what a product has or is, and *benefits* are what the product does for the customer. Finally, include proof that the product or service can deliver these benefits. Table 10-1 shows an analysis of features, benefits and proofs.

You can employ this format to examine the features, benefits and proofs for your own products or services and use the information to devise your ads. Remember, the customer pays for the benefits and the seller for the features. So the benefits provide the copy for most of your future advertising and promotional efforts.

Table 10-1	Listing Features and Benefits	
Feature	*Benefit*	*Proof*
We use a unique hardening process for our machine.	Our tools last longer and that saves you money.	We have a patent on the process; independent tests carried out by the Cambridge Institute of Technology show our product lasts longest.
Our shops stay open later than others in the area.	You get more choice of when to shop.	Come and see.
Our computer system is fault tolerant using parallel processing.	You have no downtime for defects or system expansion.	Our written specification guarantees this – come and talk to satisfied customers operating in your field.

Try this format out on your business idea. Keep at it until you really have a good handle on what makes your customers tick. To make the process work best, you need to talk to real prospective customers in your target market.

Making an exhibition of yourself

One way to gather useful market research data on customers and competitors is to attend exhibitions. Exhibitions are also a useful way of seeing whether a demand for what you have to offer is likely to exist, because hundreds of key decision makers are gathered in one place for you to make a pitch to.

Equinox, a designer furniture company, took part in a national exhibition at London's Earls Court while on an enterprise programme at Cranfield Business School. A grant paid for half the cost of its £1,200 stand and the £5,000 of firm orders it received more than covered the rest of the cost. More importantly, the founder felt more confident in his product and he took away 40 contacts to follow up later.

You can find out when exhibitions relevant to your business take place in the UK by searching Exhibitions UK (www.exhibitions.co.uk), the official website for the British exhibition industry, sponsored by UK Trade & Investment, the government organisation responsible for all trade promotion and development work. If you want to exhibit or attend a show overseas, TSNN (www.tsnn.com), which calls itself 'The Ultimate Trade Show

Resource', operates a widely consulted event database containing data on more than 15,000 trade shows, exhibitions, public events and conferences worldwide. You need to register (free) for full access to the database.

You may be able to get financial help from your trade association to attend an overseas exhibition. For example, the UK Fashion and Textile Association has grants available for eligible UK-based companies for key shows in Paris, Berlin, Florence and New York, covering menswear, womenswear, lingerie and childrenswear (go to the website www.ukft.org and select Business and then Export). See Chapter 8 for information on finding a grant to help pay for attending exhibitions at home and abroad.

Setting advertising objectives

You're wasting your time advertising your product or service unless it leads to the opportunity for a sale in a significant number of instances. Ask yourself what potential customers have to do to enable you to make these sales. Do you want them to visit your showroom, phone you, write to your office, return a card or send an order in the post? Do you expect them to order now, or to remember you at some future date when they've a need for your services?

The more specifically you identify the response you want, the better you can tailor your promotional effort to achieve your objective, and the more clearly you can assess the effectiveness of your promotion.

The more general your advertising objective is – for example, to 'improve your image' or 'to keep your name in front of the public' – the more likely it is to be an ineffective way of spending your money.

Deciding the budget

People commonly use two methods to calculate their advertising budget numbers:

- ✔ **What can we afford?** This approach accepts that cash is usually a scarce commodity and advertising has to take its place alongside a range of competing demands.

- ✔ **Cost/benefit:** This approach comes into its own when you've clear and specific promotional goals. If you've spare capacity in your factory or want to sell more out of your shop, you can work out how much it costs you to increase your production and sales, and how much you may benefit from those extra sales. You then figure out how much advertising money it's going to take to get you the extra business.

Suppose you expect a £1,000 advertisement to generate 100 enquiries for your product. If your experience tells you that on average 10 per cent of enquiries result in orders, and your profit margin is £200 per product, then you can expect an extra £2,000 profit. That benefit is much greater than the £1,000 cost of the advertisement, so the investment seems worthwhile.

In practice, you should use both these methods to decide how much to spend on promoting your products.

Defining the message

To define your message, you must look at your business and its products from the customer's standpoint and be able to answer the question, 'Why should I buy your product?' The best way is to consider the answer in two stages:

1. **'Why should I buy your *product or service*?'**

   The answer comes naturally when you look carefully at customers' motives for buying and the benefits they get from the product.

2. **'Why should I buy *your* product or service?'**

   The only logical and satisfactory answer is: 'Because it's better and so it's different.'

   The difference can arise in two ways:

   - You, the seller, are different. To achieve this, you establish a particular niche for your business.

   - Your product or service is different. Each product or service should have a unique selling point, based on fact.

Your promotional message must be built around the strength(s) of your product or service and must consist of facts about the company and about the product or service.

The stress here is on the word *fact*. Although many types of fact may surround you and your products, your customers are only interested in two – the facts that influence their buying decisions, and the facts of how your business and its products stand out from the competition.

The assumption is that everyone buys for obvious, logical reasons only, but of course innumerable examples show that people don't. Does a woman buy a new dress only when an old one is worn out? Do bosses have desks that are bigger than their subordinates' because they have more papers to put on them?

Choosing the media

Broadly, your advertising choices are *above-the-line* media, which is jargon for the Internet, newspapers and magazines, television, radio and other broadcast media, and *below-the-line* activities such as distributing brochures, leaflets and visiting cards, stationery, letterheads and the way you answer the phone.

The printed word (the Internet, newspapers and magazines) probably takes most of your above-the-line advertising budget. Print is the accepted medium to reach the majority of customers. Most people read a newspaper, especially on Sunday, and magazines cater for every imaginable interest and range from parish magazines to Sunday supplements. News and articles are also increasingly available on the Internet, as online versions of conventional papers or via blogs.

You must advertise where your buyers and consumers are likely to see your message. Your market research (which I talk about in Chapter 4) tells you where your likely prospects lie. Before making your decision about which paper or journal to advertise in, you need to get readership and circulation numbers and the publication's reader profile.

You can get this information directly from the journal or paper, which should be able to access through your local business library. The Audit Bureau of Circulations Electronic (`www.abc.org.uk`) audits website traffic, among other media, and Rajar (Radio Joint Audience Research) independently compiles radio audience statistics every quarter, providing an industry benchmark (`www.rajar.co.uk`). Newsgator (`www.newsgator.com`) and Blog Catalogue (`www.blogcatalog.com`) operate social network and blog indexing services that can help you filter through the myriad of social media to let you home in on the ones that operate in your business sector. (See also Chapter 21, where I cover the whole social networking scene.)

When considering below-the-line advertising, identify what business gurus call *moments of truth* – contact points between you, your product or service and your customer. Those moments offer you a chance to shine and make a great impression. You can spot the difference immediately when you get a really helpful person on the phone or serving you in a shop. The same is true of product literature that's actually helpful, a fairly rare event in itself.

Some of the most effective promotional ideas are the simplest; for example, a business card with a map on the reverse showing how to find you, or thank-you cards instead of letters on which you can show your company's recently completed designs.

Choosing the frequency

Think carefully about the timing of your advertising in relation to the kind of media you're considering. The copy dates of some monthly publications are two months before publication; trade exhibitions often only occur once or twice a year. This scarcity poses problems if you're waiting on a shipment or uncertain about a product change. Daily or weekly publications allow much prompter changes. The ultimate kinds of media are probably the Internet, which can be updated minute by minute, and radio, where messages can be slotted in on the same day. Yearbooks, diaries and phone directories require a lot of forward notice.

Writing a leaflet

Whether or not you actually use a leaflet as part of your advertising strategy, I always recommend writing one. The process forces you to think about what you have to tell potential customers about your product or service and, most importantly, what you want them to do next when they know of your existence. So if you want them to buy now, you need to give prices, availability, delivery times and so forth.

A leaflet doesn't have to be big – both sides of a sheet of A4 paper is as much as you can hope to get most readers to plough through, even if you're peddling the elixir of life. As well as carrying text, leaflets are a great way to get across more complex messages that a picture or diagram delivers best.

The leaflet content needs to be

- ✔ Clear, in straightforward English, simply laid out and easy to read

- ✔ Concise, using as few words as possible, and jargon free

- ✔ Correct, because spelling mistakes and incorrect information destroy confidence in you and your product or service

- ✔ Complete, providing all the information needed for the reader to progress to the next stage in the buying process

 Flyerzone (`www.flyerzone.co.uk/catalogue/designs`) has hundreds of ready-made designer templates for hundreds of different types of business from bars to wedding services. You can use their free online template to create your own leaflet, flyer or poster.

Using the Internet for viral marketing

The Internet is now central to the marketing process for most businesses. Even where customers don't buy online, most consumers and all business buyers check out products and services using the Internet to check price, quality and competitive offers. Increasingly, products that used to have a physical presence are disappearing from the shelf. Music, software, film and now even books are available in 'soft' form to try or buy and download online. (This whole subject is so vital to a small firm's ability to compete that I dedicate two whole chapters to the subject; flick to Chapter 15, which covers doing business online, and Chapter 21, where I look at social media.)

Viral marketing is a term that describes the ability of the Internet to accelerate interest and awareness in a product by rapid word-of-mouth communications. To understand the mathematical power behind this phenomena, take a look at the sidebar 'How viral marketing works'.

The birth of viral marketing, using the power of Reed's Law to the full (see the sidebar 'How viral marketing works' for details of this law), has been attributed to the founder of Hotmail, who insisted that every email sent by a Hotmail user should incorporate the message: 'Get your free Web-based email at Hotmail.' By clicking on this line of text, the recipient would be transported to the Hotmail home page. Although this email sent by the company itself wouldn't have had much effect, at the foot of an email sent by a business colleague or friend it made a powerful impact. The very act of sending a Hotmail message constituted an endorsement of the product and so the current customer was selling to future customers on the company's behalf just by communicating with them. The recipient of a Hotmail message discovered that the product works, but also that someone she respected or liked was a user.

You only have to see how quickly a harmful computer virus can spread in hours and days, to cover the whole world, to see the potential of viral marketing. For a small firm, this technique has the added advantage of being inexpensive and easy to execute. Just look at a few major sites on the Internet to get ideas. Book e-tailors all have links for you to email a friend about a book you've 'stumbled' across on their site. Travel sites encourage you to email any of their special offers that you don't plan to take up to a friend. However, the beauty and limitation of viral marketing is that it only works when you're talking about a good product. People don't recommend something they don't like using themselves.

Providing opportunities to see

The more opportunities you give potential customers to see your name or your product, the greater the chance of them remembering you, which is why direct mail letters usually involve more than one piece of literature. The theory is that the recipient looks at each piece before discarding it. The recipient may only give it a brief scan, but each scan gives the seller another chance to hook a customer. So, rather than using different advertising messages, try getting the same or a similar message to one customer group several times.

How viral marketing works

Take a look at recent communications networks and how they work.

The simplest are the 'one-to-one' broadcast systems such as television and radio. In such systems, the overall value of the network rises in a simple relationship to the size of the audience; the bigger the audience, the more valuable your network. Mathematically, the value rises with N, where N represents the size of the audience. This relationship is known as Sarnoff's Law, after a pioneer of radio and television broadcasting.

Next in order of value comes the telephone network, a 'many-to-many' system where everyone can get in touch with anyone else. Here the mathematics are subtly different. With N people connected, every individual has the opportunity to connect with N–1 other people (you exclude yourself). So the total number of possible connections for N individuals is N (N–1), or N^2-N. This relationship is known as Metcalf's Law,

after Bob Metcalf, an inventor of computer networking. The size of a network under Metcalf's Law rises sharply as the value of N rises, much more so than with simple one-to-one networks.

The Internet, however, has added a further twist. As well as talking to each other, Internet users have the opportunity to form groups in a way they can't easily do on the telephone. Any Internet user can join discussion groups, auction groups, community sites and so on. The mathematics now becomes interesting. As David Reed, formerly of Lotus Development Corporation demonstrated, if you've N people in a network, they can in theory form 2^n-N-1 different groups. You can check this formula by considering a small N, of say three people, A, B and C. They can form three different groups of two people, AB, AC and CB, and one group of three people, ABC, making a total of four groups as predicted by the formula. As the value on N increases, the size of the network explodes.

One claimed benefit of breakfast television is that it can get your message out before the shops open. In business-to-business sales, trade buyers are deluged with calendars, diaries, pen sets and message pads in the hope that when the buyer is making a decision, the promotional materials are still close at hand and have an influence on that decision.

Figuring your bang-for-the-buck ratio

You should only undertake advertising where you can realistically measure the results. Everything else is self-indulgent. The formula to keep in mind is:

Effectiveness = Total cost of the advertising activity concerned ÷ Results (in measurable units such as customers, new orders or enquiries)

A glance at the advertising analysis in Table 10-2 shows how one organisation went about measuring and comparing the effectiveness of different advertising methods. Table 10-2 shows the advertising results for a small business course run in London. At first glance, the Sunday paper produced the most enquiries. Although it cost the most, £340, the cost per enquiry was only slightly more than the other media used. But the objective of this advertising wasn't simply to create interest; it was intended to sell places on the course. In fact, only 10 of the 75 enquiries converted into orders – an advertising cost of £34 per head. On this basis, the Sunday paper was between 2.5 and 3.5 times more expensive than any other medium.

Table 10-2		Measuring Advertising Effect			
Media Used	*Enquiries*	*Cost of Advertising (£)*	*Cost per Enquiry*	*No. of Customers*	*Advertising Cost per Customer (£)*
Sunday paper	75	340	4.50	10	34
Daily paper	55	234	4.25	17	14
Posters	30	125	4.20	10	12
Local weekly paper	10	40	4.00	4	10
Personal recommendation	20	N/A	N/A	19	N/A

Getting into the News

Getting your business into the news is one of the most cost-effective ways to get your message in front of both actual and potential customers. People see papers, TV and journals, online and off-line, as being unbiased, and so they've a greater impact on their audiences than pure adverts. It goes without saying that what you're looking for is favourable news. If you do have bad news coming through, check out this website: www.aboutpublicrelations.net/crisis.htm.

The surest way to get in the news is to write a press release. Better still, write lots of them. To be successful, a press release needs to get attention immediately and be quick and easy to digest. Studying and copying the style of the particular journals (or other media) you want your press release to appear in can make publication more likely.

The introduction is the most vital part. Ask yourself, 'Will what I write make the reader want to read on?' Avoid detail and sidetracks. The paragraphs should have bite and flow. Keep the sentences reasonably short. State the main point of the story or information early on. Follow these suggestions for a successful press release:

- Type the release on a sheet of A4 paper headed 'Press Release' or 'Press Information' and email it to the News Editor, News Desk or a named journalist.

- Use double spacing and wide margins to allow for editorial changes and printing instructions, respectively. Use one side of the paper only.

- Date the release and put a headline on to identify it. This must persuade the editor to read on. If it doesn't attract interest, it'll be quickly 'spiked'. Editors are looking for topicality, originality, personality and, sometimes, humour.

- Tell your story in three paragraphs. The substance should come in the first one. The first paragraph must say who, what, why, when and where, and succeeding paragraphs can fill in the detail. If space is short, a sub-editor deletes from the bottom and papers are always looking for fillers – short items that they can drop into gaps. Even if the paper cuts the bulk of the story, at least it may print the main facts.

- Include at least one direct quotation or comment, always from a named individual and ideally from someone of standing or relevance.

- Keep the press release simple and write for the readership. The general public prefers images or descriptions to technical facts. For example, you can describe a new car lock as being able to keep out a professional thief for 30 minutes for a story in the general press. For the trade press, the same story may be better supported by facts about the number of levers, codes and so forth that are involved in beefing up the lock's security system.

- Finish with a contact for more information. Give phone numbers for work and home and a mobile number, as well as your email and website addresses. Doing so helps a journalist looking for more detail – if a gap occurs suddenly and you're available for further information, your story may be more attractive.

- Submit the release before the paper or journal's deadline. All the media work to strict deadlines. Many local papers sold on a Friday are printed on a Tuesday or Wednesday morning. A release that fails to make it by then probably gets ignored. The national dailies, of course, have more flexibility and often have several editions. At the other end of the scale, many colour supplements and monthly journals have a cut-off date six weeks in advance.

✔ Steer away from selling your firm and product, and write news. Anything else is advertising and may be discarded. You're not writing an advertisement, you're telling a story to interest readers.

✔ A good picture is worth a thousand words, as the adage goes. Certainly, from a journalist's point of view, your picture is worth half a page of text she doesn't have to write herself.

Deciding who to contact

Remember that the target audience for your press release is the professional editor, who is the person who decides what to print. With British editors receiving an average of 80–90 press releases per week, make sure that you're publicising your latest newsworthy item and that your press release is free of puffery and jargon.

Do your research to find not only the right newspapers or journals, but also the right journalists. Read their columns, or listen to or watch their programmes, and become familiar with their style and approach to news stories. Your goal is to write a press release that's so close to a journalist's own style that she has almost no additional work to do to make your news usable.

Following through

You get better results if you follow up your press release with a quick phone call. Journalists get bogged down and distracted like everyone else, so don't be too surprised if your masterpiece sinks to the bottom of a pile of prospective stories before the day is out. That phone call, or even an email if you can't get through, is often enough to keep up interest and get your story through the first sifting.

When you start getting results, you want to keep the effort going. But even if you aren't successful at first, don't be disappointed or disheartened. Keep plugging away. Try to find a story regularly for the local press and get to know your local journalists and editors. Always be truthful, helpful and available. If a media contact rings you and you're in a meeting, make sure that you ring back.

Some companies seem to get a piece in the paper every week. The stories published aren't always earth-shattering news, but the continuous drip of press coverage eventually makes an impact. For example, Virgin Airways was boosted immeasurably by successful press coverage. Few of the millions of words of copy written about Branson or Virgin have been paid for.

Using Blogs and Social Networks

Consumers increasingly get influenced by their peers' views as to what to buy and do. This process of disseminating information was at one time the exclusive domain of mainstream advertising and of comment in the press or on the news. The Internet has changed the game and now everyone can find out from consumers how good or bad a product or service is.

Blogs, Facebook, Foursquare, Twitter and a host of other social networks are now an important way to get your message across. In some cases – such as when marketing to the under 25s – they're the *only* way. Often systematic processes are in place; TripAdvisor's information on hotel users' experiences is a good example, where users rate on a points scale different aspects of a hotel experience – accommodation, service, value for money. This information allows potential customers to see whether the particular aspect or aspects they're looking for in a hotel are likely to be delivered.

So you need to build these social network routes into your marketing plans. Shiv Singh's *Social Media Marketing For Dummies* (Wiley) contains everything you need to know about this vital topic. Also check out Chapter 21 on this subject.

Selling and Salesmanship

More direct than advertising or publicity, selling is at the heart of every business. Whatever kind of selling your business involves, from moving goods over a counter to negotiating complex contracts, you need to understand the whole selling process and be involved with every aspect of it.

Telling the difference between selling and marketing

Marketing involves the whole process of deciding what to sell, who to sell it to and how. The theory is that a brilliant marketing strategy should all but eliminate the need for selling. After all, selling is mostly concerned with shoe-horning customers into products that they don't really want, isn't it? Absolutely not! Although the more effort you put into targeting the right product or service to the right market, the less arduous the selling process is, you still have a selling job to do.

The primary job of the sales operation is to act as a bridge or conduit between the product and the customer. Across that gulf flows information as well as products and services. You need to tell customers about your great new ideas and how your product or service performs better than anything they've seen to date.

Most businesses need selling and marketing activities in equal measure to get their message across effectively and get goods and services into their markets.

Selling yourself

One of the most important operational issues to address is your personal selling style. If you've sold products or services before, you may have developed a successful selling style already. If not, you need to develop one that's appropriate for your customers and comfortable for you. Regardless of your experience, assessing your selling style helps define and reinforce your business goals.

Check that you and your salespeople always see things from the customer's point of view. Review the sales styles of your salespeople to see how they can improve. Consider whether your own and your salespeople's selling styles are *consultative*, where you win the customer over to your point of view, or *hard*, where you try forcing the customer to take your product or service.

In assessing your selling style, consider the following:

- ✔ Always have a specific objective for any selling activity, together with a fall-back position. For example, your aim may be to get an order, but you may settle for the chance to tender for a customer's business. If you don't have objectives, much of your sales activity may be wasted on courtesy calls that never reach the asking-for-an-order stage.

- ✔ The right person to sell to is the one who makes the buying decision. You may have to start farther down the chain, but you should always know who you finally have to convince.

- ✔ Set up the situation so you can listen to the customer. You can best do this by asking open questions that look for long answers as opposed to closed questions that solicit a 'yes or no' response. When the customer has revealed what her needs really are, confirm them back to her.

- ✔ Explain your product or service in terms of the customer's needs and requirements.

- ✔ Deal with objections without hostility or irritation. Objections are a sign that the customer is interested enough in what you have to say at least to discuss your proposition. After you've overcome the customer's objections and established a broad body of agreement, you can try to close the deal.

- ✔ Your approach to closing can be one of a number of ways. The *assumptive close* takes the tack that because you and the customer are so much in agreement, an order is the next logical step. If the position is less clear, you can go for the *balance sheet close*, which involves going through the pros and cons and then arriving at a larger number of pros. So again, the most logical way forward is for the customer to order. If circumstances allow, you can use the *special situation* closing technique. This may be appropriate if a product is in scarce supply or on special offer for a limited period.

- ✔ If you're unsuccessful, start the selling process again using your fall-back objective as the goal.

Outsourcing selling

Hiring sales people can prove to be too costly for a new or small business. A lower-cost and perhaps less-risky sales route is via agents. Good agents should have existing contacts in your field, know buyers personally and have detailed knowledge of your product's market. Unlike someone you recruit, a hired agent should be off to a flying start from day one.

The big difference is that agents are paid purely on commission – if they don't sell, they don't earn. The commission amount varies, but is rarely less than 7 per cent of the selling price, though 25 per cent isn't unknown.

You can find an agent as follows:

- ✔ Advertise in your specialist trade press or newspapers such as the *Daily Telegraph* and *Exchange and Mart.*

- ✔ Use the search facility on the website of the Manufacturers' Agents' Association (www.themaa.co.uk), whose membership consists entirely of commission agents selling in all fields of business. The fee is £175 plus £35 VAT to contact up to 20 agents in one search.

- ✔ Check out the International Union of Commercial Agents and Brokers (www.iucab.com), which has details on around 470,000 commercial agents in Europe and North and South America.

- ✔ Look in trade directories that list other agents' associations.

- ✔ Approach outlets where you want to sell (this method is the most reliable one). They know the honest, competent and regular agents who call on them. Draw up a shortlist and invite those agents to apply to you.

When interviewing potential sales agents, you should find out:

- What other companies do they work with and products do they already sell? You want them to sell related but not competing products or services to yours.

- What's their knowledge of the trade and geographical area that you cover? Sound them out for specific knowledge of your target market.

- Who are their contacts?

- What's their proven selling record? Find out who their biggest customers are and talk to them directly.

- Do they appear honest, reliable and fit to represent your business? Take up references and talk to their customers.

Finding professional representation is a challenge, so your product has to be first class and your growth prospects good, with plenty of promotional material and back-up support.

When you do find someone to represent your product, draw up an agreement to cover the main points, including geographical area, commission rates, when commission is payable, customers you want to continue dealing with yourself, training and support given, prohibition of competing agencies and periods of notice required to terminate. Also build in an initial trial period after which both parties can agree to part amicably.

Measuring results

Sales results can take time to appear. In the meantime you need to make sure that you (or your agent) are doing things that eventually lead to successful sales. You should measure the following:

Activities:

- Sales appointments made
- Sales calls made per day, per week, per month (monitor trends, because last quarter's sales calls give you a good feel for this quarter's sales results)
- Quotations given

Results:

- New accounts opened
- Old accounts lost
- Average order size

Settling On a Price

Pricing is another element of the marketing mix and it represents the biggest decision you have to make about your business and the one that has the biggest impact on company profitability. You need to keep pricing constantly under review.

To get a better appreciation of the factors that may have an influence on what you charge, keep these factors in mind. (I cover the accounting aspect of pricing in Chapter 13.)

Caring about business conditions

Obviously, the overall conditions in the marketplace have a bearing on your pricing policy. In boom conditions, where products are so popular that they're virtually being rationed, you can expect the overall level of prices for some products to rise disproportionately. And conditions can vary so much from place to place that they've a major impact on pricing. For example, one business starter produced her beauty treatment price list based on prices near to her home in Surrey. However, she planned to move to Cornwall to start her business, where prices were 50 per cent lower, reflecting lower rates of pay in the county. So although she got a boost by selling her Surrey home for much more than she paid for a house in Cornwall, that gain was offset by having to charge much lower prices for her services.

Seasonal factors can also contribute to changes in the general level of prices. A turkey, for example, costs less on the afternoon of Christmas Eve than it does at the start of Christmas week.

Working to your capacity

Your capacity to produce your product or service, bearing in mind market conditions, influences the price you set. Typically, a new venture has limited capacity at the start. A valid entry strategy may be to price high enough to just fill your capacity, rather than so low as to swamp you.

A housewife started a home ironing service at £5.50 per hour's ironing, in line with competition, but because she only had 20 hours a week to work in, she rapidly ran out of time. It took six months to get her price up to £7 an hour and her demand down to 20 hours per week. Then she was able to recruit some assistance and had a high enough margin to pay outworkers and make a bit of profit herself.

Understanding consumer perceptions

A major consideration when setting your prices is customers' perception of the value of your product or service. Their opinion of value may have little or no relation to its cost, and they may be ignorant of the price that the competition charges, especially if your product or service is a new one.

Skimming versus penetrating

The overall image that you want to portray in the marketplace influences the prices you charge. A high-quality image calls for higher pricing, naturally. However, within that pricing policy you've two options: set a high price, which just *skims* the market by only being attractive to a small population of wealthier customers; or go for a low price to *penetrate* the market, appealing to the mass of customers.

Businesses often adopt skim pricing with new products with little or no competition that are aimed at affluent buyers who are willing to pay more to be the trendsetters for a new product. After the innovators have been creamed off the market, you can drop the price to penetrate to lower layers of demand.

The danger with this strategy is that high prices attract the interest of new competitors. If you've a product that's easy to copy and impossible to patent, you may be better off setting the price low to discourage competitors and to spread your product throughout the market quickly.

Avoiding setting prices too low

The most frequent mistake that companies make when setting a selling price for the first time is to pitch it too low. Through failing to understand all the costs associated with making and marketing your product or through yielding to the temptation to undercut the competition at the outset, you set your price so low that you risk killing your company.

Pondering Place and Distribution

Place is the fourth 'p' in the marketing mix. Place makes you review exactly how you get your products or service to your customers.

If you're a retailer, restaurateur or garage proprietor, for example, then your customers come to you. Your physical location is probably the key to success. If your business is in the manufacturing field, you're more likely to go out and find customers. In this case, your channels of distribution are the vital link.

Even if you're already in business and plan to stay in the same location, you may benefit from taking the opportunity to review that decision. If you're looking for additional funds to expand your business, your location is undoubtedly an area that prospective financiers will want to explore.

Choosing a location

From your market research data, you should be able to come up with a list of criteria that are important to your choice of location. The factors you need to weigh up when deciding where to locate include:

- ✔ If you need skilled or specialist labour, is it readily available?

- ✔ Are the necessary back-up services available, such as computer support, equipment repairs and maintenance?

- ✔ How readily available are raw materials, components and other supplies?

- ✔ How does the cost of premises, rates and utilities compare with other areas?

- ✔ How accessible is the site by road, rail and air?

- ✔ Are there any changes in the pipeline that may adversely affect trade? Examples include a new motorway bypassing the town, changes in transport services and the closure of a large factory.

- ✔ Are there competing businesses in the immediate neighbourhood? Are these competitors likely to have a beneficial or detrimental effect?

- ✔ Is the location conducive to the creation of a favourable market image? For instance, a high-fashion designer may lack credibility trading from an area famous for its heavy industry and infamous for its dirt and pollution.

- ✔ Is the area generally regarded as low or high growth? Is the area favourable to businesses?

- ✔ Can you and your key employees get to the area easily and quickly?

You may even have spotted a role model – a successful competitor, perhaps in another town, who appears to have got the location spot on. You can use its location criteria as a guide to developing your own.

Using these criteria, you can quickly screen out most unsuitable areas. You may have to visit other locations several times, at different hours of the day and on different days of the week, before screening them out too.

Selecting a distribution channel

When you know where you want to locate, selecting a distribution channel involves researching methods and deciding on the best way to get your product to your customers.

Moving a product through a distribution channel calls for two sorts of selling activity. *Push* is the name given to selling your product in, for example, a shop. *Pull* is the effort that you carry out on the shop's behalf to help it sell your product. Your advertising strategy or a merchandising activity may cause the pull. You need to know how much push and pull are needed for the channel you're considering. If you aren't geared up to help retailers sell your product, and they need that help, this channel may be a poor choice for you.

The way in which you have to move your product to your end customers is an important factor to weigh up when choosing a channel. As well as such factors as the cost of carriage, you also have to decide on packaging materials. As a rough rule, the more stages in the distribution channel, the more robust and expensive your packaging has to be.

Not all channels of distribution settle their bills promptly. For example, mail-order customers pay in advance, but retailers can take up to 90 days or more to pay. You need to take account of this settlement period in your cash-flow forecast.

Consider these factors when choosing channels of distribution for your particular business:

- ✓ **Does the channel meet your customers' needs?** You have to find out how your customers expect their product or service to be delivered to them and whether they need that particular route.

- ✓ **Will the product itself survive?** Fresh vegetables, for example, you need to move quickly from where they're grown to where they're consumed.

- ✓ **Can you sell enough this way?** 'Enough' is how much you want to sell.

- ✓ **Is the channel compatible with your image?** If you're selling a luxury product, then door-to-door selling may spoil the impression you're trying to create in the rest of your marketing effort.

- ✓ **How do your competitors distribute?** If they've been around for a while and are obviously successful, you may benefit from looking at how your competitors distribute, and then using that knowledge to your advantage.

✔ **Is the channel cost-effective?** A small manufacturer may not find it cost-effective to supply retailers in a particular area because the direct 'drop' size – that is, the load per order – is too small to be worthwhile.

✔ **Is the mark-up enough?** If your product can't bear at least a 100 per cent mark-up, then you're unlikely to be able to sell it through department stores. Your distribution channel has to be able to make a profit from selling your product too.

Part III
Staying in Business

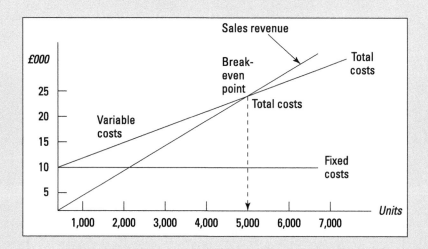

In this part . . .

✔ See how to recruit, manage and motivate employees.

✔ Decide where to set up your business and calculate the space and equipment that you need at the outset.

✔ Keep on top of your accounts and taxes, including value added tax (VAT), pay as you earn (PAYE) and national insurance (NI).

Chapter 11

Employing People

In This Chapter

▶ Finding the best employees for your business

▶ Deciding on motivations and rewards

▶ Keeping on the right side of employment law

*U*nless you intend to work on your own, when running a business you're involved in employing and motivating others to do what you want them to do. Even if you don't employ people full-time, or if you outsource some portion of your work to others, you have to choose who to give those tasks to, how to get the best out of people and how to reward their achievements.

In recent years with high levels of unemployment, even among well-qualified graduates, recruitment has been a buyer's market. But times change, and sometimes faster than you believed possible. Who'd have imagined in June 2013 that by September the number of jobs in real estate would have grown by 50,000 over the quarter to 562,000, the highest level since records began in 1978!

In any event, you'll never find it easy to get the best people to work for a new or small enterprise. Poor promotion prospects and low job security, both hallmarks of the sector, aren't exactly great pullers. So, you may find it better to work at getting your work proposition polished up.

In this chapter, I show you how to find the right people for your business, what to pay them and how to motivate and retain them.

Finding Great Employees

You may need to change your attitude to the whole hiring process. Most entrepreneurs dislike hiring employees, so they do it as little as possible and fit it around their other 'more important' tasks. You have lots of important factors to consider here: Do you need full-time or part-time employees, or a mix of both? How do you go about finding them? What exactly do you want your employees to do and how can you build that into a job description and your selection criteria?

Finding good staff is *the* number one job for a boss. You need good people to delegate to. And bringing new people into your current team can bring fresh and innovative ideas to stimulate everyone on to greater heights.

If you hope to grow your business, recruitment will become a routine task, like selling or monitoring cash flow, which you do every day. Furthermore, you need a budget to carry out recruitment and selection, just as you need a budget for equipment or rent. If you don't have a recruitment budget, you shouldn't be surprised if a task for which you've not allocated any money goes wrong.

Deciding on full- or part-timers

One important decision you need to make before you can start your search for staff is whether you need to hire a full-time person. Some good reasons may exist for not doing so. If, for example, the demand for your products is highly seasonal and has major peaks and troughs, keeping people on during slack periods may make no sense. This scenario may be the case if you're selling heating oil, where you can expect demand to peak in the autumn and tail off in the late spring because of variations in the weather. Other examples of seasonal fluctuations are increased sales of garden furniture and bar-beques in summer, and toys and luxury items before Christmas.

Using part-timers can open up whole new markets of job applicants, some-times of a higher quality than you may expect on the general job market. Highly skilled and experienced retired workers, or women who've given up successful careers to have a family, can be tempted back into temporary or part-time work. You may sometimes be able to have two members of staff sharing one job, each working part-time. You can also use this tactic to retain key staff members who want to leave full-time employment. This solution makes for continuity in the work, allows people to fit in their job around their personal circumstances and brings to the business talents that it may lose if it insists on full-time work.

Part-time work is more prevalent than many people think. Up to a third of all those in employment in certain countries are working part-time. Most are working in small firms whose flexibility in this area can often be a key strength over larger firms when it comes to recruiting and retaining employees.

You can find part-time staff using the same methods as for full-time employees, which I discuss in the next sections.

Recruiting and selecting

To make sure that you get great people into your business, follow the tips in these sections.

Reviewing your business goals

The starting point for any recruitment activity is a review of your short- and medium-term business goals. If you've recently updated your business plan (see Chapter 6), your goals should be fresh in your mind. If not then you need to do so. You need to be sure of exactly who you're going to recruit. For example, if you plan to sell and service software via your website, the people you need may be quite different from those required if you plan to supply physical products.

Defining the job (s)

Set out the scope and responsibilities of the job before you start recruiting. The job description should include the measurable outcomes that you expect, as well as a description of the tasks the person is to do. So, for a salesperson, spell out what the sales target is, how many calls you expect the person to make, what the customer retention target is and so on.

Too many small firms don't get round to preparing a job description until the person is in place, or worse still they don't have job descriptions at all. They argue that because jobs in the small business world have a short shelf-life because the company is growing and changing all the time, why bother? Well, if you don't know what you want the person you recruit to be doing, he won't know either.

Profiling the person

Flesh out your idea of the sort of person who can do the job well. If you're looking for a salesperson, communication skills and appearance are important factors to consider, as are the person's personal circumstances, because he may have to stay away from home frequently. Make sure that you pay regard to discrimination legislation when looking at candidates' personal circumstances (I cover this topic in the section 'Avoiding discrimination', later in this chapter).

As well as qualifications and experience, keep in mind the person's team skills and that all-too-rare attribute, business savvy.

Advertising the job

You can fill positions from outside your company but also from inside it – don't overlook your existing staff. You may be able to promote from within, even if you have to provide additional training. Also, your staff, suppliers or other business contacts may know of someone in their network who may be suitable.

You can advertise in newspapers and also on the Internet, which has a proliferation of recruitment websites and is a major source of staff.

The type of vacancy you have determines the medium that's best for you. The Internet may be right for design engineers, but a leaflet drop on a housing estate can be better when looking for shift workers.

Advertising for recruitment is subject to legal restrictions that vary from country to country. The laws most likely to apply are those relating to discrimination on the grounds of gender, race, age, religion or sexual orientation. Avoid sexist language or *he* or *she*, and select your words carefully to avoid stipulating characteristics that exclude potential applicants of a specific sex or race or in a particular age range. If in doubt, consult the Advertising Standards Authority (www.asa.org.uk) or take legal advice. Most restrictions apply to newspapers, magazines, radio and television; however, you're wise to include the Internet on that list.

Making your selection

When you have a number of applicants, your first job is to screen out the people who don't meet your specifications. Phone them if you need to clarify something; for example, to establish whether they've experience of a particular software package. Then interview your shortlist, perhaps using a test where relevant to your business. Many self-administered tests are available, designed for different types of work – I talk about tests in 'Testing to find the best', later in this chapter.

If the search process has been successful, you probably end up with more good applicants than you've time to interview. You need to evaluate all the applicants against cut-off criteria such as qualifications, experience, potential to grow with the job and travel time to work.

Set your criteria into a short-listing matrix – a table with criteria in the rows and candidates in the columns – and score candidates between one and three against each criterion, with three being a good rating and one being barely acceptable. (The Start Up Donut, a resource provided by the National Enterprise Network, has a number of useful recruitment templates at www.startupdonut. co.uk/startup/employees/hiring-employees.) You can set the cut-off point where applicants below a certain standard wouldn't be offered a job under any circumstances. Raise the standard if this cut-off point still leaves you with an overly large list of candidates to interview.

You need to thoroughly prepare before interviewing job applicants. When interviewing:

- ✔ **Have a pre-prepared list of the key questions you plan to ask.**

- ✔ **Allow the candidate to talk freely as long as he sticks to the point.** If the candidate strays from dealing with areas on your list, bring him back by asking your questions.

✔ **Give the applicant time to reply to your questions.** Don't fill every silence with another question, but if the silence persists for about ten seconds ask the candidate whether he'd like you to clarify the question.

✔ **Look for specific evidence of the skills you're seeking.** Without this evidence, you can't be sure that the candidate is suitable.

✔ **Ask questions that give you an impression of the candidate's motivation**, such as, 'What made you decide to . . . ?'

✔ **Avoid asking leading questions, and be sensitive to potential discriminatory questions** (for example, age, sex, religion and ethnic group).

✔ **Avoid dominating the interview.** The candidate should speak for at least 75 per cent of the interview.

✔ **Close the interview on a positive note.** Leave the candidate feeling that he's had a fair hearing and has no further questions to ask. Indicate approximately when the candidate is likely to hear from you and what the next stage in the selection process is.

You may want to let the applicants meet other people in the business. Doing so gives them a better feel for the company and you can get a second opinion on them. When Apple was developing the Macintosh, the entire Mac team was involved in every new appointment. Applicants spent a day with the team, and only when the team decided that people were suitable did they let them in on the project.

Ideally, you end up with at least three people whom you'd be happy to appoint. Offer the job to the best candidate, keeping the others in reserve. You must have a reserve in case your first choice lets you down, accepts but then changes his mind or quits or is fired after a week or two.

Always take up references, preferably on the phone. Don't accept 'testimonials' at face value.

Welcoming new employees

Having got the right people to join you, make sure that they become productive quickly and stay for a long time. The best way to ensure that they do is to have a comprehensive induction process showing them where everything is and the way things are done in your business. Keep them posted about developments – put them on the email circulation list straight away. Set them short-term objectives and monitor performance weekly, perhaps even daily at first, giving praise or help as required. Invite them to social events as appropriate.

TIP

Six good interview questions

A good interview question gives you the specific information that you seek, and helps you to form a view about how the candidate's mind works, the type of person he is and whether or not he'd fit into your business. Here are a few suggestions. You don't have to use them all, but review them to see which you can use in an interview and add questions of your own, based on the job and your reading of the candidate's CV. You can also check out Rob Yeung's *Answering Tough Interview Questions For Dummies* (Wiley) for many more great interviewing questions.

✔ **What are your greatest strengths and weaknesses?** You need to look behind the reply to see what the candidate really means. If a candidate claims to have no weaknesses, or admits only to a weakness that's just a thinly disguised strength, you should on your guard. Tie any claimed strengths back to specific achievements mentioned on the application form.

✔ **How could your current employer be more successful?** This question is designed to see whether the applicant has thought about the bigger picture of what his employer's core competence is or should be. You want people to do their jobs well, but you need every employee in a small firm to know what your mission and goals are, so they can play a full part in the business.

✔ **What was your greatest achievement and greatest failure?** Change the wording of this question depending on whether you're talking to a delivery driver or an export sales manager, but the thinking is the same. You need to find out whether the candidate has done anything to make a difference by using his own initiative. Look for measurable factors. Watch out for candidates who present their failures as someone else's fault because they may not be up to accepting personal responsibility.

✔ **What do you know about our business and why do you want to work here?** If a candidate can't answer this question well, you know that he isn't interested and that this post is just any old job to him.

✔ **What do you see yourself doing in three years' (or three months', if appropriate) time?** Here you're trying to find out about a candidate's ambitions and then see whether they're realistic and likely to be achievable in your business. If the candidate can't achieve these goals, then his stay with you might be a short one. Remember, you need low flyers too.

✔ **If you were to be hired, in which areas can you contribute immediately?** This question gives you an idea of how ready the applicant is now and what kind of short-term payback you might get from having him work for you. You also see how much he's absorbed about your business and the job on offer.

Testing to find the best

You can supplement the classic trio of selection methods – application letter or CV, interviews and references – with other tools that can improve your chances of getting the right candidate for most of the jobs you may want to fill. These tools are often clustered under the general heading of *psychometric tests,* although most of the tests themselves have less to do with psychology than with basic aptitude.

Although tests are popular and becoming more reliable, they're neither certain to get selection decisions right nor risk-free.

Dozens of commercial test publishers exist, producing collectively over 3,000 different tests. You can locate a test and guidance on which is best for your business needs through the British Psychological Society (www.psychtesting.org.uk) or the Chartered Institute of Personnel and Development (www.cipd.co.uk/hrsuppliers/listing/guide/assessment-psychometric-testing).

Exploring Other Ways of Recruiting

You don't have to do everything involved in recruiting employees yourself. You can find a recruitment consultant or use a government Job Centre to do much of the hard work for you. In fact, they may even be better at recruitment than you, because they recruit and select every day of the week. Research suggests that recruitment consultants, for example, are twice as successful at filling vacancies than are entrepreneurs on their own. You can also consider taking the job in question out of your business and paying someone else to do it. The following sections take you through your options.

Using agencies

Occasions may well occur when you feel that you're unable or unwilling to do the job of recruiting yourself. In such circumstances, you may find it useful to use a recruitment agency. The costs involved may sound high, but when you reckon up your internal costs you may find that an agency isn't that expensive. Doing the recruiting yourself can take several days of your time and that of others in your firm. If you're working on your own or with just one or two others, this work may be too great a distraction from other key tasks.

 The Recruitment and Employment Confederation (www.rec.uk.com) has a searchable database of recruitment consultants listed by postcode, region and business sector. Also check out the Online Recruitment Resource (www.onrec.com) for information and resources on many aspects of recruitment.

Using Job Centre Plus

Job Centre Plus is the government-run employment service that has professionally run offices with a growing number of staff specialising in small and medium enterprises (SMEs). Typically, the service operates out of 1,000 Job Centres based in towns where job seekers are likely to live. At any one time, it has around 400,000 job seekers on its database.

Job Centre Plus is particularly helpful to small firms with little experience of recruiting, because it offers a wide range of free help and advice on most matters concerned with employing people as well as signposting to other related services.

The Job Centre Plus range of services includes everything you expect of a recruitment consultant. But unlike other recruitment agencies, many of its services are free and in any event cost less than using any other external recruiter. You can find details of all services for employers at the Job Centre Plus website (www.gov.uk/jobcentre-plus-help-for-recruiters).

Recruiting over the Internet

The fastest-growing route to finding new job applicants is via the Internet. The number of websites offering employment opportunities has exploded in recent years. The advantages of Internet recruitment to both candidates and clients are obvious. Internet recruitment offers a fast, immediate and cheap service compared to more traditional methods of recruitment. A number of recruitment sites have established formidable reputations in Europe and the US. These sites include

- **Futurestep** (www.futurestep.com), which covers all job functions and industry sectors.

- **Monster** (www.monster.co.uk), which attracts approximately 100,000 visits per month and contains over a million CVs. Its vacancies cover every industry sector and regional area.

- **Web Recruit** (www.webrecruit.co.uk), which offers to fill your vacancy through its online service for £695, or give you your money back.

Another option is to have a job-listing section on your own website. This solution is absolutely free, although you're certain to be trawling in a really small pool. However, it may not matter if the right sort of people are already visiting your site. At least they know something about your products and services before they apply.

Outsourcing jobs

If you want to, you can probably buy in almost every part of the work you do from external sources. Other companies can design and host your website and you can rent other technology. External warehouses can hold stock of your product. Transport companies can deliver on your behalf. Third-party call centres can handle your customer services. Online banks compete with traditional banks to offer online payment processing. You can outsource almost every other aspect of business – from accounting and recruitment, to payroll and human resource services.

Motivating and Rewarding Employees

After you've recruited the staff you want, you need to manage them in the most suitable way for your business. Management is the art and science of getting people to do what you want them to do because *they* want to do it; something, of course, that is easier said than done.

Most entrepreneurs believe that their employees work for money and their key staff work for more money. Pay them enough and they'll jump through any hoop. In contrast, most research ranks pay as third or even fourth in the reasons for people coming to work.

If they don't necessarily work for money, why do people work in a particular organisation? I provide some of the answers in the following sections.

Getting the best out of employees

My best advice for getting the best out of your employees is: get to know everyone. This statement may sound insane in a small firm – after all, you almost certainly recruited them all in the first place. However, by observing and listening to your employees you can motivate them because you make them feel special.

The starting point in getting people to give of their best is to assess them as individuals and to recognise their specific needs and motivations. A person's age, gender or job influences these differences, as does the individual's personality. You need to tailor your actions to each person to get the best results.

Some practical tools and techniques can help you get the most out of your employees. For example:

✔ **Show an interest in people's work.** This interest has nothing to do with monitoring performance and more to do with managing by walking about, seeing everyone and talking with them as often as possible.

   If you employ fewer than five people, you need to spend time with each of them every day; up to ten people, spend time with them every week. After that, you should have managers doing much the same thing, but you still need to get around as often as possible.

✔ **Give praise as often as you can.** The rule is simple: minimise your reaction to bad results and maximise your appreciation of good results. Autocratic employers continually criticise and complain, finding only poor performance wherever they look. Criticism reinforces poor behaviour. Everyone wants to be recognised, and strangely enough people often prefer to be shouted at than ignored. So, if doing things wrong is the only way to get noticed in your company, that's what may well happen.

   If you do need to criticise, keep it constructive and lighten it with a favourable comment. For example, if an employee is making some progress but is short of being satisfactory, saying something like 'This is certainly an improvement, but we still have a way to go. Let's spend a little time together and I'll see whether we can't get to the bottom of what's holding you back' may produce a better level of motivation than just shouting out your criticism.

✔ **Create a no-blame culture.** Everything in business is a risk. To a greater or lesser extent, you delegate some of the responsibility for taking risks to your employees. But how should you react when the inevitable happens and things go wrong? If you jump up and down with rage, no one will ever take a risk again. They'll leave all the decisions to you and you'll become even more overworked. Good people will get highly demotivated and leave. If you take a sympathetic and constructive attitude to failure, you motivate and encourage employees to try again.

   You need to make clear that tolerance of mistakes has its limits and that repetition of the same mistake won't receive an equally tolerant reaction.

✔ **Reduce demotivation.** Often the problem isn't so much motivating people, but avoiding demotivating them! If you can keep off employees' backs, they're more likely to motivate themselves. After all, most people want the same things – a sense of achievement or challenge, recognition of their efforts, an interesting and varied job, opportunities for responsibility, advancement and job growth.

Dealing with difficult or demotivated employees

Difficult or demotivated people need prompt and effective managing. Dissatisfaction can spread quickly and lower other people's motivation levels. The first step is to identify the causes of the problem – is it to do with the employee or with the job itself? The problem may be brought about by illness, stress or a personality clash between people working together.

Whatever the cause, the initiative for re-motivating an employee has to come from you. However, the only reason for going through this effort is that the employee has delivered satisfactory results in the past or you believe he has the potential to do so, if you can only find the key.

Keeping motivation in the family

Over 80 per cent of small businesses are family businesses in which one or more relatives work in the organisation. Family businesses have both strengths and weaknesses when it comes to motivation. By being aware of these factors, you can exploit the former and do your best to overcome the latter to give your business a better chance of prospering.

The factors that motivate or demotivate family members can be different to those affecting non-family members.

The overwhelming strength of a family business is its different atmosphere and feel. A sense of belonging and common purpose usually leads to good motivation and performance. Another advantage is that a family firm has greater flexibility, because the unity of management and shareholders provides the opportunity to make quick decisions and to implement rapid change if necessary.

On the downside, several weaknesses exist. Although these weaknesses aren't unique to family businesses, family firms are particularly prone to them.

- ✔ **Unwillingness to change is the single most common cause of low motivation in family firms.** Family firms often do things the way they've always done them just because that's the way they've always done them. This attitude can lead to stagnation in the market place and failing confidence in investors. Resistance to change is exacerbated by diminishing vitality, as the founders grow old.

✔ **Family goals and commercial goals can come into conflict.** Unlike other businesses, family firms have additional objectives to their financial performance targets, such as building family reputation and status in the community; providing employment for the family; protecting family wealth; ensuring independence; and a dynastic wish to pass on a position, in addition to wealth, to the next generation. However, superimposing these family values on the business can lead to difficulties. For example, nepotism may lead to employment of family members at a level beyond their competence, or a salary above their worth. This unfairness can lead to discontent and be demotivational for non-family members.

✔ **Conflict may exist between growth and ownership.** Families prefer majority ownership of a small company to minority holdings in a big company where they're answerable to outside shareholders. A dilemma that all family managers face is growing the company, keeping purely commercial goals in mind at whatever risk to family control, or subordinating the firm's welfare to family constraints. This dilemma affects all areas of the business, from recruitment through to management.

✔ **The impact and career prospects of non-family employees may be limited.** At management level, family pride sometimes doesn't allow a situation where its members are subordinate to an outsider – even if the outsider is a better person for the job. Also, reliance on family management to the exclusion of input from outsiders may starve a growing firm of new ideas. A family firm may become inward looking, insensitive to the messages of the marketplace, unreceptive to outside ideas and unwilling to recruit competent outside managers. None of these factors is likely to be motivational to others in the business.

A family firm must address these problems to avoid all the effort it puts into motivating employees being seen as a cynical deception. Having a clear statement of family policy on the employment of family members, succession and ownership can be helpful. If these things are in place, non-family members can buy into this policy or not join the company in the first place.

Rewarding achievements

Different types of work have different measurable outcomes. You need to identify the outcomes you want and arrive at a scale showing the base rate of pay and payment above that base for achieving particular objectives. Different types of 'payment by results' schemes are in common use, and you need to make sure that you pick the right mix of goals and rewards.

Setting pay scales

People don't come to work just for money, but they certainly won't come if you don't pay them, and they won't stay and be motivated to give of their best if you don't give them the right pay. But how much is the right amount? Get it too low and you impair your ability to attract and retain productive and reliable people capable of growing as your business grows. But pay too much and your overheads rise so high that you become uncompetitive. Small firms face the real danger of a wage bill that represents their largest single business expense.

The ground rules for pay aren't complicated but they're important:

- ✔ Pay only what you can afford. Don't sink the company with a wage bill that it can't meet.

- ✔ Make sure that pay is fair and equitable and that everyone sees it as such.

- ✔ Let people know how you arrive at your pay scales.

- ✔ See that pay scales for different jobs reflect the relative importance of the job and the skills required.

- ✔ Ensure that your pay scales are in line with the law on minimum wage requirements. The UK has a *statutory minimum wage* whose amount is governed by the age of the employee and whether an employee is undergoing training. The hourly rate changes over time, so you need to keep abreast of the latest rates (`www.gov.uk/national-minimum-wage-rates` has information on current rules in this area).

- ✔ Ensure that your pay scales are competitive with those of other employers in your region or industry. PayScale (`www.payscale.com/hr/index`) is a useful website for getting accurate, real-time information on pay scales.

Here are a few ways to find out the going rate for a job:

- ✔ Read articles on pay, as well as job advertisements on the Internet, in local papers and in the relevant trade journals. You may have to correct some pay rates to allow for variations. For example, pay rates for similar jobs are often much higher in or near major cities than they are in rural areas.

- ✔ Talk to your chamber of commerce or trade association, some of which publish salary surveys, and to other local employers and business owners in your network.

- ✔ Contact employment agencies, including those run by the government. They're usually a bit ahead of the rest of the market in terms of pay information. Other employers know only what they're paying their present staff. Recruitment agencies know what you have to pay to get your next employee.

Deciding the pay rates of people who work for you arbitrarily may appear to be one of the perks of working for yourself. But inconsistent pay rates quickly upset people and staff members tend to jump ship at the first opportunity.

Matching pay to performance

You may want to add to people's salaries by rewarding them with money or benefits for the level of performance they achieve. I discuss various reward approaches in this section, which all follow the same ground rules for matching pay to performance:

- ✔ Make the rules clear so that everyone knows how the reward system works.
- ✔ Make the goals to be achieved specific and if possible quantifiable.
- ✔ Make the reward visible so that everyone knows what each person or team receives.
- ✔ Make the reward matter. It has to be worthwhile and commensurate with the effort involved.
- ✔ Make the reward fair, so that people believe you've calculated it correctly.
- ✔ Make the goals realistic, because if you set the target too high no one will try to achieve it.
- ✔ Make the reward happen quickly.

Paying a commission

Paying commission is perhaps the easiest reward system, but it really only works for those directly involved in selling. A *commission* is a payment based in some way on the value of sales that the individual or team concerned has secured.

You have to make sure that the order is actually delivered or executed before you pay any commission and you may even want to make sure that the customer has paid up. However, as with all rewards, you must keep the timescale between doing the work and getting the reward as short as practicably possible, otherwise people forget what the money is for.

Base the commission on your gross profit (the value of sales less the cost of generating those sales) rather than your sales turnover – otherwise you can end up rewarding salespeople for generating unprofitable business.

Awarding bonuses

A *bonus* is a reward for successful performance, usually paid in a lump sum related as closely as possible to the results that an individual, team or the business as a whole has obtained. In general, bonuses are tied to results, so that how an individual contributed directly to the result achieved is less obvious. For example, a company bonus may be paid to everyone if the firm as a whole achieves a certain level of output. Keeping everyone informed about how the firm is performing towards achieving that goal may well be motivational, but the exact role that, say, a cleaner or office worker has in helping to attain that goal isn't easy to assess – not as easy as it is to calculate a salesperson's commission.

You can pay bonuses periodically or as a one-off payment for a specific achievement.

Sharing profits

Profit sharing involves giving a specific share of the company's profit to its employees. The share of the profits can be different for different jobs, length of service or seniority. This type of reward has the great merit of focusing everyone's attention on the firm's primary economic goal – to make money. One or more employees can be performing well while others drag down the overall performance. In theory, in such circumstances, the high-performing staff put pressure on the others to come up to the mark.

If profits go up, people get more; but profits can also go down, which can be less attractive. Also, the business can miss profit targets for reasons outside of employees' direct control. If your company depends on customers or supplies from overseas, for example, and the exchange rate moves against you, profits, and hence profit-related pay, can dip sharply. However unfair this situation may seem to a receptionist who's been hoping for extra cash to pay for a holiday, it shows the hard reality of business. If you think that your employees are adult enough to take that fact on board, then profit sharing can be a useful way to reward staff.

Sharing ownership

Share option schemes give employees the chance to share in the increase in value of a company's shares as it grows and prospers. The attraction of turning employees into shareholders is that doing so gives them a long-term stake in the business, hopefully makes them look beyond short-term issues and ensures their long-term loyalty. Of course, unwelcome side effects can occur if the value of the business goes down rather than up. Share schemes also have important tax implications that you need to take into account. You can find out all about these implications on the HM Revenue and Customs website (www.hmrc.gov.uk/shareschemes).

Giving skill and competence awards

You can give a skill or competence award when an employee reaches a certain level of ability. These awards aren't directly tied to an output such as improved performance, but you must believe that raising the skill or competence in question ultimately leads to better business results.

The award itself can be cash, gift certificates, extra days of holiday, a trip to a show or sports event or whatever else your employees may appreciate. Bottles of wine always seem to be well received!

Creating a menu of benefits

A *benefit* is defined as any form of compensation that's not part of an employee's basic pay and isn't tied directly to his performance in his job. Non-salary benefits such as a pension or changes in working conditions can also play a part in keeping people on your side. A wide range of other perks is on offer to employees, ranging from being allowed to wear casual dress to on-site childcare. Other benefits available in some organisations include personal development training, company product discounts, flexible hours, telecommuting and fitness facilities.

You're now obliged to consider flexible working if an employee requests it and has sufficient reason, and setting up some form of pension scheme looks set to become compulsory for most businesses soon.

Staying on the Right Side of Employment Law

All businesses operate within a legal framework whose elements the owner-manager must be aware of. The areas I cover in the following sections summarise only a few of the key legal issues. Different types of business may have to consider different legal issues, and employment law itself is dynamic and subject to revision and change.

The government website www.gov.uk/browse/employing-people provides the definitive, up-to-date guidance on current employment legislation, covering every aspect from recruiting to dismissing staff and everything in between. The Advisory, Conciliation and Arbitration Service (ACAS; www.acas.org.uk) and the British Safety Council (www.britsafe.org) are useful organisations that can help with aspects of employment issues. Emplaw (www.emplaw.co.uk) is a website covering basic British employment law information and can direct you to a lawyer in your area who specialises in the aspect of employment law you're concerned with.

Keeping employment records

You need to keep records about your employees, both individually and collectively. Keeping records makes the process of employing people run smoothly. Some of the data you need to keep is a legal requirement, such as information on accidents. Some of the information is also invaluable in any dispute with an employee; for example, in a case of unfair dismissal.

The individual employee information you retain should include

- ✔ Application form
- ✔ Interview record and results of any selection tests used
- ✔ Job history, including details of promotions and assignments
- ✔ Current and past job descriptions
- ✔ Current pay and bonus details and a record of the amount and date of any changes
- ✔ Details of skills and competences
- ✔ Education and training records, with details of courses attended
- ✔ Details of performance assessments and appraisals
- ✔ Absence, lateness, accident, medical and disciplinary records, together with details of any formal warnings and suspensions
- ✔ Holiday entitlement
- ✔ Pension contribution data
- ✔ Termination record giving date, details of exit interview and suitability for re-engagement
- ✔ Copies of any correspondence between you and the employee

Collective information should include

- ✔ Numbers of staff, grades and job titles
- ✔ Absenteeism, staff turnover and lateness statistics
- ✔ Accident rates
- ✔ Records on age and length of service
- ✔ Wage and salary structures
- ✔ Employee costs
- ✔ Overtime statistics showing hours worked and costs
- ✔ Records of grievances and disputes
- ✔ Training records showing how many person days have been devoted to training and how much that's cost
- ✔ Gender, ethnic and disability profiles

Employees have three basic rights over the information an employer keeps in their employment records:

- ✔ To be able to obtain access to their personal data
- ✔ To be able to claim damages for losses caused by the use of inaccurate data or the unauthorised use of data, or by loss or destruction of data
- ✔ To apply to the courts if necessary for rectification or erasure of inaccurate data

These rights mean that an employee is entitled to gain access to his personal data at reasonable intervals without undue delay or expense. This request must legally be put in writing, although you may choose not to insist on this, and you must provide the information within 40 days of the request.

Preparing contracts of employment

You have to give an employee a written statement of certain terms and conditions of his employment within two months of starting work for you.

The list of terms that form part of this statement include the following:

- ✔ The employee's full name
- ✔ When the employee started working for you
- ✔ How and how much you pay your employee
- ✔ Whether pay is weekly or monthly
- ✔ The hours you expect the employee to work
- ✔ The number of days' holiday the employee is allowed, including public holidays, and how that holiday is accumulated
- ✔ The employee's job title or a brief description of his work
- ✔ Where you expect the employee to work and what conditions apply if you expect him to work elsewhere
- ✔ Whether you intend the employment to be permanent or, if it's for a fixed term, when it starts and finishes
- ✔ Details of who manages the employee and who he can talk to if he has any dispute with that person
- ✔ Any terms and conditions relating to sickness or injury, including any provision for sick pay
- ✔ Any terms and conditions relating to pensions and pension schemes
- ✔ Any disciplinary rules applicable to the employee

✔ The period of notice required, which increases with length of service; a legal minimum of one week's notice per year of service is required up to a maximum of twelve weeks (express terms in the contract may override this)

The job description forms the cornerstone of the contract of employment that exists between employer and employee. However, the contract is rarely a single document and may not even be completely documented. A contract comes into existence as soon as someone accepts an offer of paid employment, even if both offer and acceptance are only verbal. In practice, the most important contractual document may be the letter offering the person the job, and detailing the salary and other basic employment conditions. Many employers don't document the contractual relationship with employees properly and end up with disputes. A contract of employment consists of four sets of terms:

✔ **Express terms:** Terms specifically agreed to between employer and employee, whether in writing or not.

✔ **Implied terms:** Terms considered to be so obvious that they don't need spelling out. These terms include such matters as the employee complying with reasonable instructions and taking care of business property and equipment. For the employer, these terms can include taking reasonable care of the employee and paying him for work done.

✔ **Incorporated terms:** Terms from outside sources, most commonly from trade union agreements, which are included in the contract.

✔ **Statutory terms:** These include any work requirements laid down by law – safety regulations, for example.

The government provides an online toolkit to help first-time employers with a step-by-step guide to hiring staff: www.gov.uk/government/news/help-in-hiring-your-first-employee.

Working legal hours

Although the owner of a business may be content to work all hours, the law strictly governs the amount of time employees can be asked to put in. The Working Time Regulations apply to any staff over the minimum school-leaving age. This group includes temporary workers, home workers and people working for you overseas.

As an employer, you must keep records that show you comply with the working-time limits and that you've given night workers the opportunity for a health assessment.

This website has information on everything you need regarding working hours: www.gov.uk/maximum-weekly-working-hours/overview.

Granting leave

Occasions are bound to arise when you're obliged to give your staff time off work other than their usual holidays or when they're unwell. You have to meet statutory obligations of course. Otherwise you may not have to pay them when these occasions occur, but you do have to respect their right to be absent for compassionate or sickness reasons. And if they're off sick, always meet up with them when they return, just to make sure that all's well and that no underlying problems exist.

Protecting parents

Employees who become parents naturally or by adopting a child are entitled to paid time off and other benefits, including Statutory Maternity, Paternity and Adoption Pay. The employee may also be entitled to have his job back at some later date.

Work Smart, a Trade Union Council-run website, has a full description of the latest rules and regulations on these ever-changing topics. (Go to www.worksmart.org.uk, click on Your Rights and then Working Life and Family-friendly Policies.)

Recognising emergency leave

Employees have the right to reasonable unpaid leave where their *dependants* – spouses, children, parents, other people living in an employee's house (except lodgers) and others who rely on an employee in emergencies, such as elderly neighbours – are affected by

- ✔ Illness, injury, assault or childbirth
- ✔ Breakdown in childcare/other care arrangements
- ✔ The consequences of a death
- ✔ A serious incident at school or during school hours

To take this leave, your employee should give notice as soon as reasonably practical, giving the reason for, and likely duration of, his absence. The legislation doesn't define *reasonable* time off, but usually one or two days should suffice.

Avoiding discrimination

By and large business owners can employ whoever they want. However, when setting the criteria for a particular job or promotion, discriminating on the grounds of sex, race, age, marital status, religious beliefs, sexual orientation or union membership is usually illegal. Regulations also prevent you from treating part-time employees less favourably than comparable full-time employees – that is, someone doing broadly similar work and with a similar level of skills and qualifications.

Discrimination starts right from when vacancies are advertised – you can't include such phrases as 'women required' or 'young person sought', or 'no blacks' or 'no whites'. The rules extend to the pay, training and promotion of those who work for you.

Victimising someone who's complained about being discriminated against is illegal. Sexual harassment is also a form of discrimination, defined as the 'unwanted conduct of a sexual nature or other conduct based on sex affecting the dignity of men and women at work'. This description can include unwelcome physical, verbal or non-verbal conduct. Finally, you mustn't include in your reason for dismissing an employee that he's a member of a particular minority group protected by law.

To avoid discriminating in your employment, you need to ensure that all your policies and procedures meet the following criteria:

- ✔ They're applied equally to all who work for you irrespective of sex, race and so forth.
- ✔ They don't limit the proportion of one group who comply compared with another.
- ✔ They don't disadvantage any individual.
- ✔ They can be objectively justified. For example, no argument exists when being a man or a woman is a genuine occupational qualification – for example, for the purpose of a particular photographic modelling assignment or an acting role. The same is true when you've a part-time vacancy so have no need of a full-time employee.

To make sure that you're not discriminating, follow this six-point checklist:

- ✔ Ensure that your business has an equal opportunities policy. You can find a sample policy on the Equality and Human Rights website (www.equalityhumanrights.com).
- ✔ Train staff in equal opportunities policies.
- ✔ Keep records of interviews showing why you rejected candidates.
- ✔ Ensure that you take complaints about discrimination seriously, fully investigate them and address any problems that emerge.
- ✔ Conduct staff surveys to help determine where discrimination may exist within your business.
- ✔ Examine the payroll – pay should reflect employees' job titles, not their gender.

The Equality Act 2010 is the law that protects people from discrimination in the workplace and in wider society. Under the law, organisations that do business with any public body – government, local government, hospital trust, school, university and so forth – as well as the public themselves have to have an equality policy and equality objectives. You can find out more about who's protected from discrimination, the types of discrimination under the law and what action people can take if they feel they've been unfairly discriminated against at www.gov.uk/equality-act-2010-guidance. Visit www.bl.uk/aboutus/stratpolprog/diversity/equdivpol to see an example of a public sector policy. Also check out VentureNavigator, a free equality monitoring form (available online, at www.venturenavigator.co.uk/content/539).

Keeping healthy and safe

By law you have to provide a reasonably safe and healthy environment for your employees, visitors and members of the public who may be affected by what you do. This obligation applies to the premises you work from and to the work itself. An inspector has the right to enter your premises to examine it and enforce legal requirements if your standards fall short in any way.

When you have employees you must take some or all of the following measures, depending on the number of employees. A prudent employer should take all these measures whether or not the law requires them. Doing so sets a standard of behaviour that's common in the very best firms.

- ✔ Inform the organisation responsible for health and safety at work for your business of where you are and what you do. For most small businesses, this organisation is the Environmental Health Department of your local authority (you can find contact details in your local telephone directory). The Health and Safety Executive website (www.hse.gov.uk) has a section devoted to small firms, covering both regulations and advice on making your work environment safer.

- ✔ Get employer's liability insurance to cover you for any physical injury or disease your employees may suffer as a result of their work. The amount of coverage must be at least £2 million and the insurance certificate must be displayed at all your places of work.

You, as an employer, can in turn expect your employees

- ✔ To take reasonable care of their own health, safety at work and of other people who may be affected by their acts or omissions

- ✔ To co-operate with the employer in ensuring that they comply with the requirements imposed by the relevant statutory provisions

Chapter 12

Operating Effectively

. . . .

In This Chapter

▶ Selecting premises

▶ Opting to make it yourself or buy from outside

▶ Choosing and using suppliers

▶ Deciding on key business advisers

▶ Dealing with cyber security

. . . .

*A*lthough you've decided to go into business, it doesn't necessarily mean that you have to make your own product, carry out every aspect of the business yourself or even work from dedicated premises. The best use of your time may be to outsource the most time-consuming and least valuable aspect of your business. For example, I bet you can't get a package from Milton Keynes to Penzance in under 24 hours and see change from a £20 note! But a delivery service can.

Whether you buy in most of what you sell, or just components and assemble them yourself, you have to choose between the dozens if not hundreds of suppliers in the market. Price alone is rarely a good enough guide to which supplier to choose. If they can't deliver on time, price is irrelevant. You may also find it expedient to consider their green credentials and how those fit with yours.

You have to face risks in your business, including those in areas you might not at first consider, such as cybersecurity, and not all of which you want to or are able to shoulder yourself. For these, you have to make choices about insurance types and levels to cover you. Even if you're a director of your limited company, some of those company risks fall on you and the consequences of getting things wrong can be serious, even catastrophic.

Fortunately, you don't have to face all these decisions alone. Plenty of advisers are there to help. This chapter looks at the decisions and risks involved in running a business and helps you to choose someone to assist you through the minefield.

Proposing Premises

If you can avoid taking on premises when starting up your business, perhaps by working from home, so much the better. (See 'Working from home' in Chapter 3 for more information.) If that's not an option, read on.

Buying or *leasing*, the term used for renting a business premises, entails navigating through a number of important and often complex regulations, as well as the practical nuts and bolts of finding, fitting out and settling in to the premises. These regulations go way beyond the scope of the physical premises into areas such as opening hours and health and safety.

The key decisions to make are how much space you need, whether you want to rent or buy and what equipment you need to fit into your premises.

Calculating requirements

The first decision to make is how much space you actually require and what other facilities you need. The space is the easy bit. You can take the steam age route and make cut-out scale models of the various items you need – chairs, desks, tables and so forth – and set them out on scaled drawings of the premises. By a process of trial and error, you should be able to arrive at an arrangement that's flexible, convenient to work in and meets the needs of customers and staff alike. You can also take the high-tech route and use a software program to save on the scissor work. Try Google's free program Sketchup (www.sketchup.com), a 3D-modelling software tool that's easy to learn and simple to use. Alternatively, for around £90 you can buy a package from Smart Draw (www.smartdraw.com/specials/officeplanning. asp); you can try it for free before you buy.

Finding the right premises

As soon as you know where you want to be, how much space you need and any special requirements, you can hit the trail visiting local estate agents, reading the local press and generally keeping your ear to the ground. You can, of course, get someone else to do much of the donkey work for you and put your valuable time to more productive work such as finding customers or raising dosh. Office Planet (www.office-planet.net) and Official Space (www.officialspace.co.uk), for example, provide free office-finding services. You can search through their databases of available properties and create a shortlist of solutions that meet your needs, or simply call an adviser.

If you're looking for a workshop, warehouse or showroom that doesn't have to be in the centre of a town, Ashtenne (www.ashtenne-online.co.uk; an Industrial Fund Unit Trust that owns 500 industrial estates around the UK ranging in size from 500 to 50,000 square feet) and Comproperty (www.comproperty.com) operate online databases for buying, selling or leasing commercial property and businesses in the UK.

For retail premises, Shop Property (www.shopproperty.co.uk) and Daltons Business (www.daltonsbusiness.com) have online databases of shops for sale and rent, searchable by price, size and location throughout the UK.

Renting or owning?

This question is another imponderable one. Buying a premises gives you all sorts of advantages, not least that you can make any alterations you want (if the law allows) without going cap in hand to a landlord, and of course no one can kick you out. On the downside, you have to invest a substantial amount of money upfront and you have to sell up if you outgrow the premises. You of course enjoy any rise in the value of the property, but if you really believe that property is a better bet than investing in your own business, perhaps you should rethink your business proposition.

Renting isn't without its problems, however. You have to take on the property for a number of years, and even if you sublet with the landlord's permission, you're liable for rent for the full period should the person you sublet to default. Rents are reviewed, almost invariably upwards, every three to seven years. You're expected to keep the property in good repair and return it to the landlord at the end of the lease period in the condition it was in at the outset. That can prove expensive if the landlord doesn't share your opinion that any changes you've made constitute an improvement.

Net Lawman (www.netlawman.co.uk/ia/business-property-lease) provides free advice and information to both landlords and tenants about business leases. Also, the Department for Communities and Local Government website has a guide to the law governing commercial property leases (www.gov.uk/government/publications/renewing-and-ending-business-leases-a-guide-for-tenants-and-landlords).

Sorting out equipment

After you've found the right premises, you need to furnish them. A number of items such as furniture, shelving, filing and computing equipment are common to many types of business. Some require more specialised items, including cookers, commercial printers and machine tools. Only in the most exceptional cases should a start-up business buy new equipment. Aside from the basic economics – new may cost two to three times as much as used – until you get trading, you've no real idea of what you actually need.

The following are useful sites, apart from the ubiquitous eBay, on which to search out second-hand business equipment:

✔ Auction Guide (www.auctionguide.com)

✔ Greasy Machines (www.greasymachines.com)

✔ MM Börse Online (www.gebrauchtmaschinen.de/en/1284) for used machines

✔ Office Furniture Desks and Chairs (www.officefurnituredesksand chairs.co.uk)

Searching for suppliers of new products is best done using a business-to-business directory, such as those provided by Business Magnet (www. businessmagnet.co.uk), Kelly Search (www.kellysearch.co.uk) and Kompass (http://gb.kompass.com), which between them have global databases of over 2 million industrial and commercial companies in 200 countries, listing over 200,000 product categories. You can search by category, country and brand name.

Taking the Make-or-Buy Decision

If your business involves making or constructing products, you should address the issue of whether to make the product yourself or to buy it, ready to sell or as components for assembly.

Making it yourself – pros and cons

If you decide to make the whole of your product yourself, or at least a major part of it, you need to decide exactly what plant and equipment you need and how many pieces you can produce at what rate. Then you have to consider such factors as what engineering support, if any, you need and how to monitor and control quality.

The great advantage of manufacturing your product yourself is that you have control over every aspect of the business and its products. You can, in theory at least, step up production to meet extra demand, make minor modifications to a product to meet a customer's particular needs and have the resources in-house to develop prototypes of new products to respond to changing market conditions.

However, some possible disadvantages of making products yourself in a start-up business are

- The large outlay of money needed from day one

- The deflection of management time, mostly your own, to looking inwards at processes rather than outwards at the market place

- Established manufacturers being better and cheaper than you are at various elements of the production process – after all, they've been at it longer than you and have the benefit of being farther up the learning curve and farther down the cost curve than any start-up can realistically expect to be

Outsourcing – a low investment option

Outsourcing, contracting out the production of your product or the supply of your service, has become a buzzword. Thousands of articles and hundreds of books have been written on the subject and you can attend countless related seminars. An Internet search on *outsourcing* brings up more links than you can ever hope to handle.

Outsourcing work means that you don't always have to take on premises big enough to meet your peak requirements, as this story shows. Lean and mean were key watchwords for Nick Jenkins, the Cranfield MBA founder of Moonpig, the online greetings cards business. Capacity proved problematic in the early years because of the ebb and flow of Moonpig's business. The business typically sold up to 15,000 cards a day in the run-up to Christmas, for example, but at other times of the year it sold only between 1,500 and 2,000 cards a day. So Nick had to be flexible and creative when it came to office space. At Moonpig's busiest times, when its office was near capacity with people stuffing envelopes, many other employees worked from home to free up desk space. This outsourcing strategy clearly worked. Moonpig now accounts for over 90 per cent of the online greetings card market and sells more than 10 million cards a year (which, if laid out end to end, would stretch from London to Moscow!). In July 2011 the company was bought out by PhotoBox, a digital photo service provider, for £120 million.

One way to set the boundaries for outsourcing is to decide what you're good at, and then outsource everything else. In other words, focus your company on your core competency, and 'stick to the knitting'. That logic is sound in theory, and to a certain degree in practice, but like everything else you can take it too far. The key is to understand your business and its goals and decide how outsourcing can help you attain them.

Some things are central to your business and you shouldn't outsource them, at least at the outset. You need to keep an eye (your eye!) on such things until you have them fully under control. These things include cash-flow management and most aspects of customer relations. Later on you may consider, for example, outsourcing collecting cash from customers to an invoice discounter or factoring service (which I talk about in Chapter 8), which may have better processes in place to handle larger volumes of invoices than you can afford.

Some tasks make sense to outsource initially and bring them in-house later. If you plan to offer a product or service that you're not expert at, you may benefit from contracting out this core function, at least until you gain confidence and expertise. For example, if you plan to start an upmarket soup kitchen but aren't experienced at making soup, you can turn to an established soup chef to cook for you. The outside expert charges you a premium, but for that you get significant value – the contractor understands your requirements, produces the product and delivers it to your site with little risk to you. If the quality is wrong, you send it back. If you need more product, you order it. You don't have to wait for your new equipment to arrive before you can step up production.

Setting quality standards

Quality may well be, like beauty, in the eye of the beholder, but you're wise to set clear standards that you expect every aspect of your end product or service to conform to. You need to set these standards whether you make in-house or outsource.

A number of well-regarded quality standards may help you monitor and control your quality. The BS EN ISO 9000 series provides perhaps the best-known standards. They can ensure that your operating procedure delivers a consistent and acceptable standard of products or services. If you're supplying to large firms, they may insist on your meeting one of these quality standards, or on auditing your premises to satisfy themselves. The British Standards Institute (www.bsigroup.com) can provide details of quality standards.

A number of commercial organisations provide user-friendly guidelines and systems to help you reach the necessary standard. Searching the Web using keywords such as 'Quality standards' or 'Measurement' brings up some useful sites.

Choosing a Supplier

Selecting the wrong supplier for your business can be a stressful and expensive experience. This section offers pointers on how to find a supplier and make sure that your supplier can meet your business needs. (Chapter 4 talks about similar issues, so you may want to consult that chapter too.)

Look for value in the service a supplier offers rather than just the price you pay. Here are the key questions you should ask about any prospective suppliers to your business:

- ✔ Do they offer a guaranteed level of service?

- ✔ Do they have a strong business track record and evidence of financial stability? Check out their accounts at Companies House (`www.companies house.gov.uk`).

- ✔ Do they have clients in your business sector and local area?

- ✔ Can they provide you with client references and impartial evidence of their quality? You should check out references to make sure that suppliers are reliable and can meet deadlines.

- ✔ Can they meet rushed deliveries in case of emergency?

- ✔ What level of after-sales support do they provide?

- ✔ Do they offer value for money when compared to competitive services?

- ✔ Do you think that you can enjoy working with them? If so, the relationship is going to be more productive.

Thomas's Register (`www.thomasnet.com`), Kelly's (`www.kelly.co.uk`) and Kompass (`http://gb.kompass.com`) between them have details on over 1.6 million British companies and hundreds of thousands of US and Canadian manufacturers, covering 23 million key products and 744,000 trade and brand names. If someone makes a particular product, you can find their details in one of these directories.

Some free search facilities are available online. Your local business library also holds hard copies of directories and may even have Internet access to all the key data you'll ever need on suppliers.

Evaluating trading terms

Buying is the mirror image of selling. Remember that as you negotiate with suppliers, who are essentially selling their services. Even if they have no deliberate intention to mislead, you may be left thinking that a supplier isn't committed to doing what you want in the way you want it. So get any agreement in writing.

The starting point in establishing trading terms is to make sure that suppliers can actually do what you want and what they claim to be able to do. You do so by checking them out and taking up references.

The next crunch point is price. As a small business, you may feel you're fairly short on buying power. That may be true, but room for negotiation always exists. All suppliers want more customers and sometimes they want them badly enough to shift on price.

If you do your research by contacting several suppliers so that you've a good idea of the price parameters before you talk seriously to any supplier, set yourself a target discount price and start negotiating 10 per cent or so below that. In any negotiation you may well have to give ground, so if you start at your target price you end up paying more.

The supplier's opening claim is likely to be that it never negotiates on price. Don't be deterred. Many ways exist to get your costs down without changing the headline price. Here are a few examples:

- Allowing a certain percentage of free product, along the line of a free bottle of wine with every half case, can nudge the price down by15 per cent.

- Agreeing to hold stock in the supplier's warehouse saves you from the need to rent your own warehouse.

- Benefiting from an extra 30 days' credit eases your cash flow and may be the difference between growing your young business and standing still.

You need to examine all the contract terms, such as delivery, payment terms, risk and ownership (the point at which title to the goods passes from the maker to you), warranties and guarantees, termination, arbitration rules if you fall out and the governing law in dealings with overseas suppliers. These issues are the same ones you deal with when you set your own terms of trade, so turn to Chapter 5 for a detailed review.

Building a relationship

To ensure that you handle any problems you have with your suppliers effectively, you need to build relationships with them. That means talking to them and keeping them informed of your plans and intentions. If you're planning a sales drive, new price list or other similar activity, let suppliers know so that they can anticipate the possible impact on them. Keeping them informed doesn't commit you to buying extra product, or indeed any product beyond what you've contracted for, but it does make your suppliers feel part of the value chain between you and your customers. By involving suppliers, you're indirectly encouraging them to commit to helping you meet your goals.

Many businesspeople pay too much for the goods or services they purchase, which shows up as lower gross margins and poorer performance than the competition. Many of these people don't raise the issue with their supplier but instead start looking elsewhere for an alternative source. Don't make this mistake. More often than not, your supplier will prefers to discuss the terms of your arrangement than lose your business. In many cases, you both end up with a better deal than before.

Buying online

Buying online has a range of important benefits for a small firm. Big companies have buying departments whose job is to find the best suppliers in the world with the most competitive prices and trading terms. A small firm can achieve much the same at a fraction of the cost by buying online – doing so can lower costs, save scarce management time and get supplies just in time, hence speeding up cash flow and reducing stock space, along with many other benefits.

The range of goods and services that you can buy online is vast and getting larger. As well as office supplies you can buy computer equipment, software, motor vehicles, machine tools, vending equipment, insurance, hotel accommodation, airline tickets, business education, building materials, tractors, work clothing and cleaning equipment, to name but a few.

You can use several methods to buy business supplies online. I explain the most useful methods in the following sections.

Joining an e-buying group

Online buying groups go by various names, including trading hubs, e-marketplaces, online communities, aggregators and cost reducers.

Buying in this way allows you to collect information from potential vendors quickly and easily. These online markets gather multiple suppliers in one place so that you can comparison shop without leaving your office or picking up the phone. For example, if you need to buy toner cartridges for your office laser printer, you can go to an online marketplace and search the catalogues of multiple office supplies vendors, buying from the one that offers the best deal. You can also use the same method for bigger-ticket items such as office furniture or photocopiers. No more calling a handful of potential suppliers, sitting through sales presentations and negotiating prices. Comparison shopping saves you time for more valuable business activities and gets you a better rate.

Buying Groups (`www.buyinggroups.co.uk`) offers an online guide to British buying groups and purchasing consortia. Also, Enrich (`http://enrich.com/what-we-do/procurement-in-a-box`) offers a service to facilitate collaboration with other organisations to leverage purchasing volumes and so secure more competitive prices and terms.

Going in for auctions

You can buy supplies online through online auctions. The advantage is that you pay only as much as you're willing to. The disadvantage is that you may have to wait for the right deal to come up.

Auctions are a great way to significantly reduce the funds you need to purchase items on your business *wish list* – items you want now or need eventually but that aren't a current necessity. (See 'Sorting out equipment', earlier in this chapter.)

Bartering online

You can avoid using hard cash by taking advantage of online barter exchanges. These e-exchanges let you trade your company's products and services for those of other businesses. You can swap ad space for accounting services, or consulting for computers. For start-ups or cash-strapped companies, barter can be an effective way to get products or services you may otherwise be unable to afford. An organisation that can help you get started with bartering is Bartercard (www.bartercard.co.uk).

Minimising Risk and Assessing Liability

As the saying goes, no pain, no gain. Some of the pain is routine and you can allow for it in the normal course of events. Employees come and go, you have to pay suppliers, you have to move into and out of premises. But some events are less easy to predict and can have serious if not disastrous consequences for your business. What happens if the warehouse burns down or your pizzas send a few customers to hospital?

You can't be expected to know that such things will happen ahead of time, but you can be reasonably sure that *something* will happen *sometime*. The laws of probability point to it and the law of averages gives you a basis for estimating your chances. You have to be prepared to deal with the unexpected, which is what this section helps you do.

Insurance forms a guarantee against loss. You must weigh up to what extent your business assets are exposed to risk and what effect a particular event may have on the business if it occurs.

One simple way to assess risk is to get an insurance quote to cover the risk. Insuring against an earthquake in London is cheap, but the same cover in Istanbul costs a significant sum, which tells you a lot.

Insurance is an overhead, producing no benefit until a calamity occurs. How much insurance to carry is therefore a commercial decision, and although the temptation exists to minimise cover, you should resist it. You must carry some insurance cover, by employment law or as an obligation that a mortgager imposes.

Establish your insurance needs by discussing your business plans with an insurance broker. Make sure that you know exactly what insurance you're buying; and, because insurance is a competitive business, get at least three quotations before making up your mind.

The Association of British Insurers (ABI; www.abi.org.uk) and the British Insurance Brokers' Association (BIBA; www.biba.org.uk) can put you in touch with a qualified insurance expert.

Protecting your employees

You must carry at least £2 million of liability insurance to meet your legal liabilities for death or bodily injury incurred by an employee during the course of business. In practice, this cover is usually unlimited, with the premiums directly related to your wage bill.

Employer's liability covers only those accidents in which the employer is held to be legally responsible. You may want to extend this cover to any accident to an employee while on your business, whoever is at fault. You may also have to cover your own financial security, particularly if the business depends on your being fit and well.

Covering yourself against an employee suing

The growing burden of employment legislation facing small firms is forcing more and more businesses to take out legal expense insurance as the risk for being prosecuted for breaking the law rises.

One area of concern to small business owners is the cost of unfair dismissal. The maximum penalty in 2012 was £72,300; however, the average actually paid out was less than £5,000 for each successful case. Trade unions represented 5,500 claimants (down from 10,000 in 2010/11), and lawyers represented 72,600 (down from 142,700 in 2010/11). An additional 34,900 claimants represented themselves (down from 40,400 in 2010/11).

The Job Rights website has an unfair dismissal calculator. (`www.jobrights.co.uk/unfair-dismissal-calculator.htm`). Just put in age, years of service, pay and a number of other factors, including how long it may take for the person to get another job, and – hey presto! – a number appears. The figure may not match the actual bill when it comes in, because the law is an uncertain arena. But it gives you something to work with from a budgeting perspective.

The remedy for the small firm without its own human resources department to keep it operating clearly within legal boundaries and a legal department to fend off any legal threats is to take out legal expenses insurance. Firms that sign up for this type of insurance can expect the insurance company to pay not only any fines and awards they incur but also their costs associated with defending themselves against allegations.

Protecting assets

Obviously, you need to insure your business premises, plant and equipment. However, you can choose between a couple of ways to do that:

- ✔ **Reinstatement** provides for full replacement cost.
- ✔ **Indemnity** meets only the current market value of your asset.

You also have to consider related costs and coverage. For example, who pays for removing debris? Who pays the architect to design the structure if you have to rebuild? Who reimburses employees for any damaged or destroyed personal effects? And potentially the most expensive of all: who covers the cost of making sure that a replacement building meets current, possibly more stringent and more expensive, standards?

The small print of your insurance policy covers these factors, so if they matter to your business, check them out.

From raw materials through to finished goods, stock is as exposed as your buildings and plant in the event of hazards such as fire and theft. Theft from commercial property runs to hundreds of millions of pounds per annum. When you're in business, you can expect threats from within and without. You can take out a *fidelity guarantee* to protect you from fraud or dishonesty on the part of key employees. You can also take out normal theft cover to protect your business premises and their contents.

Covering loss of profits

Meeting the replacement costs of buildings, plant, equipment and stock doesn't compensate you for the loss of business and profit arising out of a fire or other disaster. Your overheads, employees' wages and so on may have to continue during the period of interruption. You may incur expenses such as getting subcontracted work done. Insurance for *consequential loss*, as this type of insurance is known, is intended to restore your business's finances to the position they were in before the interruption occurred.

Goods in transit

Until your goods reach your customers and they accept them, the goods are still at your risk. You may need to protect yourself from loss or damage in transit.

Protecting yourself

Anyone who puts a substantial amount of money into your business – a bank or a venture capitalist, for example – may require you to have *key man insurance*. This type of insurance provides a substantial cash cushion in the event of your death or incapacity – you being the key man (even if you're a woman) on whom the business's success depends.

Key man insurance is particularly important in small and new firms where one person is disproportionately vital in the early stages. In a partnership, your partners may also consider this a prudent protection.

Guaranteeing goods and services

As well as your own specifications confirming how your products or services perform, you may have legal obligations under the *Consumer Protection Act*, which sets out safety rules and prohibits the sale of unsafe goods, and the *Sale of Goods Acts*, which govern your contractual relationship with your customer. In addition, the common-law rules of negligence apply to business dealings.

If you're a principal in a partnership with unlimited liability, a lawsuit concerning product liability is quite likely to bankrupt you. Even if you carry out the business through a limited company, although the directors may escape personal bankruptcy, the company doesn't. If you believe that real risks are associated with your product, then you need to consider taking out product liability insurance.

If your business involves foodstuffs, you must also pay close attention to the stringent hygiene regulations that now encompass all food manufacture, preparation and handling. If you've thoroughly examined and identified all the hazard points yet something unforeseen goes wrong, you can claim the defence of 'due diligence', insofar as you've done everything you could reasonably have been expected to do. Trading Standards (www.tradingstandards. gov.uk) and environmental health officers based in your local government office are there to help and advise you in a free consultative capacity.

Producers or importers of certain types of goods face obligations under both the Consumer Protection Act 1987 and the Sale of Goods Act 1979. Importers can be sued for defects; they can't disclaim liability simply because they haven't been involved in manufacture.

The Office of Fair Trading has produced a no-nonsense guide to the sale of goods legislation. Download a copy at www.oft.gov.uk/shared_oft/ 738369/738375/OFT002_SOGA_explained.pdf. Here are other liabilities you should consider taking insurance cover against:

- ✔ **Public liability:** A legal liability to pay damages for bodily injury, illness or disease contracted by any other person, other than employees, or loss of or damage to their property caused by the insured.

- ✔ **Professional indemnity:** Provides protection against any legal action by clients who believe they received bad or negligent services, and incurred a loss as a result. Most professional companies have professional indemnity cover – in some industries this cover is compulsory. Anyone who supplies advice or services such as consultancy should consider professional indemnity insurance.

The main points of liability law in the UK are as follows:

- ✔ Don't make claims such as, 'So simple a child could understand.' You're laying yourself wide open to rebuttal.

- ✔ Instructions should be crystal clear both on the packet and on the article if possible.

- ✔ Textiles must carry fibre content, labelling and washing instructions.

- ✔ Because the Acts cover the European Union, if you're exporting to another country in the Union you must double-check translations. It can now happen, for example, that a German person sues you as manufacturer in a German court for goods exported to Germany that have a product defect.

- ✔ You must keep records for ten years and be ready to institute a product recall operation if necessary.

Dissecting Directors

If you decide to trade as a *limited liability company* (see Chapter 5), then in all probability you have to become a director of the business. You may be the only director, or you may be one of several, but as well as the status you have responsibilities.

Here are a few of a director's duties, responsibilities and potential liabilities:

- ✔ To act in good faith in the interests of the company; this duty includes carrying out duties diligently and honestly

- ✔ Not to carry on the business of the company with intent to defraud creditors or for any fraudulent purpose

- ✔ Not knowingly to allow the company to trade while insolvent ('wrongful trading'); directors who do so may have to pay for the debts incurred by the company while insolvent

- ✔ Not to deceive shareholders

- ✔ To have regard for the interests of employees in general

- ✔ To comply with the requirements of the Companies Acts, such as providing what's needed in accounting records or filing accounts

In practice, a director's general responsibilities are much the same as those for a sole trader or partner (outlined in Chapter 5). By forming a company, you can separate your own assets from the business assets (in theory at any rate, unless they're covered by your personal guarantee). However, a director also has to cope with more technical and detailed requirements; for example, sending your accounts to Companies House. More onerous than just signing them, a director is expected and required in law to understand the significance of the balance sheet and profit and loss account and the key performance ratios.

You can insure directors' risks using directors' insurance, which covers negligent performance of duties and breach of the Companies Acts – particularly the Insolvency Act, which can hold directors personally liable to a company's creditors. The company bears the cost of the insurance because the directors are acting on its behalf.

The most dangerous areas of a director's responsibilities are ones that can get you disqualified. In summary, the following are areas to avoid at all costs:

- ✔ **Trading while insolvent** occurs when your liabilities exceed your assets. At this point the shareholders' equity in the business has effectively ceased to exist, which puts directors personally at risk. Directors owe a duty of care to creditors – not shareholders. If you find yourself even approaching this area, you need the prompt advice of an insolvency practitioner. Directors who act properly aren't penalised, and live to fight another day.

✔ **Wrongful trading** can apply if, after a company goes into insolvent liquidation, the liquidator believes that the directors ought to have concluded earlier that the company had no realistic chance of survival. In these circumstances the courts can make directors personally liable for the company's debts.

✔ **Fraudulent trading** is rather more serious than wrongful trading. Here the proposition is that the director(s) were knowingly party to fraud on their creditors. The full shelter of limited liability can be removed in these circumstances.

Former directors of insolvent companies can be banned from holding office as a company director for periods of up to 15 years. Fraud, fraudulent trading, wrongful trading or a failure to comply with company law may result in disqualification.

If you're concerned about anyone you're going to do business with and believe they are or have been a company director, you can check in the Disqualified Directors Register on the Companies House website (`http://wck2.companieshouse.gov.uk//dirsec`).

Finding and Choosing Business Advisers

You need lots of help to get started in business, and even more when you're successful – and this help can come from accountants, banks, lawyers and management consultants, as well as possibly tax consultants, advertising and public relations consultants, technology and IT advisers, and so on. The rules and tips in the following sections should steer you through dealing with most situations involving choosing and using outside advisers.

Tallying up an accountant

Keeping your financial affairs in good order is the key to staying legal and winning any disputes. A good accountant inside or outside your company can keep you on track. A bad accountant is in the ideal position to defraud you at worst, or to derail you through negligence or incompetence.

What attributes should you look for and how can you find the right accountant for your business? Here are the key steps to choosing a good accountant:

✔ Check that the accountant is a member of one of the recognised accounting bodies such as the Chartered Institute of Management Accountants (`www.cimaglobal.com`) or the Institute of Chartered Accountants in England and Wales (`www.icaew.com`).

✔ Have a clear idea of what services you require. You need to consider how complete your bookkeeping records are likely to be, whether you need your value added tax (VAT) returns completed or budgets and cash-flow forecasts prepared and updated, as well as whether you require an annual audit.

✔ Clarify the charges scale at the outset. Spending a little more on book-keeping, both staff and systems, may make more sense than leaving it all to a much higher-charging qualified accountant.

✔ Use personal recommendations from respected fellow businesspeople, particularly fellow clients of the accountant you're considering. Pay rather less attention to the recommendation of bankers, government agencies or family and friends, without totally ignoring their advice.

✔ Take references from the accountant's clients as well as from the person who recommended the accountant. They may just get on well – they may even be related!

✔ Find out what back-up the accountant has for both systems and people. The tax authorities aren't sympathetic if you're late with your records, whatever the reason. It would be doubly annoying to be fined for someone else's tardiness.

✔ See at least three accountants before making your choice, ensuring that they deal with companies of your size and a bit bigger – not so much bigger that they've no relevant advice and help to offer, but big enough for you to have room for growth without having to change accountants too quickly.

✔ Find out which other companies the accountant acts for. You don't want the accountant to be so busy she can't service your needs properly, or to be working for potential competitors.

✔ Make the accounting appointment for a trial period only, and set a specific task to see how the accountant gets on.

✔ Give the accountant the latest accounts of your business and ask for her comments based on her analysis of the figures. You can quickly see whether she's grasped the basics of your financial position.

Investing in a bank

You may wonder why I list selecting a bank in a section covering choosing business advisers. The answer, crazy as it may seem, is that your banker is almost invariably the first person you turn to when the chips are down. You may not find this answer so surprising when you think about it. After all, most big business problems turn on money, and bankers are the people who turn the money on.

Go for the wrong bank and you can lose more than your overdraft. You may lose the chance to acquire a free, or at least nearly free, business adviser.

Here are the top ten questions to ask before taking on a bank manager:

- ✔ **How quickly can you make decisions about lending?** Anything longer than ten days is too long.

- ✔ **What rate of interest do you charge?** Around 2 or 3 per cent above the Bank of England base rate is fairly normal. Above 4 per cent is on the high side.

- ✔ **What factors do you take into consideration in arriving at that rate?** If the bank proposes a high rate of interest, say 4 per cent above the Bank of England base rate or higher, then you need to know why. It may be that all the bank is asking for is further security for its loan, which you may think worth giving in return for a lower interest rate.

- ✔ **What other charges are there?** For example, does the bank charge for every transaction in and out of an account and if so how much?

- ✔ **Do you visit your clients and get to know their business?** If the bank doesn't visit, how can it ever get to understand your business in depth?

- ✔ **Under what circumstances does the bank want a personal guarantee?** When the bank is feeling exposed to greater risk than it wants to take, it may ask you to shoulder some of that risk personally. Under the terms of a bank's loan to your business, it may state that its lending shouldn't exceed a certain sum. You need to be clear what that sum is.

- ✔ **What help and advisory services do you have that may be useful to me?** Banks often provide advice on export trade, currency dealing, insurance and a range of other related services.

- ✔ **What's unique about your banking services that may make me want to use you rather than any other bank?** This factor rather depends on what you consider to be valuable. A bank that delivers all its services on the Internet may be attractive to one person and anathema and a turnoff to another.

- ✔ **How long may it be before my present manager moves on?** If the bank routinely moves managers every few years, forming personal relationships may not be particularly valuable.

- ✔ **Do any situations exist when you're likely to ask for early repayment of a loan?** A bank may insist that if you break any major condition of the loan, such as the overdraft limit or repayment schedule, the whole loan is repayable. You need to find out whether this condition applies, and what sum or event may cause this to happen.

Soliciting for a lawyer

Lawyers or solicitors are people you hope never to have to use and when you do need one you need her yesterday. Even if you don't appoint a company lawyer, you may well require one for basic stuff if you're forming a company or setting up a partnership agreement. Follow the same rules as you do for choosing an accountant (refer to 'Tallying up an accountant', earlier in this chapter).

The fact is that, in business, one day you're going to need a lawyer. The complexity of commercial life means that sooner or later you may find yourself initiating or defending legal action. It may be a contract dispute with a customer or supplier, or perhaps the lease on your premises turns out to give you far fewer rights than you hoped. A former employee may claim that you fired her without reason. Or the health and safety inspector may find some aspect of your machinery or working practices less than satisfactory. When things do go wrong, the time and money required to put them right can be an unexpected and unwelcome drain. By doing things right from the start, you can avoid at least some of the most common disputes and cope more easily with catastrophes.

In addition to ensuring that contracts are correctly drawn up, that leases are free from nasty surprises and that you're following the right health and safety procedures, a solicitor can also advise on choosing the best structure for your company, on protecting your intellectual property and on how to go about raising money.

It makes sense to see your solicitor before your problems arise and find out what she can do for you, or, at least, to make yourself conversant with the relevant laws. Taking timely action on legal issues may help you gain an advantage over competitors and almost certainly saves you money in the long run.

If you're going to see a lawyer, make sure that you're well prepared. Have all the facts to hand and know what you want help with.

 Lawyers For Your Business (`www.lawsociety.org.uk/for-the-public/ common-legal-issues/setting-up-business`) represents some 1,400 firms of solicitors in England and Wales that have come together to help ensure that all businesses, especially the smaller owner-managed ones, get access to sound legal advice whenever they need it.

Managing a consultant

If you're facing a new major problem in which you have no expertise, particularly a problem you don't expect to experience again, then hiring a consultant is an option worth considering. For example, if you're moving premises, changing your computing or accounting system, starting to do business overseas or designing an employee share-ownership scheme, getting the help of someone who's covered that area several times before and who's an expert in the field may well make sense.

The time a consultant takes to carry out most tasks a small business may require is likely to be between a fortnight and three months. Anything much longer is too expensive for most small firms and anything much shorter is unlikely to have much of an impact on the business. However, the consultant isn't working continuously on your project for that time. After an initial meeting, a consultant may do much of the work off site and in chunks of time. Costs vary depending on both the skill of the consultant and the topic covered. A tax consultant, for example, can cost upwards of £450 an hour, and a training consultant may cost the same sum for a day.

Take on a consultant using the same procedures as for a key employee (see Chapter 11). Brief the consultant thoroughly, and don't expect to dump the problem on the consultant's doorstep and walk away. Set the consultant a small, measurable part of the task first to see how she performs. Never give the consultant a long-term contract or an open-ended commitment.

You can't delegate decision making, you can only delegate the analysis of problems and the presentation of options. In the end, you have to choose which way to go. Don't let consultants implement decisions on their own. The line of responsibility between yourself and your staff needs to be preserved. Seeing someone else giving orders undermines the chain of command. If the consultant's solution is so complex it needs her expertise to implement, you have the wrong solution.

The Institute of Consulting (www.iconsulting.org.uk) provides guidelines for choosing a consultant as well as a fully searchable database of consultants providing information by region and specialisation.

Taking Cyber Security Seriously

The government ranks hostile attacks upon UK cyber space as a Tier One Priority Risk, just after international terrorism and well ahead of disruption to oil or gas supplies. The government claims that cyber crime costs as much as $1 trillion per year globally, with untold human cost. Implementing *cyber security* means taking measures to protect websites, networks, computers, programs and data from such attacks, and from damage and theft.

Major British companies are increasingly anxious about the impact of cyber crime on their bottom line and the resilience of the networks upon which commerce relies. But small businesses are also at risk. In 2012, the Federation of Small Businesses published findings of a survey that showed

✔ Around three in ten members had been a victim of online crime over the last year. Businesses had particularly had issues with virus infections (20 per cent), hacking or electronic intrusions (8 per cent) and system security breach or loss of availability (5 per cent).

✔ The average annual cost to small businesses of fraud and online crime was just under £4,000 per year.

✔ In terms of action to minimise online crime, four in five members had acted in some way, including regular updates of virus scanning software (59 per cent), using a firewall (47 per cent) and using spam filtering software (43 per cent). Written formal information security plans and the introduction of information security standards were less common.

The following sections help you understand and protect your business against the risks.

Recognising common types of cyber crime

The following are some of dangers that you should be ready for when working and doing business online:

✔ **Bring your own devices (BYOD):** Mobile phones, laptops and tablets used by employees on or away from business premises pose a serious risk because they usually lack the professional security protection used on business-owned hardware.

✔ **Card not present (CNP):** Fraudsters steal genuine card details to make a purchase, usually over the phone or Internet, both circumstances where the card isn't present at the point of sale. This fraud accounts for more than half of all card fraud, but has been diminishing since 2008 with the introduction of MasterCard SecureCode and Verified by Visa.

✔ **Network access control (NAC):** With the explosion of devices regularly in use, you can't really know with certainty who's accessing your network, where, when and how. Fraudsters can use USB memory sticks, laptops, tablets and smartphones to access your network, so you need a security system that protects your business network.

✔ **Spoofing, phishing and pharming:** These dangers are varieties of the same generic fraud whose aim is to lure the recipient into believing she's dealing with the genuine article – a website or email. Fraudulent emails or web links that appear to be from genuine individuals or companies try to persuade people to reveal personal financial information such as card numbers, account information, PINs or passwords.

✔ **Spyware:** This malicious software is designed to penetrate data, applications or operating systems to get through to sensitive data. The software may be a

- **Virus:** *Computer viruses* are software programs that can get into your computer when you operate online. They're designed to interfere with your computer's operations in some harmful way, such as diverting traffic to another website, hacking into data or causing computer programmes and systems to fail.

- **Keystroke logger:** Sneakily installed on a computer, often by a virus, and used to capture and record a user's keystrokes when she enters confidential data, such as passwords or bank details, and transmit that to a fraudster's computer.

- **Trojan:** Like the Trojan horse of Greek mythology, it masquerades as a legitimate program but it contains an invisible program that gives hackers a secret way into a computer system to gain access to information or take control in some way.

Adopting preventative measures

Use these measures to ensure that you're not the victim of cyber crime:

✔ **Employ a blend of security protection solutions,** including anti-virus and firewalls, and carry out security updates on all software and hardware regularly. Most security software comes with a program that regularly updates, so keeps abreast of the latest threats. Check at least once a month that updates are taking place.

A *firewall* is a cordon around your PC or network, sitting between it and the Internet, designed to prevent unauthorised access to your PC or network and hide your Internet-connected PC from prying online eyes.

✔ **Have a robust password policy,** ideally using a combination of letters and numbers, changing at least twice a year. You can use sites such as Password Meter (`www.passwordmeter.com`) to get a feel for the strength of certain types of password, without, of course, actually putting in the password you'll be using finally.

Passwords should be in place at every point where your hardware comes in contact with the Internet, from your servers or wireless connection through to individual areas such as your website transaction areas.

✔ **Have clear, documented security procedures** for email, Internet and mobile devices, and train your staff in good security practices.

✔ **Carry out regular security testing** on your email systems and website. You may consider doing a live test, as did Tom Cochran, Chief Technical Officer (CTO) at Atlantic Media and former director of new media technologies at the White House. One Friday afternoon he sent a phishing email to his entire company. Within two hours almost half of the company had opened the email, and 58 per cent of those employees had clicked the false malicious link designed to lure them into the hacker's clutches. Cochran's phishing experiment got the crucial buy-in of employees who now personally understand the dangers online.

Cloud computer services may open your business up to cyber risks. Along with the benefits of the cloud – ease of access to data and constantly updated software – comes the additional risk of having all your sensitive data away from your in-house computer and your own security systems. Satisfy yourself that your cloud provider is on top of security. Check out Intel's guide to cloud security planning at `www.intel.co.uk/content/www/uk/en/cloud-computing/cloud-security-planning-guide-infographic.html`.

Making a Virtue Out of Going Green

Over the past decade, the business community has experienced what amounts to a green revolution. Pressures on business abound: to produce less waste, use less energy, consume less water, encourage employees to walk or cycle to work, or to facilitate working from home for at least part of the time. That this green wave has received the enthusiastic support of business is in large measure because many of these activities are consistent with aggressive long-term cost cutting.

The beauty, from a business perspective, is that this pressure to go green comes from outside and is supported in many cases by legislation. Companies such as 3M, DuPont, IBM and, latterly, Google, Cisco and Microsoft are enthusiastic green cost cutters. They've even managed to save billions as a result of measures to reduce waste and energy consumption. Toyota, with innovative hybrids such as the Prius, has created what amounts to new streams of revenue while greatly enhancing the value of its brand.

And the evidence is that employees like working for green businesses. A global study by corporate communications firm Hill & Knowlton revealed that four in every ten MBA students wouldn't take 'a great offer' from a company with a poor environmental reputation. Another survey covering college students found that 92 per cent want to work for a green company.

Under the Climate Change Act, the government has introduced carbon reporting across all businesses. So get to grips with your business's carbon footprint. Here are some tips for doing so:

✔ **Get greener vehicles.** Low-emission vehicles cost less to tax and insure, are fuel efficient and attract fast tax write-down rates, in some cases as much as 100 per cent of the purchase price in the first year.

✔ Buy from businesses with good green credentials where possible.

✔ Recycle paper and take measures to reduce paper use in your business, such as by putting technical literature and other material on your website.

✔ Review your packaging and use only biodegradable materials where possible.

✔ Improve the insulation of your premises and consider using solar panels or other forms of low-carbon heating.

Look at GreenWise (www.greenwisebusiness.co.uk), an independent daily information service for businesses – large and small – that want to find out more about the opportunities and challenges of moving to a low-carbon economy. And if you're thinking of basing your business on a green product or service, check out the Carbon Trust's Entrepreneurs Fast Track service (www.carbontrust.com), which helps early-stage companies make the transition from low-carbon concepts to commercialisation. Often such ventures are high risk in nature and find it difficult to attract finance and managerial talent. As well as expert advice and networking opportunities, the Fast Track service channels £5 million a year into clean-tech ventures with the highest growth potential.

Greening up Daily Bread

Daily Bread was started in 1986 in the basement of a Chelsea deli. Thirty-five delicious sandwiches were made up and taken around local offices with the aim of selling them. The business was part of the Hain Celestial Group until August 2012, when it was sold to a strategic buyer, a leading natural and organic food and personal-care products company. The group's other brands include the New Covent Garden Soup Company and Linda McCartney, and it has operations in North America and Europe. Daily Bread still makes delicious sandwiches and has earned a royal warrant to prove it, but more conventional routes to market have supplanted basket deliveries.

As with all companies that supply sandwiches to Marks & Spencer, Daily Bread is required to discard four slices from each loaf, the crusts and the first slices in. As well as wasting food, the company was paying around £65,000 a year to send this food to be turned into gas for power generation. Then, as a result of advice from a UK-government-sponsored body called Environwise, Daily Bread started to sell its unwanted bread to a local farmer for use as animal feed. The company turned a cost into a revenue stream (it gets £25 a tonne from the farmer). Also, the process emits no carbon dioxide, so the shift contributed to its green strategy, culminating in it being named the tenth greenest company in the UK and *the* greenest company in the food and drink sector in the *Sunday Times* Best Green Companies Awards 2009.

Chapter 13

Keeping Track of Finances

*E*very business needs reliable financial information for both decision making and accountability. No one is going to be keen to pump money into your venture if you can't demonstrate that you know what's likely to happen to it. Reliable information doesn't necessarily call for complex book-keeping and accounting systems: simple is often best. As the business grows, and perhaps takes on outside investors, you require more sophisticated information. That's when using a computer and some of the relevant software packages may be the best way forward. But even with a computer errors can occur, so you have to know how to recognise when financial information goes wrong and how you can correct it. You've a legal obligation in business to keep accounting records from the outset and not just wait until your business runs into serious problems. If, as a director or owner of a business, you can't see when you're heading for a financial reef, you may find yourself in deep trouble, if not actually heading for jail – and definitely not collecting £200 on the way.

This chapter gives you a good grounding in keeping track of finances, but keep in mind that now's not the time to be shy in coming forward for advice. According to the 2012 Small Business Survey carried out for the UK Government, 46 per cent of new business sought advice from an accountant, mostly on financial matters to do with running the business. One hundred per cent would be a far preferable figure.

Keeping the Books

To survive and prosper in business you need to know how much cash you have, and what your profit or loss on sales is. You need these facts on at least a monthly, weekly or occasionally even a daily basis to survive, let alone grow.

Recording financial information

Although bad luck plays a part in some business failures, a lack of reliable financial information plays a part in most. However, businesses have all the information they need to manage well close at hand. Among the bills you have to pay, invoices to raise, petty cash slips to file and bank statements to diagnose, you've enough to give you a true picture of your business's performance.

All you need to do is record and organise that information so that the financial picture becomes clear. The way you record financial information is called *bookkeeping*.

Not only the business owner needs these financial facts. Bankers, shareholders and tax inspectors are unsympathetic audiences to anyone without well-documented facts to back them up. If, for example, a tax authority presents a business with a tax demand, the onus then lies with the businessperson, using his records, to agree or dispute the sum claimed.

In any event, if you plan to trade as a limited company (see Chapter 5), the Companies Act 1985 requires you to 'keep adequate records sufficient to show and explain the company's transactions'.

Reasons for keeping proper records:

- ✔ To know the cash position of your business precisely and accurately
- ✔ To discover how profitable your business really is
- ✔ To see which of your activities are profitable and which aren't
- ✔ To give bankers and other sources of finance confidence that your business is being well managed and that their money is in good hands
- ✔ To allow you to calculate your tax bill accurately
- ✔ To help you prepare timely financial forecasts and projections
- ✔ To make sure that you both collect and pay money due correctly
- ✔ To keep accountancy and audit costs to a minimum

Starting simple with single entry

If you're doing books by hand and don't have a lot of transactions, the single-entry method is the easiest acceptable way to go.

Single entry means that you write down each transaction in your records once, preferably on a ledger sheet. You record the flow of income and expenses through your business by making a running total of money taken in (gross receipts) and money paid out (payments or, as they're sometimes called, *disbursements*). You should keep receipts and payments and summarise them daily, weekly or monthly, as the business needs require. At the end of the year, you total up the 12 monthly summaries. You're ready for tax time.

You may benefit from separating different types of income and expense into categories – for example, stock, vehicles, telephone – as in Figure 13-1. This separation lets you see how much you're spending or receiving in each area.

Figure 13-1:
An example
of an anal-
ysed cash
book.

Payments				Analysis			
Date	Name	Details	Amount £	Stocks	Vehicles	Telephone	Other
4 June	Gibbs	Stock purchase	310	310			
8 June	Gibbs	Stock purchase	130	130			
12 June	ABC Telecoms	Telephone charges	55.23			55.23	
18 June	Colt Rentals	Vehicle hire	87.26		87.26		
22 June	VV Mobiles	Mobile phone	53.24			53.24	
27 June	Gibbs	Stock purchase	36.28	36.28			
Totals			672.01	476.28	87.26	108.47	

You need to keep copies of paid and unpaid sales invoices and the same for purchases, as well as your bank statements. You then reconcile (match) bank statements to your cash book to tie everything together.

Dealing with double entry

If you operate a partnership or trade as a company, you may need a double-entry bookkeeping system from the start.

A *double-entry bookkeeping system* requires two entries for each transaction – hence the name – and every transaction has two effects on the accounts. For example, when you buy an item of stock for sale and pay for it in cash, your cash balance goes down and your amount of stock goes up by the same amount, keeping everything in balance.

Choosing the right accounting program

With the cost of a basic computerised accounting system starting at barely £100, and a reasonable package costing between £200 and £500, planning to use such a system from the outset is sensible. If you're at all concerned as to whether such software represents value, try out Intuits SimpleStart on a free trial basis (`http://quickbooks.intuit.co.uk`). Thereafter it costs around £8 a month. Or, if you can face having adverts pop up from time to time, Wave, which makes cloud-based, integrated software and tools for small businesses, offers a free-forever accounting package at `www.waveapps.com/accounting`.

Using a computerised accounting system means no more arithmetical errors. As long as you enter the information correctly, the computer adds it up correctly. With a computer, the £53.24 mobile phone expenditure in Figure 13-1 is input as an expense (a debit), and then the computer automatically posts it to the mobile phone account as a credit. In effect, the computer eliminates the extra step or the need to master the difference between debit and credit.

A computerised accounting program is only as good as the data you enter into it. Introduce strict end-of-month controls to make sure that you've counted and valued all stock, dealt with all the month's invoices and so on. Without this, your computer program reflects inaccurate data.

Routine tasks, such as filling in tax and value added tax (VAT) returns, take minutes rather than days with a computer. The system can ensure that your returns are accurate and fully reconciled. With a computerised system, invoices are always accurate. You can see at a glance which customers regularly take too long to pay. You've two main options in your choice of your first accounting system:

- ✔ **Manual:** If you think that a manual system is best for your purposes, you can get sheets of analysis paper with printed columns for accounting entries, and put in your own headings as appropriate. Or you can buy off-the-shelf sets of books from any office stationer's outlet. These cost anything from £10 to £20 for a full set of ledgers. Hingston Publishing (`http://hingston-publishing.co.uk/accounts-books`) produces small business accounts systems for both VAT and non-VAT registered businesses for about £15.

- ✔ **Accounting software:** If you decide to take the plunge and go straight for accounting software, you've a myriad of software providers to choose from that serve the small business market with software for bookkeeping. These are a selection of the more popular packages and providers:

  - • **Mamut** (Formerly Mind Your Own Business; `www.mamut.com/uk`) offers a range of accounting package systems, starting with its Mamut One Office Accounting costing £118.80 including VAT.

- **QuickBooks** (`http://www.intuit.co.uk/quickbooks/accounting-software.jsp`) offers a range of products from around £8 a month up to £30 a month for a system that can automate the VAT return as well as help with budgeting, purchase orders and stock holding. The software is cloud-based.

- **Sage One** (`http://shop.sage.co.uk/accountssoftware.aspx`) is Sage's entry-level product. It costs £5 a month plus VAT, with more sophisticated desktop-based products available for a one-off purchase price of up to £619 plus VAT.

- **TAS FirstBooks** (`http://shop.tassoftware.co.uk/firstbooks.aspx`) is aimed specifically at the needs of new, smaller companies. Online support within the product is generally comprehensive, and a manual helps to explain more advanced features. This fairly basic system costs £99 plus VAT to purchase one licence.

If you plan to submit your accounts online, you need an accounting system that meets the requirements of Her Majesty's Revenue and Customs (HMRC). A range of Internet-filing-enabled software and forms is available from HMRC and commercial software and service suppliers. You can use these to file company tax returns, including accounts and computations, online. HMRC provides a list of software suppliers at `www.hmrc.gov.uk/efiling/ctsoft_dev.htm`, but doesn't take responsibility for loss, damage or costs incurred by using the software.

Outsourcing bookkeeping

Accountants and freelance bookkeepers can do all your bookkeeping work – at a price. The rate is anything from £20 per hour upwards.

Bookkeeping services range from a basic write-up of the entries and leave-the-rest-to-you approach, through to providing weekly or monthly accounts, perhaps with pointers as to what may be going wrong. Services even exist that act as a virtual finance director, giving you access to a senior accountant who may sit on your board.

Most bookkeeping services have a computer system into which you have to plug your records, so if you're thinking of going down this route, check out which software you require first.

The bookkeeper's most routine but vital task may be doing the payroll. If you don't get this done on time and correctly, both staff and HMRC, for which you have to collect pay as you earn (PAYE), become restless. A weekly payroll service for up to ten employees costs upwards of £85 per month. If you pay everyone monthly, the cost drops to about a third of that figure.

If you go down this route, you probably need someone local, so ask around to find someone who uses a bookkeeper and is satisfied. Alternatively, turn to the phone book, or use Service Start (http://uk.servicestart.com), which gets up to five price quotes from rated bookkeeping service providers all over the UK.

As with an accountant, make sure that a prospective bookkeeper is adequately qualified. The International Association of Book-keepers (IAB; website www.iab.org.uk) and the Institute of Certified Bookkeepers (www.bookkeepers.org.uk) are the two professional associations concerned.

You can check out the letters that anyone in the accounting profession uses after his name or the bodies he claims to be a member of at the Directory of Essential Accountancy Abbreviations, maintained by the Library and Information Service at the Institute of Chartered Accountants in England and Wales (www.icaew.com/en/library/subject-gateways/accounting/abbreviations).

Understanding Your Accounts

Keeping the books is one thing, but being able to make good use of the information those accounts contain is quite another. You need to turn the raw accounting data from columns of figures into statements of account. Those accounts in turn tell you how much cash your business has, its profit or loss numbers and how much money you've tied up in the business to produce those results. The following sections discuss some of the key accounting statements and performance analyses.

Forecasting cash flow

In the language of accounting, income is recognised when a product or service has been sold, delivered or executed, and the invoice raised. Although that rule holds good for calculating profit (see 'Reporting Your Profits', later in this chapter), it doesn't apply when forecasting cash flow.

Chapter 8 covers how to prepare a cash-flow forecast. Profit is what may be generated if all goes well and customers pay up, and you can think of cash flow as the cold shower of reality, bringing you sharply back to your senses.

Overtrading describes a business that's expanding beyond its financial resources. As sales expand, the amount of cash tied up in stocks and customers' credit grows rapidly. Pressure also comes from suppliers of goods and services and from additional employees, who all expect to be paid. The natural escape valve for pressures on working capital is an overdraft (or a substantial increase in the existing one). Monitoring cash flow reduces the risk of overtrading.

Reporting your profits

A key use of bookkeeping information is to prepare a profit and loss account.

In carrying out any business activity, two different actions go on. One is selling your goods and services and getting paid for them. Money comes in – perhaps not immediately, but it usually shows up eventually. This money goes by a variety of names, including *revenues, income* and *sales income.* The second transaction is the outlay you make in order to provide the goods and services you sell to your customers. Some of the costs you incur are for raw materials, salaries, rents and so forth. These costs are known as *expenses.* By deducting your expenses from your income, you end up with the profit (or loss) for the particular period under review.

At its simplest, the profit and loss account has at its head the period covered, followed by the income, from which you deduct all the expenses of the business to arrive at the profit (or loss) made in the period. Figure 13-2 shows a sample account.

Figure 13-2: A basic profit and loss account.

Profit and Loss Account for year to 31 March 201X	£
Income	1,416,071
Less expenses	1,389,698
Profit	26,373

Although the information shown in the profit and loss account is certainly better than nothing, you can use basic bookkeeping information to give you a much richer picture of events within the business. Provided, that is, that you've set up the right analysis headings in the first place.

The following sections show, step by step, how to build up a profit and loss account to give you a more complete picture of the trading events of the past year at Safari Europe, the example I use in the following sections.

Calculating gross profit

One of the most important figures in the profit and loss account is the gross profit. Whatever your activity, you have to buy certain 'raw materials'. Those include anything you have to buy to produce the goods and services you're selling. So if you sell cars, the cost of buying in the cars is a raw materials cost. In Safari's case, because the company is in the travel business, the costs of airline tickets and hotel rooms are the raw material of a package holiday.

The amount left from the sales revenues after deducting the cost of sales, as these costs of 'making' are known, is the *gross profit.* This is really the only discretionary money coming into the business, where you have some say over how it's spent. Figure 13-3 shows a sample profit calculation.

Safari Europe

Profit and Loss Account for year to	31 March 201X

Income

Tours sold	1,402,500
Insurance & other services	13,571
Non-operating revenue	0
Total income	1,416,071

Less **Cost of goods sold**

Tours bought	1,251,052
Insurance & other services	4,071
Total cost of goods sold	1,255,123
Gross profit	160,948

Figure 13-3:
An example gross profit calculation.

In the account shown in Figure 13-3, you can see that Safari has two sources of income, one from tours and one from insurance and other related services. It also, of course, has the costs associated with buying in holidays and insurance policies from suppliers.

The difference between the income of £1,416,071 and the cost of the 'goods' the company has sold is just £160,948. That's the sum that the management has to run the business, not the much larger, headline-making figure of nearly £1.5 million.

Figure 13-4 shows how to calculate gross profit in a business that makes things rather than selling services.

Figure 13-4:
A manufacturer's gross profit.

	£
Sales	100,000
Cost of goods sold	65,000
Gross profit	35,000

In the example in Figure 13-4, the basic sum is the same as for a service business, as shown in Figure 13-3. Take the cost of goods from the sales income and what's left is gross profit. The cost of goods is calculated by noting the stock at the start of the period, adding in any purchases made and deducting the closing stock.

You also need to build in the labour cost in production and any overheads, such as workshop usage, and deduct those in order to arrive at the gross profit, as shown in Figure 13-5.

	£	£	£
Sales			**100,000**
Manufacturing costs			
Raw materials opening stock	30,000		
Purchases in period	25,000		
	55,000		
Less Raw materials closing stock	15,500		
Cost of materials used		39,500	
Direct labour cost		18,000	
Manufacturing overhead cost			
Indirect labour	4,000		
Workshop heat, light and power	3,500		
Total manufacturing costs		7,500	
Cost of goods sold			65,000
Gross profit			35,000

Figure 13-5: Expanded gross profit calculation.

Reckoning expenses

After you calculate the gross profit, you have to allow for all the expenses that are likely to arise in running the business. Using the Safari case as a working example, Figure 13-6 shows all the costs usually associated with running the business, such as rent, rates, telephone, marketing and promotion, and so forth. Although all these expenses are correctly included, they aren't all allowable for tax purposes in every country. I look at taxation in Chapter 14.

The 'Total expenditure' heading isn't quite accurate. Other expenses associated with running a business aren't included here, but these expenses are treated in a slightly different way, for reasons that should become apparent as you read on about the different types of profit.

Appreciating the different types of profit

You can measure profit in several ways:

- ✔ **Gross profit** is the profit left after you've deducted all costs related to making what you sell from income (see the beginning of this section, 'Reporting Your Profits', for what represents income).

✔ **Operating profit** is what's left after you take the expenses (or expenditure) away from the gross profit.

✔ **Profit before tax** is what you get after deducting any financing costs. This is a measure of the performance of the management, which is important if the owners and managers aren't the same people, as may be the case when you start to employ staff. The reasoning here is that the operating management can have little influence over the way in which the business is financed (no borrowings means no interest expenses, for example), or the level of interest charges.

Safari Europe

Profit and Loss Account for
the year to 31 March 201X

	Year 1
Income	
Tours sold	1,402,500
Insurance & other services	13,571
Non-operating revenue	0
Total income	1,416,071
Less **Cost of goods sold**	
Tours bought	1,251,052
Insurance & other services	4,071
Total cost of goods sold	1,255,123
Gross profit	160,948
Expenditure	
Rent & rates	18,000
Heat, light & power	3,500
Telephone system lease	2,000
Computer leasing	5,000
Marketing & promotion	12,500
Postage & stationery	3,250
Telephone	3,575
Insurance & legal	3,500
Wages (not owner's)	36,000
Consultancy services	25,000
Membership & subscription	1,500
Travel & subsistence	4,250
Training & staff development	6,000
Depreciation of fixtures	5,500
Total expenditure	129,575

Figure 13-6:
Business
expenses.

Interestingly enough, when it comes to valuing the business, the operating profit is generally used as the multiplying factor (so, many times earnings is a typical valuation mechanism and operating profit is used to represent earnings).

In Figure 13-7, taking away the financing costs, in the example £5,000 interest charges, leaves a profit before tax of £26,373. Finally, you deduct tax to leave the net profit after tax, the bottom line. This sum belongs to the owners of the business and, if the company is limited, is what dividends can be paid from.

Safari Europe

Profit and Loss Account for the year to 31 March 201X	
Income	
Tours sold	1,402,500
Insurance & other services	13,571
Non-operating revenue	0
Total income	1,416,071
Less **Cost of goods sold**	
Tours bought	1,251,052
Insurance & other services	4,071
Total cost of goods sold	1,255,123
Gross profit	160,948
Expenditure	
Rent & rates	18,000
Heat, light & power	3,500
Telephone system lease	2,000
Computer leasing	5,000
Marketing & promotion	12,500
Postage & stationery	3,250
Telephone	3,575
Insurance & legal	3,500
Wages (not owner's)	36,000
Consultancy services	25,000
Membership & subscription	1,500
Travel & subsistence	4,250
Training & staff development	6,000
Depreciation of fixtures	5,500
Total expenditure	129,575
Operating profit	31,373
Less interest charges	5,000
Net profit before tax	26,373
Tax	5,538
Net profit after tax	20,835

Figure 13-7: Levels of profit.

Accounting for Pricing

Setting a selling price for your wares is one of the most important and most frequent business decisions that anyone running a business has to make. At first glance, it doesn't seem such a big deal. Just add up all the costs, add a healthy profit margin and as long as the customers don't rush for the exit you're in business. Unfortunately, the first part of that sentence contains a few traps for the unwary.

Complications start when you have to get to grips with the characteristics of costs. Not all costs behave in exactly the same way. For example, the rent on a shop, office or workshop is a fixed sum, payable monthly or quarterly. Your landlord doesn't usually expect you to pay more rent if you get more customers, nor is he especially generous if you've a particularly lean period. (One exception to this rule comes if you're able to negotiate a rent geared to performance, an offer landlords have been known to make to some retailers.) The business rates on any premises and the cost of an advertisement in the local paper are also *fixed costs*. That term shows that the cost in question doesn't vary directly with the volume of sales, not that the cost itself has been immutably settled and you're committed to pay it. You don't have to advertise and you do have to pay business rates, but both are fixed costs.

Contrast that with the cost of the products you plan to sell. Assume for a moment that you're selling just one product, a bottle of wine costing £3 to buy in. The more you sell, the more your stock costs to buy. That type of cost varies directly with the volume of sales you achieve, and in a rare display of user-friendliness from the accounting profession is known as *variable*. The cost of each individual bottle may or may not vary – your supplier may or may not change the price, perhaps lowering it to win more business from you or upping it to meet the chancellor of the exchequer's ever-growing demand for more tax. But the nature of the cost means that the total cost does vary as your sales volume changes.

The main tool that can help you with pricing decisions is breakeven analysis. Using that tool, which I explain in the following sections, helps you to set the best price for single or multiple products, to see how much you have to sell to hit your profit goals and to deal with changing your prices.

Breaking even

To keep things simple: your business plans to sell only one product, for example the wine I mention in the previous text, and you only have one fixed cost, the rent. Figure 13-8 sets out a graphical picture of how your costs stack up.

The vertical axis shows the value of sales and costs in thousands and the horizontal axis shows the number of units sold, in this case bottles of wine. The rent is £10,000 for the year, represented by a straight line labelled 'fixed costs'. The angled line running from the top of the fixed costs line shows the amount of the variable costs. Sell zero bottles and you incur zero additional costs. In this case, the total costs are £10,000 plus £0 equalling £10,000. Every bottle you buy in adds £3 of variable costs (you have to buy the wine in!!) to the total costs.

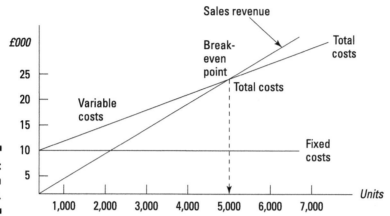

Figure 13-8: Breakeven chart.

You need to calculate the breakeven point – that is, when you've made enough money from selling wine to pay the rent. The sales revenue line moves up at an angle from the bottom left-hand corner of the graph. If you plan to sell your wine at £5 a bottle, you calculate the figures for this line by multiplying the number of units sold by that price.

The breakeven point is the stage at which a business starts to make a profit – when the money coming in from sales is higher than the fixed and variable costs added together. For your wine business, you can see from the chart that this point arises when you've sold 5,000 bottles. You don't have to draw a chart every time you want to work out your breakeven point – you can use a simple formula.

$$\text{Breakeven point} = \frac{\text{Fixed costs}}{\text{Selling price} - \text{Unit variable cost}}$$

$$= \frac{10,000}{5 - 3} = 5,000 \text{ units}$$

Pricing for profit

You have to break even if you want to remain in business, but doing so isn't enough on its own. You need to make a profit over and above your breakeven point.

Profit isn't an accident of arithmetic discovered by your accountant at the year end. Profit should be a specific, quantified goal that you set in advance. Look again at the earlier wine selling example: you plan to invest £10,000 in a year's rent, and you need to hold at least £5,000 worth of stock too, making £15,000 total costs. So what return can you expect on the money you're investing? If you invested the same amount in other people's businesses by buying an average bundle of shares on the stock market, you may expect to get a return of £1,200, around 8 per cent. If you went for more risky start-up and early-stage ventures, a venture capital firm may recommend that you look for a return of between 20 and 30 per cent.

To keep the numbers simple again, say your profit goal is to make £4,000 profit, a return of 27 per cent (4,000 ÷ 15,000 x 100). How many bottles of wine do you need to sell to break even and meet your profit goal? The new equation must include your desired profit, so it looks like this:

$$\text{Break-even profit point (BEPP)} = \frac{\text{Fixed costs} + \text{Profit goal}}{\text{Selling price} - \text{Unit variable cost}}$$

$$= \frac{10{,}000 + 4{,}000}{5 - 3} = \frac{14{,}000}{2} = 7{,}000$$

From the formula, you now know that to reach your profit goal you have to sell 7,000 bottles of wine. Better still, this powerful little equation allows you to change each element and experiment to arrive at the optimum result. For example, say that after doing market research you conclude that you're unlikely to sell 7,000 bottles of this wine, but that you can sell 6,000. What does your selling price have to be to make the same profit?

Using the BEPP equation and inserting 'x' for the element you're changing, you can calculate the answer:

$$\text{Break-even profit point (BEPP)} = \frac{\text{Fixed costs} + \text{Profit goal}}{\text{Selling price} - \text{Unit variable cost}}$$

$$= 6{,}000 = \frac{10{,}000 + 4{,}000}{x - 3}$$

$$\text{Therefore } x - 3 = \frac{10{,}000 + 4{,}000}{6{,}000} = 2.33$$

$$x = 3 + 2.33 = 5.33$$

So your new selling price has to be £5.33 a bottle if you need to make £4,000 profit from the sale of 6,000 bottles. If the market can bear that price, great; if not, then you need to look for ways to decrease the fixed and variable costs, or to sell more, if you're to meet your profit goal.

Working with that formula may have frightened you if your algebra is a bit rusty! The easy option is to use a spreadsheet to take the pain out of the number crunching. So far you've only been working with one fixed cost and one variable cost; in practice you obviously have many more, and using a spreadsheet makes changing the calculation much easier. Harvard Business School offers a free, downloadable, interactive breakeven workbook (`http://hbswk.hbs.edu/archive/1262.html`), one of several workbooks/tutorials from the HBS Toolkit used by its students. Bankrate, a leading aggregator of financial rate information, also has a number of financial spreadsheets on its website including a neat tool for working out your breakeven point (`www.bankrate.com/brm/news/biz/Cashflow_banking/breakeven.XLT`). And your second option? Of, if you're a glutton for punishment and want to do the sum yourself, boost your algebra at the BBC's Bitesize website (`www.bbc.co.uk/schools/gcsebitesize/maths/algebra`).

Building in more products

The example so far has been for a one-product company, but what if you plan to sell more than just one type of wine – or perhaps even add crisps and chocolates too? When you reach this stage, you need to work from your gross profit percentage (for how to calculate this percentage see 'Analysing Performance', later in this chapter).

If, for example, you're aiming for a 40 per cent gross profit, your fixed costs are £10,000 and your profit goal is £4,000, then the sum is as follows:

$$\text{BEPP} = \frac{10,000 + 4,000}{0.4} = \frac{14,000}{0.4} = £35,000$$

If you got a bit lost about where the 0.4 came from, don't worry; that's just 40 per cent expressed as a decimal, a step you need to take before you can use the number. What you now know is that at a 40 per cent gross profit margin you need to sell £35,000 worth of wine, chocolates and crisps to hit your profit goal. Your accountant can help with these calculations, and the Harvard Business School website has a useful tutorial that links with its breakeven spreadsheet (see the preceding section).

Handling price changes

The most sensitive and revisited area of business strategy is pricing. You can check out the impact of a particular pricing policy on your profitability using breakeven analysis (see 'Pricing for profit', earlier in this chapter, for more details). As part of your strategy, you may consider changing your price. All things being equal, a lower price should open up a bigger market and so increase sales. But should you reduce your price?

As a rule of thumb, if you decrease your prices by 5 per cent you have to increase your sales by three times that percentage, just to make the same level of profit. This increase depends on the gross profit you're achieving, but the figure given holds good for gross profits of 30 to 40 per cent.

Conversely, if you push your prices up by 5 per cent, you can lose around a seventh of your business before you're any worse off in terms of profit.

BizPep has a useful piece of software that allows you to calculate your optimal selling price under a wide range of business conditions (www. bizpeponline.com/PricingBreakeven.html). A fully functioning download is available free for a seven-day trial. The outputs include breakeven charts for current, increased, decreased and optimum pricing calculated for prices ranging from –50 to +50 per cent of your current actual or proposed price. You can carry out the same analysis yourself using the free software from the Harvard Business School (see the earlier section 'Pricing for profit'), but BizPep's templates do some of the grunt and groan for you.

Balancing the Books

You have to know where you are now before making any plans to go anywhere else. Without a starting point, any journey is bound to be a confusing experience. A business sums up its current position in a balance sheet, the business's primary reporting document. The balance sheet contains the cumulative evidence of financial events, showing where money has come from and what's been done with that money. Logically, the two sums must balance.

In practical terms, balancing your sums takes quite a bit of work, the hardest bit of which isn't necessarily the balancing part, but figuring out the numbers. Your cash-in-hand figure is probably dead right, but can you say the same of the value of your assets? Accountants have their own rules on how to arrive at these figures, but they don't pretend to be anything more than an approximation. Every measuring device has inherent inaccuracies, and financial controls are no exception.

To help balance the books, the *balance sheet* sets out a business's assets and liabilities in way that makes it easier to understand crucial relationships. In the following sections, I look at the balance sheet and the essential technical terms that you need to grasp in order to get the full picture of how a business is faring.

A balance sheet

In formal accounts the figures are set out vertically rather than in horizontal fashion, as reflected in Figure 13-9. The business's long-term borrowings, in this case the mortgage and hire purchase charges, are named *Creditors, amounts falling due in over 1 year* and deducted from the total assets to show the *Net total assets* being employed.

	£	£
NET ASSETS EMPLOYED		
Fixed assets		
Premises	150,000	
Car	7,000	
Furniture	1500	
Jewellery and paintings	350	
Book value		158,850
Current assets		
Money owed by sister	135	
Cash	50	
Total current assets	185	
Less Current liabilities		
Overdraft	100	
Credit cards	50	
Total current liabilities	150	
Net current assets		35
Total assets		158,885
Less: Creditors, amounts falling due in over 1 year		45,500
Net total assets		***113,385***
FINANCED BY		
My capital	113,385	
Total owners' funds		113,385

Figure 13-9: Jane Smith Limited Balance Sheet at 5 April 201X.

The bottom of the balance sheet in Figure 13-9 shows how the owners of the business have supported these assets, in this case by their own funds. As you can see later, they could also have invested profit made in earlier years back into the business (see the later section 'Understanding reserves'). I've also assumed that the owner's house is now a business premises owned by her company. (This assumption has wider implications, but none relevant to the arithmetic or the balance sheet.)

Categorising assets

Accountants describe *assets* as valuable resources, owned by a business, that were acquired at a measurable monetary cost.

The exception to the *paid for* part is the grey area of goodwill. *Goodwill* is the value placed on the business's reputation and other intangible assets – a brand name, for example. Assessing the value of this asset is of particular interest to those buying or selling a business.

One useful convention recommends listing assets in the balance sheet in their order of permanence; that is, starting out with the most difficult to turn into cash and working down to cash itself. This structure is practical when you're looking at someone else's balance sheet, or comparing balance sheets. It can also help you recognise obvious information gaps quickly.

Accounting for liabilities

Liabilities are claims against the business. These claims may include such items as tax, accruals (which are expenses for items used but not yet billed for, such as telephone and other utilities), deferred income, overdrafts, loans, hire purchase and money owed to suppliers. Liabilities can also be less easy to identify and even harder to put a figure on, bad debts being a prime example.

Understanding reserves

Reserves are the accumulated profits that a business makes over its working life, which the owner has ploughed back into the business rather than taking them out.

Jane Smith's balance sheet (see the earlier section 'A balance sheet') shows her capital as being the sole support for the liabilities of the business. The implication is that she put this whole sum in at once. In practice, this sum is much more likely to have been paid over time, and in a variety of ways.

Perhaps she started out in business – because that's how you must now look at her affairs – with a sum of £25,000. In the period since she's been in business, she's made a net profit after tax of £50,000 and put this amount back into her business to finance growth. In addition, the premises that she bought a few years ago for £111,615 have just been re-valued at £150,000, a paper gain of £38,385.

The bottom portion of her company balance sheet may now look as shown in Figure 13-10.

	£	£
FINANCED BY		
Capital introduced		25,000
Reserves		
Capital reserve	38,385	
Revenue reserve	50,000	88,385
		113,385

Figure 13-10: Jane's reserves.

The profit of £50,000 ploughed back into the business is called a *revenue reserve*, which means that the money actually exists and can be used to buy stock or more assets. The increase in value of the business premises is, on the other hand, a *paper* increase. Jane can't use the £38,385 increase in *capital reserves* to buy anything, because it's not in money form until the premises are sold. However, she can use that paper reserve to underpin a loan from the bank, so turning a paper profit into a cash resource. Both reserves and the capital introduced represent all the money that the shareholder has invested in this venture.

Analysing Performance

Gathering and recording financial information is a lead-up to analysing a business to see how well (or badly) it's doing. This analytical process requires tools, in this case ratios, and you need to understand their usefulness and limitations before you can use them to good effect.

Using ratios

All analysis of financial information involves comparisons. Because a business is constantly changing, the most useful way to measure activity is through ratios. A *ratio* is simply one number expressed as a proportion of another. Travelling 100 miles may not sound too impressive, until you realise it took one hour. The ratio here is 100 miles per hour. If you know that the vehicle in question has a top speed of 120 miles per hour, you've some means of comparing it to other vehicles, at least in respect of their speed. In finance, too, ratios can turn sterile data into valuable information in a wide range of different ways and help you make choices.

I describe the key financial ratios you need from the outset in the following sections. Monitor all these at least on a monthly basis.

Gross profit percentage

To calculate gross profit percentage (*percentage* is one form of ratio where everything is described in terms of a relationship to 100), you deduct the cost of sales from the sales and express the result as a percentage of sales. The higher the percentage, the greater the value you're adding to the goods and services you're producing. Figure 13-11 shows the calculation.

Figure 13-11: Formula for calculating gross profit percentage.

$$\text{Gross profit percentage} = \frac{\text{Profit}}{\text{Sales} - \text{Cost of sales}} \times 100$$

Operating profit percentage

Calculating the operating profit percentage gives you a measure of how well the management is running the business, because operating expenses for which the management is responsible form a component of the calculation. Financing decisions are presumed to be the owner's responsibility; interest and taxation are set by the government, so those numbers are out of management control and accountability.

To calculate this number, you deduct from profit not only the cost of sales but also expenses, as Figure 13-12 shows.

Figure 13-12: Calculating operating profit.

$$\text{Operating profit percentage} = \frac{\text{Profit}}{\text{Sales} - (\text{Cost of sales} + \text{Cost of operations})} \times 100$$

Net profit percentage

Working out your net profit essentially gives you your business's *bottom line,* telling you how much money is left for you to take out or reinvest in your business. A higher percentage means that you're making more money from each pound of sales generated.

You can calculate net profit after you pay tax or before – earnings before interest and tax, known as EBIT.

In its after-tax form, which Figure 13-13 shows, net profit percentage represents the sum available for the business to distribute as dividends or retain to invest in its future.

Figure 13-13:
Calculating
net profit
percentage.

$$\text{Net profit percentage} = \frac{\text{Profit}}{\text{Sales} - (\text{Cost of sales} + \text{Cost of operations} + \text{Taxes paid})} \times 100$$

Return on capital employed

This number, frequently abbreviated to ROCE, is the primary measure of performance for most businesses. If, for example, you invested £10,000 in a bank and at the end of the year it gave you £500 interest then the return on your capital is 5 per cent (£500 ÷ 10,000 x 100 = 5 per cent).

A business calculates this ratio by expressing the operating profit (profit before interest and tax) as a percentage of the total capital employed – both in fixed assets and in working capital, called *net current assets* in the balance sheet. Figure 13-14 shows the formula for calculating ROCE. Refer to Figure 13-12 to work out the operating profit number.

Figure 13-14:
Calculating
return on
capital
employed.

$$\text{ROCE} = \frac{\text{Operating profit}}{\text{Fixed assets} + \text{Working capital}} \times 100$$

If you think about it, return on capital employed is the same as the return on the shareholders' funds plus the long-term loans, or the 'financed by' bit of the balance sheet.

Current ratio

You calculate the current ratio by dividing your current assets by your current liabilities. Only one rule exists about how high (or low) the current ratio should be. It should be as close to 1:1 as the safe conduct of the business allows. This rule isn't the same for every type of business, though. For example, a shop buying in finished goods on credit and selling them for cash can run safely at 1.3:1. A manufacturer, with raw material to store and customers to finance, may need over 2:1. This difference is because the period between paying cash out for raw materials and receiving cash in from customers is longer in a manufacturing business than in a retail business.

Average days' collection period

Any small business selling on credit knows just how quickly cash flow can become a problem. You calculate the average collection period ratio by dividing the value of your debtors by the value of credit sales, and then multiplying that by the days in the period in question. The result is expressed in days, so you can see in effect how many days it takes for your customers to pay up, on average.

A period of 60 days is fairly normal for customers to take before paying up. Around 45 days is a good target to aim for and 90 days is too long to let payment go without chasing. The above is a good control ratio, which has the great merit of being quickly translatable into a figure any businessperson can understand, showing how much giving credit costs you.

If you're selling into overseas markets, the practice on punctual payments can vary widely. Knowing your average collection period for these markets can help you to plan cash flow more effectively.

Stock control ratio

A simple way to tackle stock control is to see how many times your business turns its stock over each year. Dividing the cost of sales by the value of your stock gives you this ratio. The more times you can turn your stock over, the better.

Gearing down

The more borrowed money a business uses, as opposed to the money the shareholders have put in (through initial capital or by leaving profits in the business), the more highly *geared* the business is. Highly geared businesses can be vulnerable when sales dip sharply, as in a recession, or when interest rates rocket, as in a boom. Figure 13-15 shows how to calculate gearing percentage.

Figure 13-15:
Calculating gearing percentage.

$$\text{Gearing percentage} = \frac{\text{Debt (long-term borrowings)}}{\text{Debt + Shareholders' funds}} \times 100$$

Gearing levels in small firms average from 60 per cent down to 30 per cent. Many small firms are probably seriously over-geared, especially when they're in the first stages of growth.

Try these tools:

- ✔ **Bankrate.com,** an aggregator of financial rate information, has seven free small business ratio calculators that cover all aspects of measuring financial performance (http://www.bankrate.com/brm/news/biz/bizcalcs/ratiocalcs.asp).

- ✔ **SME Toolkit,** by the International Finance Corporation (IFC), a member of the World Bank Group, includes free ratio calculator tools (go to www.smetoolkit.org, Accounting and Finance, and then Financial Management and Reporting).

Keeping on the Right Side of the Law

Whether the money in the business is yours alone, provided by family and friends or supplied by outside financial institutions, you've a legal responsibility to make sure that you keep your accounts in good order at all times. If you're successful and need more money to expand, you need financial information to prove your case. If things aren't going so well and you need to strengthen your position to weather a financial storm, you've even greater need of good accounting information.

Whatever the circumstances in the background, tax and VAT authorities need to be certain that your figures are correct and timely.

Carrying out an audit

Companies with balance sheet totals in excess of £3.26 million or annual turnovers above £6.5 million are required to appoint an auditor and have their accounts audited. However, a large number of much smaller businesses still have to have their accounts audited. If, for example, you've shareholders owning more than 10 per cent of your firm, they can ask for the accounts to be audited.

You can check whether your business is exempt from having to be audited at
www.gov.uk/audit-exemptions-for-private-limited-companies.

The auditor's job is to report to the members (shareholders) of the company
as to whether the accounts have been properly prepared, taking notice of
the appropriate accounting rules. The auditor must also report as to whether
the accounts give a *true and fair* view of the state of the company's affairs. In
order to arrive at a conclusion, the auditor examines the company's records
on a test basis to ensure that the accounts aren't materially incorrect. This
examination doesn't mean that the auditor checks every detail, but he does
look at a representative sample of transactions to get a feel for whether or
not the books are being properly kept.

Filing your accounts

If you're trading as a company then you have to file your accounts with
Companies House (www.companieshouse.gov.uk) each year.

Unless you're filing your company's first accounts, the time normally allowed
for delivering accounts to Companies House is ten months from the end of the
relevant accounting period for private companies. If you're filing your company's first accounts and they cover a period of more than 12 months, you must
deliver them to the registrar within 22 months of the date of incorporation for
private companies. Late filing attracts financial penalties, details of which you
can find on the Companies House website.

All companies must prepare full accounts for presentation to their shareholders, but small and medium-sized companies can send abbreviated accounts
to the registrar of companies. Abbreviated accounts contain little information that can be of use to a competitor. Nothing is given away on turnover or
margins, for example, a luxury denied to larger companies. Small companies'
accounts (ones with less than £6.5 million turnover, balance sheet total less
than £3.26 million and fewer than 50 employees on average, to be precise)
delivered to the registrar must contain

- ✔ An abbreviated balance sheet

- ✔ Selected notes to the accounts, including accounting policies, share
   capital, particulars of creditors payable in more than five years and the
   basis of any foreign currency transactions

- ✔ A special auditor's report (unless exempt from audit; see the preceding
   section on audits)

The rules of disclosure are complex and the above is only a brief outline of the requirements. If you're unsure about the information that you have to provide, you should take professional advice.

Managing Your Accountant

Accountancy is just another business discipline, like selling, research, administration or production. So you need to manage, motivate, reward and appraise your accountant, like any other member of staff. Whoever acts as your company accountant, be he a part-timer from outside or a fellow director, you as the owner must take the lead.

✔ Your monthly management accounts should be available within a week of the end of each month. You have the wrong accountant or the wrong accounting system if you can't achieve this standard. If you don't yet have monthly management accounts, make that your accountant's next measurable goal.

✔ Accounting systems and reports should be simple, free of jargon and supported by clear written explanations of the key issues to consider. For example, if profits are down by 10 per cent, as well as the bald figures an explanation that this reduction was caused by a 5 per cent reduction in sales of product X and a 5 per cent increase in raw material costs gives a clear indication of responsibilities and possible remedies.

✔ Your accountant should also ensure that your books and records are kept to the standard required by company law. He must also see that your accounting policies meet the required standards and that accounts, VAT returns, and PAYE and tax demands are dealt with in a timely manner.

Chapter 14

Managing Your Tax Position

. . . .

In This Chapter

▶ Finding out how much tax you have to pay

▶ Seeing how to cut that bill, legally

▶ Knowing how to handle employment taxes

▶ Getting through a tax investigation intact

. . . .

*T*he government raised £591.7 billion in 2012/13 in one form of tax or another, equivalent to roughly £11,500 for every adult in the UK. Not only is the amount colossal but now about a zillion ways exist in which tax is raised. Aside from income tax, which only accounts for £154.8 billion of the money raised, you have value added tax (VAT) and national insurance (NI), which most people brush across. Then you have taxes or reliefs from paying tax on fuel, capital gains, capital expenditure, research and development, business rates, excise duty, a climate change levy, air passenger duty, landfill tax, an aggregates levy, small company tax relief, vehicle excise duties and stamp duties, to mention but a few that the successful owner manager can expect to encounter. Each of these tax categories in turn has a number of its own categories. VAT, for example, is levied at a standard rate, reduced rate, zero rate and exempt from VAT altogether, and the government shifts about the 50 or so product and service categories within each VAT category from time to time. The government has made 44 major changes to the tax system in the UK since 1979 and a couple of thousand minor ones.

If you think that all, or even most, of the profit you make in your business comes your way, think again. The government takes a sizeable slice of everything you make, in one way or another, and gets very nasty if you try to evade its clutches. You may be starting your first business, but government agencies have had centuries to hone their skills in extracting their pound of flesh. Since 1842, when income tax was reintroduced into Britain, everyone in business has been required to account for their income and profits.

Before you reach for your passport and head offshore, taxing entrepreneurs is a fact of life in almost every country in the world, though both the amounts and methods of assessment vary widely. Surprisingly enough, the tax climate in the UK is relatively benign and people here pay less than most. So although you may have to pay tax, you don't have to pay too much. As a Morgan Stanley advert succinctly puts it, 'You must pay taxes. But there's no law that says you gotta leave a tip.'

What follows is a guide to the taxes you should prepare to face, rather than an accurate statement of the amounts involved. In any normal year many tax rates change, and since the credit crunch the pace of those changes has accelerated sharply. VAT, for example, moved from 17.5 per cent, to 15 per cent and then back to 17.5 per cent, and is currently at 20 per cent as I write this edition – and all that in the space of a year or so. Add that to the changes that will come in if Scottish devolution comes to pass and their strong case for devolving corporation tax to the Scottish Parliament is upheld, and the next few years should be even more volatile. (Scotland, by the way, is pushing for a lower rate of corporation tax than that applying to the UK as a whole, as indeed is Northern Ireland. We may soon have some new tax havens close to home.)

A survey of the UK tax system as it stood at October 2012 (www.ifs.org.uk/bns/bn09.pdf) by the Institute for Fiscal Studies outlines the amount of tax raised by category and the changes and new taxes introduced since 1979. Not exactly bedtime reading, more a horror story.

You can keep up to date with all the taxes that apply to business in the UK on the Gov.uk website (www.gov.uk/browse/business/business-tax).

Tackling Taxes for Different Types of Businesses

The government treats sole traders, partnerships and limited companies differently for tax purposes, so I look at each in turn.

Managing your tax position is one area in which timely professional advice is essential. Advice is even more important because tax rules can change every year. Good advice can both help to reduce your overall tax bill and increase the value of profits to the business. Head to Chapter 12 for details on finding good advisers.

Figuring out sole traders and partnerships

A partnership is treated as a collection of sole traders for tax purposes, and each partner's share of that collective liability has to be worked out. If you're a *sole trader* (in other words, self-employed), your income from every source is brought together and the profit is taxed altogether. Income from business is one of a number of headings on your general tax return form.

In the UK, the key taxes that you need to calculate are

- ✔ Income tax on profits
- ✔ Class 4 NI on profits
- ✔ Capital gains tax, on the disposal of *fixed assets* such as property at a profit, or when the whole business is sold
- ✔ Inheritance tax, paid on death or when certain gifts are made

Neither of the last two taxes is likely to occur on a regular basis, nor do they occur in the first few years in business, so I don't cover them here. When those taxes do come into play, the sums involved are likely to be significant and you should take professional advice from the outset.

Adding up income tax

Under the self-assessment tax system in the UK, you pay taxes for your accounting year in the calendar year in which that accounting year ends. Special rules apply for the first year and the last year of trading to ensure tax is charged fairly.

If your turnover is low – currently in the UK less than the VAT threshold of £77,000 per year – you can summarise your income on three lines: sales, expenses and profit (see this factsheet for details: www.hmrc.gov.uk/ factsheet/three-line-account.pdf). If your turnover is above the minimum, you have to summarise your accounts to show turnover, gross profit and expenses by account categories, such as vehicle running costs, advertising, telephone and rent.

No matter how you account for your business income, as a sole trader or partnership you get to deduct a personal allowance amount from your profit figure, paying income tax on your profit minus your personal allowance. The personal allowance is the current threshold below which you don't pay tax.

Calculating class 4

You calculate class 4 NI based on taxable profits. The percentage you pay depends on what range your profits fall in. Expect to pay around 9 per cent if the number falls in a range from approximately £7,000 to £43,000. Above that figure, you pay 2 per cent. The percentage is paid in addition to the flat-rate Class 2 NI contributions of about £2.50 per week.

All these rates and amounts change in March of every year, but the broad principles remain the same. You can find the latest NI contribution rates on the website of HM Revenue and Customs (HMRC) at www.hmrc.gov.uk/rates/nic.htm.

Looking at levies on companies

Companies have a legal identity separate from those who work in them, whether or not those workers also own the company. Everyone working in the business is taxed as an employee. The company is responsible through the pay as you earn (PAYE) system for collecting tax and passing it to the tax authorities.

Directors' salaries are a business expense, just as with any other wages, and are deducted from the company's revenues in arriving at its taxable profits.

Companies in the UK pay tax in three main ways at rates that can change each year. The current company tax rates are published on the HMRC website (www. hmrc.gov.uk/rates/corp.htm).

- ✔ **Corporation tax** is paid on the company's profits for the year, as calculated in the tax-adjusted profits. The rate of corporation tax in the UK, and in many other countries, depends on the amount of profits made. In the UK, if the profits are less than £300,000, the small companies rate applies, currently 20 per cent. Above £1.5 million, the full rate of around 23 per cent is charged (at the time of writing that rate was due to fall to 21 per cent in 2014). For figures in between, a taper applies (all these figures are subject to annual review in the budget). Corporation tax is payable nine months after the end of the accounting period.

- ✔ **Dividend payment taxes** are levied on the distribution of profit to shareholders. This arrangement gives the appearance of taxing the same profit twice, but through a process of tax credits this double taxation doesn't generally occur. When a shareholder gets a dividend from a company, it comes with a tax credit attached, which means that any shareholder who pays the basic rate of tax won't have to pay any more tax. Higher-rate taxpayers, however, do have a further amount of tax to pay.

- ✔ **Capital gains tax** is owed if a company sells an asset, say a business property, at a profit. This capital gain is taxed along the general lines of corporation tax, with lower rates applying to smaller companies.

Assessing the best legal structure

The most important rule is 'never let the tax tail wag the business dog'. Tax is just one aspect of business life. If you want to keep your business finances private, the public filing of accounts required of companies isn't for you. However, if you want to protect your private assets from creditors if things go wrong, being a sole trader or partner probably isn't the best route to take.

Company profits and losses are locked into the company, so if you've several lines of business using different trading entities, you can't easily settle losses in one area against profits in another. But because sole traders are treated as one entity for all their sources of income, they've more scope for netting off gains and losses. Here are a few other points to bear in mind:

- ✔ If your profits are likely to be small, say well below £50,000, for some time, then from a purely tax point of view you may pay less tax as a sole trader, because as an individual you get a tax-free allowance. Your first few thousand pounds of income aren't taxable. This amount varies with personal circumstances and can change in the budget each year.

- ✔ If you expect to be making higher rates of profit (above £50,000), and you want to reinvest a large portion of those profits back into your business, then you may be better off forming a company. Companies don't start paying higher rates of tax until their profits are £300,000. Even then, they don't pay tax at 40 per cent. A sole trader is taxed at the 40 per cent rate by the time her profits reach about £30,000, taking allowances into account. So a company making £300,000 taxable profits can have £54,000 more to reinvest in financing future growth than does a sole trader in the same line of work.

- ✔ Non-salary benefits are more favourably treated for the sole trader. You can generally get tax relief on the business element of costs that are only partly business related, such as running a vehicle. A director of a company is taxed on the value of the vehicle's list price and isn't allowed travel to and from work as a business expense.

However, the whole area of company structure is complicated and depends heavily on what you want to achieve. For example, if you want to maximise your entitlement to make pension contributions, then a strategy that's tax efficient – for example, incorporating (as turning yourself into a limited company is known) – may be a bad idea. Get professional financial advice before you make any decision in this area.

Whiting Partners, a firm of chartered accountants and business advisors, has a useful guide to help you decide, from a tax perspective, which legal structure would be best for you at various levels of annual profits. Check out www.whitingandpartners.co.uk/News/Limited-Company-v-SoleTrader.

Paying Taxes

Most businesses encounter two taxes at some point; the more successful you are, the sooner you get swept into the taxman's net. Value added tax (VAT) is a tax based on your turnover, and the second – business tax – is based on the profit you make. The HMRC website (www.hmrc.gov.uk) contains all the latest tax rates and details of almost everything you're likely to need to complete your tax returns correctly.

Valuing VAT

As well as paying tax on profits, every business over a certain size has, in effect, to collect taxes too. Value added tax (VAT) is a tax on consumer spending. VAT is a European system, although most countries have significant variations in VAT rates, starting thresholds and the schemes themselves.

HMRC produces a range of leaflets, factsheets and booklets on VAT and other areas of taxation for guidance only (www.hmrc.gov.uk/leaflets). For the latest rules and rates go to www.hmrc.gov.uk/businesses. If in doubt (and the language isn't easy to understand), ask your accountant or the local branch of HMRC; after all, they prefer to help you to get it right in the first place than have to sort it out later when you've made a mess of it.

You get no reward for collecting VAT, but you're penalised for making mistakes or for sending returns in late. Read on for the nitty-gritty of what you need to do.

Registering for VAT

VAT is a complicated tax. The general rule is that all supplies of goods and services are taxable at the standard rate (anything between 5 and 20 per cent is possible) unless the law specifically states they're to be zero rated or exempt.

You can register voluntarily for VAT at any time at the HM Revenue and Customs website (www.hmrc.gov.uk/vat/start/register/signup-online.htm), but you must register your business for VAT if your taxable turnover – that is, your sales (not profit) – exceeds £77,000 in any 12-month period (£70,000 if you sell by mail order or via the Internet) or looks as though it may reasonably be expected to do so. This rate is reviewed each year in the budget and changes frequently. (The UK is significantly out of line with many other countries in Europe, where VAT entry rates are much lower.)

In deciding whether your turnover exceeds the limit, you must include your zero-rated sales (things like most unprocessed foodstuffs, books and children's clothing) because they're technically taxable; but the rate of tax is 0 per cent. Leave out exempt items like the provision of health and welfare, finance and land. Currently, you don't have to include business done overseas in your VAT calculations.

It sometimes pays to register even if you don't have to – if you're selling mostly zero-rated items, for example, because you can reclaim VAT that you've paid out on purchases. Also, being registered for VAT may make your business look more professional to your potential customers.

You can find out how and when to register for VAT at the HM Revenue and Customs website (www.hmrc.gov.uk/vat/start/register/).

Calculating VAT

You may need to extend the simple bookkeeping system I describe in Chapter 13 to accommodate VAT records. For example, the analysed cash book you use in a simple system needs additional columns to accommodate the pre-VAT sales, the amount of VAT and the total of those two figures.

Calculating the VAT element of any transaction can be confusing. Following these simple steps helps you always get it right:

1. Take the gross amount of any sum (items you sell or buy) – that is, the total including any VAT – and divide it by 120, if the VAT rate is 20 per cent. (If the rate is different, add 100 to the VAT percentage rate and divide your transaction amount including VAT by that number.)

2. Multiply the result from Step 1 by 100 to get the pre-VAT total.

3. Multiply the result from Step 1 by 20 to arrive at the VAT element of the bill.

Completing the VAT return

VAT returns are where a computer-based bookkeeping system wins hands down. The accounting package automatically generates VAT returns. All you have to do is enter the current VAT rate. If you get web-enabled software updates, you may not even have to do this.

Basically, VAT inspectors are interested in three figures:

✔ The amount of VAT you collected on the goods and services you sold.

✔ The amount of VAT collected from you by those who've sold you goods and services.

✔ The difference between those two sums. If the difference is positive, that's the amount of VAT due to be paid. If the number is negative, you're entitled to reclaim that amount.

For a business, VAT is a zero-sum game – you don't make money and you don't pay money – the end consumer picks up the tab.

The final two numbers are a check on the reasonableness of the whole sum. You have to show the value of your sales and purchases, minus VAT, for the period in question.

The person registered for VAT has to sign the VAT return. Remember that a named person is responsible for VAT – a limited company is treated as a person in this instance. Not only are you acting as an unpaid tax collector, but you also face penalties for filing your return late or incorrectly. You have to keep your VAT records for six years and periodically you can expect a visit from a VAT inspector.

Sending in VAT returns

Each quarter, or each year if you take that option, you have to complete a return that shows your purchases and the VAT you paid on them, and your sales and the VAT you collected on them. The VAT paid and collected are offset against each other and the balance sent to HMRC. If you paid more VAT in any quarter than you collected, you get a refund.

To help smaller businesses that may struggle with the more traditional VAT return, HMRC has introduced the Flat Rate Scheme (FRS), which enables eligible businesses to calculate their VAT payment as a percentage of their total turnover. You still have to put VAT on your sales invoices, but you don't have to do the input and output tax return to settle up your VAT. Your VAT liability is agreed as a percentage of all your sales. This percentage is allocated by HMRC based on the type of trade your business carries out. You can find out more about the Flat Rate scheme at www.hmrc.gov.uk/vat/start/schemes/flat-rate.htm.

Virtually all VAT-registered businesses must submit their VAT returns online and pay any VAT due electronically. The very few exceptions include businesses going into insolvency and those businesses run by practising members of a religious society whose beliefs prevent them from using computers. You can find out all about completing your VAT return online and paying the tax due electronically at www.hmrc.gov.uk/vat/vat-online/moving.htm.

Choosing cash or income accounting

Generally, VAT is levied on invoiced sales, so in theory and often in practice occasions can arise when you have to pay VAT on sums you haven't collected yourself. This unhappy state of affairs can happen if you send out an invoice at the end of the quarter and your customer hasn't paid by the time you have to make the VAT return. If this situation proves a major problem, you can usually elect to pay VAT on a cash basis, rather than the strictly more correct income recognition basis that's triggered when you send out your invoices.

You can find out whether you're eligible to operate a cash VAT scheme at www.hmrc.gov.uk/vat/start/schemes/cash.htm.

Minimising tax on profit

You have no reason to arrange your financial affairs in such a way that you pay the most tax! While staying within the law by a safe margin, you can explore ways to *avoid* as opposed to *evade* tax liabilities. This avoidance is a complex area and one subject to frequent change. The tax authorities try most years to close loopholes in the tax system, while highly paid tax accountants and lawyers try even harder to find new ways around the rules.

Here are some of the areas to keep in mind when assessing your tax liability:

- ✔ Make sure that you include all allowable business expenses. Especially when you've recently set up in business, you may not be fully aware of all the expenses that you can claim. Discuss this with your accountant and check out HMRC's website (www.hmrc.gov.uk/incometax/relief-self-emp.htm) for more information.

- ✔ If you've made losses in any tax period, under certain circumstances you may carry them forward to offset future taxable profits or backward against past profits.

- ✔ You can defer paying capital gains tax if you plan to buy another asset with the proceeds. This arrangement is known as *rollover relief* and you can use it normally up to three years after the taxable event. Check out this website for the latest position on this and other capital gains tax reliefs: www.hmrc.gov.uk/cgt/businesses/reliefs.htm.

- ✔ Pension contributions reduce your taxable profits. You may even be able to set up a pension scheme that allows you some say over how those funds are used. For example, your pension fund can be used to finance your business premises. The pension fund in effect becomes your landlord. The company then pays rent, an allowable business expense, into your pension fund, which grows tax free.

- ✔ If you do intend to buy capital assets for your business, bring forward your spending plans to maximise the use of the *writing-down allowance*, which is the portion of the cost of the asset you can set against tax in any year. For example, if you propose to buy a computer or a very low-emission motor vehicle, you may be allowed to charge 100 per cent of the cost in the year you make the purchase. And if you know in March that you intend to buy a new computer later that year, by making the purchase before 5 April you can take the writing-down allowance in that tax year. If you delay until after that date, you have to wait until the following tax year to get the benefit of a lower tax bill. Find out more on this subject at www.hmrc.gov.uk/capital-allowances/basics.htm.

- ✔ Identify non-cash benefits that you and others working for you can take instead of taxable salary. For example, a share option scheme may achieve the same, or better, level of reward, with less tax payable.

✔ Examine the pros and cons of taking your money out of a limited company by way of dividends or salary. These routes are taxed differently and may provide scope for tax reduction.

✔ If your spouse has no other income from employment, she can earn a sum equivalent to her annual tax-free allowance (currently about £8,000) by working for your business. HMRC is currently looking hard at the taxation of husband and wife partnerships and companies, so check with your accountant to confirm what is allowed. The HMRC website (www. hmrc.gov.uk/manuals/bimmanual/BIM72065.htm) gives you its take on the subject.

✔ If you incurred any pre-trading expenses at any stage over the seven years before you started up in business, you can probably treat them as if you incurred them after trading started. Such expenses can include market research, designing and testing your product or service, or capital items such as a computer bought before you started trading and then brought into the assets of your business.

✔ You may be able to treat the full purchase price of business assets you bought through hire purchase in your capital allowances calculation.

This list is indicative rather than comprehensive. Taxation is a field in which timely professional advice can produce substantial benefits in the form of lower tax bills.

Tax Cafe (www.taxcafe.co.uk/business-tax.html) publishes a range of regularly updated business tax advice guides aimed at anyone wanting to find out how to pay less tax legally.

Handling Employment Taxes

Not only must you pay tax on your business profits and collect VAT from suppliers for onward transmission to an ever-hungry exchequer, but you also have to look after your employees' tax affairs too. As an employer you have a legal responsibility to ensure that an employee's taxes are paid, and you can end up picking up the tab yourself if the employee fails to. So ensure that you collect tax from employees' pay before paying them.

Paying PAYE

HMRC collects income tax from employees through the pay as you earn (PAYE) system. The employee's liability to income tax is collected as it's earned instead of by tax assessment at a later date. If the business is run as a limited company, then the directors of the company are employees. PAYE must be operated on all salaries and bonuses paid to directors, yourself included.

HMRC now issues booklets in reasonably plain English about how PAYE works. The main documents you need to operate PAYE are

- A deduction working sheet (Form P11) for each employee
- The PAYE Tables – two books of tax tables are in general use, which are updated in line with the prevailing tax rates:
  - Table A Pay Adjustment Table shows the amount that an employee can earn in any particular week or month before paying tax
  - Tables B to D and LR Taxable Pay Tables show the tax due on an employee's taxable pay
- Form P45, which is given to an employee when transferring from one employer to another
- Form P46, which is used when a new employee doesn't have a P45 from a previous employer (such as a student starting work for the first time)
- Form P60, which is used so that the employer can certify an employee's pay at the end of the income tax year in April
- Form P35, the year-end declaration and certificate for each employee – this form is used to summarise all the tax and NI deductions from employees for the tax year
- Form P6, the tax codes advice notice issued by the inspector of taxes telling you which tax code number to use for each employee

You work out the tax deduction for each employee using the following steps. (For _week_ read _month_, if that is the payment interval you use.)

1. Add the current week's gross pay to the previous total of gross pay to date, to show the total gross pay up to and including this week of the tax year.

2. Check the tax code number of the employee in Table A, to arrive at the figure of tax-free pay for that particular week.

3. Deduct the amount of tax-free pay from the total pay to date, to get the amount of taxable pay.

4. Work out the tax due on the total taxable pay for the year to date using Table B. Then make the appropriate deduction to allow for the tax due.

5. Deduct the amount of tax already accounted for in previous weeks from the total tax due, to work out the tax due for the week.

Allocating national insurance

As well as deducting income tax, as an employer you must also deduct national insurance (NI) contributions. Three rates of contributions apply for NI purposes:

- Table A – the most common rate, used in all cases except for those who qualify for Table B or C
- Table B – used for certain married women who have a certificate for payment at a reduced rate
- Table C – used for employees who are over pension age

For Tables A and B, you need to calculate two amounts: the employee's contribution and the employer's contribution. For Table C, no employee's contribution is payable. You record the amounts of contributions on the same deduction working sheets that you use for income tax purposes.

You can find the amounts of NI due by referring to the appropriate table. The tables show both the employee's liability and also the total liability including the employer's contribution for the week or month. You must record both these figures on the deduction working sheet.

Accounting for employment taxes

When you pay out wages and salaries to your staff, you need to record the net pay in your cash book as well as the PAYE and NI you've paid to the collector of taxes.

If you've only one or two employees, then the record of the payments in the cash book, together with the other PAYE documentation, is probably sufficient. But if you've any more, you should keep a wages book.

The deductions working sheet gives you a record of the payments made to each employee throughout the year. You also need a summary of the payments made to all employees on one particular date.

The law requires that employers *must* provide their staff with itemised pay statements, known as payslips. These payslips must show

- Gross pay
- Net pay
- Any deductions (stating the amounts of each item and the reason the deductions are made)

As an employer, you've a legal obligation to operate PAYE on the payments you make to your employees if their earnings reach the NI lower earnings limit (LEL). The HMRC website has details on the basics of employment taxes and related matters (www.hmrc.gov.uk/payerti/forms-updates/rates-thresholds.htm).

Surviving a Tax Investigation

If your books are in good order and you honestly report your income and expenses, you should have little trouble from the authorities. However, serious penalties exist for tax misdemeanours, and you're required to keep your accounts for six years. So if at any point tax authorities become suspicious, they can dig into the past even after they've agreed your figures – back six years if they suspect you've been careless, and back twenty years if they believe you've intentionally filed false accounts.

If you're found to have underpaid tax, you have to pay any tax you owe, plus interest, as well as a penalty of up to 100 per cent of the tax owed. These penalties are big business for HMRC: research published in October 2012 by UHY Hacker Young, an accounting firm, indicates that HMRC netted £434 million in extra tax and fines for small and medium-sized companies in the preceding year.

A tax investigation can be triggered for a variety of reasons, ranging from the banal to the frankly terrifying. A number of businesses are put under the spotlight each year, and you may just be pulled out of the hat. Or you may be in an industry that for one reason or another is being investigated generally. However, the more likely reason is that your accounts have shown major and unexplained changes (unusually high expenses, for example) or that you've been noticed for having a lifestyle inconsistent with the profits you're reporting. This revelation can come about through a diligent tax inspector, an envious neighbour, a disgruntled former spouse or employee, or indiscreet gossip in the pub.

However the investigation is triggered, you need professional advice from your accountant immediately. And it would certainly be prudent to protect yourself from any problems by getting insurance against a tax, VAT or NI investigation.

Joining the Federation of Small Business gives you immediate professional support and essential protection for tax matters (www.fsb.org.uk/tax-protection). Membership starts at £120 a year, plus a £30 joining fee, plus VAT. Also check out Tax Donut, which has useful advice on dealing with a tax enquiry (www.taxdonut.co.uk/tax/tax-problems-and-investigations/tax-investigations).

Part IV
Making the Business Grow

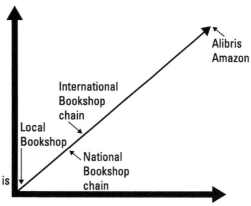

Richness

(Characteristics of)
- Bandwidth or amount of data that can be transmitted
- Ability to customize product or service to an individual buyer's needs
- Interactivity between 'buyer' and 'seller'
- Reliability of the service
- Security of data and transaction processes, including payment systems
- Currency — how current the data is
- Operating hours 24/7
- Ease with which languages can be added to facilitate global reach

Local Bookshop

International Bookshop chain

National Bookshop chain

Alibris Amazon

Reach (Characteristics of)
- Number of people/customers who can be approached
- Geographic spread
- New intermediaries in the distribution channels

For a look at some handy tools to help you work out your options for growing your business, go to www.dummies.com/extras/startingabusinessuk.

In this part . . .

✔ See how getting your business online creates growth.

✔ Get a handle on building teams and delegating tasks for them to carry out, and become an effective leader and motivator.

✔ Understand ways to get the best performance out of your business.

✔ See why growing your business matters and how to safely achieve it.

Chapter 15

Doing Business Online

. . . .

In This Chapter

▶ Understanding the power of the Internet and how to use it

▶ Checking out how you can add value to your business online

▶ Getting help with your website

▶ Making sure that you get seen online

▶ Analysing traffic

. . . .

According to the Office for National Statistics, the average weekly value of Internet retail sales in the UK in August 2013 was £586.6 million. That's an increase of 10.7 per cent compared with July 2012. Some 60 per cent of people in the UK have bought goods and services online, and the average adult spends £2,180 each year online.

The range of products sold online is extending considerably, and with it the way business does business is changing. For example, car buyers used to make five or more visits to a dealer while making up their mind, but now, according to research by the University of Buckingham, 86 per cent do most of their tyre kicking online, making barely one showroom visit before making their choice. So showrooms have been supplanted by websites and social media work on platforms like Facebook and Twitter.

Making your online presence effective, then, is vitally important. This chapter gives you a good grounding in what you need to know to harness the power of the Internet.

 Social media is part of your online presence. Read Chapter 21 for my take on that way to reach customers.

Appreciating the Power of the Internet

So just how big is the Internet? Well, in August 2013 over 2.8 billion people, more than a third of the world's population, were online and using methods of connectivity infinitely superior to the early primitive telephone links.

According to new global estimates by digital marketing data analyst eMarketer, in 2012 business-to-consumer e-commerce sales grew 21.1 per cent to top $1 trillion for the first time, and in 2013/14 sales will grow 18.3 per cent to $1.298 trillion worldwide.

As well as reaching virtually every corner of the planet, the Internet is now able to deliver a rich seam of valuable products in their own right. For example, when the first Internet bookshop opened up in 1982 they simply took orders for physical books by email. By 2010, however, Amazon was selling more Kindle editions than hardback versions of its books.

Ruminating on richness versus reach

The Internet has largely changed the maths of the traditional trade-off between the economics of delivering individually tailored products and services to satisfy targeted customers ('richness') and the requirement of businesses to achieve economies of scale ('reach'). Figure 15-1 shows how as the richness grows, so too does the number of potential customers. The Internet is the perfect medium to enable richness and reach to extend. The near-impossible-to-find second-hand book that you had to track down laboriously and at some cost is now just a mouse click away. The cost of keeping a retail operation open all hours is untenable, but sales can continue online all the time. At one time, a small business couldn't have considered going global until many years into its life. But thanks to the Internet, today the business can sell its wares to anyone, anywhere, with a basic website costing a few hundred pounds and with little more tailoring than the translation of a few dozen key words or phrases and a currency widget that handles its payments. Internet has made real what in the 1970s Marshall McLuhan, a Canadian visionary of marketing communications, called the 'Global Village'.

The book business is a powerful illustration of the way a product and its distribution systems endure in principle while changing in method over the centuries. From 1403, when the earliest known book was printed in Korea, through to Gutenberg's 42-line Bible printed in 1450, which in turn laid the foundations for the mass book market, the product, at least from a reader's perspective, has had many similarities. Even the latest developments of in-store print-on-demand and ebook delivery such as that by Amazon's Kindle look like leaving the reader holding much the same product. What has, however, transformed the book business is its routes to market, the scope of its reach and the new range of business partnerships and affiliate relationships opened up by the Internet.

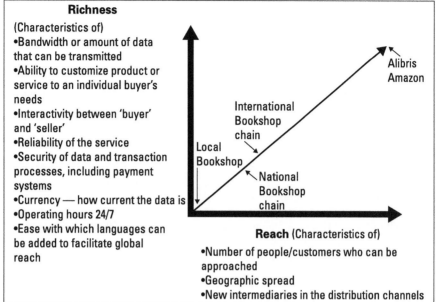

Figure 15-1: Richness versus reach in the book business.

Richness

(Characteristics of)
•Bandwidth or amount of data that can be transmitted
•Ability to customize product or service to an individual buyer's needs
•Interactivity between 'buyer' and 'seller'
•Reliability of the service
•Security of data and transaction processes, including payment systems
•Currency — how current the data is
•Operating hours 24/7
•Ease with which languages can be added to facilitate global reach

Local Bookshop

International Bookshop chain

National Bookshop chain

Alibris
Amazon

Reach (Characteristics of)
•Number of people/customers who can be approached
•Geographic spread
•New intermediaries in the distribution channels

Checking out clicks and bricks

Of course the Internet business world and the 'real' world overlap and, in some cases, overtake. Jessops, for example, died on the UK high street in January 2013, closing 187 stores, only to be born again on 28 March that year with a slimmed-down estate of 30 shops and a major presence on the Internet, under a new owner, Peter Jones of *Dragons' Den* fame. Many of the old economy entrants to the e-economy have kept the 'mortar' as well as acquiring 'clicks'. Trust stems from customers being able to physically see what the company stands for. Tesco, a UK-based international retailer, uses specially developed software to offer an intelligent Internet tool that reacts to customers' shopping habits, suggesting different sites related to subjects or products they're interested in. In this way, Tesco hopes to build a similar level of trust to that achieved in its stores, but over the Internet. The firm uses its local stores for 'pick and pack' and delivers locally using smaller vehicles.

Not on the High Street

When Holly Tucker and Sophie Cornish launched their online retail venture in 2006, they knew they were innovators. Their business, Not on the High Street, puts hundreds of personalised and unique gifts – gold rings, linen shawls, organic scented candles, overnight bags and more – all on the one website. Rather than trudging around dozens of shops or scouring the Internet, the pair has brought a near-inexhaustible choice of gifts under the umbrella of a single online shopping centre. In fact, the collections of gifts they offer are unlikely to feature on many high streets, now almost exclusively the domain of big multiples with standardised product ranges. The flood of charity shops that fill up vacant slots left by the growing band of failed retailers are unlikely to appeal to the discerning gift buyer either.

It's hardly surprising then that the business hit a £6.4 million turnover in year two, in 2010 it reached £14 million, and is expected to break the £100 million barrier in 2013/4. The founders put in £70,000 of their own money as an initial investment, raised by mortgaging their homes. The rest of the funds, some £7.5 million, came from venture capital firm Index Ventures, which has a track record of success in the sector having previously backed Betfair, Net-a-Porter and Last.fm. Ben Holmes, a partner at the venture capital firm, recognised that Tucker and Cornish were onto something with their idea of putting 35,000 products sourced from small businesses around the country on a single website, available to drop into one online shopping basket. Most of Not on the High Street's 3,200 suppliers have no online presence themselves or are too small to have much visibility in a crowded Internet marketplace.

In 2011 the business hired Jason Weston, formerly of Amazon, and Mark Hodson from PayPal, and their presence is beginning to shine through.

Recognising the limits – you have none!

Even if you think that e-business offers you few advantages, you can find yourself facing a range of unexpected threats and competitors heading your way courtesy of the Internet. For example, the competitors that a new offline business currently faces are probably small, and perhaps even big, firms in its own country or area and large international firms from elsewhere in the world. But with the Internet, the new business may now have small firms similar to itself, but based anywhere in the world, entering its market. Potentially, this reality can put the business starter up against hundreds if not thousands of competitors, all with the advantages of nimbleness and being driven by hungry entrepreneurs just like the business starter – you too, of course.

Your business faces dangers as a consequence of the Internet by virtue of its near unlimited capacity for penetrating and opening up markets to new entrants and innovations. Not only can competitors of all sizes from around the world attack your market using the Internet, but if you don't have an Internet presence, your company may also

> ✔ Appear old fashioned and out of date compared with other firms that do have websites.
>
> ✔ Miss out on some business that may only go to firms with an Internet presence. This problem is particularly true of rural markets, where the Internet has offered a degree of choice that's otherwise only available to customers in major cities.
>
> ✔ Lose its best staff, who leave in search of more stimulating and forward-thinking places to work.
>
> ✔ Miss out on the operational cost saving that can be made using e-business, which may make you uncompetitive so you lose out to other firms.

Reviewing What You Can Do Online

You can be forgiven for thinking that a website is just for those who plan to sell on the Internet. That's certainly a powerful argument for getting online and perhaps the easiest one to justify financially. Using a website to sell is so important that I've given that topic a whole section to itself in this chapter (see 'Selling Goods and Services'). But selling isn't the only valuable use your business can get from being on the Internet.

Generating advertising revenue

When you have a website, you have 'readers' who other people will pay to reach, just as they would if you had a hard-copy magazine. You can sell space on your website yourself, but you should be too busy running your business to get diverted with this type of distraction. The easiest way to get advertising revenue is to get someone else to do the hard work. Google Adsense (www.google.com/AdSense), for example, matches advertisements to your site's content and you earn money every time someone clicks an ad on your site.

You can check out the dozens of other affiliate advertising schemes at AssociatePrograms.com (www.associateprograms.com/directory), a site that has an affiliate program directory with 13,756 programmes listed.

Recruiting staff

When you start to grow your business, you can advertise for staff on your own website. In that way, you can be sure that applicants know something of your business and you can cut out most of the costs of recruitment. In addition, nearly a quarter of all jobs are filled using *job boards,* websites where employees and employers can get together much along the lines of a dating agency. The Internet's advantages are speed, cost and reach. You can get your job offer in front of thousands of candidates in seconds. The fees are usually modest, often less than regional paper job adverts. Services through job boards range from the passive, where employers and employees just find each other, to the proactive, where the website searches online candidate databases and makes suitable candidates aware of your vacancy.

I look at recruiting staff online in full in Chapter 11, along with other aspects of recruiting staff.

Answering frequent questions

Businesses get dozens of phone calls and letters asking essentially the same questions. By having an frequently asked questions (FAQ) section on your website you can head off most of those enquiries and save time and money.

CSGNetwork (`www.csgnetwork.com/csgfaqsgen.html`) has a free FAQ generator. Just enter the questions you receive frequently and their respective answers, click the generate button and the script outputs a complete FAQ page for you.

Carrying out market research

The Internet is a rich source of market data, much of it free and immediately available. But you can't always be certain that the information is reliable or free of bias because it can be difficult if not impossible to always work out who exactly is providing the information. That being said, you can get valuable pointers as to whether or not what you plan to sell has a market, how big that market is and who else trades in that space.

I look in detail at the sources of market data on the Internet, and at market research in general, in Chapter 4.

Establishing an Internet Presence with a Website

Thousands of small companies seduced into having a presence on the Internet quickly become disappointed. Part of the reason is that in the rush to put together a website, they end up with little more than an online leaflet or brochure. *E-commerce,* which is where the real value from being on the Internet arises, only comes about when you can buy and sell products and services, just as you can with any other route to market, and equally importantly when you can open up a dialogue with customers. That conversation can be as simple as a strong FAQ section, a blog or an invitation to ask for specific information.

Persevere because the gain is almost always worth the pain. Here are a few of the other benefits of being on the Internet for a small business:

- ✔ You can have global reach from day one, without the bother of getting a passport, a visa or turning up at an airport.

- ✔ You can extend your working time to 365 days a year, 24 hours a day, without creating an enormous wages bill or imposing impossible demands on the few people you have who can deal with sales enquiries or handle customer support.

- ✔ Things can change quickly in a small business. If you do business online, you can make changes to your product and service offers or prices quickly and inexpensively and fine-tune your propositions.

- ✔ You can reduce human error by eliminating certain stages in each transaction. The more times a piece of information is handled between a customer's enquiry and the order being fulfilled, the greater the chances are of something going wrong.

Read Ben Carter, Gregory Brooks, Frank Catalano and Bud Smith's *Digital Marketing For Dummies* (Wiley) to get a thorough insight into co-ordinating your website with your overall marketing plan.

As well as deciding exactly what copy you want on your website, you need to figure out what the website should look like and what you want people to do on it – whether you just want them to read, or to place orders, get into discussions and so on. At this point, you may well decide that you want a helping hand, so read on . . .

Deciding on content

The danger with producing content for websites is that you fall into the trap of believing that because it costs virtually nothing to load your site up with copy, pictures, diagrams and videos, you should do so. As I explain in Chapter 10, when it comes to marketing messages, less is best. Think through what you want website visitors to do as a result of arriving at your site – place an order, ask a question, gather more information, see a demonstration and so forth – and then produce the minimum clear content to achieve those goals. Make the content credible, original, current, varied and concise – readers typically ignore content beyond the first one-and-a-half to two page lengths.

Information on your site needs to be fresh and informative. Nothing is quite so off-putting as being on the fastest method of global communication known to humanity and seeing an invitation to a seminar that's already taken place or a special offer that expired weeks ago. You can buy in a news feed covering topics related to your business such as finance, travel or politics, or just general news, to ensure that your front page is always busy and topical, without you having to do a single thing. Check out sites such as Yellowbrix (www.yellowbrix.com) that harvest hundreds of thousands of news articles every day from the most respected news sources and categorise them into topics covering virtually every industry.

Designing the website

You probably already have a basic website writing tool with your office software. If you use Microsoft Office, you can find free web design tools in the Publisher section of your software. Basic stuff, but it gets you up and running. For more on building a website for free, check out David Crowder's excellent *Building a Web Site For Dummies* (published by Wiley).

You can also find hundreds of packages from £50 to around £500 that, with varying amounts of support, help you create your own website. Also take a look at these sites:

- ✔ **BT Broadband Office** (http://business.bt.com) has dozens of articles on how to improve your website design.

- ✔ **Top Ten Reviews** (www.top10bestwebsitebuilders.co.uk) provides a regular report on the best website creation templates rated by ease of use, help and support, value for money and a score of other factors. The best buy as I write this edition is available on an indefinite free trial, albeit on a slightly cut-down basis. You won't get an e-commerce facility unless you upgrade to a plan costing £6.39 a month.

- ✔ **Web Wiz Guide** (www.webwiz.co.uk/kb/website-design) has a tutorial covering the basics of Web page design and layout.

More expensive options come with access to an editor, hours of webmaster assistance per month, a domain name, hosting, email and more.

Good website design is essential to having a successful experience online. Here are some website design dos and don'ts:

- ✔ **Do think about design.** Create a consistent visual theme, grouping elements together so that your reader can easily follow the information you're presenting.

- ✔ **Do plan your site navigation.** Research shows that visitors have to be hooked within three clicks or they jump ship to a more user-friendly website. So, clear signposting is essential, with a simple menu of options on every page and a link back to your homepage so visitors can get back to their starting point. Your pages need to be organised intuitively so they're easy to navigate.

✔ **Do consider *loading time* (how long it takes the recipient's computer to download your data).** If loading takes too long, people may leave without looking at your site at all and you may have lost an opportunity for a sale. Use graphics rather than photographs, which take up too much memory. Optimise your hypertext mark-up language (HTML), especially on your home page, to minimise file size and download time by removing excess spaces, comments, tags and commentary. You can check your website's loading time at the search engine optimisation company 1-Hit's website: www.1-hit.com/all-in-one/tool.loading-time-checker.htm (I explain search engine optimisation in the later section 'Gaining Visibility').

✔ **Do optimise for searching.** Build in key words and tags and markers so that search engines easily find your site (see the later section 'Gaining Visibility').

✔ **Don't have pointless animation.** Many are distracting, poorly designed in terms of colour and fonts, and add unnecessarily to file size, slowing down your reader's search.

✔ **Don't use the wrong colours.** Colour choice is crucial; black text on a white background is the easiest to read and other colours, such as reds and greens, are harder to read. Check out Visibone's website (www.visibone.com/colorblind) for a simulation of the web designer's colour palette of browser-safe colours.

✔ **Don't waste your reader's time.** Making readers register on your site may be useful to you, but unless you have some compelling value to offer, don't. If you absolutely must, keep registration details to a couple of lines of information.

Check out The World's Worst Websites Ever (www.theworldsworstwebsiteever.com) to see how to avoid the biggest howlers, and in consequence how to get your website design right.

Checking out competitors

To get an idea of what to include and exclude from your website, check out your competitors' websites and those of any other small business that you rate highly. You can also get a few pointers from the Web Marketing Association's Web Award (www.webaward.org). Take a look at the Winners section where you can see the best websites in each business sector. Also check out The Good Web Guide (www.thegoodwebguide.co.uk), whose site contains thousands of detailed website reviews.

You can keep track of how many times your competitors change information on their websites by using the services on offer from companies such as Update Patrol (www.updatepatrol.com) or WebSite-Watcher (www.aignes.com).

Don't get into the habit of constantly changing the fundamental layout of your website. Customers may wonder if it's still you that's running the show! Customers expect consistency as well as currency when they come to your website.

Using a consultant

Thousands of consultants exist who claim to be able to create a website or you. Prices start from £499, where a consultant tweaks an off-the-peg website package slightly to meet your needs, to around £5,000 to get something closer to tailor-made for you. The Directory of Design Consultants (www.designdirectory.co.uk/web.htm) and Web Design Directory (www.web-design-directory-uk.co.uk) list hundreds of consultants, some one-man or one-woman bands, others somewhat larger. You can look at consultants' websites to see whether you like what they do. Web Design Directory also has useful pointers on choosing a designer.

If you're working within a set budget, you can consider auctioning off your Web design project. Make sure, though, that those you offer the auction to are going to do the job that you need. Using People Per Hour (www.peopleperhour.com), you state how much you're prepared to pay with a description of the project, and freelancers around the world bid under your price, with the lowest bidder winning.

If you decide to use a consultant to create your website, make sure that he builds it on a widely used platform such as Wordpress so that after it's up and running you can make small updates yourself. Otherwise, you incur further expense and delays every time you want to make a change such as changing a price, adding a product or revising a specification.

Registering domains

Having an Internet presence means that you need a *domain name* – the name by which your business is known on the Internet and that lets people find you by entering your name into their browser address box, such as example.com. Ideally, you want a domain name that captures the essence of your business neatly so that you come up readily on search engines, and one that's as close as possible to your business name (see Chapter 5 where I cover naming your business).

Domain names come in all shapes and sizes. Those such as '.com', exude an international/US flavour, and '.co.uk' implies a UK orientation. Charities usually opt for '.org', or '.org.uk', and '.net' or '.net.uk' are used by network service providers. Businesses often use '.biz', but it doesn't really matter what domain you use: what you want is to be seen.

Some domains are restricted. For example '.ac.uk' is used by higher education institutes in the UK and '.gov.uk' is used by UK government departments.

If your business name is registered as a trademark (see Chapter 5), you may (as current case law develops) be able to prevent another business from using it as a domain name on the Internet.

After you've decided on a selection of domain names your Internet service provider (ISP), the organisation that you use to link your computer to the Internet, can submit a domain name application on your behalf. Alternatively, you can use

- ✔ **Nominet UK** (`www.nominet.org.uk`), the registry for British Internet domain names, where you find a list of members who can help you register (though you can do so yourself if you're web aware).

- ✔ **A world directory of Internet domain registries** if you want to operate internationally; for example, by using a '.com' suffix or a country-specific domain. Check out `www.internic.net` and `www.norid.no/domenenavnbaser/domreg.html`.

- ✔ **A company that sells domain names,** such as Own This Domain (`www.ownthisdomain.co.uk`) and 123 Domain Names (`www.names.co.uk`), which provide an online domain-name registration service, usually with a search facility so you can see whether your selected name has already been registered. Electric Names (`www.electricnames.co.uk`) has a detailed domain name registration on its websites as well as offering a same-day registration service for prices between £10 and £25 per annum.

- ✔ **Free domain** that you obtain along with free web space by registering with an Internet community. These organisations offer you web pages within their community space as well as a free domain name, but most communities only offer free domain names that have their own community domain tagged on the end – this addition can make your domain name rather long and hard to remember, and unprofessional.

Hosting your website

As well as a domain name, you need to make your website visible to people searching on the web. Doing so is the function of a *host,* a service that stores all your website pages and makes them available to any computer connected to the Internet. Think of hosting as a sort of telephone exchange that makes sure that people can connect with each other.

Expect to pay a monthly fee that varies depending on how much information you plan to put online. Less than £5 per month should meet the needs of most new businesses putting their toe in the water.

Read *Web Hosting For Dummies* by Peter Pollock (Wiley) for the lowdown on everything about web hosting.

Selling Goods and Services

Everything from books and DVDs, through computers, medicines and financial services and on to vehicles and real estate are sold or have a major part in the selling process transacted online. Holidays, airline tickets, software, training and even university degrees are bundled in with the mass of conventional retailers such as Tesco that fight for a share of the ever-growing online market. The online gaming market alone has over 217 million users.

Not all business sectors are penetrated to the same extent by the Internet. According to Internet research company Forrester (www.forrester.com), although sales of clothing and footwear online is a multi-billion-pound business, it only accounts for 8 per cent of total sales. Contrast that with computers, where 41 per cent of sales occur online.

You may decide that you want to handle sales from your website yourself. Doing so certainly puts you in control, but it's not the only way to get business online. You can sell through other people's websites and even get someone else to despatch your goods and collect the cash. These options have their strengths and weaknesses, which I explore in this section.

Using third-party websites

Selling online may be a sound way into market, but you still have another option: tag along with someone else, much as you would if you were selling a product into a shop. That way you don't have to deal with the procedures of selling on the Internet that, aside from having your own website, require systems for showing and describing the goods and services on offer, as well as ordering payment and fulfilment facilities (these topics are the subject of the following sections).

The main advantages to setting up your own selling procedures are that you've greater control over where your products appear, which can be important to people passionate about their venture, and you get to keep the whole profit margin rather than sharing it with others in the channels of distribution. Setting up your own online sales operation requires several thousand pounds of investment upfront and a continuing stream of investment to keep your systems up to date, much as a retailer would need new shop fittings.

The other way of getting your goods and services to Internet markets is to piggyback on established, ready-built e-tail platforms:

- ✔ **Amazon** (www.amazon.co.uk/gp/seller/sell-your-stuff.html) will list, take payment, insure and, if required, pick, pack and deliver your products through its distribution system. Amazon provides tools to make it easy for you to upload inventory onto the website and you can have an unlimited number of listings to sell to its millions of customers. No fixed- term contract exists and charges depend on the type of products sold.

- ✔ **eBay** (http://pages.ebay.co.uk/businesscentre) isn't just a place to pick up a bargain and sell last year's ski gear when you move on to a snowboard. Sure, that's one side of the businesses. The other is the 160,000 or so people in the UK, Power Sellers as they're known, who make anything from a few hundred to tens or even hundreds of thousands of pounds. You can become Bronze-level Power Seller when your minimum value of sales reaches £750. (*eBay.co.uk For Dummies* (Wiley) by Marsha Collier, Jane Hoskyn and Steve Hill is a good place to find out more about selling on eBay.)

- ✔ **IBidFree.com** (www.ibidfree.com) was set up by Shane McCormack, a former eBay seller, with the proposition that you can have all the features of eBay but for free. IBidFree.com was created as a perfect opportunity for the person working from home trying to market their products without all their profits being swallowed up by charges and fees. The rules are few and, unlike eBay sellers, sellers are encouraged to place a link in their auctions back to their own websites. They're also allowed to directly email each other to allow for better communication.

Building a store front

Okay, so you've decided to take the plunge and set up your own shop front. If you were selling from a shop, you'd set out your window display and have a basket for customers to drop their shopping into prior to checking out and paying. Your online store has much the same features, with buttons and boxes around your order page allowing customers to select colours, sizes and quantities, place their order, pay and track the progress of their delivery. You need to decide what you want your online store to do because with linkages to other services you can arrange payment, delivery and even stock re-ordering, all of which come at an increasing price, eating into your profit margin.

You can choose between dozens of companies in the field such as Altcom (http://altcom.co.uk) and ekmpowershop (www.ekmpowershop.com), which offer turnkey online shop fronts from £19.99 a month. GoECart (www.goecart.com), founded in 2000, doesn't charge any listing or transaction fees and a merchant can open a store for around £600 a month. That fee includes all you need: a shop front, trolley buying system, payment acceptance, fraud protection, compete order and stock management and Web traffic statistics. This fee covers up to five admin users. GoECart also claims to have the most search-engine-friendly architecture.

Getting paid online

If you're going to trade on the Internet, you need some form of online payment such as a credit card merchant account. An alternative is one of a new breed of businesses tailored expressly for the Internet. The leader of the pack is PayPal (www.paypal.com). It claims to have 100 million accounts around the world and that firms using its services get an average of 14 per cent uplift in sales.

Using PayPal you can in effect get a merchant account with all major credit and debit cards in one bundle, without set-up fees or a lengthy application process, and start accepting payments within minutes. PayPal isn't free; you pay 20p per transaction and a sliding charge ranging from 3.4 per cent if your transactions amount to £1,500 in any month down to 1.4 per cent if sales are above £55,000 a month.

PayPal's Micropayments provides special rates for your low-value transactions, which is cost effective for items selling for less than £8.

eBay's international payments incur additional costs. PayPal charges a standard cross-border fee of between 0.4 and 1.5 per cent and a foreign currency conversion fee of up to 4 per cent.

WorldPay (www.worldpay.com), Click and Buy (www.clickandbuy.com) and Durango (www.durango-direct.com) offer similar services.

You can keep up with all the various services by reading the Merchant Account Forum (www.merchantaccountforum.com), a free newsletter set up by Richard Adams, who was so frustrated in his efforts to set up a merchant account for his first online business that he decided to launch a site to review merchant accounts.

Fulfilling orders

You've two main options when it comes to actually getting products and services to customers after they've bought online. The simplest way is doing it yourself. Take the orders, clear the payment and despatch the product.

Alternatively, MetaPack (www.metapack.com) automates and improves customer delivery using one or more of 23 carriers that provide between them around 590 services. You detail what you're sending, to whom, when you want it delivered and any other particulars such as security and the MetaPack software recommends a solution and can do anything from printing off a despatch label to booking a courier pick-up. Or, if you don't want the hassle of managing your own fulfilment, you can ship your products to an outsourced fulfilment business that handles as much or as little of the process as you want. Contact International Logistics (www.ilguk.com), or search the UK Warehousing Association's membership database (www.ukwa.org.uk), where you can look for a company in your area by specific tasks such as garment hanging, order picking, shrink wrapping and cold storage.

Amazon (http://services.amazon.co.uk/services/fulfilment-by-amazon/features-benefits.html) has its own fulfilment service. When you include the cost of overheads such as warehouse costs, packing supplies, postage and labour, dealing with customer service enquiries and returns handling, letting Amazon do the job may actually be a cheaper option than doing it yourself. Amazon claims to be able to get a small electronic item through its entire system, from stock held in its warehouse to cash in your bank, for around £1.85.

Gaining Visibility

Unless the world that matters to you knows how to find your website, you're winking in the dark. The tricks of the trade start with ensuring that your *homepage* is chock full of words and phrases that people would put into their search pane to find your website and that their chosen search engine can find. That's where this section comes in.

As well as ensuring that people find your website through a web search, promote it offline such as by featuring your website address on all products and publications. For more on promotion, head to Chapter 10.

Understanding search engines

Online searching services are often grouped under the single heading of *search engines.* However, two distinct services exist, directories and search engines, that both contain the key to unlocking the wealth of information contained across the Internet. Directories and search engines differ mainly in the way that each compiles its database of information.

✔ **Directories:** These depend on people to compile their information. You submit your *URL* (your website address; 'www.mybusiness.com' for example, with a brief description of your content. Editors view the website, see whether it's appropriate for the directory and place it in a category. Each category is subdivided into more specific categories. Dmoz (www.dmoz.org) claims to be the largest human-edited directory, followed in size and range by WoW (www.wowdirectory.com) and Web Directory List (www.webdirectorylist.co.uk).

✔ **Search engines:** Unlike directories, no human interaction takes place with the websites submitted. Instead, search engines have three major elements that attempt to arrive where the surfer is trying to get to:

- **The spider (also called the crawler):** The spider visits a web page, reads it and follows links to other pages within the site. The spider is looking for HTML tags or markers that the website creator weaves in to a web page, making it more likely that the spider finds a particular page.

- **The index:** Everything the spider finds goes into the *index,* which is a bit like a big digital book holding a copy of every web page the spider finds. This 'book' is updated every time a web page changes. Until a web page is entered into the index, it's not available to those searching with a search engine. Hence, the longer the interval between a site being *spidered,* as this process is known, the less likely that information searched for is relevant or current.

- **Search engine software:** This program is the one that sifts through the index to find search matches. It also ranks matches according to criteria to suggest which pages are most relevant. Some give a percentage score to each result, suggesting which is most likely to be the site with the information you require.

Check out Search Engine Watch (http://searchenginewatch.com) to keep abreast of major search engines and *meta search engines* (sites that give you results from several search engines at once). The site has tips for moving up search engine rankings.

Optimising your website

Search engine optimisation (SEO for short) is the best way to be sure of getting ranked highly in the results returned by the various search engines in order to attract potential customers. Some of the work you can do yourself, without shelling out pounds; other work costs you. The following sections lay out your options. (The bible on this subject is *Search Engine Optimization For Dummies* by Peter Ketn (Wiley) with the absolute beginner in mind. Now in its fifth edition, the book walks you through increasing your online ranking and explains the ins and outs and best practices of successful SEO.)

Doing what you can for free

Start by brainstorming how customers can enquire about your products or services, as well as key words and phrases used in your industry. Then make a list of the words that a searcher is most likely to use when looking for your products or services. As a rule of thumb, for every 300 words on your web page you need a key word or phrase to appear between 10 and 15 times. Search engines thrive on content, so the more relevant content, the better.

Good Keywords (www.goodkeywords.com) has a programme to help you find words and phrases relevant to your business and provides statistics on how frequently these words are used. Good Keywords also has several additional filters and tools to help you refine your key word lists, but these come at a price, as you may expect. Expect to pay upwards of £35.

Search engines also like important, authoritative and prestigious terms. So although you may not be able to boast 'by Royal Appointment', if can get your press releases quoted in the *Financial Times,* your comments included on popular blogs or your membership of professional associations mentioned on your home page, your chances of being spidered rise.

Another way to gain visibility is to search out other websites with which you can swap links for free. For example, you may be able to persuade a company selling marine insurance to put a link on its site to your boat-selling website in a reciprocal arrangement. Such relationships are known as *affiliate marketing,* which is new speak for a kind of finder's fee.

A variation of affiliate marketing is banner advertising on sites that you can't get onto for free. You can even sell advertising yourself, but you need to prove a substantial volume of visitors to your site first. A number of online UK business directories exist, such as UK Business Directory (www.business-directory-uk.co.uk) and Free Index (www.freeindex.co.uk), offering free listings to UK businesses and companies in exchange for a link from your company website linking to their directory.

As you may expect, Google has a service to help you connect to online searchers. You can pay for an advert to appear next to or above the search results any time the key words you've selected to promote your business come up in a Google search. A click on that ad takes searchers to your website. You pay Google when someone sees the ad and clicks through to your website and Google auctions off the key words, with the winners appearing earlier in the search list. Check out www.google.co.uk/ads/adwords/ for an explanation of how the process works.

Using a submissions service

You can build words into your website to help search engines find you. You can also go to a professional. Submission services such as Submit Express (www.submitexpress.co.uk), Rank4u (www.rank4u.co.uk) and Wordtracker (www.wordtracker.com) have optimisation processes that aim to move you into the top ten ranking in key search engines. 'Aim' is the important word here. These services don't guarantee anything, so the proof of the pudding is in the eating. If it works, you can always go back for a second helping.

Payment methods vary. For example, Rank4u has a no-placement, no-fee deal where you pay only after it's achieved the positioning you want. This service isn't on offer to every business all the time, so you need to check it out yourself.123 Ranking (`www.123ranking.co.uk`) has optimisation packages aimed at small and new businesses from £344 per annum. Search Engine Guide (`www.searchengineguide.com`; go to Search Engine Marketing) has a guide to all aspects of search engine marketing.

Paying for placement

If you don't want to wait for search engines to find your website, you can pay to have your Web pages included in a search engine's directory. That won't guarantee you a position; so, for example, if your page comes up at 9,870 in Google's list then the chance of a customer slogging his way to your page is zero. The only way to be sure you appear early in the first page or two of a search is to advertise in a paid placement listing. Major search engines such as Google AdWords (`https://adwords.google.co.uk`) and Microsoft's Bing (`https://secure.bingads.microsoft.com`) invite you to bid on the terms you want to appear for, by way of a set sum per click.

If you have a compelling proposition, you may persuade a search engine to offer you a 'pay-for-performance' deal, where it takes a share of the profits you make from having extra visibility. You can check out companies working this way at `http://pay-for-performance-seo.topseosratings.com`. *Digital Marketing For Dummies* (Wiley) provides a primer on this complex subject.

Tracking Traffic

A wealth of information is available on who visits your website: where they come from in terms of geography, search engine and search term used; where they enter your website (homepage, FAQs, product specifications, price list, order page); and how long they spend in various parts of your website. That information is aside from the basic information you automatically receive from orders placed, enquiries made or email contacts.

You can use visitor data to tweak your website and content to improve the user experience and so achieve your goals for the website. For example, you may find that lots of visitors are entering your website via a link found on a search engine that takes them to an inappropriate section of your site, say the price list, when you want them to start with the benefits of your product or success stories. By changing the key words on which your website is optimised, or by putting more visible links through the site, you can drive traffic along your chosen path.

Check that your website is accessible and user friendly at all times. Many people are impatient when it comes to web usage, and if a website doesn't work immediately, go elsewhere!

A good way to measure the success of your website is to make use of the free Google Analytics package available from the Google website (www.google. com). Google Analytics tracks the traffic that comes to your website from all *referrers* – that is, email marketing, search engines, pay-per-click downloads, display advertising and links from PDF documents. In doing so, Google Analytics gathers and reports data that shows how well your website is doing and enables you to make sense of all this information. The package also serves up statistics that provide details about the people who visit your website and allows you to track your landing page quality, and to see the specific pages that your visitors are viewing.

Google Analytics is aimed at marketers and business types, rather than webmasters and technologists – techie types – which makes it easy to use.

Chapter 16

Improving Performance

· ·

In This Chapter

▶ Seeing why retaining customers matters

▶ Measuring customer satisfaction

▶ Discovering ways to cut costs and work smarter

▶ Setting budgets

· ·

*A*n unpleasant truism in business, and in much else, is that after resources are allocated they become misallocated over time. Another way of looking at this problem is to say that just because something 'ain't broke', it doesn't mean you can't make it perform better still. To get your business to grow and keep growing needs a continuous effort to improve every aspect of that business.

In this chapter, I tell you how to boost your business by keeping your customers happy, improving your efficiency and effectiveness, and increasing and expanding your business.

Checking Your Internal Systems

In order to improve performance, you have to have systems in operation that help you measure performance in the first place. The following sections give you tips for evaluating how you spend your time and how to keep on top of your markets.

Keeping track of your routine

A good test of whether you're allocating enough time to the task of improving performance is to keep a track of how you spend your time, say, over a month. As well as recording the work you do and the time you spend on each major task, put the letter 'R' for routine, 'S' for strategic or 'I' for improving performance next to the task.

A routine task is something like meeting a customer or the bank manager, delivering a product or service, or taking on a new employee. Strategic tasks include considering a major shift of activities, say from making a product to just marketing it, forming a joint venture or buying out a competitor. Improvement activities include all the elements I talk about in this chapter – activities focused on getting more mileage, lower costs or higher yields out of the existing business.

Most owner-managers spend 95 per cent of their day on routine tasks and only tackle improvement and strategic issues when they hit the buffers. For example, most entrepreneurs don't worry too much about cash until it runs out. Then they pick up the phone and press customers into paying up. What they should have done, however, is introduce new procedures for collecting cash *before* the crunch.

If you're not spending at least 30 per cent of your time on improving your business and strategic issues, then you're probably heading for the buffers.

Analysing market position

A *SWOT analysis* is a way of consolidating everything you know about your competitive market position. SWOT stands for Strengths, Weaknesses, Opportunities and Threats. Many businesses use SWOT analysis regularly, and few people try it once and never again. For my money, SWOT is the way to go.

Discovering strengths and weaknesses

A strength or weakness is an element that matters to the customers concerned. In fact, it has to be such an important factor in customers' minds that they don't buy without it. These factors are known as critical success factors.

Find out the five or so things that you have to get right to succeed in your market. For retail booksellers, location, range of books, hours of operation, knowledgeable staff and ambiance may be the top five elements. Rank how well you think your competitors perform in these critical areas – or better still ask their existing, soon-to-be-your, customers. If they score badly, you may possess a strength.

Keeping an eye on opportunities and threats

You need to recognise that an idea, invention or innovation isn't necessarily an opportunity to grow your business. An opportunity has to be attractive, durable and timely. It centres on a product or service that creates or adds value for its buyer or end user.

Working out what's attractive to you is fairly straightforward. Estimating the likely life of an opportunity or whether the time is right for its launch isn't so easy. In a way, that's the essence of an entrepreneur's skill. You're looking for opportunities that bring the maximum benefit to the business while at the same time having a high probability of success. The benefits you're looking for may vary over time. In the early years of a business, cash flow may feature high on the list. Later, fast growth and high margins may be more important.

Threats can come from all directions. Changes in the political or economic climate, new legislation, and hackers and computer viruses can all have an impact on your business. For example, one business founder found to his dismay that his new website linked into dozens of pornography sites – the work of professional hackers. This disaster set his operation back months. Changes in the demographic profile of populations (more older people and fewer of working age) or changing fashions also hit all businesses.

Too many potential threats always exist for you to consider, so you need to focus on those with the greatest possible impact and that seem most likely to occur.

Doing the analysis

In the actual SWOT process you ask various groups to share their thoughts on your company's greatest strength, its most glaring weakness, the area of greatest opportunity and the direction of the greatest threat.

You need to consider each element separately for each major market segment. You can't carry out a SWOT analysis on the business as a whole. Because customer needs in each segment are different, you have to do different things in each segment to satisfy those needs. You may be up against different competitors in each segment, so your strengths and weaknesses are particular to that competitive environment. For example, look at travel methods – for families, car, coach and to a lesser extent train compete with each other; for businesspeople, car, plane and first-class rail travel are the biggest competitors.

Use the following steps to find out your SWOT quotient in each SWOT area:

1. **Determine your own view.**

   Decide what you think your business's best feature is, what its greatest weakness is, where your opportunities to gain more customers lie and what the biggest threat facing your business is.

2. **Find out what other entrepreneurs and your management team think about these issues.**

3. **Ask your newest front-line staff the same questions.**

4. **Form a customer focus group to consider the same questions.**

5. **Analyse how far apart the views of each group are.**

   If you're close to your customers and to your market, little difference should exist among the various groups. If a large difference exists, figure out what you can do to make sure that the gap narrows and stays that way.

The question 'So what?' is a good one to apply to all aspects of your SWOT analysis. That helps you concentrate only on the important issues. When completed, the SWOT provides the ingredients and framework for developing your marketing strategy, which I look at in Chapter 10.

Retaining Customers

Businesses spend an awful lot of time and money on winning customers and nothing like enough time and money on keeping them. This behaviour is as pointless as pouring water (or perhaps molten gold may be a better material to keep in mind) into a bucket with a big hole in the bottom. You need most if not all the flow to keep the bucket partially full. However fast the flow in, the flow out is just as fast.

Virtually all managers agree that customer care is important. A recent survey of major British companies showed that 75 per cent had recently instituted customer-care quality schemes. Sadly, another survey, conducted by American consultancy company Bain, also revealed that less than a third of those companies saw any payback for their efforts in terms of improved market share or profitability.

Bain suggests that the reason companies are disappointed with their attempts to improve customer care is that they don't have anything tangible to measure. To help overcome that problem, it suggests that managers focus on the Customer Retention Ratio, a Bain invention. For example, if you've 100 customers in January and 110 in December, but only 85 of the original customers are still with you, then your retention rate is 85 per cent. Bain's study demonstrated that a 5 per cent improvement in retention had a fairly dramatic effect on clients. For a credit card client it boosted profits by 125 per cent; for an insurance broker a 5 per cent increase in profits occurred; and a software house benefited from a 35 per cent improvement in profits. Bain claims that the longer customers stay with you, the more profitable they become.

The next sections explain why and how you should improve customer retention rates.

Realising why retaining customers matters

Studies and common sense indicate several principal reasons that retaining customers is so vital:

✔ Acquiring new customers costs more than retaining the ones you have. What with market research, prospecting, selling time and so on, acquiring a new customer costs between three and seven times as much as retaining an old one.

✔ The longer you retain a customer, the more years you have to allocate the costs of acquiring that customer to. By spreading the costs of acquiring new customers over ten years, instead of one or two, the annual profit per customer is higher. Suppose it costs you £500 to get a new customer, and that customer makes you £1,000 profit each year you keep her. If you keep the customer for one year, your annual profit is £500 (£1,000 minus £500). However, if you keep the customer for ten years, your annual profit is £950 (£1,000 minus £500 ÷ 10). Also, customers who stay tend, over time, to spend more.

✔ Regular customers cost less to serve than new customers. Insurance and underwriting costs as a percentage of sales fall by 40 per cent for renewal policies, for example. You don't incur upfront costs again.

✔ Long-term customers are often willing to pay a premium for service. They're also less prone to check your competitors because they know and like you.

Avoiding the consequences of losing customers is a powerful motivator for keeping in your customers' good graces. Here are a couple of those consequences:

✔ Dissatisfied customers tell between 8 and 15 others about their experience. Just avoiding this negative publicity has a value.

✔ Your former customers are fertile ground for your competitors. If you keep your customers, your competitors have to offer inducements to dislodge those customers, and doing so is expensive and time consuming.

Working to retain customers

Use these five rules to make sure that you retain customers and so improve your profit growth:

✔ Make customer care and retention a specific goal, and reward people for keeping customers, not just for getting them in the first place.

✔ Find out why you lose customers. Don't just let them go – send them a follow-up questionnaire or get someone other than the salesperson concerned to visit former customers to find out why they changed supplier. You may be surprised how pleased people are to tell you why they didn't stay with you, if you explain that it may help you serve them better the next time. QuestionPro, a web-based service for conducting online surveys, has a number of customer satisfaction survey templates that you can download for free (go to `www.questionpro.com/a/showArticle.do`). Also see 'Conducting the research' in Chapter 4 for more ideas.

- ✔ Research your competitors' service levels as well as their products. If practical, buy from them on a regular basis. If you can't buy from competitors, keep close to people who do.

- ✔ If one part of your organisation is good at caring for customers, get people there to train everyone else in what they do.

- ✔ Recognise that the best people to provide customer care are those who work directly with customers. But this means that you have to train them and give them the authority to make decisions on the spot. Aloof or indifferent employees don't convince customers that you really want to keep their business.

Retaining customers isn't the passive activity it sounds. The next sections offer concrete ways to keep your customers happy.

Monitoring complaints

One terrifying statistic is that 98 per cent of complaints never happen. People just don't get round to making the complaint, or worse still, they can find no one to complain to. You'd have to be a hermit never to have experienced something to complain about, but just try finding someone to complain to at 8:00 p.m. on a Sunday at Paddington Station and you get a fair impression of how being in the Gobi Desert feels.

You can never be confident that just because you're not hearing complaints, your customers and clients aren't dissatisfied and about to defect. Not making complaints also doesn't mean that they may not run around bad mouthing you and your business. Remember that on average people share their complaint with a score of others, who in turn are equally eager to share the bad experience. The viral effect of email has the potential to make any particularly juicy story run around the world in days if not hours.

Set up a system to ensure that your customers have ample opportunity to let you know what they think about your product or service. This opportunity may involve a short questionnaire, a follow-up phone call or an area on your website devoted to customer feedback. As a bonus, you may find you get some great ideas on how to improve your business.

Ninety-eight per cent of customers who have a complaint are prepared to buy from you again if you handle their complaint effectively and promptly. Not only do they buy from you again, but they also spread the gospel about how clever they were in getting you to respond to their complaint. Nothing makes people happier than having something to complain about that ends up costing them next to nothing.

Giving customers opportunities to complain

One entrepreneur who's more than aware of the problems (and, incidentally, opportunities) presented by complaints is Julian Richer, founder of the retail hi-fi chain Richer Sounds. His maxim is that his staff should maximise customers' opportunities to complain. The operative word in that sentence is *opportunities*, which you shouldn't confuse with *reasons*. In order to put this policy into effect, Richer uses a range of techniques. The whole customer satisfaction monitoring process starts from the moment customers enter one of his retail outlets. A sign near the door invites people to ring a bell if they've had particularly good service or help while in the shop. That help may be simply getting some great advice or finding a product they want to buy at a highly competitive price.

Customers find that, when they get their hi-fi equipment home, it contains a short questionnaire on a postcard asking them for their immediate post-purchase feelings. Does the product work as specified, is it damaged in any way, were they delighted with the service they received? The postcard is addressed to 'Julian Richer, Founder' and not, as is the case with so many other big businesses, to 'Customer Services, Department 126754, PO Box, blah blah blah'.

Richer does surveys on customer satisfaction and encourages his staff to come up with their own ideas for monitoring customer reactions. In fact, he insists that they hit minimum targets for getting customer feedback. Silence on the customer satisfaction front isn't an option for management in his business.

Setting customer service standards

Customer service is all those activities that support a customer's purchase, from the time she becomes aware that you can supply her with a particular product or service, to the point at which she owns that product or service and is able to enjoy all the benefits she was led to believe were on offer.

The largest part of the value of many products and services lies in how the company delivers customer service. Customer service is also the area most likely to influence whether customers come back again or recommend you to others. Customer service works best when

✔ Customers are encouraged to tell you about any problems.

✔ Customers know their rights and responsibilities from the beginning.

✔ Customers know the circumstances under which they're entitled to get their money back and how to take advantage of other rights.

✔ Customers feel in control. You're far better advised to provide a full refund if the customer is dissatisfied than to demand that they come up with a good reason for the refund. A refund, or any other recourse you offer, should be prompt.

Repeat business is a key profit maker. Repeat business comes from ensuring that customers are genuinely completely satisfied with – and preferably pleasantly surprised by – the quality of your product. Repeat sales save unnecessary expenditure on advertising and promotion to attract new customers.

As standards of living rise, quality, convenience and service are going to become even more important relative to price. An investment in a strategy of quality customer service now is an investment in greater future profitability.

Customer service is often the difference between keeping customers for life and losing customers in droves. You and your staff have to deliver outstanding customer service at all times. In order to do this, everyone has to know what the important elements of good customer service are and everyone needs to incorporate those elements into their everyday customer interactions.

The key elements of your customer service plan should include

- ✔ **Initial contact:** The customer's first contact with staff creates a lasting impression and can win and sustain customers. All your staff need to be aware of how to handle enquiries quickly and competently. They should know how to leave potential customers feeling confident that their requirements can be met.

- ✔ **Information flow:** Keeping customers informed of where their orders are in the process influences their feelings about the way you do business. Your action plan needs to specify each step of your process – quotation, order confirmation, delivery notification and installation instructions. A regular flow of information throughout this period makes your customers feel that they matter to you.

- ✔ **Delivery:** Delivering the goods or service is a key part of customer service. Your product needs to be available in a timely manner, delivery lead times must be reasonable and the delivery itself must be in a way that meets the customer's requirements.

- ✔ **After-sales support:** Good coverage in areas such as maintenance, repairs, help-lines, upgrade notification, instruction manuals, returns policy and fault tracing helps customers feel that you care about their total experience with your products and business.

- ✔ **Problem solving:** Often the acid test of customer service; your staff need to be able to recognise when customers have a real crisis and what your procedure is for helping them.

High customer service standards enable many firms to charge a premium for their products. Yet in many ways, good customer service can be a nil-cost item. After all, answering the phone politely takes as much effort as doing so with a surly and off-putting tone. So improved customer service is one route to increased profitability.

Rewarding loyalty

Loyalty improves profitability because

- ✔ Retaining customers costs less than finding and capturing new ones.

- ✔ Loyal customers tend to place larger orders.

- ✔ Loyal customers don't always place price first, but new ones usually do.

So what works and what doesn't when it comes to keeping customers loyal?

One of the ideas that hasn't lived up to its promise is customer loyalty cards. When they were launched, retailers made big claims about how they were going to gather tons of invaluable data about customers. But mostly they possess no more than huge virtual warehouses of information that hasn't been used. Analysing the buying habits of millions of shoppers as their cards are swiped at the till can be prohibitively expensive, and few companies have used much of the data gathered to make their customers feel special and hence want to stay loyal.

Asked to give reasons for their loyalty, the top five elements consumers list are

- ✔ Convenience

- ✔ Price

- ✔ Range

- ✔ Customer service

- ✔ Quality

What the above list means is that you have to get your basic marketing strategy right and understand what your customers want and how much they're pre-pared to pay. If that's wrong, no loyalty scheme is going to keep them on board. Customer service and quality are about getting things right first time, every time. So, always under-promise and over-deliver.

Care- and help-lines that customers are encouraged to call for advice, infor-mation or help with problems can keep customers loyal and make them more likely to buy from you in the future. If the line is a freephone service, it's even more effective.

Keeping in touch with customers can also bind them more securely. Ques-tionnaires, newsletters, magazines, letters about incentives, customer service calls, invitations to sales events and 'member-get-member' schemes are all ways of achieving this result.

Improving Productivity

Improving productivity is a constant requirement for a growth-minded business, not simply an activity during periods of economic recession (when it is still, nonetheless, important – much better than adopting the 'turtle position', pulling in your head and your hands and getting off the road!). You need to improve productivity by acting on both your costs and your margins.

You can increase margins by changing the mix of products and services you sell to focus on those yielding the best return, or by raising your selling price. Also look at ways to work smarter and cut costs. These strategies can help make you more productive.

Cutting costs

People often see cost cutting as a routine part of the budgeting process or a response to an external crisis. The recent credit crunch is a good example of when almost every type of organisation had costs squeezed hard. Companies consider nothing sacred in a downturn and sacrifice almost anything to ensure corporate survival. The people usually charged with doing the squeezing are the chief executive officer (CEO), who sets the target, and the chief financial officer (CFO; accountant to you and me), who decides whose pips will be squeezed the hardest. At best, the company assembles a task force to carry out the work, but usually the role of Mr Nasty is left to the CFO. After the crisis has passed everyone breathes a sigh of relief and gets back to business as usual, which usually involves spending more.

Cost cutting, however, is a permanent management process, and by concentrating its execution only when doing the budget (see the later section 'Budgeting for Beginners') or during periods of distress or economic downturn, a business can miss out on major opportunities to pay less for more.

Cost cutting plays a vital role in ensuring a business becomes or remains competitive, an argument that I expand upon in Chapter 1. Staying competitive means that fewer reasons exist for a knee-jerk reaction when the going gets tough.

Read on for pointers on how to keep control of your costs.

Reducing variable and fixed costs

Variable cost cutting is always in evidence in a recession; witness the automotive and banking staff cuts in the early 1990s, in 2002–2003 and with a vengeance in 2009–2010. Cutting variable costs includes such things as wages and materials that are directly related to the volume of sales (for full details of variable and fixed costs, take a look at Chapter 13).

Cutting fixed costs such as cars, computers and equipment – costs that don't change directly with the volume of sales – shouldn't include scrapping investments in technology that may bring economies and extra nimbleness in the future (like flexible-manufacturing facilities, where, for example, Peugeot has invested in product lines that can turn out two models of vehicle at once).

Equally, alliances between firms, aiming to reduce fixed-cost investments, can be advantageous. In the soft drinks industry, Perrier provides distribution for Pepsi in France, and Bulmers reciprocates for Perrier in England, avoiding the need for extra investment in warehousing and transport.

Focusing attention on the 20 per cent of items that make up 80 per cent of your costs probably yields your biggest savings.

Adopting a frugal culture

Successful owner-managers follow three guiding principles: they're honest, a sure-fire way to keep customers happy and employees onside; they're pre-pared, because life is full of uncertainties; and, importantly, they're frugal. Being frugal isn't the same as being mean. *Frugal* means encouraging a culture where people recognise that costs matter and they're everybody's business. Think for a moment: if you're running a business that makes 20 per cent profit and through carelessness you waste £1,000, through poor stock management or sloppy manufacturing processes, you have to sell £5,000 more product to just stand still.

Clearly, you can't do everything at once when it comes to cutting costs, so it makes sense to prioritise the tasks in some way that recognises that not all actions are equally easy to carry out, nor do they have equal cost savings potential. Figure 16-1 provides a framework to help with such decisions by ranking actions using two basic criteria: the ease or difficulty of carrying out the task, and the likely savings you achieve after accomplishing the task.

Potential Cost Saving

		Low		High	
Slow and Difficult	**Catch Ups**		**Priority 2**	
	Action	Cost Saving	Action	Cost Saving
	1. Buy better	£10,000 p.a.	1. Renegotiate supplies	£350,000 p.a.
	2.		2.	
	3.	_____	3.	_____
	Total cost savings	_____	Total cost savings	_____
Easy and Quick	**Quick Wins**		**Priority 1**	
	Action	Cost Saving	Action	Cost Saving
	1. Reduce shrinkage	£2,000 p.a.	1. Strip out waste	£200,000 p.a.
	2.		2.	
	3.	_____	3.	_____
	Total cost savings	_____	Total cost savings	_____

Ease of Implementation

Figure 16-1: Setting cost-cutting priorities.

Starbucks: Where less can mean more . . . profit, that is

Most people believe Howard Schultz to be the founder of Starbucks, but that accolade belongs to Jerry Baldwin, Zev Siegl and Gordon Bowker, three friends who shared a passion for fresh coffee. They opened their first outlet in Seattle in 1971, and by the time Shultz, a plastics sales-man for Hammarplast, saw the opportunity to roll the business out, in was 1981 and Starbucks was the largest business in Washington with six retail outlets selling fresh coffee beans. Shultz's vision was to create community gathering places like the great coffee houses of Italy and transplant them to the United States.

The idea didn't strike a chord with Baldwin, who had hired Shultz in as his marketing man-ager, but he let him try out the concept of sell-ing espresso by the cup in one of his stores. Baldwin remained unconvinced, so Shultz started out on his own, opening a coffee house he named Il Giornale, after Italy's then biggest selling newspaper.

In 1987 the owners of Starbucks wanted to sell out, and Schultz convinced a group of local investors to stump up $3.7 million (£2.22 million) with the goal of opening 125 outlets over the fol-lowing five years. Shultz abandoned the name Il Giornale in favour of Starbucks, and he's gone on to open more than 15,000 retail locations in North America, Latin America, Europe, the Middle East and the Pacific Rim.

But Starbucks doesn't just open outlets, it closes them too. When a lease comes up for renewal, or sales dip, the outlet's viability is reviewed. Sometimes the problem is that the customers have moved away, and sometimes it's that rents that are out of line. Globally, Starbucks launched a programme in September 2009 to slash costs by $500 million (£306 million), which involved selling or agreeing lower rents in around 50 loss-making stores in the UK alone.

In January 2013, Starbucks extended its cost-cutting strategies when it introduced re-usable cups in the USA to replace the old dispos-able paper ones. As well as earning brownie points from the environmental lobby who see tonnes less waste in landfill sites, the company expects to save millions on buying in disposable cups and make tens of millions by selling the reusable ones at $1 a shot. Two further benefits accrue: customers owning their own Starbucks cup are expected to be more loyal to the brand, and because the cup has a short useful life, a sizeable replacement market exists.

The example in Figure 16-1 shows that you can make some sizeable savings quickly by stripping out waste, which puts it in the Priority 1 quadrant. Rene-gotiating with suppliers can make even larger savings, but these savings take time because the business has contracts to unwind, making this a candidate for the Priority 2 quadrant. Reducing shrinkage is labelled as a 'Quick Win', because it may be easy to implement but doesn't reduce costs significantly. You can implement Quick Wins alongside Priority 1 tasks; or at any stage that you need morale-boosting savings to reassure managers that cost-cutting targets can be met; or when political signals are required, to demonstrate, for example, to shareholders that a cost-saving programme is underway. The savings from Quick Wins are usually too small to spend much time on, but they can prove valuable nevertheless. The final quadrant headed 'Catch Ups' comprises difficult tasks that won't reduce costs by much and that you should leave to last.

Increasing margins

To achieve increased *profit margins*, which is the difference between the costs associated with the product or service you sell and the price you get in the market, you need first to review your sales. Reviewing your sales requires accurate costs and gross margins for each of your products or services (see Chapter 12). Armed with that information, you can select particular product groups or market segments that are less price sensitive and potentially more profitable.

No one rushes out to buy expensive, overpriced products when cheaper alternatives that are just as good are readily available. The chances are that your most profitable products are also the ones that your customers value the most. You should start your efforts to increase margins by concentrating on trying to sell the products and services that make you the most money.

Pricing is the biggest decision your business has to make, and one it needs to keep constantly under review. Your decision on pricing is the one that has the biggest impact on company profitability. Try the consultants' favourite exercise of computing and comparing the impact on profits of a 5 per cent

- ✔ Cut in your overheads
- ✔ Increase in volume sales
- ✔ Cut in materials purchased
- ✔ Price increase

All these actions are usually considered to be within an owner-manager's normal reach. Almost invariably, the 5 per cent price increase scores the highest, because it passes straight to the net profit, the bottom line. Even if volume falls, because of the effect that price has on growth margin, you usually gain more profit from selling fewer items at a higher price. For example, at a constant gross margin of 30 per cent with a 5 per cent price increase, profits are unchanged even if sales decline 14 per cent. Yet if prices are cut 5 per cent, you need an extra 21 per cent increase in sales to make the same amount of profit. (See also the section about accounting for pricing in Chapter 13.)

Frequently, resistance to increasing prices, even in the face of inflationary cost rises, can come from your own team members, eager to apportion blame for performance lapses. In these instances, making detailed price comparisons with competitors is important.

Working smarter

Making more money doesn't always have to mean working longer hours. You can just work smarter – and who knows, you may even end up working fewer hours than you do now and still make more money.

One way to get everyone's grey matter working overtime is to create 'smart circles', comprising people working in different areas of your business who you challenge to come up with ideas to make the business better (and smart rewards, which include extra resources, holidays and recognition for their achievements, rather than cash). You can formalise the process of encouraging employees to rethink the way they work and reward them in a way that makes their working environment better still.

Rewarding results

If you can get the people who work for you to increase their output, you can improve productivity. The maxim 'What gets measured gets done and what gets rewarded gets done again' is the guiding principle behind rewards, and setting objectives is the starting point in the process. You can read about some of the types of reward schemes common in small businesses in Chapter 11.

The objectives you want people to achieve in order to reward them beyond their basic pay need to be challenging but achievable too, which is something of a contradiction in terms. Problems start to arise as soon as professional managers and supervisors come on board with experience of working in big companies. They, and probably you, tend to take objectives and the ensuing budgets really seriously. You have to hit the budgets, so it makes sense to pitch them on the conservative side.

But in a small business, growth and improvement percentages have the potential to be much greater than in larger firms. A big business with a third of its market can grow quickly only by acquisition or if the market itself is growing particularly fast. A small firm, on the other hand, can grow by large amounts quickly. Moving from 0.01 per cent of a market to 0.02 per cent is hardly likely to upset many other players, but it can represent a doubling in size for a small firm. However, exceptional performance, even in a small firm, is only attainable with breakthrough thinking and performance. The question may not be how to grow the business by 20 per cent a year, but how to grow it by 20 per cent a month.

Nevertheless, if you set goals too aggressively people may leave. Even, perhaps especially, great performers balk if the hurdle is put too high.

Rewarding excellent results

Nick White's Ecotravel company sends people to off-the-beaten-track, exotic locations and to conservation areas where money goes into research projects. Ecotourists who book with Ecotravel pay to see animals in conservation areas and a proportion of the money they spend on the holiday goes directly to conservation projects.

White expanded the business slowly, until two years ago when he introduced a 'rewarding excellence' initiative and sales shot up by 40 per cent in just six months. The basis of the reward is an accelerating bonus. If the company hits its sales targets, staff share in a 5 per cent bonus. If it exceeds targets, the bonus rates rise too. For every 20 per cent of achievement above target, the bonus rate goes up 1 per cent. Targets are reset each year using a similar formula, but starting from a new and higher base level.

One way to get the best of both worlds is to have a performance band rather than just one number. The reward for achieving a really great result should be massive, but if the employee misses this high goal slightly, you reward her as if the goal had been set at the level she reached. The reward is proportionately smaller, so your rewards budget still balances. This technique can get an 'inspiration dividend'. You can persuade teams to set higher goals than they may otherwise have set, and even if they miss them, the year-on-year improvements can be stunning.

Budgeting for Beginners

One sure-fire way to get poor performance back on track – or, better still, to turn satisfactory results into exceptional ones – is to set specific goals to make that happen. Sure, you have a long-term business plan that looks out to the distant horizon (I cover this in Chapter 6). But you also need something with a bit more immediacy and a whole lot of bite. In the business world, this process is known as *budgeting*. Budgets set goals in terms of revenues and expenses for the year ahead and are usually reviewed at least halfway through the year and often quarterly. At that review, you can add a further quarter or half year to the budget to maintain a one-year budget horizon – known in the trade as a *rolling quarterly (half yearly) budget*.

You can think of a budget as doing much the same as a coach does with an athlete in setting improvement targets to be achieved by a specific date in the future. Then the coach gets a stopwatch out, checks on performance and cheers or cajoles as the situation warrants. In business, you set financial goals for the period ahead, then see how you've performed against them while trying to understand where things haven't gone to plan and learning from the experience.

Setting the guidelines

Your budget should adhere to the following general principles:

- ✔ **Based on realistic but challenging goals.** Those goals are combine both a top-down aspiration of the boss (you) and a bottom-up forecast of what the employees or departments concerned see as possible.

- ✔ **Prepared by those responsible for delivering the results.** The salespeople should prepare the sales budget and the production people the production budget.

- ✔ **Agreed by those involved.** During the budgeting process, several versions of a particular budget should be discussed. For example, the boss wants a sales figure of £20,000 but the sales team's initial forecast is for £15,000. After some debate, £18,000 is the figure agreed upon. After a figure is agreed, a virtual contract exists that declares a commitment from employees to achieve the target and commitments from the employer to be satisfied with the target and to supply resources in order to achieve it. It makes sense for this contract to be in writing.

- ✔ **Finalised at least a month before the start of the year,** not weeks or months into the year.

- ✔ **Reviewed periodically** throughout the year to make sure that all the basic assumptions that underpin it still hold good. Accurate information reviewing performance against the budget should be available seven to ten working days after the month's end.

Analysing the variances

Understanding variances is a key task. As the boss, you need to carefully monitor and compare performance against the budget as the year proceeds, taking corrective action where necessary. You do this monitoring on a monthly basis (or using shorter time intervals if required), showing both the company's performance during the month in question and throughout the year so far.

Looking at the fixed budget

Looking at Table 16-1, you can see at a glance that the business is behind on sales for this month, but ahead on the yearly target. The convention is to put all unfavourable variations in brackets. Hence, a higher-than-budgeted sales figure doesn't have brackets, but a higher materials cost does. You can also see that although profit is running ahead of budget, the profit margin is slightly behind (–0.3 per cent). It is behind partly because other direct costs, such as labour and distribution in this example, are running well ahead of budget.

Table 16-1	The Fixed Budget in £'000s					
	Month			Year to Date		
	Budget	**Actual**	**Variance**	**Budget**	**Actual**	**Variance**
Sales	805	753	(52)	6,358	7,314	965
Materials	627 (78%)	567	60	4,942	5,704	(762)
Less cost of materials	178 (22%)	186	8	1,416	1,610	194
Direct costs	74	79	(5)	595	689	(94)
Gross profit	104	107	3	820	921	101
Percentage	12.92	14.21	1.29	12.90	12.60	(0.30)

Flexing the figures

A budget is based on a particular set of sales goals, few of which are likely to be exactly met in practice. Table 16-1 shows a company that's used £762,000 more materials than budgeted (see variance column under Year to Date). Because more has been sold than was budgeted for, this is hardly surprising. The way to manage this situation is to flex the budget to show what, given the sales that actually occurred, would be expected to happen to expenses. Applying the budget ratios to the actual data does this. For example, materials were planned to be 78 per cent of sales in the budget. By applying that to the actual month's sales, you arrive at a materials cost of £587,000 (78 per cent of £753).

Looking at the flexed budget in Table 16-2 , you can see that the company has spent £19,000 more than expected on the material given the level of sales actually achieved, rather than the £762,000 overspend shown in the fixed budget.

The same principle holds for other direct costs, which appear to be running £94,000 over budget for the year. When you take into account the extra sales shown in the flexed budget, you can see that the company has actually spent £4,000 over budget on direct costs. Although this situation is serious, the problem is not as serious as the fixed budget suggests.

The flexed budget allows you to concentrate your efforts on dealing with true variances in performance.

Table 16-2	The Flexed Budget in £'000s					
	Month			**Year to Date**		
	Budget	**Actual**	**Variance**	**Budget**	**Actual**	**Variance**
Sales	753	753	-	7,314	7,314	-
Materials	587	567	20	5,685	5,704	(19)
Materials	166	186	20	1,629	1,610	(19)
Direct costs	69	79	(10)	685	689	(4)
Gross profit	97	107	10	944	921	(23)
Percentage	12.92	14.21	1.29	12.90	12.60	(0.30)

The SCORE website has a downloadable Microsoft Excel spreadsheet from which you can make sales and cost projections on a trial and error basis (www.score.org; go to Templates and Tools, and then Sales Budgeting). When you're satisfied with your projection, use the profit and loss projection (Template Gallery, and then Profit and Loss Projection [3 Years]) to complete your budget. You may also want to have a rummage around the hundreds of other useful tools and tips on the SCORE website.

The figures shown for each period of the budget aren't the same. For example, a sales budget of £1.2 million for the year doesn't translate to £100,000 a month. The exact figure depends on two factors:

✔ The projected trend may forecast that although sales at the start of the year may be £80,000 a month, they'll change to £120,000 a month by the end of the year. Sure, the average would be £100,000, but month by month the budget figure against which performance should be measured is going up.

✔ By virtue of seasonal factors, each month may also be adjusted up or down from the underlying trend. For example, you can expect sales of heating oil to peak in the autumn and tail off in the late spring.

Budgeting from zero

When you sit down with your team and discuss budgets, the arguments always revolve around how much more each section needs next year. The starting point is usually this year's costs, which are taken as the only facts on which to build. So, for example, if you spent £25,000 on advertising last year and achieved sales of £1 million, your advertising expense was 2.5 per cent of sales. If the sales budget for next year is £1.5 million, then it seems logical to spend £37,500 next year on advertising. That, however, presupposes that you spent last year's sum wisely and effectively in the first place, which you almost certainly did not.

Zero-based budgeting turns the cost argument on its head. It assumes that each year every cost centre starts from zero spending and, based on the goals of the business and the resources available, presents arguments for every pound you're planning to spend, *not just for the increase*. So each year starts out with a blank sheet of paper rather than last year's figures.

Chapter 17

Exploring Strategies for Growth

. . . .

In This Chapter

▶ Seeing why market share matters

▶ Recognising the value in brands

▶ Discovering ways to sell more

▶ Checking out market growth strategies

▶ Getting into alliances

▶ Looking at franchising opportunities

. . . .

*I*f you thought it was hard work getting your business off the ground, 'you ain't seen nothing yet'. In periods when economic growth is strong, it may be possible to increase sales without too much effort, being swept along on a benevolent tide. But that route to increasing sales won't help a business to outperform its competitors or to increase market share, which is vital if a business is to achieve superior long-term performance. Nor will going with the flow be a great success if the economy is experiencing a downturn. In this chapter, I tell you why growth is vital to maintain a firm's competitive edge.

Also, without growth you can't provide opportunities for development and advancement for the staff you took so much care in recruiting (I cover recruitment in Chapter 11) and a business is only as good as the people it employs. The budget (see Chapter 16) sets the goals for the business and allows you to track performance against those goals. But you still need strategies to meet your goals, and that's what this chapter is all about.

Understanding the Importance of Growth

Growth is the natural path for a healthy business. Too little and the firm atrophies and dies; too much and it's in danger of exploding. How much growth is enough depends on market conditions, the aspirations of the boss – you – and your key employees. You hopefully want to enjoy the fruits of your labours and have a valuable business that you pass on to your family or sell up and then retire on the proceeds. To achieve those aims, the business needs to grow.

Back in the 1960s a smart firm of American management consultants, Boston Consulting Group (BCG), observed a consistent relationship between the cost of producing an item (or delivering a service) and the total quantity produced over the life of the product or service concerned. BCG noticed that total unit costs (labour and materials) fell by between 20 per cent and 30 per cent for every doubling of the cumulative quantity produced. So any company capturing a sizeable market share has an implied cost advantage over any competitor with a smaller market share. You can then use that cost advantage to make more profit, lower prices and compete for an even greater share of the market or invest in making the product better, so stealing a march on competitors. And so it became imperative for firms to get on the growth treadmill.

The starting point is to get a handle on your present business in terms of market share and brand position. These things are important measurements that you need to aim to improve.

You can read industry-specific case studies on how BCG has helped businesses achieve sustainable competitive advantage at www.bcg.com/expertise_impact/impact_stories/default.aspx.

Measuring market share

You can't set any realistic market share goals until you've made an attempt at measuring the size of the market. Now, in principle this measurement isn't too difficult. I cover the market research process that helps you unravel such facts in Chapter 4.

Here's an example. Using market research, you'd be able to discover that the consumption of bread in Europe in 2013 was worth £10 billion a year.

First, to make much sense of that bald figure, you need a definition of bread. The industry-wide definition of *bakery*, a term used to cover the whole bread market, includes sliced and un-sliced bread, rolls, bakery snacks and specialty breads. It covers both plant-baked products, those that are baked by in-store bakers and products sold through craft bakers.

You probably won't, as a newish small firm, be in every segment of that market. So you need to sift through the figures to arrive at the market relevant to you. This sifting involves refining global statistics down to provide the real scope of your market. If your business only operates in the UK, the portion of the European market open to you is worth around £2.7 billion, equivalent to 12 million loaves a day, one of the largest sectors in the food industry. If you're only operating in the craft bakery segment, then the data shows that the relevant market shrinks down to £13.5 million; this amount contracts down still further to £9.7 million if you're, say, only operating within the radius of the M25 ring road. That in turn means that if you've annual sales of £500,000, you've just over 5 per cent of the market (500,000 ÷ 9,700,000 x 100). Now 5 per cent isn't a dominant market share by any measure, but is a whole lot bigger than the share you'd have if you used £10 billion as the base line.

Various competing businesses share your relevant market in different proportions. Typically, you find a market leader, a couple of market followers and a host of businesses trailing in their wake. The slice each competitor has of a market is its *market share*. You find that marketing people are fixated on market share, perhaps even more so than on absolute sales. That may appear little more than a rational desire to beat the 'enemy' and appear higher in rankings, but it has a much more deep-seated and profound logic, as BCG uncovered.

You can read up more on the importance of market share and how BCG used it to evaluate product growth strategies at the NetMBA website (`www.netmba.com/strategy/matrix/bcg`).

Building a brand

People consider the brand to be the holy grail of successful business growth. A brand encompasses not just what a product is or does but all the elements such as logo, symbols, image, reputation and associations. Branding is an intangible way of differentiating a product in a way that captures and retains markets through loyalty to that brand. McDonald's arches represent its brand as a welcoming beacon, drawing customers in. Coca-Cola tastes little different from a supermarket brand, but the promotion that supports the brand confers on the consumer the chance to share the attractive lifestyle of those 'cool' people in the adverts. Apple's iPod is differentiated from just any old MP3 player in much the same way. Intel and Audi are examples of branding designed to reassure consumers in unfamiliar territory that a product will deliver. And Body Shop International exudes ethics and concern for the environment, where other cosmetics concentrate on how they make the wearer look beautiful.

The economic crisis that engulfed the world at the end of the first decade of the 21st century proved the enduring value of having a successful brand. Here you can aptly apply investor Warren Buffet's statement, 'It's not until the tide goes out that you can see who is swimming naked.'

Building a brand takes time and a considerable advertising budget. But by creating brand value – that's the price premium commanded by that product over its unbranded or less appealing competitors – a business can end up with a valuable asset.

Superbrands (`www.superbrands.com`) has a listing of the top brands by country, often with a case study supporting the top brands in any country.

Increasing Sales

The most obvious way to grow a business and improve market share is to get more sales. This is often easier said than done, but some tried and proven techniques usually deliver the goods. A helpful framework to keep in mind is the growth matrix developed by business guru Igor Ansoff.

Ansoff's model has four main elements:

- ✔ **Business development,** which is about getting more customers like the ones you already have and getting them to buy more from you.
- ✔ **Market development,** which involves entering new markets in your home country or overseas.
- ✔ **Product or service development,** which involves launching new products or extensions to existing products or services. A courier service adding an overnight delivery service to its existing 48-hour service is an example of this activity.
- ✔ **Diversification,** which means, in a nutshell, launching off into the unknown.

In the sections that follow, I look at these different elements, and how you can use them to increase your sales.

Getting customers to buy more

This starting point is a no-brainer for achieving profitable growth. Winning a new customer can be an expensive and time-consuming activity, so when you have a customer, the more you can get him to spend with you rather than a competitor, the better your bottom line is going to be.

Use this framework to categorise your customers and so ensure that you keep them longer and that they buy more from you:

- ✔ **Courtship:** This stage is the one before a customer has bought anything from you. At this stage the customer is suspicious and your objective is to get your first order. Any order is okay, just to get the relationship underway.
- ✔ **Engagement:** Having got your first order in the bag, your customer may still be moderately suspicious of you and unsure whether your intentions are wholly honourable. Your goal is to get your first repeat order and cement the relationship. Getting to this stage means that your first order must go well and your customer must be at least satisfied, or delighted if you want to get to the honeymoon stage in your relationship. To make that happen, you need to stand out from the crowd and go the extra mile to make that customer feel special by meeting his particular needs.

✔ **Honeymoon:** With several repeat orders successfully fulfilled, your customer now trusts you and is susceptible to new ideas. Here you should be looking to increase sales volume. Almost certainly, as a new supplier your customer hasn't put all his eggs in your basket. Now your task is to get as many eggs as you can and build up to being the customer's preferred and perhaps only supplier.

✔ **Wedlock:** When you first started talking to your customer you were the new kid on the block, to the customer at least. Your ideas and products or services were refreshingly new and the customer's existing suppliers had had ample opportunity to disappoint him and let him down. Now you've become, or are fast becoming, that old, boring supplier. You need to think of ways to keep your relationship exciting and fresh.

✔ **Deadlock:** Your customer has become disenchanted and is considering divorce. The time has come to bring on new products and services to whet the customer's appetite and make him see you as the exciting, vigorous supplier you appeared to be when your relationship started.

Encouraging referrals

Referrals are the most valuable marketing asset any business can have. Whether you're selling direct to an end consumer or user, or operating in the business-to-business arena, your goal is the same – to get those using your product or service to talk in glowing terms about their experience with your business.

Passive word of mouth is rarely as effective as encouraging satisfied customers to pass on the glad tidings. Happy customers tell an average of seven other people if they've had a positive experience with you. Unhappy customers tell 11 to 20 other people.

You can make word-of-mouth advertising work, however. You just require discipline and a programmed effort to ask your customers for referrals. Make it easy for them – give them brochures, flyers, samples or whatever they need to make your case. Then follow up.

Angus Thirlwell and Peter Harris, founders of Hotel Chocolat (www. hotelchocolat.com), have a neat method of getting customers to promote their luxury home-delivered chocolate business. They started a number of tasting clubs that have attracted well over 100,000 regular members, who enjoy a brand new selection of exciting, artisan chocolates every month. The idea is that members receive a selection of chocolates together with a scoring card, and then invite their friends to taste and rate the selection. In the process, new members are recruited to the club.

Discounts for introductions come out of your advertising budget. So you need to work out how much an introduction to a prospect is worth before you can decide on the discount. The rules are as follows:

- Be specific in the type of introductions you want. In particular, make the sales volume and product specifications clear. Giving a discount for products on which your margins are already tight is a pointless exercise.

- Have a sliding scale of discounts. The more introductions you get, the more discount you give.

- Make giving you introductions easy for people. Send them fax-back forms or have a place on your website for them to tap in minimal details. A name and company should be enough for you to find the other details you need.

- Follow up and let people know that their introduction paid off. People are usually interested in more than just the discount when they give introductions.

- Have a specific programme such as member-gets-member and run it as a campaign for a set period. Then change the programme and the discounts. That keeps people interested.

- Give the discount promptly, but not until the new introduction has bought and paid his bill.

- Give extra discounts for introductions to loyal customers, perhaps when the new customer has placed his third or fourth order.

- Research the market and find out what introductory schemes are on offer in your sector.

- Set up a database to monitor the effectiveness of your introductory discount scheme.

Entering new market segments at home

Generally, the most rewarding market growth for small businesses comes in its first few months and years, when you tackle the low-hanging fruit. Later on, you may find it profitable to enter new markets, which can take a number of shapes. The two most common are

- **Geographic:** When you're confident that you've extracted as much business as you can from your immediate business area, be that a town, city or region, move on to another one. You need to make sure that the new geographic area is broadly similar to the one you've been successful in already. For example, Bristol and Bath are broadly similar to Bradford and Sheffield as cities, but if your business has tourists as customers, the last two cities are less appealing as a new market than the first two.

> ✔ **Demographic:** This covers factors particular to customer groups. If you make clothes for women in Bristol, you can consider making clothes for children, men or teenagers, sticking to the Bristol area.

Selling overseas

A recent 'Made in the UK' report by the Federation of Small Businesses showed that barely a quarter of its 200,000-plus members sold anything outside of the UK. Only 10 per cent of the smallest members sold anything abroad, a figure that had grown to over a third by the time annual turnover reached £5 million. The message here seems clear: if you want to get big, you should explore the possibilities of expanding your business to other countries.

Financial information website Motley Fool's entry into the German market involved a modest change in a well-proven product, as for its entry into the British, French and Italian markets, changing little except the language on its website. But expanding overseas isn't quite as easy as it looks. Marks & Spencer made a mess of its foray into the USA and retired in some ignominy from the French market, closing 38 stores virtually overnight and exciting the wrath of the French trade unions on the way. The Body Shop, a world business if ever there was one, found the French market hard going, because in France people take beauty, as they do wine, rather more seriously than most.

Don't let these stories of failure discourage you. After all, millions of businesses export successfully, and you can always find some help. The following sections give you a few pointers to start you off.

Researching overseas markets

The good news about checking out overseas markets is that you don't have to go far – not at first, that is. Sure, boots on the ground have to follow, but for now stick to your computer screen or your local library and do the following:

> ✔ **See the big picture.** If you think that the US Central Intelligence Agency (CIA) is an unlikely source of business facts on overseas markets, you're wrong. The US government is more interested than most in new business opportunities and so the CIA hoovers in that data. The CIA World Factbook (www.cia.gov/library/publications/the-world-factbook) offers data on 267 countries or regions. Each country has around half a dozen pages of basic economic, political and demographic information – population size, education levels, income and so forth – as well as information on political disputes that may cause business problems in the future. The CIA keeps the Factbook up to date, so you can be reasonably confident of having the most current information to hand.

✔ **Get to the nitty-gritty.** A country may be full of people who have enough of the readies to buy your products and are well enough educated to understand and value your proposition. But can you really do business there? That's where the aptly named Doing Business (www.doingbusiness.org) comes in. Doing Business is the World Bank's database and it provides objective measures of business regulations across 185 countries. You can find out everything from the rules on opening and closing a business to tax rates, employment laws, investor protection, enforcing contracts and much more. You can also use a tool to compare countries, ranking them by the criteria you consider most important.

✔ **Know the enemy.** After you've set your eyes on a particular country to sell into, you can bet that local firms are doing a pretty good job already. The World Industrial Reporter (www.worldindustrialreporter.com/solusource) is the place to find industrial product and company information from around the world. This site is an online directory in 11 languages with details of over 700,000 suppliers in 28 countries. You can search by industry subsector or name, for the world or by country. Also look for sections on new products, market trends and country profiles, and a calendar of global trade shows.

Ninety per cent of small firms who sell overseas sell into another European country. Only 23 per cent sell into the African continent, most of those into just one country, South Africa. There must a clue there.

Finding the right way in

If you're taking your first shot at selling overseas, you want to keep your costs to a minimum until you're sure of a welcome. Here are some inexpensive ways to get started in this area.

Start by translating your website into the language of the country you want to sell into. Companies such as Global Voices (www.globalvoices.co.uk) and Motion Point (www.motionpoint.com) can get your website translated and localised so that it deals with all the issues, sales tax, delivery options, currencies and trading laws.

Then optimise your website for international business by identifying relevant key words in the language concerned. Webcertain has a guide to international SEO that describes the collection of activities that, combined, enable a website to reach its target markets in multiple countries or regions (www.webcertain.com/international-seo-guide.html). (For more on search engine optimisation, go to Chapter 15.)

Lastly, and before reaching for the big guns, find a local sales agent to handle business for you in your target market(s). International United Commercial Agents and Brokers can put you in contact with agents in most countries using their online international database (www.iucab.com/en/looking_for_agents.php).

Getting government help with going global

UK Trade and Investment (www.ukti.gov.uk), the government's export advisory organisation, can put a package of help together for you. And it's keener than ever to help. The government's stated ambition in its National Export Challenge is to boost the UK's export performance. So it set a target for UKTI to increase the number of firms it assists from 25,000 to 50,000 by 2015, and for 100,000 more companies to be exporting by 2020. Currently, around 960,000 small and medium-sized businesses export, so UKTI's target is a tough one by any standards.

To help UKTI achieve its goal, it has more resources:

- ✔ An additional 50 international trade advisers (taking the total to 270)

- ✔ An additional £8 million per year to enable 5,000 more companies to benefit from the Tradeshow Access Programme (TAP)

- ✔ A 50 per cent discount on Overseas Market Introduction Service (OMIS) for up to 2,500 new users

UKTI's assistance comes in the following forms:

- ✔ **Aid Funded Business** helps British companies win business that's being funded by aid agency money. Multilateral agencies (such as the United Nations and the World Bank) spend £60 billion every year on everything from tents to telecommunications, and this scheme puts you in contact with people who can help you enter these markets.

- ✔ **Export Marketing Research Scheme (EMRS)** provides independent advice, at no charge, on carrying out marketing research, whether you're looking at new markets or re-evaluating an existing one. In addition, companies may be eligible for a grant of up to 50 per cent of the cost of conducting market research.

- ✔ **International Trade Teams** are located in over 40 local offices around the country. Every UK region also has dedicated sector specialists who can provide support tailored to your industry.

- ✔ **Open to Export** provides information and advice from experts across the public and private sector to small and medium-sized businesses that are new to doing business abroad or are looking to enter new markets.

- ✔ **Passport to Export** is an assessment and skills-based programme that provides new and inexperienced exporters with the training, planning and ongoing support they need to succeed overseas.

- ✔ **Tradeshow Access Programme (TAP)** provides grant support for eligible small and medium-sized businesses to attend trade shows overseas.

You can find out more about the help UKTI provides for small businesses trying to crack overseas markets at www.ukti.gov.uk/export/howwehelp.html. You can also tap into its network of market specialists based in the UK and across the globe at www.ukti.gov.uk/export/contactus.html.

Adding new products or services

At one end of a spectrum of innovation are truly new products; at the other end are relatively modest product or service line extensions. For example, Amazon's music and video/DVD business can be seen as a product line extension of its book trade. Its tools and hardware operation looks more like a new product – new to that company, of course, not to the thousands of other businesses in that sector.

Most new products are unsuccessful. A new product has to be two or three times better in some respect – price, performance, convenience, availability – to dislodge a well-entrenched rival.

But these unsuccessful products don't necessarily have to be *your* new products and services, of course. Alliances, affiliations, joint ventures and the like abound and may help you to be even more successful.

Here are some sources of successful new products:

- ✔ Customers can tell you their needs and dissatisfactions with current products and services, if you listen to them.

- ✔ Your sales team are close to the market and can form a view as to what may sell well.

- ✔ Competitors who are first to market usually make lots of mistakes on the way. Following in their wake, you can avoid the worst of their errors and succeed where they haven't.

- ✔ Exhibitions and trade fairs are where other firms, not necessarily competitors but those on the margins of your sector, meet and exchange ideas. You can adapt products and services that work well in one environment for use in your market at little cost.

- ✔ Other markets may be in advance of your own. Many new ideas start their lives in the USA and only arrive in Europe 18 months to 5 years later. Following trends there can give you useful pointers for successful new products in your own market.

- ✔ Research and development departments often throw up innovative ideas for which no obvious market need exists. You may know of profitable ways to exploit those technologies.

Diversifying as a last resort

Diversification involves moving away from the products, services and markets in which you currently operate to completely new areas of business.

This strategy is the riskiest of all – selling things you know little about to people you know even less about. Sure, you can do market research and buy in industry expertise, but risk still exists.

Companies that succeed in diversifying do so slowly, sometimes by acquisition, and above all by listening to customers and front-line staff.

Unless you can quantify the value added in an acquisition or diversification – for example, in better buying with quantity discounts or by being able to spread your costs over a bigger sales volume – don't bother.

However, if you can get acquisitions right, the growth through diversification can be phenomenal.

Forming Alliances

Alliances come in a variety of different forms and in theory can prove one way of pumping steroids into your growth strategy.

Before I look at this strategic option in a little more detail, I need to make clear what types of alliance are usually on offer:

- An *acquisition* occurs when one company buys another – more often than not in a 'friendly' deal, but sometimes events aren't so harmonious. After the acquisition, only the parent company usually exists in any real legal sense and the top management of the 'victim' usually departs quickly.

- *Mergers* are friendly bids where companies join forces and the separate identities of the businesses of the companies concerned continue after the deal is consummated.

- *Joint ventures* occur when two or more companies decide to set up a separate third business to exploit something together. There may be no attempt to harmonise the whole of the two parent businesses, and the joint venture may be disbanded when the reasons they joined forces in the first place disappear.

Going on the alliance trail

Okay, so you parked your worries about the relatively low chances of success and decided to get out in the big outside world and buy or buddy up with other players. Here are the ground rules.

Tying in with Tesco

Australian-born Nick Tolley founded Harris + Hoole, the artisan-style coffee shop with his two younger siblings Laura and Andrew. In 2013 the company was turning over the equivalent of £5 million a year, but had ambitious expansion goals. With 18 standalone stores in the south east of England since launching, Tolley wanted to treble his business over the next three years. The coffee market is a crowded retail space, with Starbucks, Costas and a host of other players crammed into every nook and cranny. Tolley decided that he needed a strategic partner to supercharge business growth.

That's where an alliance with Tesco came in. By the autumn of 2013, Harris + Hoole had opened outlets on five Tesco sites or within

Tesco stores, the most recent in a Tesco Extra hypermarket in Watford. The partnership with Tesco provides benefits for both parties. Tolley and his team get to sit alongside some of the smartest guys in the retail room, as well as access money in a climate where small firms aren't exactly the flavour of the month with bankers. Tesco gets a chance to see how another business works at first hand. That's what it did with Dunnhumby, the firm that created its loyalty card, which they bought into in stages. Tesco also has an 80 per cent stake in movie-streaming site Blinkbox, a stake in family-friendly restaurant chain Giraffe and a slice of Euphorium Bakery, recently opened in Tesco's Kensington outlet.

Knowing why you want to buy or buddy up

Ideally, the reasons to buy or buddy up to a business need to be practical and down-to-earth and embedded in the firm's core strategy. Sound reasons for acquisitions include the following:

- ✔ To increase market share and eliminate a troublesome competitor

- ✔ To broaden your product range or give you access to new markets

- ✔ To diversify into new markets, acquiring the necessary management, marketing or technical skills to enable you to capture a reasonable slice of the market, relatively quickly

- ✔ To get into another country or region

- ✔ To protect an important source of supply that may be under threat from a competitor

- ✔ To acquire additional staff, factory space, warehousing or distribution channels, or to get access to additional major customers more quickly than by starting up yourself

Produce a written statement explaining the rationale behind your reason to buy or buddy before you start looking for targets. Otherwise you may end up pursuing a bargain that has absolutely nothing to do with your previously defined commercial goals just because it seems cheap. Also remember that companies available at knockdown prices are likely to need drastic surgery. So unless you fancy your chances as a company doctor, stay well away.

Deciding what you want to buy or buddy with

It can take over one year of work, on average, to find and buy a business. The more accurately you describe your ideal purchase, the simpler, quicker and cheaper your search is. Just imagine trying to buy a house without any idea where you want to live, how much you want to spend, how many bedrooms you need, whether you want a new house or a listed building, or whether you want a garden. The search would be near-impossible to organise, it may take forever and the resultant purchase would almost certainly please no one. The same problem is present when buying a company. The definition of what you want to buy should explain

- Business area/products/service the company is in

- Location

- Price range and the cash you have available

- Management depth and the management style you're looking for

- Image compatibility between your company and any target

- Scope for integration and cost savings

- Tax status – for example, a business nursing a substantial loss can be worth looking at if you can offset the loss against your company's profits and so reduce tax due

- Minimum profitability and return on capital employed you can accept

If the company you plan to buy only makes 1 per cent profit but you make 5 per cent, and you're of equal size, the resultant profit will be 3 per cent (5 + 1 ÷ 2). I cover this subject in Chapter 13.

Outside of the factors listed in these bullet points, you may have vital reasons that, if not met, would make the target a poor bet. For example, if you want to iron out major cash flow or plant capacity cycles, there's little point in going for a business similar to your own. That only makes the peaks and troughs more pronounced.

The Leadership Factor (www.leadershipfactor.com), founded in Huddersfield in 1996 by Nigel and Janet Hill, specialises in a niche area of market research: customer satisfaction. Nigel got the idea from the US where it was already a well-established business, and he could see he could start the business with relatively little upfront investment. The Leadership Factor now conducts 500 customer satisfaction surveys each year, using a database of 250,000 respondents. With a multi-million turnover and a blue-chip customer base that includes LV=,the UK's largest Friendly Society (that is, a body owned by its members) and the Youth Hostel Association, the Hills have fuelled their expansion by buying stakes in similar companies selling the same product in Spain, Australia and the USA. They're licensing their business model in other less developed markets such as Russia and the Ukraine. This strategy of buying into competitors has added £1 million to turnover.

Investigating and approaching

After you have your shopping list of prospective targets, you need to arm yourself with everything you can find out about them. Get their literature, samples of any products, copies of their advertising, press comments and, of course, their accounts. Then go and see their premises and as much of their operation as you can. If you can't get in, get one of your salespeople in to look the business over for you. This investigation helps you both to shorten your shopping list and to put it into order of priority. Now you're ready for the approach. I cover the research tools you need to deploy here in Chapter 4.

You've three options as to how to make the initial approach and each has its merits:

- ✓ **Telephone,** giving only the broadest reason for your approach – saying, perhaps, that you want to discuss areas of common interest.

- ✓ **Write** and be specific on your purpose, following that up with a phone call to arrange a meeting, perhaps over lunch.

- ✓ **Use a third party** such as an accountant or consultant (reasons of secrecy can make this method desirable) or a corporate finance house. If executive time is at a premium, no other practicable way may exist.

The first meeting is crucial and you need to achieve two objectives. First, you must establish mutual respect, trust and rapport. Nothing worthwhile follows without these. Then you need to establish in principle that both parties are seriously interested. You can sidestep time scale, price and methods of integration until later, except in the most general sense.

Valuing a target

Forming an alliance, be it a merger, acquisition or joint venture, involves you stumping up money. You need to be sure that you're getting good value for your investment. I cover the tools for valuing a business in Chapter 22 and for assessing return on investment in Chapter 13.

Managing an alliance

However well negotiated the deal, most acquisitions and venture relationships that go wrong do so because of the human factor, often in the first few weeks and months after the deal is done. Have an outline plan for how to handle the relationship and be prepared to be flexible. (Interestingly enough, only one buyer in five has a detailed operational plan of how to manage their acquisition, yet 67 per cent of those being bought believe that the buyer has such a plan, so the plan is psychologically important.)

Franchising Your Way to Growth

If your business concept looks as though it can be replicated in several other places, you've a number of choices. The most obvious is to open up more branches. But you can consider a faster, and in some ways safer, route by franchising your business for others to roll out and share the risk.

Franchising is a great way into business and a great way to grow a business too. Over 700 different types of franchise are on offer somewhere in the world, so you can almost certainly find one that suits your needs and aspirations.

As a *franchiser* you supply a product or teach a service to a *franchisee*, who then sells your product or service to the public. In return for your input, the franchisee pays you a fee and a continuing royalty, based usually on turnover. You may also make additional money by ensuring that the franchisee buys materials or ingredients from you.

You've two possible strategies for harnessing the power of franchising to your business. You can consider taking on a franchise or master franchise that's complementary to your existing business, or you can franchise your own business concept, taking on self-employed franchisees instead of hired-in managers to run your new branches or outlets.

Bolting on a franchise

Adding a franchise to your own business is a safer way to grow than franchising your own business idea. After all, after a franchise is up and running you can see how well it works. You can assess the franchise's track record, and though no guarantee of success exists, at least the franchise has ironed out many of the unknowns associated with any new venture. The following sections outline the two routes to deploying this growth strategy.

Adding a franchise

A few years back Harrods, London's upmarket department store, opened the first British outlet of Krispy Kreme Doughnuts. For Harrods, the sale of doughnuts is complementary to its other food and beverage sales, so the addition represented pure extra revenue. For Krispy Kreme, the venture represented a chance to enter the British market, which it believed was ripe for development with no dominant doughnut brand in the market.

The aim in adding a franchise to your existing business is to leverage, as the business gurus say, your customer or resource base, in order to get more sales per customer or square metre of space.

So if your customers are buying chocolate, sweets and stationery from you, adding a freezer with ice cream is no big deal. Chances are that the ice cream supplier is so keen to extend its distribution that it throws in the freezer cabinet for free. You're taking someone else's business model, product and support systems and bolting them on to your business to add turnover and profits.

Taking out a master franchise

Instead of just adding a franchise to complement your business, you can consider rolling out a chain of franchises. Doing so involves taking a master franchise for a country or region. You can also look on this option as a strategy for rapidly expanding your own business, if you can put it into a franchise format. I cover that aspect of expansion in 'Rolling out the franchise', later in this chapter.

You can find out more about taking on a master franchise from Master Franchises for Sale (www.masterfranchisesforsale.com), Franchise Solutions (http://uk.franchisesinternational.com) and Franchise Direct (www.franchisedirect.co.uk).

Weighing the advantages and disadvantages

From the franchiser's point of view, one huge financial advantage is that you don't have any direct investment in any of your franchises. The franchisee owns the inventory and equipment.

Because of the shortage of prime sites, one growing trend is for franchisers to acquire leases on behalf of franchisees, or at any rate to stand as guarantors. Nevertheless, the effect on the liquidity of the franchiser, in contrast to expansion by opening branches, is enormous.

However, you do face heavy start-up costs in piloting the franchise and in setting up and maintaining training if you do the job properly. Thereafter you incur further costs in providing a continuing service to franchisees in such matters as research and development, promotion, administrative back-up, and feedback and communication within the network.

As a franchiser, you're dependent on the willingness of the franchisee to observe the rules and play the game, and any failure of the franchisee to do so is equally, or perhaps more, damaging to you and to other franchisees than to the wayward franchisee.

Doing the pilot

After you've developed a franchise concept, you should run a pilot operation for at least a year. Someone as similar to the intended typical franchisee for the chain as is practical should run the pilot. The aim isn't just to test the business concept, but to see whether you've described the operating systems well enough for people outside the founding business organisation to run them.

Take as an example a fast-food outlet offering slimmers' lunches. You already own a couple of outlets for which you've found a catchy name, Calorie Counter. You've established a standard image in terms of decor, layout, tableware, menus and graphics, and your staff members have a stylish uniform. Your gimmick is that on the menu every dish has a calorie rating and a breakdown of the fibre and salt content, and along with their bill customers get a calorie and fibre count for what they've bought. You also have some recipes that you've pioneered.

In the year since you opened, you've ironed out most of the start-up bugs and learned a lot about the catering, accounting and staffing problems in running a business of this kind.

The indication is that demand exists for more restaurants like yours, but you've neither the capital nor the inclination to take on restaurant managers. Being a thorough sort of person, you've documented every aspect of running your restaurant, covering everything from recipes, ingredients and cooking times, to opening hours, wages, incentives and dress code. You've also standardised your accounting system and linked the electronic till to your raw material and stock systems, so that you can order key ingredients automatically. From your experience of opening two of your own restaurants you know how and where to advertise, how much to spend and how sales demand is likely to grow in the early weeks and months. You've captured all this knowledge in a sort of manual, which you propose to use as a guide for whoever you select to open your next outlet.

You're now ready to run your first pilot franchise. This pilot involves using your manual and procedures with a real live franchisee. True, you may have to give the franchisee an incentive to join you in the risk. But whatever you end up negotiating, as long as it gives you the benefits of franchising that I list in 'Weighing the advantages and disadvantages', earlier in this chapter, you're ahead of the game.

When your pilot franchisee gets underway, you have the opportunity to test your manual in action. You, after all, invented the business, so you should know what to do in every situation – but seeing whether a green franchisee straight off the street can follow your 'map' and get a result is the acid test.

Put what you learn from the pilot into a revised franchise manual, sort out your charging and support systems, and you're ready to start to roll the franchise out.

Finding franchisees

Sorry, but the last sentence in the previous section was a bit misleading. Despite having a great business, a robust and proven business manual and a couple of pilot runs under your belt, you aren't quite ready to roll the franchise out around the world, or even around your neighbourhood. The NatWest / British Franchise Association survey (they do one every year and have done for the last 20) asked franchisers what they consider to be the biggest barrier to the growth of the number of franchises they operate. By far the greatest number of respondents cited the lack of suitable franchisees.

Visit any franchise exhibition – and you visit many if you're serious about growing in this way – and the thousands of people milling around the stands and in the seminar rooms may convince you that no lack of interest exists among the general public to taking up a franchise.

Finding potential franchisees isn't a problem. Use the contact details in 'Finding your way to franchising' in Chapter 5 to advertise for applicants and attend as many exhibitions as you can, and you should have applicants coming out of your ears. Yet turning that latent demand into done deals isn't so easy. One international franchise chain only offers franchises to 30 per cent of the people it interviews, and it only interviews a small fraction of the number of people it sees at exhibitions.

This begs the obvious question: what sort of person makes the ideal franchisee? Well, looking at past career patterns may not be much help. Les Gray, chairperson of Chemex, formerly Chemical Express, a 104-outlet cleaning products franchise chain, lists a postman, a sales manager, a buyer, a farmer and a shipping agent as the occupations of his most successful franchisees.

Franchisers say that they have the most success with franchisees who are motivated and able to work hard, and who have some management aptitude and good communication and people skills, but are *not* too entrepreneurial. They aren't looking for people with relevant industry skills and experience, because they want to inculcate candidates into their own formula.

Look at Chapter 11 for tips on how to recruit and select great people.

Rolling out the franchise

So now you've a proven formula and a steady stream of candidates, you really are ready for the big roll-out. Carefully select locations and areas that most closely fit your business model. For example, the Hard Rock Cafe model is known as a capital city business. In other words, room only exists for one in each major international city. Prontaprint, on the other hand, can accommodate an outlet in each major business area within a city, or a single outlet in any major town with a population over around 30,000 people.

Your equation depends on your customer profile. A fast-print outlet may find the going tough in a seaside town with 20,000 pensioners and 10,000 holidaymakers.

Chapter 18

Becoming a Great Manager

· ·

In This Chapter

▶ Seeing why you need a team and how to build one

▶ Planning for your own successor

▶ Delegating effectively

▶ Developing the right leadership style

▶ Preparing for change

· ·

*I*n business, one of the simplest profit calculations is profit per employee. Until you become a massive company with more than 500 employees, each employee you add increases your profit. Still, you needn't worry too much about what happens when you have 500 employees on your hands. Well, not in this book, anyway.

But employees aren't a trouble-free resource. To maximise the employee–profit ratio, you have to manage your employees so that they produce quality work for you. You have to build them into teams, and lead and manage them to prepare them for the roller-coaster life of change that is the inevitable lot of a small, growing business.

In this chapter, I give you the tools you need to become a successful and effective manager.

Building a Team

Teams are a powerful way to get superb results out of even the most average individual employees. With effective teamwork, a small firm can raise its efficiency levels to world-class standards. Some small firms have built their entire success around teams.

A group of people working together isn't necessarily a team. A successful sports team has the right number of players for the game, each with a clearly defined role. The team has a coach, to train and improve players' performances, and measurable goals to achieve in the shape of obvious competitors to beat. Contrast that with the situation that usually prevails in a typical small firm. The number of players is the number who turn up on a particular day, and few have specific roles to play. Some are trained and properly equipped and some aren't. For the most part the business's objectives aren't clearly explained to employees, nor are any performance-measuring tools disclosed. Most of the players in the home team are highly likely not even to know the name or characteristics of the enemy against whom they're competing.

Clearly, a successful sports team and an unorganised group of co-workers have little in common, but you can clearly see what you need to do to weld people at work into a team.

Successful teams have certain features in common. They all have

- ✔ A good balance of team members, with complementary skills and talents
- ✔ A size appropriate to the task
- ✔ Appropriate resources
- ✔ Clear objectives
- ✔ Strong and effective leadership
- ✔ The ability to communicate freely throughout the organisation
- ✔ The ability to work collectively
- ✔ The authority to act quickly on decisions

However talented the soloists are in a small business, in the end orchestras are what make enough noise to wake up slumbering customers and make them aware of your virtues as a supplier. But teams don't just happen. However neat the curricula vitae and however convincing the organisational chart, you can't just turn out a team-in-a-box. The assumption that people are naturally going to work together is usually a mistake. Chaos is more likely than teamwork.

Founding principles

Successful teams share common principles, outlined in the following list.

- ✔ **Balanced team roles:** Every team member must have a valuable team role. Experts in team behaviour such as Meredith Belbin have identified the key team profiles that are essential if a team is to function well (you can find full details on Belbin's widely used team role evaluation system at www. belbin.com or by calling 01223 264975). Any one person may perform more than one of these roles. But if too many people are competing to perform one of the roles, or if one or more of these roles is neglected, the team is unbalanced. Its members then perform in much the same way as a car does when a cylinder misfires. The key roles that Belbin describes are

- **Chairperson/team leader:** Stable, dominant, extrovert. Concentrates on objectives. Does not originate ideas. Focuses people on what they do best.

- **Plant:** Dominant, high IQ, introvert. A 'scatterer of seeds' who originates ideas. Misses out on detail. Thrusting but easily offended.

- **Resource investigator:** Stable, dominant, extrovert and sociable. Lots of contacts with the outside world. Strong on networks. Salesperson/diplomat/liaison officer. Not an original thinker.

- **Shaper:** Anxious, dominant, extrovert. Emotional and impulsive. Quick to challenge and to respond to a challenge. Unites ideas, objectives and possibilities. Competitive. Intolerant of woolliness and vagueness.

- **Company worker:** Stable, controlled. A practical organiser. Can be inflexible but likely to adapt to established systems. Not an innovator.

- **Monitor evaluator:** High IQ, stable, introvert. Goes in for measured analysis, not innovation. Unambiguous and often lacking enthusiasm, but solid and dependable.

- **Team worker:** Stable, extrovert, but not really dominant. Much concerned with individuals' needs. Builds on others' ideas. Cools things down when tempers fray.

- **Finisher:** Anxious introvert. Worries over what may go wrong. Permanent sense of urgency. Preoccupied with order. Concerned with 'following through'.

✔ **Shared vision and goal:** The team members must have ownership of their own measurable and clearly defined goals. This requirement means involving the team in business planning. It also means keeping the communication channels open as the business grows. Those in the founding team knew clearly what they were trying to achieve, and because they probably shared an office, they shared information as they worked. But as the group gets larger and new people join, you have to help the informal communication systems work better. Briefing meetings, social events and bulletin boards are all ways to get teams together and keep them facing the right way.

✔ **Shared language:** To be a member of a business team, people have to have a reasonable grasp of the language of business. Extolling people to improve return on capital employed or reduce debtor days isn't much use if they've only the haziest notion of what those terms mean, why they matter or how they can influence the business's results. So you need to develop rounded business skills across all the core team members through continuous training, development and coaching.

✔ **Compatible personalities:** Although having different team profiles is important, having team members who can get on with one another is equally vital. Team members have to be able to listen to and respect each other's ideas and views; support and trust one another; and accept conflict as a healthy reality and work through it to a successful outcome.

✔ **Good leadership:** First-class leadership is perhaps the most important characteristic that distinguishes winning teams from the also-rans. However good the constituent parts, without leadership a team rapidly disintegrates into a rabble bound by little but a pay cheque.

You can't just pick people and put them into teams because of their particular professional or job skills. If the team is to function effectively, its balance of behavioural styles has to mesh too.

Coaching and Training

Coaching and training are two ways to help individuals and teams improve their performance.

A *coach* is a skilled and experienced person who watches an individual or small group performing a task. The coach shows them individually how they can improve their performance. The emphasis is on personalised instruction. *Training* is usually a more formal process, where the trainer has a set agenda for the event based on the knowledge required by the trainees. Everyone being trained goes through much the same process, at the same time.

Small firms are notoriously bad at recognising the need for training of any type. Over 40 per cent of small firms devote only one day or less to staff training each year. Only 13 per cent invest five days or more in training. Amateur football teams spend more time in training than the average small firm, so the fact that few teams in that firm ever realise their true potential, or come anywhere near becoming professionals, is hardly surprising.

And yet all the evidence is that training pays a handsome and quick return.

The choices a small firm has for training include the following:

✔ **On-the-job coaching:** This type of training is where people learn from someone more experienced about how a job should be done. The advantages are that this kind of coaching is free and involves no time away from work. It should also directly relate to an individual's training needs. However, the coaching is only as good as the coach, and if the coach is untrained you may end up simply replicating poor working standards.

✔ **In-house classroom training:** This type is the most traditional and familiar form of training. Some, or all, of your employees gather in a 'classroom', on your premises or in a local hotel. You hire in a trainer or use one of your own experienced staff. This method provides plenty of opportunity for group interaction, and the instructor can motivate the class and pay attention to individual needs. The disadvantages, particularly if you hold the training away from your premises, are that you incur large costs that are more to do with hospitality than training, and for a small firm releasing a number of employees at the same time is time consuming and difficult.

✔ **Public courses:** These courses are less expensive than running a training programme in a hotel. You can also select different courses for different employees and so tailor the training more precisely to their needs. However, most public courses are generic and the other attendees are more likely to come from big business or even the public sector, so much of what is covered may be of little direct relevance to your business. Quality can be patchy.

✔ **Interactive distance learning:** This kind of training can be delivered by a combination of traditional training materials, teleconferencing and the Internet and email discussions. You miss out on the personal contact, but the costs are much lower than traditional training. Most of the learning programmes are aimed at larger firms, so some material may not be relevant.

✔ **Off-the-shelf training programmes:** These programmes come in packaged kits, which may consist of a training manual, video and/or a CD-Rom. The cost is lower than for face-to-face training, but you miss out on a professional trainer's input.

✔ **College courses:** Many universities and business schools now offer programmes tailored to the needs of small firms. Professional instructors who understand the needs of small firms deliver these courses. They're relatively expensive, but can often be effective.

✔ **Government initiatives:** National governments have an interest in encouraging training in small firms. As well as providing information on where their training schemes are being run, governments often provide training grants to help with the costs.

To make sure that you get the best out of your training, follow these guidelines:

✔ Introduce a routine that ensures that all employees attending training are briefed at least a week beforehand on what to expect and what you expect of them.

✔ Ensure that all employees discuss with you or their manager or supervisor what they got out of the training programme – in particular, did it meet both their expectations? This discussion should take place no later than a week after the programme.

✔ You or the manager need to check within a month, and then again at regular intervals, to see whether their skills have improved, and that employees are putting those skills into practice.

Evaluate the costs and financial benefits of your training and development plans, and use this information to help set next year's training budget.

You can find a training course or programme for yourself and anyone you employ from Training Directory UK (www.trainingdirectoryuk.com). Their advisers can help you search for the training courses you need through their network of around 5,000 UK training providers, offering more than 57,000 UK courses. They search on your behalf and email you training course quotes to review and compare. If you want to proceed, they can book the training course for you; they claim the cost will be no more than had you booked direct. The following are a few sources of free business training materials:

- ✔ The Massachusetts Institute of Technology (http://ocw.mit.edu/index.htm) makes virtually all its courses freely available on the web for non-commercial use.

- ✔ Open Culture (http://www.openculture.com/business_free_courseswww.openculture.com/business_free_courses), the brainchild of the director of Stanford University's Continuing Studies Program, offers over 150 free online business courses.

- ✔ On the website of the US Small Business Administration's Small Business Learning Center (www.sba.gov/sba-learning-center/search/training), you can find over 30 free courses.

Appraising Performance

Appraising the performance of both teams and individuals isn't primarily concerned with blame, reward or praise. Its purpose is to develop people and help them perform better and be able to achieve their career goals. The result of an appraisal is a personal development plan.

Appraisal lies at the heart of assessing, improving and developing people's performance for the future of the business. However, for it to be an effective tool, everyone involved needs to approach appraisal seriously and professionally. The appraisal has to be a discussion between people who work together rather than simply a boss dictating to a subordinate. It should be an open, two-way discussion for which both the appraiser and appraisee prepare in advance. Successful appraisals are

- ✔ **Results oriented:** The appraisal interview starts with a review against objectives and finishes by setting objectives for the year to come.

  Set intermediate goals and objectives for new staff even if you can't realistically set final goals. For example, challenge new salespeople to acquire product knowledge and visit all the key customers, leaving actual sales achievement objectives until later in the year.

✔ **Separate from salary review:** A discussion about salary is unlikely to encourage people to be open and frank, but an appraisal must be both those things. The salary review and the appraisal must be different events, if possible carried out at different times of the year.

✔ **Narratives:** They don't consist of tick boxes and ratings schedules. The appraisal covers a discussion of achievements, areas for improvement, overall performance, training and development, and career expectations.

Allow plenty of time for each appraisal interview (one and a half hours on average). The setting should be free from interruptions and unthreatening.

Carry out appraisals at least once a year, with more regular quarterly reviews – you should review new staff after three months. Some owner-managers question the necessity of a formal annual appraisal when they feel that they're already appraising their team informally on a day-to-day basis. That approach is rather like trying to assess a business by its daily trading figures rather than its annual profit and loss account. The changes in behaviour and performance you're trying to assess happen over a longer time span and may not be easy to see on a day-to-day basis. Also, your daily assessments are likely to be influenced by pressures and feelings on the day and they may not reflect the true longer-term picture.

Use appraisals to identify training needs and incorporate any deficiencies into a personal or company-wide training plan.

The HR Council, an organisation funded in part by the government of Canada, has as useful toolkit to help with setting up an appraisal process as well as a sample performance assessment form; see `http://hrcouncil.ca/hr-toolkit/keeping-people-performance-management.cfm`.

Developing a Leadership Style

Most large organisations have grown up according to basic management principles. If you started your business career working for a bigger firm, or your present managers worked in such enterprises, you know the scenario. Managers in these organisations plan, organise and control in a way that produces consistent if unexciting results. The formula worked remarkably well for much of the 20th century, when all a successful company had to do to prosper was more of the same. But management that's all about maintaining order and predictability is ill-equipped to deal with change, which is the order of the day in the 21st century. To cope with change effectively, you need to be a leader as well as a competent manager – and young businesses are in greater need of leaders than they are of managers, at the outset at least.

Understanding leadership

Leadership and management aren't the same, although many businesspeople fail to make the distinction. The late management professor Peter Drucker summed up the difference between leaders and managers thus: 'A leader challenges the status quo; a manager accepts it.'

In a world where product lifecycles are shrinking, new technologies have an ever shorter shelf life and customers demand faster delivery and higher quality, the leader's job increasingly means defining and inspiring change within a company. By setting a company's direction, communicating this this direction to its workforce, motivating employees and taking a long-range perspective, a leader adapts the firm to whatever volatile environment it does business in. In short, leaders become the change masters in their own firms.

Delegating

Overwork is a common complaint of those running their own business. They never have enough time to think or plan. But if you don't make time to plan, you can never move forward.

Delegating certain tasks eases the stress. *Delegation* is the art of getting things done your way by other people. Or, as one entrepreneur succinctly put it, 'making other people happy to make you rich'.

Many owner-managers are unable to delegate, either because they draw comfort from sticking to routine tasks such as sending out invoices, rather than tackling new and unfamiliar ones such as keeping up with developments in the industry, or because they just don't know how to delegate. Either way, neither the business nor those in it can grow until delegation becomes the normal way to operate.

Seeing the benefits of delegation

Delegating brings benefits to everyone involved in the process.

Benefits for the boss include

- ✔ **More time to achieve more today and to plan for the future:** In this way you can free up time to tackle high-value-added tasks such as recruitment and selection, or motivation.

- ✔ **Back-up for emergencies and day-to-day tasks:** By delegating, you have a reserve of skilled people who can keep the business running profitably if you're not there. This reserve can also give customers and financial backers the comfort of knowing that they aren't dealing with a one-person operation that would fall apart without you.

Benefits for employees include

✔ **The opportunity to develop new skills:** Failing to delegate deprives employees of the opportunity to learn discover new skills and to grow themselves, and drives good employees, just the ones a growing organisation desperately needs, away in search of greater challenges. Employees who have assumed the responsibility for new tasks train their staff in the same way. Then the organisation can grow and have in-depth management.

✔ **Greater involvement:** Research consistently shows that employees rank job satisfaction to be of equal or greater value than pay. Delegation encourages people to take ownership of their decisions and increases their enthusiasm and initiative for their work, so they get more satisfaction from their work.

Benefits for the business are

✔ **Efficiency improves** by allowing those closest to the problems and issues being faced to take the decisions in a timely manner.

✔ **Flexibility of operations increases** because several people are able to perform key tasks. In this way, you can rotate and expand or contract teams and tasks to meet changing circumstances. Delegation also results in more people being prepared for promotion.

Delegating successfully

Delegation is a management process that you shouldn't confuse with 'dumping', in which you shove unpopular, difficult or tedious tasks unceremoniously onto the shoulders of the first person who comes to hand. To make delegation work successfully, adopt the following five-point plan.

1. **Decide what and what not to delegate.**

   Here are the general questions for deciding what to delegate:

   - Can anyone else do or be trained to do the work to a satisfactory standard?

   - Is all the information necessary to carry out the task available to the person(s) to whom you're planning to delegate the task?

   - Is the task largely operational rather than strategic?

   - Would delegating the task save you a reasonable amount of time?

   - Would some initial teething problems while the new person settles into the task cause undue problems? Delegation itself is a form of risk taking, so if you can't deal with a few mistakes then delegation proves difficult.

   - Can someone other than you properly exercise direct control over the task?

Usually, you can readily delegate any routine jobs, information gathering or assignments involving extensive detail or calculations. Tasks that are less easy to delegate include all confidential work, discipline, staff evaluation, and complex or sensitive issues.

2. **Decide to whom to delegate.**

The factors to consider here are the following:

- Who has the necessary skills?

- Who could or should be groomed for future promotion?

- Who's most likely to respond well to the challenge?

- Who's most likely to be, or continue to be, a loyal employee?

- Whose workload allows her to take on the task(s)?

3. **Communicate your decision.**

Factors to consider here are the following:

- Discuss the task you propose to delegate one to one with the individual concerned.

- Confirm that she feels up to the task or agree any necessary training, back-up or extra resources.

- Set out clearly in writing the task, broken down into its main components, the measurable outcomes, the timescales and any other important factors.

- Allow time for the implications to sink in and then discuss with the person concerned how she proposes going about the task.

- Let others in the business know of your decision.

4. **Manage and evaluate.**

From the beginning, clearly establish set times to meet with the person delegated to and review her performance. Make the intervals between these reviews short at first, lengthening the period when the person's performance is satisfactory. The secret of successful delegation is to follow up.

5. **Reward results.**

Things that get measured get done and those that are rewarded get done over again. The reward need not be financial. Recognition or praise for a job well done are often more valuable to an ambitious person than money.

Evolving leadership styles for growth

All businesses require leadership, but they don't require the same type or amount of leadership all the time. As with children, businesses don't grow seamlessly from being babies to adulthood. They pass through phases – infancy, adolescence, teenage years and so on. Businesses also move through phases if they're to grow successfully. Each of these phases is punctuated by a *crisis*, used in this sense to signify a dangerous opportunity.

Researchers have identified several distinctive phases in a firm's growth pattern that provide an insight into the changes in organisational structure, strategy and behaviour that you need to move successfully on to the next phase of growth. The inability to recognise the phases of growth and to manage the transition through them is probably the single most important reason for most owner-managed firms failing to achieve their true potential, let alone their founder's dreams.

Typically, a business starts out taking on any customers it can get, operating informally, with little management and few controls. The founder, who usually provides all the ideas, brings all the drive, makes all the decisions and signs the cheques, becomes overloaded with administrative detail and operational problems. Unless the founder can change the organisational structure, any further growth leaves the business more vulnerable. Crises of leadership, autonomy and control loom large.

Over time, the successful owner-manager tackles these crises and finds a clear focus, builds a first-class team, delegates key tasks, appraises performance, institutes control and reporting systems, and ensures that progress towards objectives is monitored and rewarded. The firm itself consistently delivers good results.

Each phase of growth calls for a different approach to leading the business. At times strong leadership is required; at others a more consultative approach is appropriate. Some phases call for more systems and procedures, some for more co-operation between staff. Unfortunately, as the business gets bigger, most founders try to run their business in much the same way as they did when it was small. They end up with a big-small company, rather than the small-big company that they require if they're to achieve successful growth. They believe that taking on another salesperson, a few hundred square metres of space or another bank loan can solve the problems of growth. This approach is rather like suggesting that the transition from infancy to adulthood can be accomplished by nothing more significant than providing larger clothes.

Finding a mentor

You can read heaps of books on leadership and attend multiple training programmes and still be a poor leader. Why? Because a gap exists between what you know and what you do. A great way to bridge that gap is to find a mentor to inspire and guide you. The mentor is someone with greater experience and wisdom who's sufficiently independent to be able to offer impartial advice and support. If you know someone who fits the bill, so much the better. If not, contact Get Mentoring (`http://getmentoring.org`), a big network with a lot of impressive strategic partners that recruits and trains business mentors in the UK from the small, medium and micro business communities.

Managing change

The late professor Peter Drucker claimed that the first task of a leader is to define the company's mission. In a world in which product and service lifecycles are shrinking, new technologies have ever shorter shelf lives and customers demand ever higher levels of both quality and innovation, entrepreneurial leadership means inspiring change.

Being flexible enough to change

In adapting the business to an increasingly volatile and competitive environment, the boss must become the change master in the firm. Small firms are usually better at handling change than big firms. A speedboat can always alter course faster than a supertanker. However, small firms often have to adapt to much more change than big, established firms. Big firms usually define the standards in an industry and the small firms have to scramble to keep up.

The turbulence created by changes in the economy can also create a wash that can sink small firms unless they can adapt and change quickly. Those small firms most able to adapt and change, and of course those that are most prepared, are most likely to survive and prosper during turbulent times.

But recognising the need for change falls a long way short of being able to implement it successfully. Few people like change and even fewer can adapt to new circumstances quickly and without missing a heartbeat.

By definition, a small business seeking growth must be able to manage a fast rate of change. Entrepreneurs must see change as the norm and not as a temporary and unexpected disruption that goes away when conditions improve.

Planning for change

Change management is a business process, like any other business process. Following a tried and proven procedure can improve your chances of getting it right more often.

These four steps show how you can break down change management into its elements.

1. **Tell staff why change is necessary (or better still, help them to find out for themselves).**

   The benefits of change aren't always obvious. So spell them out in much the same way as you explain the benefits of your product or service to a prospective customer.

   Explaining the background to the changes you want to make helps people see the changes as an opportunity to be competitive rather than a threat to existing work practices.

   Better than just explaining is to encourage staff to look outside the business for themselves, identify potential problems and suggest their own solutions. Not only may they have great ideas for change – perhaps better than yours – but they may be more willing to take responsibility for making the changes succeed.

2. **Make the change manageable.**

   Even when people are dissatisfied with the present position and know exactly what needs to be done to improve things, the change may still not happen. The change may be just too big for anyone to handle. But if you break the change down into manageable bits, you can make it happen.

3. **Take a shared approach.**

   Involve people early on. Asking them to join you in managing change only at the implementation stage is too late to get their full co-operation. Give your key participants some a say in shaping the change right from the start. This involvement means that nobody feels that you're imposing the change and more brains are brought to bear on the problem.

   Individual resistance to change is a normal reaction. By understanding why people are resisting, you can help them overcome their doubts and embrace the change. Try to anticipate the impact of the change on the people involved:

   • Get an overview of the forces at work, both in favour of and against the change.

   • Make a list of those most affected by the change. Put each person into one of four categories – no commitment; will let it happen if others want it; will help it happen; will make it happen.

     Examine how each person is likely to be affected by the change. Look at career prospects, working hours and conditions, team membership and so forth.

   • Anticipate retraining. Often a fear of failing is the principal reason for people not trying something new.

Open, face-to-face communication is the backbone of successful change. It gets across the 'why' of change and allows people to face up to problems openly. It also builds confidence and clears up misunderstandings.

Open communication is vital, but announcing intended changes before you have some committed participants alongside you is risky.

4. Reinforce individual and team identity.

People are more willing to accept change and to move from the known to the unknown if they have confidence in themselves and their boss. Confidence is most likely to exist where people have a high degree of self-esteem. Building up self-esteem involves laying stress on the positive rather than the negative aspects of each person's contribution. Exhortations such as 'you guys have had it too easy for too long' are unlikely to do much for people when you're faced with major competitive pressure.

You need to emphasise the importance to the change project of each person, both as an individual and, where appropriate, as a team member. A positive, confident climate for change needs lots of reinforcement, such as the following ideas:

- Reward achievement of new goals and achieving them quickly.

- Highlight success stories and create as many winners as possible.

- Hold social events to celebrate milestones.

- Pay personal attention to those most affected by the change.

Change takes longer than you think. Most major changes make things worse before they make them better. More often than not, the immediate impact of change is a decrease in productivity, as people struggle to cope with new ways of working while they move up their own learning curve.

The doubters can gloat and even the change champions may waver. But the greatest danger now is pulling the plug on the plan and either adopting a new plan or reverting to the status quo.

To prevent this 'disappointment', you have to set realistic goals for the change period and anticipate and plan how to handle the time lag between change and results.

Measuring Morale

How your employees feel about their jobs, their co-workers, the company and you and other bosses has a direct effect on how well or poorly they do their jobs. You need to stay on top of morale issues to keep your business running smoothly.

The most reliable way to measure morale at work is to carry out an attitude survey. In a big company, one-to-one interviews and focus groups may accompany such surveys. But in a small firm, that's not really an option.

In much the same way as you may survey customers to find out how happy they are with your products and services, survey your employees to find out what they feel about their employment conditions. Attitude surveys provide an objective measure to counterbalance the more descriptive view that you can obtain from discussions and gossip. They also provide a useful way to see whether morale is getting better or worse over time.

You may decide to introduce attitude surveys because of a particular event, such as a number of key staff leaving at the same time or some other obvious problem. Change can upset morale and that can have a knock-on effect on business performance. But after you've started, keeping the practice up makes sense. At the very least, surveying your employees demonstrates your concern, and at the best it gives you valuable pointers to raising morale, output and profits.

A word of warning: your attitude surveys are inevitably going to reveal two basic facts that are fairly normal:

- **All employees believe that they're underpaid.** Most people believe that they're underpaid both by market standards and in relation to the effort they put in. They also believe that the gap between levels in the company is too great. This belief that they're poorly rewarded exists irrespective of how much people are actually paid, or indeed how hard they work. If you ask them why they don't leave, they tell you about loyalty to a small firm or perhaps, more flatteringly, loyalty to you.

- **All employees believe that communication is awful.** Employees think that their boss knows a secret that directly affects them that the boss isn't willing to divulge. This belief may be about restructuring, moving, merging or outsourcing. This phenomenon happens at all levels. The shop floor believes that supervisors have secrets; supervisors believe that managers withhold crucial information on plans that involve them; and the remaining managers know that the directors are planning their future in secret. So they become convinced that a communication problem exists in the organisation because no one tells them what's *really* going on.

You have to take all the information from your employees into consideration when sizing up the situation, and not just the results of one attitude survey.

Introducing attitude surveys

John Huggett, a young and abrasive entrepreneur, moved south from Yorkshire and bought a small but seriously troubled engineering factory. The company employed 22 people and had shrunk over the years from more than 50. The business had suffered losses for over a year. But Huggett succeeded brilliantly in solving the problems that had built up.

In the process, by his own admission, he came close to committing murder – telephone directories and occasionally the telephone itself flew through the air. Those in the organisation perceived John – not unnaturally, given his style and the rescue job he was attempting – as a fire-eating monster. No one saw the human behind the gruff exterior.

At that time, this attitude didn't matter. However, as the factory moved into a period of growth and expansion, John recognised that he and the management team needed to make a conscious effort to change towards a more consensual style of management. People didn't feel empowered and they weren't about to stick their necks out when the blood still ran from the walls. John stood up in front of the workforce and said, 'We're going to have a different management style, and we're going to change.' He introduced an attitude survey to take the temperature of the water and committed himself, in advance of the survey, to live by its results.

He and the management team have done just that, introducing exceptionally effective team briefings, management walkabouts and other consultative mechanisms. The work force took time to be convinced, but they came to respect John's integrity and open style greatly.

HR-Survey (www.hr-survey.com) and Custom Insight (www.custominsight.com) provide fast, simple and easy-to-use software to carry out and analyse human resources surveys. Both sites have a range of sample surveys that you can see and try before you buy, which may just be enough to stimulate your thinking.

Part V
The Part of Tens

To read about preparing to move on from your business, take a look at the bonus Part of Tens chapter online, at www.dummies.com/extras/startingabusinessuk.

In this part . . .

✔ Steer clear of the most common mistakes that new business founders make.

✔ Know who to talk to before you get started.

✔ Figure out how to get social media to extend your reach out into the global market.

✔ Start planning your next big move.

Chapter 19

Ten Pitfalls to Avoid

In This Chapter

▶ Making sure that you have the right skills base

▶ Keeping track of key financial data

▶ Staying out of the failure statistics

Difficult times can cause even the biggest and apparently most established firms to hit the buffers. After all, Lehman Brothers survived the 1929 depression and Woolworths had put in time on almost every high street in the UK, yet both were swept away in the recent downturn.

Around 400,000 small businesses close down each year in the UK and over half of those closures occur in the first year of trading. Although not all the closures come under the heading of home-busting events, no business owners like to have a personal failure on their hands, even if it doesn't wipe them out financially.

This chapter lists the main problems to avoid – the ones that cripple small businesses so that they have to shut their doors in the first year or so.

Knowing Too Little

Running your own business calls for a well-rounded range of expertise. In the early morning you may have to be coach and trainer to a new employee, by mid-morning (coffee-break time in big business parlance) you can be negotiating with the bank for an extra line of credit, at midday you may be drafting a marketing strategy and the early afternoon can involve looking for suppliers for a new product you're thinking of launching. The late afternoon may find you delivering a rush order to a key customer, followed by a quick shifty around a competitor's premises and a couple of possible premises for you to move into if you grow as planned. The evening is devoted to drafting a job advertisement and a leaflet, leaving the weekend to get the books up to date and the VAT return done.

Take time out before you start your business to brush up on the range of skills you're going to need. More opportunities now exist than ever before for education and training, at every level, in the small business and management fields. You don't need any formal academic qualifications for most of the courses and costs are generally modest. In certain cases, participants may be eligible for grants or subsidised training. The bulk of the activities are concentrated in universities and colleges throughout the UK.

Find a course for yourself or employees through these websites:

✔ **The Skills Funding Agency** (`http://skillsfundingagency.bis.gov.uk`) has a mission to ensure that people and businesses can access the skills training they need to succeed in playing their part in society and in growing the economy. Their website includes advice on selecting a training programme and a directory of training providers using their impartial Skills Brokerage service. They aim to help employers and employees identify the best value for money, which may mean finding training that is partially or wholly funded by the government.

✔ **Learndirect** (`www.learndirect.com/business`) is the country's biggest national training provider, with 400 delivery locations. They've helped more than 75,000 businesses equip their staff with the skills needed to succeed, ranging from thousands of SMEs to blue-chip corporates.

In addition, a growing number of opportunities are arising for the less mobile to take up some form of home study in the business field in general, and small business opportunities in particular. With the growth of the Internet, British entrepreneurs may now find it practical and worthwhile to get their learning experience from virtually any part of the world (see Chapter 18 for information on the Massachusetts Institute of Technology, which makes available free management education materials).

Being Overly Optimistic about the Market

Business starters are, by nature, optimistic. You have to be to overcome the hurdles, both natural and man-made, that appear in your path. But the one area you can't afford to be over-optimistic about is the market itself. That's the one thing you can't change. You can replace people, you can improve products and you can find money or new premises. But the raw ingredient of any business, the potential market, is a given that you can't easily change. True, big businesses talk grandly about educating the market to appreciate their wonderful product or service. But educating markets calls for deep wallets and long-time horizons, both in short supply in the small business world.

Take care not to develop the 'iceberg syndrome'. Don't believe that the small number of customers you can see is a sure indication of the great mass of other customers lying hidden below the water-line, just waiting for you to sell to them. Believing that customers are simply waiting to be sold to and that competitors are blind or lazy is a fundamental mistake.

Underestimating Start-up Time

Everything in business seems to take longer than you think. Premises take ages to find and even longer to kit out and be ready for use. If you start up before you're ready, customers may well be disappointed and rush around sharing their displeasure.

Make a chart showing the key tasks that you have to carry out before you can launch your business in the left-hand column, with the timescale in days, weeks or months, as appropriate to your business, across the top of the chart. In the right-hand column, show who's responsible for each task.

Draw a bar between the start and finish date for each key task, showing how long the task should take. Some of the tasks overlap others and some depend on the successful completion of earlier tasks. For example, you can't install the oven in a restaurant until you've found the premises and signed the lease. You can, however, research oven suppliers and negotiate the price and delivery. Use the chart to monitor progress and take corrective action as you go.

Spending Too Much at the Start

New businesses should be lean and mean. Don't spend too much on fixtures, fittings and equipment too soon. People with a background in big business often start with extravagantly high standards. They expect the latest computer equipment, broadband Internet access, colour photocopier and cappuccino maker to be close at hand, and to sit in an executive-style office from the outset. You have to spread these overheads across the products/services that you sell and you can lose your competitive edge by being too expensive. See Chapter 8 for information on start-up costs.

Mistaking Cash for Profit

The cash that flows into the business hasn't had any of the automatic deductions knocked off it, as has a pay cheque from an employer. So the money that comes in is *gross* cash flow. It may be real cash, but it's not really yours, or at least not all of it is yours. You may be tempted to use this cash to maintain your living standards, but don't yield to it. When the bills come in – from the suppliers, for national insurance, for VAT – as they inevitably do, you may be stuck for the cash to pay them. Her Majesty's Revenue and Customs puts more businesses into liquidation than anyone else.

Maintain a cash-flow forecast on a rolling quarterly basis. In that way, you always have a one-year view of what's likely to happen to the cash in the business. Use the cash-flow projection to anticipate peaks and troughs in your cash flow.

Use a spreadsheet and write the program yourself or use the template that comes with your accounting software. Manual cash-flow systems are inefficient and discourage regular updates. On the other hand, spreadsheet updates are simple, efficient and free of arithmetical errors, at least.

Choosing the Wrong Partner

A partnership is to business life what a marriage is to the rest of your life – a long-term, all-pervading relationship that spills over into and affects everything you do. Partnerships are complicated affairs, relying as much on chemistry as on personal attributes, skills or knowledge. Just as you should never embark on a marriage without a few months of dating at least, you should find a way to test out a partnership before you formalise the relationship. (See Chapter 5 for the legal aspects of partnerships.)

Take on a project together that involves using the skills and expertise you hope your prospective partner brings to the business. If you want the person to do the buying, for example, go to a trade show together, preferably one that involves a couple of days' travelling to and from the venue. Watch him at work talking to exhibitors and opening up negotiations. Get him to meet others involved with your business – your spouse, bank manager, key clients; in fact, anyone who knows you well – and get their reaction.

The big factor to keep in mind is that a business partnership is likely to last longer than the average marriage. So if you can't face that, don't start a partnership.

You may be forgiven for thinking that Simon Nixon, the founder of Moneysupermarket.com, a European financial services price comparison website, has everything to be pleased about. Ranked in the top ten companies with the fastest profit growth in the *Sunday Times*/PricewaterhouseCoopers Profit Track 100 within seven years of starting up, the company generated annual profits of £23.4 million. It has successfully spread its price-comparison skills, launching Travelsupermarket.com and sites to compare utilities, Internet service providers, insurance, mobile phones and motor cars. But all isn't rosy in Nixon's garden. His considerable expertise is in the mortgage business, and in order to get access to the IT skills he needed to get the business launched he engaged IT expert Duncan Cameron on a 50/50 basis. Cameron, the brother of Nixon's former girlfriend, hasn't been in contact with Nixon for years and is treated as a silent partner. However, Cameron's substantial holding means that he can at any stage demand a place on the board, sway strategy or, more worryingly, block moves to float the company on the stock market.

Ignoring Accounting

Many owner-managers see accounting as a bureaucratic waste of time that they carry out only to keep the tax authorities off their backs and make it easier for those authorities to carve a deeper trough in their hard-won profits. Although you can have some sympathy with that point of view, you can't condone it. For too many new businesses, their first year's accounts are also their last. By the time they really know what's going on, it may be too late to put things right.

Forgetting Working Capital

Most business starters can work out how much the big-ticket items cost – computers, vehicles and office furniture, for example. But they often forget to allow for the recurring items such as money owed by customers, stock in trade and 'invisible' items such as insurance. To make matters more complicated, these items often have time lags associated with them. A customer who owes you money has to be financed until he pays up, as do your raw materials until you can turn them into saleable product that's been delivered and paid for. These items constitute a business's working capital (Chapter 13 talks about working capital), and the more successful you are, the more of a problem working capital becomes.

Think about it. When you get a new big order, you need the ingredients or raw materials to put it together. Your suppliers expect payment within 30 days, or perhaps even on a pro forma basis (cash with delivery) in your early months of trading. But the snag is that you have to work up your product using bought-in raw materials, which may take weeks or months, and then wait for months for payment. In the meantime, you're hung out to dry with a growing need for working capital. The paradox is that nearly as many businesses go bust with the sales curve going up as with it going down. The technical term for this problem is *over-trading*, and the cure is to allow for it in your business plans and make sure that you have sufficient working capital in place to survive.

Having No Clear Competitive Advantage

You or your product or service has to have something unique about it that makes you stand out from your competitors. It may be something as obvious as being open later or longer. Or it may be a policy such as the John Lewis Partnership's 'never knowingly undersold' message. Whatever your unique selling proposition is, communicate it effectively. Slip back to Chapter 2, where I cover this area comprehensively.

Choosing the Wrong Location

Where you conduct your business and how much rent you pay are vital factors. Don't be tempted to take premises just because the rent is cheap – a reason usually exists for this, such as few customers passing that route or poor transport links, making the premises difficult for employees and suppliers to get to. Equally, don't take on an expensive town-centre site if your turnover is unlikely to cover your outgoings.

Your market research (see Chapters 4 and 12 for more on this) should help you identify a suitable location.

Chapter 20

Ten People to Talk to Before You Start

. . . .

In This Chapter

▶ Identifying all the key people who can help you get started

▶ Leveraging your network of contacts to maximum advantage

▶ Taking advantage of free advice

▶ Getting the lowdown on what people really think are your strengths and weaknesses

. . . .

Starting up a business can be a lonely endeavour, but you don't have to do it all on your own. Hundreds of people, some just a few feet away, can give you useful insights into your skills and attributes, and they may even have a useful perspective on the viability of your business idea.

Speaking with Your Spouse

Even if you don't plan to go into business with your spouse and she doesn't know a great deal about your great business idea, you can be sure that she knows a lot about you. Your spouse can remind you of your weaknesses and help you play to your strengths. She also needs to be prepared for the long hours and lack of holidays that are sure to feature in the early months and years as you get your business established. Your venture may mean that you need to re-divide the existing sharing of household and family tasks, such as taking children to school, family visits and painting and decorating, to reflect the new balance of work. That may prove contentious, so talking the issues through at the outset can save conflict and arguments when time constraints really start to bite.

The money put into the business is going to have an impact on the money available for other areas of family expenditure, so your spouse also has to be comfortable with the financial commitments you're taking on. Unlike most other investments you may have made – on houses and cars, for example – you can lose all the money you put into a business irrevocably.

One would-be entrepreneur who set out to open a bookshop was reminded by her partner how she disliked dealing with the general public. She loved books and delighted in visiting book fairs and auctions. But when reminded that essentially the job entailed opening and closing a shop six days a week, her enthusiasm level took a dive. Better take a dive before you start up than have your cash take a dive a few weeks afterwards.

If you're thinking of taking up some franchises – Chemex (http://chemexuk. com), for example – you may be asked to bring your partner along to the initial interview even if she's not going to be involved in the running of the business. Chemex wants to make sure that your partner is backing you 100 per cent, both practically and emotionally.

Making Use of Your Professional Network

The people in your network of associates have large chunks of the knowledge you need to successfully launch your business. The ability to create and maintain strong professional relationships is an important key to business success. Networking is a vital business skill that lets you cultivate lasting business relationships and create a large sphere of influence from which you can find new clients, contacts, referrals and opportunities.

You can use a network for just about anything, from finding a new supplier to getting introductions to overseas sales agents. You can find a reliable bank manager, a new accounting software package or a great venue for your next business meeting. Your network contacts, unlike almost everyone else in the business world, are usually unbiased and authoritative. You should make few major decisions without recourse to network contacts.

Benefiting from Entrepreneurs Who Started a Similar Business

People like nothing more than talking about themselves and their successes. Obviously, if someone thinks you're going to steal her customers, she shuts up like a clam. However, if the business you plan to start is unlikely to infringe on their sphere of activities, most established entrepreneurs are only too happy to pass on some of their hard-earned tips.

First, establish that you're not going to tread on the entrepreneur's toes. For example, if you plan to start up in the same line of business 30 miles away, you've little chance of causing each other much trouble. You may even be able to open a shop at the far end of the same town as a competitor without doing the entrepreneur any serious damage.

Use your common sense as to whom to approach and, to be on the safe side, double the distance that you feel is a safe gap between you.

You may also find someone who's had a business failure in the field you plan to start up in and is prepared to talk. You can find such people by scouring the press or talking to trade associations and other operators in your sector.

Don't take everything entrepreneurs say, even the most successful ones, as inevitably right. The five businesspeople who comprise the dragons in the BBC programme *Dragon's Den,* with a combined personal wealth nearing £1 billion, can reasonably be expected to know a thing or two about new business ideas. Andrew Gordon presented to them his invention for propping up wobbly table legs and they unreservedly gave it the thumbs down. Despite being ripped to shreds as a concept, his StableTable (www.stabletable.se), eight plastic leaves pinned together, has sold in industrial volumes on the Internet and has spurred development of a new product, StableTable Extreme. The simple device earned the 34-year-old in excess of $500,000 in his first year and is now being sold in packs of 25 for use in restaurants, hotels, pubs and cafes throughout the world. Andrew is an inspiration to all would-be business starters whose ideas receive a less-than-rapturous reception from fellow entrepreneurs.

Events can be a valuable route to extending your business network. Useful organisations include the following:

- ✔ **The Glasshouse** (http://theglasshouse.net), founded in 1998, holds networking events bringing entrepreneurs, financiers and business advisers across all sectors together to provide support, encouragement and inspiration to would-be business starters.

✔ **The Junior Chamber International United Kingdom** (www.jciuk.org.uk) is a personal development and networking organisation for the under-40s. It's part of the global Junior Chamber International (JCI), which has over 250,000 members in 100 different countries.

✔ **Networking4business** (www.networking4business.com) organises business-to-business networking events that enable you to meet many other businesspeople without any commitment and in a relaxed, informal atmosphere.

Spending Time with a Friendly Banker

Despite having had a bad press during the credit crunch, these guys and girls have a lot to offer other than oodles of cash (or not!). Bankers see a lot of different people about a lot of different businesses. You can draw on their wide range of knowledge and experience. Your banker may be familiar with your type of business or the location you're interested in, or have advice on different financing options.

Start by talking with a bank manager you don't want to borrow money from. Begin the conversation by asking for advice, rather than money. Only when you've convinced yourself that your proposition is an appropriate one for a bank, should you make a pitch. (See Chapter 8 for more about banks and bank managers.)

Reaching Out to Customers

Chances are that you regularly come across people buying products or services similar to those that you plan to sell. If you can rubberneck on the transaction, without being obtrusive, you can pick up valuable insights on what people really put value on. Clearly, in some businesses doing this is easier than in others. If your competitor's products are in the high street, just park yourself nearby and watch and learn. If that isn't the case, try asking around your friends, relatives and anyone you can dig up and talk to them about their purchase experience; find out what they like and don't like.

I cover how to reach out to customers in Chapter 4, but don't wait – make sure that you grab your fair share of this expertise at the earliest opportunity.

Communicating with Your Current Boss

Deciding to talk to your boss about anything other than the job in hand is always tricky. Talk about your entrepreneurial vision too soon and you may find yourself sidetracked for promotion and pay rises, and perhaps even first in line for the next downsizing event. Leave it too late and your boss may see your action as disloyalty at best and betrayal at worst.

If you plan to start up in the same line of work and possibly even try to take some key accounts with you, then you'd better talk to a lawyer rather than your boss. But if the climate is right and you can talk to your boss, a number of valuable things may happen. You boss can be a source of investment capital, a business partner or a useful resource for business advice and contacts. Your boss may even become your first customer, if the businesses are compatible.

Calling Your Colleagues

Those you've worked alongside over the years have formed a view about your talents. Your spouse has seen you after work, but your colleagues have seen you at work. If they don't know your strengths, weaknesses, foibles and desires, then no one does. At worst, they may tell you that you're barmy and explain why; at best, they may join you in the venture or invest their hard-earned savings in your business.

If you were thinking about taking on a partner, casting your eye around your colleagues is a good start. Remember, it cuts both ways. Although they may know a lot about how you perform at work, you know as much about them.

Bringing in Your Best Friend

On the assumption that your best friend isn't your spouse, then she represents someone else who should be able to tell you whether you're the right sort of person to start up the particular business you've in mind. You can start out by asking your friend to review your skills and knowledge inventory (see Chapter 3) and so provide a valuable cross-check on your self-assessment. In fact, you should always find someone who knows you really well to go through this inventory and the business idea-evaluation process (also in Chapter 3). Unfortunately, everyone's capacity for self-deception is unlimited, and you shouldn't miss any opportunity for a reality check.

Reporting to an Accountant

You need an accountant in any event (I explain about dealing with accountants and bookkeepers in Chapter 13). However, don't miss out on making the maximum use of as many accountants as possible when researching to establish your business. Accounts are great sources of info for the following reasons:

- ✔ They're the first port of call for any entrepreneur seeking help and advice, ahead of bank managers, small firm advisers and business associates. As a consequence, they're the repositories of an enormous amount of information on every aspect of business, not just finance.

- ✔ Accountants draw an increasing amount of their revenue from non-accounting tasks, and some even make more money from providing general business advice than they do from auditing.

- ✔ Most accountants are sole traders or in small partnerships operating in much the same way as you plan to do when you set up your business. So unlike bank managers, who all work in large organisations, accountants can identify with your problems and concerns.

Take all the free advice you can get, because most accountants give you a free first meeting in the hope of signing you up as a client. Pump the accountants as much as you can for any tips, pointers or advice on the business you've in mind.

Talk to the Added Value Network (www.avn.co.uk), a network of over 5,000 accountants working in over 400 offices across the UK who are focused on helping entrepreneurs start up and grow their businesses. It offers a free 'Business Builder Review' tailored to suit your needs but based on its experiences in helping 115,000 owner-managed businesses.

Plugging into a Business Angel Network

Business angels (see Chapter 8) have some attractive attributes. They aren't as risk averse as venture capital firms; they act more quickly, putting up money in weeks rather than months; and they aren't so fussy about your pedigree. But when it comes to giving a helping hand, they're absolute stars. Using the business angel networks outlined in Chapter 8, you can find an angel with expertise in the sector in which you've an interest.

Chapter 21

Ten Reasons for Using Social Media

In This Chapter

▶ Recognising why social media matters

▶ Putting social media to work in your business

▶ Ensuring that you stay ahead of the pack

*T*he Oxford Dictionary has a suitably pithy definition of *social media* – 'websites and applications that enable users to create and share content or to participate in social networking'. Social media can be seen as a collection of online communications channels dedicated to community-based input, interaction, content-sharing and collaboration.

Social media may be still in its infancy, but it's prolific and influential. That using social media for business has become a mainstream activity is evident in the fact that the options are numerous and expanding fast. Aside from the usual suspects – Facebook, LinkedIn and Twitter – hundreds of sector-specific sites exist. Pinterest, for example, is a tool for collecting and organising pictures of things that inspire you. YouTube provides a forum for people to inform billions of people around the world by distributing videos for free. eHarmony, Match.com and 6,000 other dating sites aim to help the lonely find love. Social bookmarking sites, including Digg, Delicious, Newsvine, and Reddit allow users to recommend online news stories, music and videos. Then you have word-of-mouth forums including blogs, company-sponsored discussion boards and chat rooms, and consumer product or service ratings websites and forums like Skytrax airlines rating, TripAdvisor and local-business review site Yelp. Social media sites make up at least half of the top 20 websites in most regions of the world. So you need to incorporate social media into your marketing plan, and in chapter I offer ten reasons to back up that assertion.

Visit Social Media Examiner (www.socialmediaexaminer.com/getting-started) where you can find tips on how to get started on Facebook, Twitter, LinkedIn, Google+, Pinterest and YouTube, as well as how to get your first *blog* (a web page where people record and share opinions) and *podcast* (a digital file containing video or audio material that can be accessed online) off the ground.

Augmenting Your Marketing Budget

Offline marketing is expensive. Using conventional media such as posters, leaflets, radio or TV costs hundreds, if not thousands, of pounds up front. A small firm's marketing budget can quickly become exhausted and you may not have any certainty of results going route. Plus, measuring the response from any form of offline advertising is notoriously difficult. In contrast, you can dip your toe in the social media water for virtually no cost except a few hours' work, a worthwhile trade to make while getting your business going. Even better, social media comes with inbuilt measurement systems so you can see just how many bangs you're getting for your buck.

Companies such as Ning (www.ning.com) and Engagor (http://engagor.com) help you create social media such as podcasts, *forums* (which are like blogs where people cluster around specific interest topics) and blogs while providing tools to measure, monitor and manage your social media activity. Both sites offer a free trial and basic services from just £18 per month.

Acquiring Cost-Effective Exposure

You need exposure when starting a business. After all, how are you going to reach people and sell them your wares if they don't know that you exist? Equally, cost-effectiveness is a buzzword for business start-ups where money is often tight. The good news is that you need to devote just a few hours each week to social media activities, which cost you nothing but that time, in order to get some serious online visibility as a result of your efforts.

Social Media Examiner's 2013 report (which you can find online, at www.socialmediaexaminer.com/SocialMediaMarketingIndustryReport2013.pdf) sets out to uncover the 'who, what, where, when, and why' of social media marketing. They surveyed over 3,000 marketers and found the following:

- ✔ For 89 per cent of respondents, social media marketing has generated more business exposure.

- ✔ A total of 64 per cent saw sales-lead generation increase by using social media for six hours or less per week.

✔ For 86 per cent, social media was important for their business (up from eighty three percent the previous year).

✔ Around 79 per cent had integrated their social media marketing with their traditional marketing activities.

Different social media reach different audiences, so consider where you're retrying to gain exposure when choosing which social media to employ. Facebook dominates in the business-to-consumer space (67 per cent of marketers select it as their number-one choice). However, in the business-to-business world, LinkedIn and Facebook are in joint first place, at 29 per cent each. Blogging and Twitter play a much more important role for business-to-business marketers, at 19 per cent and 16 per cent respectively, but for business-to-consumers the shares are 11 per cent and 10 per cent.

Increasing Website Traffic

To grow your business, you want more people who can buy or tell others to buy your products to visit your website, so you've got to snare those who are idly surfing the Internet or looking at other sites and draw them to your website. Through using social media, you can put out topical and interesting messages to attract surfers' attention. As soon as they take the bait and visit your website, you can expose them to any other messages or promotional material that you want them to see. Unfortunately, general browsing covers millions of websites, making targeting users near-impossible and prohibitively expensive. Social media traffic, by contrast, is concentrated in no more than a dozen networks in the English-speaking world or in easily identified sector-specific areas such as those covered by networks like TripAdvisor or eHarmony.

Your job is to find which social media are used most by the market you sell into and put your hooks there. For most small businesses, Twitter is a good place to start. Twitter is where people read breaking news, so if what you want to communicate is topical and time-dependent, Twitter can be a useful social media for you to use. (Find out everything you need to know about building up your business profile on Twitter at the For Dummies online resource: `www.dummies.com/how-to/internet/Blogging-Social-Networking/Twitter/Getting-Started.html`.) You can monitor and manage tweets using a free online organiser such as TweetDeck (`www.tweetdeck.com`) or Hootsuite (`www.Hootsuite.com`), which has the added advantage of enabling to you manage and analyse other social media you're using, such as Facebook and LinkedIn, in one place.

Moving up Search Engine Rankings

Over 500 million different websites are on the Internet today, so when you search for something on Google, Bing or Yahoo!, a lot of activity is triggered. If you type 'greetings cards' into Google, you get 68,900,000 results, for example. If your website doesn't appear on the first few pages, however, there's little chance that anyone is going to plough on to find it. *Search engine optimisation* (SEO) helps you move up the rankings (I cover topic in Chapter 15), and an essential part of an SEO strategy these days is to ride on the back of your social media traffic to move up the rankings.

Search engines are always looking for ways to eliminate low-quality results, making algorithm changes that affect the way search marketing is conducted. If you can get influential sites such as Facebook, Twitter or Pinterest gathering attention about your business, your 'quality rating' (as far as the search engines are concerned) can go up, taking your ranking up with it. The trick is to give readers a reason to pass your message on to as many people as possible and to give them a reason to visit your website. You can achieve trick by putting high-quality copy in your social media that links back to your website. For example, you can invite your blog readers to share their experiences of using products such as those you sell and provide facts that link back to a report on the subject on your website. Having your social media linked directly through to your website in way can be an effective strategy for improving website traffic.

The online news aggregator and blog, Huffington Post, is ranked highly by Alexa (www.alexa.com/siteinfo/huffingtonpost.com), the web information company that monitors web traffic. The Huffington Post blog is on its main web page (www.huffingtonpost.co.uk), together with its Facebook and Twitter links. Interesting Huffington blogs or tweets get shared and new readers are tempted to visit Huffington's website, so increasing the traffic, which then translates into a higher overall website ranking.

The 2013 Social Media Marketing Report, sponsored by the Social Media Examiner website, reported the following:

- ✔ A total of 45 per cent of firms who used social media for less than 12 months moved up the search rankings.

- ✔ Improved search engine rankings were most prevalent among those who used social media for two years or longer, with more than 62 per cent reporting a rise.

- ✔ Marketers selling to other businesses were more likely to achieve improved rankings (60 per cent) than those selling to consumers (56 per cent).

Consider using SocialOomph (www.socialoomph.com), which enables you to automate a range of tasks including scheduling and publishing recurring tweets, updating Facebook and LinkedIn pages and a whole mass of social media activity that can save you hours of work every week. When you've registered a free account, you can take the free and fully functional trial of SocialOomph Professional. Thereafter, you pay once every fortnight payments and you don't have to enter any long-term contracts.

Improving Market Intelligence

Social media has transformed the way people exchange information. Today people with similar interests band together in different online communities, sharing information and exchanging views on blogs and forums. Both are excellent sources of continuous information on industry issues, customers and competitors. Anyone and everyone can, and does, express their comments through blogs and forums, and many blogs exist on any topic. So, you can use blogs and forums as a means to research your market.

To find blogs and forums of interest:

- ✔ Visit Globe of Blogs (http://globeofblogs.com), which has over 50,000 blogs listed.

- ✔ Simply using the Google search engine (www.google.com/blogsearch) is also a good way into the world's blogs and forums.

Use information from the blogs and forums you follow to arrive at a *crowd forecast*: one that relies on the 'wisdom of the crowd' to get sense of what people are feeling. For example, the average of estimates provided by a group of individuals is more accurate than most of the individual estimates. Crowd forecasting enables you to balance expert perspectives with that of a wider audience for a more representative view of where a trend is heading.

You can also set up your own blog. Launching your own blog needn't be hard. Blogger for example, is Google's free tool for creating blogs, and you can set up a Blogger account in three easy steps: create an account, name your blog and choose a template. Then you can start blogging, and set up other blogs with the same account. You can read stories about how other small businesses have used blogging and find the link to set up your own Google blogging account at http://buzz.blogger.com.

Why not use your blog as a platform for running a survey? Use online survey sites such as Survey Monkey (www.surveymonkey.com) and Free Online Surveys (http://freeonlinesurveys.com) to canvas your customers' opinions and even their intentions; for example, by asking when they're likely to buy your type of products again. (You can find everything you need to structure your questionnaire in Chapter 4.)

Attracting Interest to Generate Sales Leads

The trick in promoting a product or service is to recognise the stages in the sale process: attention, interest, desire and, finally, a sale. You can think of anyone who responds to a well-targeted social media initiative as being at the attention or interest stage in the selling process. Some of those people go on to look for more information on your website. Not all responses result in a purchase immediately; nevertheless, the response has a value.

Top of the scale is a person who becomes an immediate customer. Farther down, there's still value if the person becomes a customer later on or recommends you to a friend or colleague with a greater need for your product than he has himself. Finally, if he never buys or recommends you to others but you can identify the person's characteristics, you can eliminate him and others like him from your future marketing efforts and so become more effective and efficient – valuable commodities in themselves.

When starting a business or later on, when you're planning for growth – say, by launching a new product or service – social media can be a valuable way to generate that all-important initial 'buzz'. Social media provides the ideal vehicle to channel your creative juices and generate innovative ways to get the word out about your business, product or service. In that way, you can create anticipation and build up enough excitement to get people talking and so generate those vital initial sales leads.

When Ford wanted to re-enter the small car market with the Fiesta, it gave 100 social media influencers a Fiesta to test drive for six months. Every month, the influencers had to complete a mission and document their experiences on various social channels such as Twitter, Facebook, YouTube and Flickr. The effects of the campaign were sensational: Fiesta generated 6.5 million YouTube views, received 50,000 requests (sales leads, if you like) for information about the car and sold 10,000 cars in the first six days post-release.

Consider using Hootsuite (who offer a free trial to whet your appetite), an essential tool for managing Twitter and other social networks. Hootsuite produces analytic reports that show how effective your various activities are. In this way, you can see just how many potential leads you're generating. You can sign up for a 30-day free trial here: `http://signup.hootsuite.com/signup-pro`.

You find essential ideas on how to use marketing effectively, including how to get your potential customers' attention, in Chapter 10.

Growing Real Sales

Generating a buzz of interest is one thing, but you can get a lot more than that from a social media drive; you can push the real sales curve up too. In a recent analysis of more than 60 Facebook marketing campaigns, 49 per cent reported a return on investment of more than five times, and 70 per cent had a return on investment greater than three times.

You can tap forums for more than ideas; you can induce people there to part with upfront cash, given the right proposition. To give an example, Hotel Chocolat, one of the UK's prestigious 'cool brands', did just that. Angus Thirlwell, Hotel Chocolat's co-founder, launched a chocolate tasting club (you can find it at `www.hotelchocolat.com/uk/tasting-club`) to develop recipes and ideas. To join the club, you have to place an initial order for £9.95 worth of chocolates, representing a 60 per cent saving on the retail price. For that, you get a box of chocolates, tasting notes and a free gift. From there, you can continue and become a Tasting Club member and get new selections regularly sent to your door. Social media strategy is a neater and more effective way of generating a customer's first order than by using a crude discount on its own. That the tasting club now has 100,000 members is proof of that particular pudding.

As part of 'The Man Your Man Could Smell Like' campaign for Old Spice in 2010, advertising firm Wieden + Kennedy launched a social media blitz. Over three days their team filmed 180-odd videos around the clock, responding directly to fans and celebrities in near-real time. Total campaign impressions since February 2010 have now reached approximately 1.2 billion. The videos have received over 34 million aggregate views with a total of 38,535 YouTube comments. Old Spice has become the all-time most viewed sponsored channel on YouTube, and best of all, since the campaign 'Mustafa' (an Old Spice product) sales have increased by 27 per cent year on year. In the three months after the height of the social media campaign, sales were up by 55 per cent, reaching 107 per cent in the final month and making Old Spice the number one bodywash brand for men.

Keeping Pace with Market Leaders

Like it or not, social media marketing is here to stay and you have to have a strategy and presence online to be considered a serious player in the business arena today. You're 'visible' on the Internet if only by default. Your prospects, clients, potential employees, business partners or backers find it odd if they can't locate a social media presence in any of the mainstream media – Facebook, Twitter, LinkedIn or at least a blog or forum on the business's website.

Keeping pace in social media isn't just about being on a large number of media sites. That can be time-consuming for a small business founder as by having presence on a social media site, your customers expect you to be actively engaged there. You'd have to keep current, fresh conversations flowing constantly. Rather, the challenge is how to keep up-to-date with which social media sites your customers use the most. An ideal way to master challenge is to read *Social Media Marketing For Dummies* by Shiv Singh and Stephanie Diamond (Wiley). This book is an indispensable resource for small businesses and start-ups looking for low-cost online marketing strategies. It shows you how to identify social media sites that appeal to your target audience and find out which social platform works best for which objectives. You can also find out how to monitor results and assess your program's effectiveness.

You couldn't get a more conservative company than Caterpillar – the world's leading manufacturer of construction and mining equipment, diesel and natural engines and industrial gas turbines, and a name associated with yellow bulldozers and building sites. Despite its conservatism, the company has a dedicated social media program manager, and social media technologies provide them with the opportunity to publicly demonstrate their customer–business relationships. Caterpillar recognises the power of the big three social media platforms – Facebook, Twitter, and YouTube – but is also exploring other platforms used in specific areas of the world as well as social media tools such as Foursquare, Facebook Places and Gowalla. Through its careful use of social media, Caterpillar is maintaining its position as market leader.

Check out your competition's social media presence regularly, at least once a month, or when you check your own Facebook, Twitter, blogs and forums.

Creating Loyalty

Social media can be harnessed to create a devoted following, and a devoted following is as good as money in the bank (see the Hotel Chocolat example in the earlier 'Growing Real Sales' section). Acquiring customers is an expensive process: you have to find them, woo them and win their custom. Once you have them onside, they cost less to keep, they spend more money with you and are less price-sensitive than new customers. Retaining them does more than almost any other marketing strategy to grow your profit margin, and using social media is a low-cost way to keep them onside. Studies have shown that increasing customer retention rates by just 5 per cent increases profits by 25 to 95 per cent, which just goes to prove that a little more loyalty can go a long way in helping a new business to succeed.

In *Social CRM For Dummies* (Wiley), Kyle Lacy, Stephanie Diamond and Jon Ferrara take a detailed look at building a customer loyalty and advocacy programme and offer their insights on a mass of ways to harness social media tools to help you retain and harvest value from your customer base.

Generating Referrals

If you want your business to grow and prosper in the long haul, you have to build up your customer base, and that in turn means you have to carry out some form of advertising and promotion activity. The most trusted form of promotion is the unbiased recommendation of someone whose judgement is trusted and who doesn't stand to gain from their advice. That sounds much like the definition of any positive conversation stream on a blog or a substantial body of followers on Facebook. Indeed, the beauty of social media is that all the hard work – thinking up nice things to say about your products – is done by your satisfied or, better still, delighted customers. By turning your customers into evangelists for your company, you boost your bottom line. You do, however, have to get it right in the first place. Social media can be a double-edged sword. If things go wrong, the word gets out loud and clear – and at lightning speed.

In *Social Media Engagement For Dummies,* by Aliza Sherman and Danielle Elliott Smith (Wiley), you can find out how to build and grow relationships with followers and customers, craft content just for them, analyse how they're responding, and refocus and refresh your campaigns accordingly.

Harnessing the Power of *For Dummies*

Knowing more about social marketing and how to harness its power is crucial to improving your chances of getting your business off the ground. I've already mentioned a few *For Dummies* titles to dip into; here are a few other places to look within the *For Dummies* catalogue that can help you get right up to speed with social marketing:

✔ *Social Media Commerce For Dummies* by **Marsha Collier.** Marsha's book is packed full of ideas. She introduces you to social media commerce and explains how you can use social media to provide better customer service, collect payments online, and build your customer base.

✔ *Social Media Marketing For Dummies* by **Shiv Singh and Stephanie Diamond.** book is an indispensable resource for small businesses and start-ups looking for low-cost online marketing strategies. It shows you how to identify social media sites that appeal to your target audience and find out which social platform works best for which

objectives. You can also find out how to monitor results and assess your program's effectiveness.

✔ *Twitter Marketing For Dummies* by **Kyle Lacy.** In concentrating on one of the most powerful and cost-effective tools in the social media armoury, Kyle covers the latest ideas, tools, tips, and techniques that can kick-start your Twitter marketing campaign.

✔ *Facebook For Dummies* by **Carolyn Abram.** Carolyn takes another vital aspect of social media, dissecting it with her forensic skills. title offers a straightforward approach to demystifying Facebook and covers Facebook's re-launched mobile application and integration with Windows 8.

✔ *LinkedIn For Dummies* by **Joel Elad.** Joel introduces you to the key features of LinkedIn, explains how it works and offers advice for marketing your business, developing strategic partnerships, and cultivating sales leads.

Index

• **F** •

• G •

• H •

About the Author

Colin Barrow was, until recently, Head of the Enterprise Group at Cranfield School of Management, where he taught entrepreneurship on the MBA and other programmes. He is also a visiting professor at business schools in the US, Asia, France, and Austria. His books on entrepreneurship and small business have been translated into twenty languages including Russian and Chinese. He worked with Microsoft to incorporate the business planning model used in his teaching programmes into the software program, Microsoft Business Planner. He is a regular contributor to newspapers, periodicals and academic journals such as the *Financial Times, The Guardian, Management Today,* and the *International Small Business Journal.*

Thousands of students have passed through Colin's start-up and business growth programmes, going on to run successful and thriving enterprises, and raising millions in new capital. He is on the board of several small businesses, is a University Academic Governor, and has served on the boards of public companies, venture capital funds, and on Government Task Forces.

Author's Acknowledgements

I would like to thank everyone at Wiley for the opportunity to write and update this book – as well as for their help, encouragement, feedback, and tireless work to make this all happen.

Publisher's Acknowledgements

We're proud of this book; please send us your comments at http://dummies.custhelp.com. For other comments, please contact our Customer Care Department within the U.S. at 877-762-2974, outside the U.S. at (001) 317-572-3993, or fax 317-572-4002.

Some of the people who helped bring this book to market include the following:

Acquisitions, Editorial, and Vertical Websites

Project Editor: Steve Edwards

Commissioning Editor: Claire Ruston

Assistant Editor: Ben Kemble

Development Editor: Charlie Wilson

Copy Editor: Charlie Wilson

Proofreader: Kim Vernon

Publisher: Miles Kendall

Cover Photos: © iStockphoto.com/kaan tanman

Project Coordinator: Sheree Montgomery

Take Dummies with you everywhere you go!

Whether you're excited about e-books, want more from the web, must have your mobile apps, or swept up in social media, Dummies makes everything easier .

FOR DUMMIES

A Wiley Brand

BUSINESS

978-1-118-73077-5

978-1-118-44349-1

978-1-119-97527-4

MUSIC

978-1-119-94276-4

978-0-470-97799-6

978-0-470-49644-2

DIGITAL PHOTOGRAPHY

978-1-118-09203-3

978-0-470-76878-5

978-1-118-00472-2

Algebra I For Dummies
978-0-470-55964-2

Anatomy & Physiology For Dummies, 2nd Edition
978-0-470-92326-9

Asperger's Syndrome For Dummies
978-0-470-66087-4

Basic Maths For Dummies
978-1-119-97452-9

Body Language For Dummies, 2nd Edition
978-1-119-95351-7

Bookkeeping For Dummies, 3rd Edition
978-1-118-34689-1

British Sign Language For Dummies
978-0-470-69477-0

Cricket for Dummies, 2nd Edition
978-1-118-48032-8

Currency Trading For Dummies, 2nd Edition
978-1-118-01851-4

Cycling For Dummies
978-1-118-36435-2

Diabetes For Dummies, 3rd Edition
978-0-470-97711-8

eBay For Dummies, 3rd Edition
978-1-119-94122-4

Electronics For Dummies All-in-One For Dummies
978-1-118-58973-1

English Grammar For Dummies
978-0-470-05752-0

French For Dummies, 2nd Edition
978-1-118-00464-7

Guitar For Dummies, 3rd Edition
978-1-118-11554-1

IBS For Dummies
978-0-470-51737-6

Keeping Chickens For Dummies
978-1-119-99417-6

Knitting For Dummies, 3rd Edition
978-1-118-66151-2

FOR DUMMIES®

A Wiley Brand

SELF-HELP

978-0-470-66541-1

978-1-119-99264-6

978-0-470-66086-7

LANGUAGES

978-0-470-68815-1

978-1-119-97959-3

978-0-470-69477-0

HISTORY

978-0-470-68792-5

978-0-470-74783-4

978-0-470-97819-1

Laptops For Dummies 5th Edition
978-1-118-11533-6

Management For Dummies, 2nd Edition
978-0-470-97769-9

Nutrition For Dummies, 2nd Edition
978-0-470-97276-2

Office 2013 For Dummies
978-1-118-49715-9

Organic Gardening For Dummies
978-1-119-97706-3

Origami Kit For Dummies
978-0-470-75857-1

Overcoming Depression For Dummies
978-0-470-69430-5

Physics I For Dummies
978-0-470-90324-7

Project Management For Dummies
978-0-470-71119-4

Psychology Statistics For Dummies
978-1-119-95287-9

Renting Out Your Property For Dummies, 3rd Edition
978-1-119-97640-0

Rugby Union For Dummies, 3rd Edition
978-1-119-99092-5

Stargazing For Dummies
978-1-118-41156-8

Teaching English as a Foreign Language For Dummies
978-0-470-74576-2

Time Management For Dummies
978-0-470-77765-7

Training Your Brain For Dummies
978-0-470-97449-0

Voice and Speaking Skills For Dummies
978-1-119-94512-3

Wedding Planning For Dummies
978-1-118-69951-5

WordPress For Dummies, 5th Edition
978-1-118-38318-6

Think you can't learn it in a day? Think again!

The *In a Day* e-book series from *For Dummies* gives you quick and easy access to learn a new skill, brush up on a hobby, or enhance your personal or professional life — all in a day. Easy!

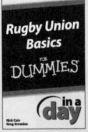

Available as PDF, eMobi and Kindle